Introduction to consciousness

Introduction to consciousness

Neuroscience, cognitive science, and philosophy

Arne Dietrich

First published 2007 by
PALGRAVE MACMILLAN
Houndmills, Basingstoke, Hampshire RG21 6XS and
175 Fifth Avenue, New York, N.Y. 10010
Companies and representatives throughout the world

PALGRAVE MACMILLAN is the global academic imprint of the Palgrave Macmillan division of St. Martin's Press, LLC and of Palgrave Macmillan Ltd. Macmillan® is a registered trademark in the United States, United Kingdom and other countries. Palgrave is a registered trademark in the European Union and other countries.

ISBN-13: 978–1–4039–9489–9
ISBN 10: 1–4039–9489–7

This book is printed on paper suitable for recycling and made from fully managed and sustained forest sources.

A catalogue record for this book is available from the British Library.

A catalog record for this book is available from the Library of Congress.

10   9   8   7   6   5   4   3   2   1
16   15   14   13   12   11   10   09   08   07

Printed in China

Brief contents

Contents

Preface

Consciousness has never been a topic that lends itself naturally to sober, intellectual discourse. This is hardly surprising, really, given that what's at stake is nothing less than the nature of our souls. But recently – since the mid-1980s, that is – people have turned up the heat another notch still. In a view approaching unanimity, consciousness has gone interdisciplinary! Long past are the days when philosophy was the sole weapon of attack. This isn't the first time, of course, that this has happened. Like other topics once exclusively in the domain of philosophy – the nature of matter, the origin of life, etc. – the mind, and its faculties, has become the domain of neuroscience, cognitive science, artificial intelligence, psychology, and several other fields of study. Some might find this takeover attitude upsetting, or at least premature, but the new weapons of choice are, no doubt, different in kind – microelectrodes, knockout mice, computer simulations, brain scanners, C++, clever questionnaires, electron microscopes, monoclonal antibodies, Lisp. Today's students of consciousness, if they are to prosper, need, in addition to philosophy, to be fluent in brainspeak, to know the nuts and bolts of artificial neural networks, to find their way around the lab, and interpret charts filled with raw data.

As we have said, this injection of a heavy dose of empirical science has done nothing to cool the debate. *Au contraire*! Consciousness remains an arena where respectable people, even those of the highest scientific standing, regularly rise to levels of speculation that can safely be called imprudent. I have personally seen otherwise calm men – the sort of Type-B personality you wouldn't want ahead of you in traffic – grow incandescent over mercurial philosophical puzzles that regular folk don't even know exist. The field of consciousness is an intellectual battleground contested as fiercely as any in war. The theoretical landscape is littered with landmines and you can be sure that there are plenty of skilled sharpshooters taking aim at you, no matter what position you defend. This book was great fun to write but when I decided to go for it, I didn't know I would need a safety helmet! I now highly recommend some form of protective headgear to anyone interested in writing about consciousness. At some point – while writing Chapter 3, specifically – I thought that the next thing in tow for me, given the drift of things, would be the witness-protection program.

I was worried because I decided to attempt the nearly impossible, a formal analysis of the mind-body problem, in 300 pages no less, that is neutral in orientation and accurately reflects what's going on, as a whole, in the field of consciousness today. This, so much I knew, would not make me any new friends on either side of the contentious mind–brain divide. I had my hopes pinned on one thing, though: to keep to a minimum the neckbreaking mental gymnastics one must perform when trying to understand the contemporary philosophical literature and feed the student a steady and thoroughgoing diet of all the new and exciting scientific hubbub that has given consciousness the kind of sex appeal usually only reserved for supermodels. Well, OK, maybe not quite. To bring you a feel for all the buzz, though, for nearly two years I sifted through mountains of data in professional journals with such fun titles as *Electroencephalography and Clinical Neurophysiology, Neuroscience and Biobehavioral Reviews* and, why not, *Pain*, spent untold hours reading my way through oodles of seriously twisted ideas, listened intently to people whose only obvious talent is to make very delicate maneuvers of logic sound terribly important, and navigated my way in, and back out of, thought experiments involving zombies, Chinese rooms, pontifical neurons, and – who knew – Martian anthropologists. The result is this book, a methodical, if slightly irreverent, trip through the hinterland of the mind, complete with an up-to-date map of neuroland.

Whether or not I succeeded in my task is, of course, your call. But before you read on, consider yourself forewarned. This book will challenge your ability to endure paradoxes, ambiguity, infinity, and nonlinearity. The good news is that all you need to bring on this journey is a sense of awe and some intrinsic curiosity about how something like a mind, with all its hopes and dreams, can possibly emerge from the 3-pound, mushy pile of electrified biochemistry inside your cranium. Neither the author nor the philosophers and scientists whose clever work is reported here can be held responsible for any mental space–time collapse leading to mystical revelations regarding the fundamental nature of consciousness, a sense of unity with the forces of nature, or profound insights into the meaning of life that may occur during the reading of this book. Finally, always remember to bring a warm blanket, plenty of patience, and your safety helmet (see above) when embarking on extended voyages through the unforgiving terrain of mindscape. If you feel dizziness or discomfort at any time we suggest you close your eyes, put your head down, and think about some easier problem, like the origin of the universe.

In a sneak preview of the journey ahead, the basic idea for this project was to create a compact, single-volume textbook for this emerging, multidisciplinary field of consciousness. To that end, I combined the relevant technical subject matter and theory with an introduction to the underlying concepts for each of the major disciplines that underpin consciousness – philosophy, psychology, neuroscience, cognitive science – without favoring any one of these. So, for example, if you are a philosophy student, you should be able to understand the higher-level content drawn from, say, neuroscience or artificial intelligence, as the text provides the background theory and research essential to grasp the more technical contributions drawn from there. This approach goes hand in hand with a concerted effort to decrypt the neurolingo that makes modern brain research seem so inaccessible to people hailing from other disciplines. All this, or so is the hope, makes the text highly flexible and allows it to be custom-fit to the very different courses that deal with the human mind nowadays. It guarantees that the student gets a good grounding in all the disciplines that make up the field of consciousness, irrespective of the area of expertise of the professor teaching the course.

The upcoming attractions are organized into four major parts, each designed to tackle a weight-bearing pillar of the study of consciousness. For Part I, I sketch out the philosophical landscape. One of the greatest pleasures in the life of a philosopher is to make ordinary matters extraordinarily complicated. There is no reason, however, to follow their example. In other words, I stick to the basics here. Instead of exploring in depth every angle of some knotty theoretical problem, the text makes choices, not to favor one view over another, but to brush aside considerations that appear, for one reason or another, minor in comparison. This simply reflects the realities on the ground, that is, the real, red-hot stuff is going on in the labs with all the snazzy gizmos mentioned earlier, and we allocate our space accordingly.

Part II introduces the student to the current thinking and research on the mechanisms of consciousness, that is, the processes that are likely to have a hand in the making of conscious experience. So, naturally, the chapters in this part contain the whole funhouse of material that has so far escaped the dustbin of wishful thinking – global workspace theory, evolution by natural selection, temporal binding, some selected computational models, a shortlist of candidates for the neural correlates of consciousness and – how could it not – chaos theory, quantum weirdness, advanced robotics, and artificial neural networks. It's the revenge of the nerds! Here, again, we stop well short of a comprehensive overview, presenting only the major proposals in roughly the proportion in which they have contributed to the current buzz.

The scenic tour through the organ of thought then continues, in Part III, to look at the content of consciousness – the actual topic of our experiences. This is not the place, as one might gather, where the connoisseur of introspection finally gets his money's worth. The subjective, first-person perspective is a philosophical tradition and, as such, belongs into Part I. Part III concerns itself, in five glorious chapters, predominantly with sound mechanistic explanations of how mental processes – perceptions, memories, emotions, thoughts, that sort of thing – are computed and made fully conscious. It is actually nothing but straight-up, mainstream cognitive neuroscience, except its focus is on consciousness. No doubt it isn't easy to imagine how thoughts and feelings come from the hustle and bustle in a cantaloupe-sized heap of meat crackling with electricity. But the full force of the gospel of modern neuroscience – the mind is the brain – does not come into clear view unless you see, bit by bit, the full-steam research program and the overpowering mountain of empirical evidence that supports this claim

Part IV, the last part of the journey, is a must for any self-respecting explorer of inner space: altered states of consciousness. After a brief opening on the nagging problem of defining and classifying these odd distortions to the fabric of mental space–time, the itinerary includes a visit to all the usual suspects – drug states, meditation, hypnosis, daydreaming, the runner's high, and the nocturnal theater of the absurd otherwise known as dreaming. Tales from the hallucination zone are nuggets of pure gold to the aficionado but certainly not the sort of scientific sound bites printed in peer-reviewed pharmacology journals. Thus, we have no time for them either. Instead, we focus heavily on the most recent scientific studies emerging from the rarefied realms of nuclear neuroimaging, electrophysiology, and neuropharmacology, which can catch a glimpse of the brain at the moment it loses its hold on ordinary reality – whatever that is.

Following tradition, this leaves the best for last. In writing this book, I had much assistance. I would like to express particular thanks to Mark Tanaka, Bill McDaniel, Narayanan Srinivasan, and Paul Frysh, among rather many others, who generously and graciously provided any help whenever I needed it. I am most indebted, however, to Reem Saab and Fida'a Chehayeb, who meticulously critiqued the entire manuscript for content and style, at times more than once. I offer them my thanks for those improvements I accepted and my apologies for those I resisted. Also, a word of thanks to Nour Saab for much of the artwork and to Yasmine Fayad for preparing the index.

Arne Dietrich
Beirut, September 2006

Acknowledgments

Figure 1.1 reprinted from F. J. Varela, Neurophenomenology: A methodological remedy for the hard problem, *Journal of Consciousness Studies*, 3 (1996), 330–49. Copyright © 1996, by permission of Academic Imprint.

Figure 3 Box based on R. Carter, *Exploring Consciousness*, Los Angeles: University of California Press, 2002

Box 5.1 from T. Bisson, They are made out of meat, *Omni Magazine*, April 1991. Copyright © Terry Bisson, reprinted by permission of the author.

Figure 4, Box 2 adapted from I. Bentov, *A Brief Tour of Higher Consciousness: A Cosmic Book on the Mechanics of Creation*, Rochester: VT: Inner Traditions, 2000. Copyright © www.InnerTraditions.com. Reprinted with permission.

Figure 6.1 from Michael S. Gazzaniga, Richard B. Ivry, and George R. Mangun, *Cognitive Neuroscience: The Biology of the Mind*, 2nd ed. Copyright © 2002 by W. W. Norton & Company, Inc. Reprinted by permission of W. W. Norton & Company, Inc.

Figure 6.2 from Michael S. Gazzaniga, Richard B. Ivry, and George R. Mangun, *Cognitive Neuroscience: The Biology of the Mind*, 2nd ed. Copyright © 2002 by W. W. Norton & Company, Inc. Reprinted by permission of W. W. Norton & Company, Inc.

Figure 7.3 from V. S. Ramachandran, Blind spots, *Scientific American*, 266 (1992), 86–91. Copyright © 1992 by *Scientific American*, Inc. Reprinted with permission.

Figure 8.2 adapted from A. M. Collins and E. F. Loftus, A spreading activation theory of semantic processing, *Psychological Review*, 82 (1975), 407–28. Copyright © 1975, by permission of the American Psychological Association.

Figure 8.3 reprinted from F. G. Ashby and E. W. Shawn, The neurobiology of human category learning, *Trends on Cognitive Science*, 5 (2001), 204–10. Copyright © 2001, by permission of Elsevier.

Figure 8.4 reprinted from C. D. Frith, R. Perry, and E. Lumer, The neural correlates of conscious experience, *Trends on Cognitive Science*, 3 (1999), 105–14. Copyright © 1999, by permission of Elsevier.

Figure 9.1 reprinted from J. E. LeDoux, Emotion, memory and the brain, *Scientific American* (June 1994), 50–7. Copyright © 1994 by *Scientific American*, Inc., courtesy of Robert Osti.

Figure 10.3 adapted from Antonio R. Damasio, *The Feeling of What Happens: Body and Emotion in the Making of Consciousness*, New York: Harcourt Brace, 1999. Copyright © 1999 by Antonio Damasio, reprinted by permission of Harcourt, Inc.

Figure 11.2 based on B. Libet, Do we have free will?, *Journal of Consciousness Studies*, 6 (1999), 47–57. Copyright © 1999, courtesy of Benjamin Libet.

Figures 11.3 and 11.4 adapted from D. M. Wegner and T. Wheatley, Apparent mental causation: Source of the experience of will, *American Psychologist*, 54 (1999), 480–92. Copyright © 1999, by permission of the American Psychological Association.

Figure 12.1 (left) adapted from C. Tart, *States of Consciousness*, New York: Dutton & Co., 1975. Reproduced by permission of Charles Tart.

Figure 12.1 (right) adapted from A. Hobson, *The Dream Drugstore*, Cambridge, MA: MIT Press, 1993. Reproduced by permission of Allan Hobson and MIT Press.

Figure 13.3 adapted from R. K. Siegel and M. E. Jarvik, Drug-induced hallucinations in animals and man, in R. K. Siegel and L. J. West (eds.), *Hallucinations: Behavior, Experience, and Theory*, New York: Wiley, 1975 (pp. 81–161). By permission of Wiley.

Every effort has been made to trace all copyright holders, but if any have been inadvertently overlooked, the published will be pleased to make the necessary arrangements at the first opportunity.

PART I

The nature of consciousness

1 Introduction

Chapter outline	

The nature of consciousness studies

What is consciousness?

Consciousness is the quintessence of philosophy, psychology, neuroscience, and several other fields of study. Traditionally known as the **mind-body problem** (although not exactly the same), it is as ancient a topic as any in the history of thought. What is the mind? How is it related to physical matter? Is the mind the workings of the body (materialism), or is the universe split into two entirely different kinds of stuff (dualism)? These questions also touch upon nearly every other ancient philosophical problem, such as the nature of the universe or the meaning of life.

Consciousness has been called "the last surviving mystery" (Dennett, 1991, p. 21). This is not to say that there aren't any great unsolved problems left in other sciences. But unlike the Big Bang or the origin of life, consciousness is truly a mystery in the sense that we do not yet even know how to think about it. Physicists and biologists have a framework in which to contextualize any phenomena they study, and they agree on the methodology that will eventually bring about a solution. In consciousness there is no such framework, and people fundamentally disagree on the approach that will bring about progress. This is ironic. The inquisitory Greeks started asking questions some 2,500 years ago, motivated by the desire to understand something about our own existence. This is what Protagoras meant when he said: "Man is the measure of all things." The late Nobel laureate Francis Crick considered consciousness the central problem of biology. Other scientists go even further. They argue that consciousness is the problem that underlies all sciences. You might think that this status is reserved for the laws of physics and the theorems of mathematics but then again, those laws and theorems are understood by the mind – *in* consciousness. Thus, the way we comprehend the universe depends on the kind of consciousness we humans have. It is entirely possible that there exist other forms of consciousness that comprehend the universe with wholly different laws and theorems.

Unlike most arcane philosophical puzzles, consciousness also has deeply personal relevance. Apart from life itself, it is arguably our most valuable possession. Imagine losing it. What do you have left if you no longer generate or use it? Would other core concepts that define us as human beings – individual freedom, memories, free will, or selfhood – still make any sense? How, for instance, should we regard a person who exists in a vegetative state (see Box 1.1)? The stream of consciousness is a never-broken succession of thoughts and feelings that accompanies us throughout life. Consciousness, then, is really at the heart of our existence.

Box 1.1   When to pull the plug?

In the spring of 2005, America was gripped by the fate of Terri Schiavo. Medicine, law, and political grandstanding all played a prominent role in the drama, but at the heart of the debate was the question of whether life is worth living at the twilight of consciousness. The tragic tale began 15 years earlier when Schiavo suffered a cardiac arrest that left her brain temporarily without oxygen. Her husband found her unconscious on the floor and rushed her to the hospital. She was resuscitated but her brain was so severely damaged from the lack of oxygen that she did not fully regain consciousness. Schiavo was not in a **coma**. Comatose patients lie motionless, neither see nor hear, and show only reflexive movements. They suffer from a complete failure of the arousal system and cannot be awakened by rigorous stimulation. This state rarely continues beyond a few weeks and patients will either die or regain full consciousness. But between these two extremes, there are two conditions of reduced states of consciousness that further question the meaning of life in the absence of full consciousness.

Terri Schiavo entered what is known as a persistent **vegetative state** (VS). In this state brain function is so compromised that patients only respond to the most elementary of stimuli, such as pain. However, patients may occasionally exhibit several behaviors that would appear – at least to the naïve observer – as signs of consciousness. They show the startle response, turn towards loud noises, open the eyes, and exhibit reflexive crying or smiling. Schiavo, for instance, seemed to comply with her doctor's request to open her eyes and appeared to gaze at her mother. The second condition is known as the **minimally conscious state** (MCS) (Giacino, 2005). In this state, patients are capable of more than simple orienteering reflexes and pain avoidance. They show a variety of contingent responding and may reach for and grasp objects, respond to verbal commands, and track visual stimuli. Clinically speaking, a patient diagnosed with VS is considered unconscious with no hope for recovery, whereas a patient with MCS is considered partially conscious

Box 1.1   *continued*

and, significantly, retains the potential for full recovery (Giacino, 2005). Schiavo was judged by neurologists to have the former, not the latter. In the absence of a unified theory of consciousness, nearly everyone in the medical community acknowledges, however, that this gradation between unconsciousness and consciousness is arbitrary at best.

Decisions to remove feeding tubes are never treated lightly by doctors. Hospitals have ethics committees that confer with family members and multiple checks exist before such a measure is taken. But end-of-life cases are also daily events in hospitals and, because several legal precedents exist, they are carried out as a matter of established law. Although Schiavo's case broke neither legal nor medical grounds, it riveted America because the family was bitterly divided over whether or not she should continue to exist in this condition. Naturally, right-to-life and right-to-die advocates lined up on either side of the heated debate. A legal battle raged for over five years that would eventually involve several instances of the courts (the US Supreme Court declined three times to review the case), the governor of Florida, the US Congress, and the President of the United States. During this period, the feeding tube was removed twice, only to be reinstated a few days later. When it was removed for the third time it was final. Terri Schiavo died on March 31, 2005 at age 41.

Aside from other grave issues concerning this case, how does one's position on the mind-body problem impact one's view of the Schiavo case? While it is one thing to commit to a dualistic position, it is quite another to accept all the logical consequences of it. For one thing, how does brain damage alter your consciousness if they are two different things? If the mind roams the body like a ghost in the machine, Schiavo's mind should be unscathed by the injury. Why didn't she behave in this way? A materialist has other matters to ponder. If Schiavo's mind is gone along with the brain, doesn't this diminish her status as a human being? Where do we draw the line? As we shall see, these are not very good arguments for or against dualism or materialism but they provide a good starting point to think about the issue.

Some clarifications

There exists no accepted definition of consciousness. We can point to two reasons for this. First, the nature of consciousness is completely unknown. Without so much as even a basic grasp of the phenomenon itself, it is not feasible to crystallize a useful definition. By virtue of the fact that consciousness has only recently become subject to empirical research, one would expect a definition to emerge with time. But in the study of consciousness there is the further dilemma that global theories of consciousness reach "all the way down" to the most basic concepts. Add to that the fact that these theories are mutually exclusive, and one can see why the attempt to derive a central definition is always filibustered by the opposition. While some take consciousness to be a unique substance, others say it is a special property, and still others claim it to be nothing more than the operation of the brain. This situation effectively preempts us to find even so much as a nuclear meaning for consciousness that could be used as a workable makeshift until we get some data on the matter. As it stands now, we have nothing of use.

Does this mean that we really do not know what, exactly, we are studying? In a way it does, but this is not a fatal problem. Einstein once quipped: "If we knew what we were doing, it wouldn't be called research, would it?" The prominent research team of Francis Crick and Cristof Koch (1998, p. 98) justified their refusal to provide a definition with the following passage:

> Everyone has a rough idea of what is meant by being conscious. For now, it is better to avoid a precise definition of consciousness because of the dangers of premature definition. Until the problem is understood better, any attempt at a formal definition is likely to be either misleading or overly restrictive, or both. If this seems evasive, try defining the word "gene." So much is now known about genes that any simple definition is likely to be inadequate. How much more difficult, then, to define a biological term when rather little is known about it.

Despite the lack of a formal definition, we can and should be more specific about what we mean by consciousness. In general, most philosophers and scientists take the term "consciousness" to be synonymous with "experience," "conscious aware-ness," and "awareness." This is consistent with the everyday usage of these terms. It does not make sense to speak of either someone who is unconscious but has experiences or someone who is conscious but lacks experiences. Accordingly, we are conscious when we experience something. Some people use the term aware-ness to refer to a lower-level form of consciousness, as in, "he is dimly aware of his feelings." However, in the absence of a clear dividing line this is not a helpful distinction. Accordingly, in this text we take awareness and consciousness to refer to the same condition. The term "mind" is also commonly used to mean consciousness. But this is not correct. The mind does not only perform mental operations that are conscious but also ones that are unconscious. So, "mind" is a broader term that encompasses consciousness as one aspect.

A further distinction is often made between being conscious and being conscious of something. This position assumes that the content of consciousness is different from consciousness itself. Naturally, others object. To them conscious-ness *is* the stream of thoughts, feelings, and actions – and nothing extra. This contention holds consciousness and phenomenal consciousness to be one and the same. This is a good example of how one's global theoretical position trickles down to basic notions. We shall see this particular issue pop up in several places, for instance, in the division between easy and hard problems of consciousness discussed later in this chapter. If you distinguish between phenomenal content and consciousness itself, you must also commit to the possibility that someone can be conscious without being conscious of something. Buddhism, for instance, does just that. Note that this contradicts equating experience with consciousness, as we did above. For our purposes, we shall presume that if a person is not conscious of something, she is also not conscious (Güzeldere, 1997). If conscious-ness and phenomenal consciousness are different, the latter being a type of the former, then consciousness must include other forms of consciousness. The philosopher Ned Block (1995) proposed that access consciousness, the ability to access information, is such a different form. Others argue against this because it imports unconscious mental processes into the ordinary usage of the term (Velmans, 2000). In this text, we shall adopt this objection and restrict the term consciousness to phenomenal consciousness, using them both interchangeably.

Some philosophers stress that two defining characteristics of consciousness are intentionality and subjectivity. **Intentionality** is the idea that mental states make a reference to something, that is, they are about something. This is not to be confused with the ordinary use of the word intentionality meaning "having intentions." Since the work of **Franz Brentano** (1838–1917), a distinction has been drawn between conscious experiences, which possess this property of "aboutness," and matter, which is not about anything. This issue comes up often in discussions on machine consciousness. As we shall see in Chapter 5, the philosopher John Searle (1992) has made the point that computers are not conscious because they lack intentionality. Human mental computations are *about* something; they are grounded in reality. In contrast, computer calculations lack this symbol grounding and they do not refer to anything in the real world. Another way of saying this is that computers have no clue what, exactly, it is they are computing.

Arguably the most contentious issue foiling the drafting of a definition is the role of **subjectivity**. On one side are theorists who believe that consciousness, by its very nature, is subjective. If we are to understand the phenomenon in all its aspects, we must include a first-person account in our explanations. The philosopher Thomas Nagel (1974) captured this sentiment in the famous proposal that consciousness includes "**what it is like**" to be something. Subjectivity, then, should be one – if not *the* – essential component of any definition of consciousness. The other camp is composed of theorists who have, to put it mildly, no time for this. They consider the inclusion of subjective data, especially as a defining element, the death of consciousness as a science. They refuse to grant consciousness any special status in the natural order. To them, all its properties, including the "what-it's-likeness," can be accounted for by objective data. We shall have the occasion to revisit this issue numerous times throughout this book.

What are the questions?

The most fundamental question in the study of consciousness is what the universe is made of. Are there two kinds of substances or just one? **Dualism** takes the view that the world can be split into two, physical-stuff and mind-stuff. **Monism** takes the view that the universe contains only one kind of substance, either physical-stuff (**materialism**) or mind-stuff (**idealism**). But even if the answer is one substance, there remains the possibility that this one substance can give rise to two kinds of properties, which brings us back to dualism. The list of primary questions appears endless. How does consciousness arise from matter? Why does it feel the way it does? Who's got it and how much do they have of it? Why do we have it? How did we come by it? What is the best way to study it? We can categorize the main questions facing the study of consciousness into five broad types.

1. What is consciousness? This is a question concerning the very nature of consciousness. What is it made of? Is it a thing? If yes, what kind of thing? Is it a process? If so, what kind of process? What are its properties?

2. How is consciousness related to physical matter and its properties? Neuroscience can ask this question in terms of very specific hypotheses. What events in the brain are associated with consciousness? What properties must neurons or networks possess to enable consciousness? How does information make the transition from an unconscious to a conscious state? Is there a threshold? Does information require representation in working memory for it to become conscious?

3. Who possesses consciousness? Is consciousness a feature of individual organisms or is it also a property of the universe as a whole? To what extent do animals have it? To what extent do computers? At which point do changes to it constitute an altered state of consciousness? Answering these questions would seem to require knowledge of what consciousness is; for how else are we to decide who to credit for it?

4. What is the function of consciousness? How did it evolve? What does it do, or more pointedly, what does it add to the organism? What is its place in the natural order? These questions are closely related to causality. Does consciousness cause thoughts and actions? Or is consciousness but an epiphenomenon with no causal role at all, a view seemingly inconsistent with the principles of evolution?

5. What are the appropriate methods to study consciousness? What aspects of it, if any, are empirical in character and can be investigated scientifically? Is neuroscience going to do all of it? What aspects, if any, will remain forever intractable to science? If there is an inexorable subjective aspect of consciousness, how should it be studied? Would progress then require new developments in epistemology? A new method of phenomenal analysis, perhaps?

The scope of the field

Some of the above questions are within the realm of science, while others are squarely in the domain of philosophy. Consciousness, then, in the most basic sense, is an interdisciplinary field. The task of philosophy is to provide the theoretical landscape, that is, sketch out the solution space and every conceivable answer within it. There is a sense in the philosophy of mind that this has been done. Progress now will have to come from advances in the sciences. The brunt of this work is done by the various subdisciplines of the neurosciences. Other fields contributing prominently to this effort are psychology and artificial intelligence, in particular domains that connect these areas, such as cognitive science. In addition, consciousness is of concern to several medical fields, including psychiatry, neurology, and anesthesiology. Here the goals of the research have practical ramifications. For instance, what implications might a better grasp of the neural substrates of consciousness have for the treatment of chronic pain, brain injury, or Alzheimer's disease? Finally, the study of consciousness cannot be divorced from its spiritual dimensions. Nearly all religions take a clear stand on issues that are at the heart of consciousness studies.

The study of consciousness by such an eclectic mixture of specialists raises the question: what is the proper place of consciousness in the edifice of human knowledge? Does it (already) belong to biology or should it be (still) part of philosophy? Alternatively, is it perhaps best categorized as a branch of psychology? Or should it, given its paramount importance to so many fields of inquiry, be a discipline on its own? Irrespective of the direction in which consciousness will develop as a field, it is quite clear that true expertise will require the student to be familiar with all these areas. No longer can philosophers operate without a working knowledge of the brain. Likewise, neuroscientists and cognitive scientists are well advised to know in detail the theoretical landscape they are beginning to conquer. How, then, should the student interested in this subject best prepare for an academic career in consciousness studies? The answer depends on who you ask. But future advances in consciousness – this much is clear – will come from empirical research. In other words, if the student wishes to make an important contribution, the best course of action is to acquire a thorough understanding of neuroscience and cognitive science.

The theoretical landscape

Clearing the ground

The first task before us is to sketch out the philosophical landscape. This, one would think, sounds like a perfectly reasonable and harmless way to start the long journey that lies ahead. But for reasons that soon will become apparent, it is a task that is anything but harmless. The field of consciousness is a conceptual muddle, an intellectual battleground contested as fiercely as any in war. Perhaps this should not be too surprising; after all, what is at stake here is nothing less than the nature of our souls. Consciousness is a swamp of conflicting theories, rival projects, controversial statements, and inflammatory accusations. With each thought experiment and data point, positions on either side of the frontline become hardened. Anyone intrepid enough to peruse the contemporary philosophical literature discovers quickly that consciousness is riddled with landmines and sharpshooters. To top it off, the battle seems to be a stalemate, with people preparing for the long haul in the trenches. Fanatical convictions and righteous attitudes can often be pacified by empirical evidence. But this is not likely to happen here, for it is science itself that is part of the conceptual mess. All this is enough to make one want to wear a safety helmet when writing a textbook about it. In the end, we must proceed one way or another and this we shall do. For Part I of this book, we will plough our way through mercurial philosophical puzzles, knotty theoretical arguments, and delicate maneuvers of logic, all in the hopeful attempt to do the nearly impossible, a formal analysis of the mind-body problem that is neutral in orientation.

Let's start with a foretaste of the principal impasse in contemporary philosophy of mind: the role of subjectivity. Consciousness poses a big problem for science; a problem unlike any it had to face before. Science is based on objective evidence. By this the scientific community means data that can be independently corroborated and replicated. For a phenomenon to fall under the purview of empirical science it must be, at a minimum, observable and quantifiable. But this is just it. Many philosophers think that phenomenal consciousness is none of the above. It is, in essence, a subjective phenomenon; it is observer-dependent and so can neither be corroborated nor replicated. It comes down to this. How can science, which relies on objective data, investigate a phenomenon in which the data in question is, by definition, subjective?

We seem to have a private, privileged view of our own conscious experience – a view from within – that cannot be seen from an external frame of reference. This personal, exclusive look into our own inner mental life is referred to as the **first-person perspective**. And it is this introspective point of view that is the central data that need to be explained in the study of consciousness. Given this apparent dimension of consciousness, the following enigma arises. If a naïve Martian anthropologist were to inspect a human being – by looking at behavior or post-mortem examination of the brain – it would not suspect that consciousness is there. But from our own point of view, the presence of conscious experience cannot be any more obvious; indeed, if we had to point to our most defining feature, that's what we would probably point to. The philosopher Max Velmans calls this the causal paradox and puts the dilemma this way (1991, p. 716):

> If one examines human information processing purely from a third-person perspective – that is, from the perspective of an external observer – consciousness does not seem to be necessary for any form of processing . . . Viewed from a first-person perspective, consciousness appears to be necessary for most forms of complex or novel processing.

Is it true, then, that the study of consciousness is different from all other disciplines in science? If the sole evidence we have of a phenomenon's existence is subjective – our own knowledge that we possess it, in this case – how can consciousness become a scientific discipline? It ought to be clear that submitting ordinary experience as empirical evidence is, by definition, not an option. It simply does not count as objective, scientific evidence. No one disputes this. Since Emmanuel Kant, especially, it is accepted that introspection only provides us with knowledge about how things seem to us but not how they really are. To paraphrase Kant, experience only tells us what is but not what necessarily is. There are no fundamental truths to be had by looking inside, only truths that apply to the one looking. But what scientists are after are universal truths, applicable to everyone, everything, and everywhere.

If you take the position that the inner and outer worlds have fundamentally different ontologies – one inherently subjective and observer-dependent, the other inherently objective and observer-independent – then the study of consciousness is different from any other field of science. It cannot be pursued by using more of the same methods that worked so well for the study of the material world –

physics, chemistry, biology, and the like. Another way of saying this is that if consciousness cannot be known from a **third-person perspective** it must be something different from the material world, which can be known that way. This is called the **knowledge argument**, and it is a position taken by philosophers such as David Chalmers, John Searle, and Max Velmans, among many others. Conscious experience, they argue, is different because it relates third-person data – brainscans, questionnaires, and so on – to first-person data. The idea that phenomenological data is a legitimate, if not preferable, source of knowledge has a long tradition in philosophy, going back at least as far as Plato. At the turn of the nineteenth century, phenomenology became a major philosophical school of thinking. Its principal proponent, Edmund Husserl, championed the experiential method as a path to true knowledge. Science relies on observation and thus sense perception. This isn't objective at all; it is, as anything else, filtered information that prevents us from seeing "the things themselves." By bracketing all preconceived notions about the world and setting aside all prior judgments, Husserl advocated what he called the epoché, the reflective analysis of conscious experience in a naïve but systematic way. This direct approach to the phenomenal field is common to many Eastern traditions and intellectual movements in the West, such as humanistic psychology or psychotherapy.

Other philosophers, including Daniel Dennett and the Churchlands, and the majority of scientists, including the Crick/Koch team, Gerald Edelman, and Bernard Baars, among rather many others, do not believe that there is such a thing as a first-person perspective to the extent that it is different in kind from a third-person perspective. They remind us of the fact that the first-person mode of existence of consciousness is revealed to us by introspection only, which is no evidence at all. Just because consciousness seems to us this way means nothing. Without some independent grounds, there is no reason to make the conjecture that consciousness is indeed something special in any way. Accordingly, we can attack consciousness by the methods of science that are available to us. The battle, then, is primarily an epistemological one. Neither camp accepts the evidence put forth by the other camps as just that, evidence. This, in a nutshell, is the standoff.

We can draw out this impasse from yet another angle: reducibility. If you think that first-person data is reducible to third-person data, it cannot be different in kind and you are effectively committed to materialism. If, on the other hand, you think that it is *irr*educible, then it *is* different in kind and you are committed to live in a dual universe. Exemplifying the latter view, Searle asks us to inspect what happens when we pinch our arm. According to him, two entirely different events occur. One can be cast in objective terms – neuronal discharges, transmitter release, and so on – while the other is a subjective event that cannot be captured with such physical descriptions; it is ineffable, requires direct access and has a mode of existence that is exclusive to the owner of the experience. He puts it this way: "Consciousness has a first-person or subjective ontology and so cannot be reduced to anything that has a third-person or objective ontology. If you try to reduce or eliminate one in favor of the other you leave something out" (Searle, 1997, p. 212). If you buy into this, experience will never fit into the existing framework of science. The problem of consciousness, then, has just become considerably bigger.

Needless to say, materialists reject the distinction and with it the whole debate. Unless shown otherwise – other than by appeal to ordinary experience – first-person, phenomenal experience is simply a product of the brain's modus operanti and there is no reason to assume that it is not reducible to an objective explanation. Thus, if we reduce or eliminate one in favor of the other, nothing is left out. It is difficult to see how your mind can be your brain, but you will encounter a mountain of evidence that significantly blurs the line between the two. This is the fascination of modern neuroscience. If you buy into this line of reasoning, experience will eventually fit smoothly into a scientific framework of the whole universe, which, of course, does not necessarily diminish the monumental size of the problem.

This is not to say that philosophers holding phenomenalist views forgo science. Most recognize that science has proven to be the most powerful tool when it comes to making real progress. They have little choice but to endorse science if they want to avoid the accusation of mysticism or intellectual stonewalling. They well remember the crippling criticisms leveled against phenomenology and qualitative psychology, which never progressed due to the inherently circular world of subjectivity. As Bertolt Brecht (1939/1966) wrote in his play *Galileo*: "The goal of science is not to open the door to everlasting wisdom, but to set a limit on everlasting error." Given the belief in the inherently subjective nature of mental phenomena, pushing for a science of consciousness is obviously a problem for these philosophers. A first-person science sounds like an oxymoron, and probably is. They, however, maintain that the evidence of ordinary experience substantiates the first-person mode of existence of consciousness beyond reasonable doubt. What we should do then, runs the argument, is to develop a science that is able to handle this kind of first-person psychological data. This amounts to nothing less than a full-fledged revolution in science. Not surprisingly, materialists have a field day with this. Dennett (2001b) calls it "the fantasy of the first-person science" and Churchland (1996, p. 405) labels it "a real humdinger of an argument." Yet some attempts have been made. For instance, the late neuroscientist Francisco Varela (1996) devised a neurologized version of phenomenology called **neurophenomenology**. As the term suggests, it is an approach to consciousness that tries to bridge the apparent divide by combining introspective reports and cognitive science in a way that validates and enhances both. As yet, this has not taken off and few people are working on it so that it might.

We shall encounter this raging battle over and over again in a seemingly infinite variety of forms. At the center is always the supposed unbridgeable gap separating the physical world from mental experience. Dennett divides the major players of this battle into the A and B teams. Team A takes a no-nonsense, scientific approach and demands from team B a positive, independent characterization of the first-person mode of consciousness. Extraordinary claims require extraordinary evidence! Team B takes it as a manifest fact that experience has an ineffable, subjective quality and so embraces the bipartite nature of the universe. It demands from team A clear evidence about how the mind can be nothing but a 3-pound pile of electrified biochemistry. Extraordinary claims require extraordinary evidence! No one budges, with each accusing the other of missing the forest for the trees.

The explanatory gap

Either way you look at it, there is an apparent gap that separates mental phenomena from solid matter. Consciousness does not seem to fit naturally into the scientific framework that explains the physical universe. The difficulty of relating the phenomenal world to the very different world described in physics is known as the **explanatory gap**. The term was coined by the philosopher Joseph Levine (1983, p. 78), who defined it as "a metaphysical gap between physical phenomena and conscious experience." It is possible to organize the current consciousness debate around the notion of the explanatory gap. A rich literature has sprung up characterizing the nature of this apparent gap and all philosophical theories take a clear stand with respect to it. For some, the gap is an ontological one. In this view, consciousness has a mode of existence different in kind to that of matter. For others the gap is merely an epistemological one. Here the view is that consciousness shares with matter the same ontology but our knowledge of its existence is subjective while our knowledge of the existence of matter is objective.

That there is a gap no one contests. The sticking point for the various philosophical positions on the nature of consciousness is what each takes to be the ultimate fate of this gap. It is at this point where temperaments can grow incandescent and the modern frontline of the mind-body problem is drawn. On one side are theorists who believe that the gap represents a fundamental barrier. The conviction arises from the claim that phenomenal consciousness – at either the ontological or epistemological level – is, in essence, a first-person phenomenon. This inherently subjective component of experience makes consciousness irreducible to a third-person perspective. Thus, consciousness cannot be explicated using the conventional methods of science, or to put it bluntly, no amount of empirical research will ever do. On the other side are theorists who believe that the gap is closable. The gap exists only because science has barely begun to look into the matter; for such gaps are to be expected in a new-established field of science. Empirical research will eventually bridge the gap, bringing experience comfortably into the framework of science. Contemporary philosophy of mind is less directed by the traditional dichotomy between dualism and monism as it is hung up on the pivotal role played by subjectivity. This can be seen in the myriad of "hybrid" theories that philosophers have recently generated. These may no longer fit into dualist or monist paradigms, yet they can still be polarized by which side of the explanatory gap they stand. There is no middle ground; either you hold the gap to be unbridgeable or you hold it to be illusory.

Chalmers (1995a) introduced a way to think about the explanatory gap that has since become popular. He divided the study of the mind into **the easy and**

the hard problems. The easy problems are those mental phenomena – attention, emotion, thinking, and so on – that lend themselves to scientific inquiry. They are, of course, not easy by any standard; they are among the toughest problems ever tackled by science. But he identified them as easy on the grounds that they are solvable, in principle, using the scientific method. In contrast, the hard problem is hard because it cannot be solved, not even in principle, using the scientific method. Once the easy problems are explicated in terms of neural or cognitive mechanisms we may be in the position to explain, say, our perceptual ability to see red, but there would still be something left over: why are mental phenomena accompanied by experience; why does seeing red feel like anything? According to Chalmers, neuroscience and cognitive science are limited to making progress on the easy problems but they cannot make headway on consciousness itself. It is a problem that is qualitatively different. Consciousness is something above and beyond the performance of our mental functions. In Chalmers's words (1995b, p. 63), "the hard problem . . . is the question of how physical processes in the brain give rise to subjective experience." One reason why the notion of a residue containing consciousness itself has resonated with people might be because modern science has indeed made no progress on this front. No brain scan or questionnaire can reveal *what it is like* to see red or to be in pain.

In spite of its popularity, the notion of splitting the study of the mind into two parts has been met with vehement opposition from many philosophers and scientists because this very distinction betrays a commitment to the belief that the explanatory gap is a permanent fixture. Many argue that separating mental events from their experiential component and placing the latter off-limits to science curtails research efforts at a time when there is no way of telling if there are indeed limits to what science can and cannot uncover. Many previous efforts to erect a fundamental barrier have turned out to be shortsighted. The division catapults consciousness, without a shred of evidence, into the category of unsolvable mystery, a status that doesn't do anyone any good. Dennett is a leading force in this attack. He believes that there is no hard problem and we are worried about nothing. The hard problem is simply a collection of easy problems that will solve itself as we make progress on those easy problems. He does not deny that some aspects of mental states have so far eluded mind scientists but it does not follow that those properties are anything extra – beyond the scope of science. In his words: "There needs to be nothing remarkable about the residue beyond it being residue" (Dennett, 1996a, p. 4). In a manner that has become his trademark, Dennett offers several analogies designed to expose what he considers an "artifact of misguided theorizing" (1994, p. 130). In the nineteenth century, a movement known as **vitalism** ignited a debate over the question of what life is. It claimed that the problem of life is intractable. Studying the processes that are part of life won't explain why the performance of these processes is accompanied by life. When biology is done with its research program, there would still be a further unanswered question. The debate raged over the better part of the century, with many falling prey to the seductive proposal that life could not possibly arise from a collection of dead molecules. Vitalists believed instead that organisms are infused with a vital force, the so-called élan vital. Imagine a vitalist arguing the following:

> The easy problems of life include those of explaining the following phenomena: reproduction, development, growth, metabolism, self-repair, immunological self-defense, . . . These are not at all *that* easy, of course, and it may take another century or so to work out the fine points, but they are easy compared to the really hard problem: life itself. (Dennett, 1996a, p. 4)

Why are there no vitalists today, asks Dennett? It is because biology solved the problem of "life itself" – along the way, so to speak – by piecemeal work of the easy problems. In the end, there were no leftovers. "The recursive intricacies of the reproductive machinery of DNA make élan vital about as interesting as Superman's dread kryptonite" (Dennett, 1991, p. 25). Dennett argues that "if you don't begin to break them [experiences] down into their (functional) components from the outset, and distribute them throughout your model, you create a monster" (Dennett, 1996a, p. 4), an imaginary problem that does not really exist. We can think of it this way: either you believe that thoughts and feelings flow past *in* the stream of consciousness or thoughts and feelings *are* the stream of consciousness.

Philosophers holding the hard problem to be a genuine troublemaker generally take one of two positions. The first bunch – the so-called new mysterians (Flanagan, 1992) – are those inclined to throw in the towel. A proponent of this camp is the philosopher Colin McGinn (1999, p. 51), who believes that we are not intelligent enough to crack the hard problem. He argues that we are "cognitively closed" with respect to the problem, which is to say, we cannot solve the hard problem for the same reason a cat cannot do trigonometry. We either do not have the right kind of cerebral equipment or not enough of it. As might be expected, this argument is dismissively rebuffed by many for the reason that naysaying at this early stage in the game is unwarranted. The second bunch are those philosophers who have not given up on a solution. But, unlike philosophers denying the existence of the hard problem altogether, they believe that the solution cannot be had using standard scientific procedures that rely on objective, third-person observation. Rather, a radical new kind of science is needed, one that takes seriously the first-person ontology of experience. Accordingly, the hard problem will not unravel with some as-yet-unrealized technology but by developing better methods for collecting first-person, phenomenological data. Chalmers (1996) argues that "this is the greatest challenge now facing a science of consciousness." As Velmans (2000) put it: "The alternative [to standard science] is not a nonscience but a non-reductionist science." Quantum approaches also fit into this category. According to Roger Penrose (1989), mental phenomena are noncomputable. They cannot be solved algorithmically and require a radical shift in scientific thinking. We return to the exciting possibility of quantum theories of mind in Chapter 4. In sum, we have three ways of dealing with the hard problem. One considers it hopeless, the second considers it solvable only if we launch a full-scale revolution in science, and a third considers it a "hornswoggle problem" (P. S. Churchland, 1996, p. 402) at best and a "major misdirector of attention, an illusion generator" (Dennett, 1996a, p. 4) at worst.

Qualia

Qualia (singular, quale) is a term of philosophical jargon. It is used to describe the fact that there seems to be an intrinsic quality to experiential states. Sensory qualia are perhaps the most obvious examples. The physical universe does not contain colors, sounds, or smells; it contains frequencies, amplitudes, and certain types of molecules. Perceptual systems decode physical energies and build representations that reflect reality. So, colors and sounds are not inherent features of the physical world; they are mental properties that exist as a result of us experiencing certain forms of energy. A tree falling in the forest makes no sound if no one is there to hear it. It makes a pressure wave traveling at 700 miles per hour; sounds are made in the brain of an observer. When they are conscious, those perceptions have a certain feel to them. Green, for example, has a quality to it that is different to that of red. Thoughts and feelings also have qualia. The thought of a loved one has a different feel to it than the thought of war. The idea of qualia, then, is that every *conscious* mental event comes with its quale or, alternatively, the quale is what makes the mental event conscious.

Most philosophers think of qualia as the quintessence of experience, the fundamental unit of consciousness. The philosopher Thomas Nagel (1974) captured this sentiment when he asked in the title of his seminal paper what it is like to be a bat; the point being, of course, that we cannot know what it is like to be somebody or something else. It isn't enough to be able to imagine what it is like to be a bat, say, envision how a sonar-generated image of external space might look like. You can really only know what it is like if you *are* the organism. Although a bit clumsy, it is generally agreed that the "what it's likeness" idea captures the essential meaning of phenomenal consciousness. Dualists take this to mean that consciousness has components to which only the subject himself is privy, that is, they require direct access. Thus, qualia are fundamentally subjective, which makes experience a phenomenon requiring a first-person view.

When this issue is put to materialists, be they of a reductionist or functionalist persuasion, the typical response is to deny that qualia exist. Again, what is denied here is not that mental states *seem* to have private aspects but that such first-person seemings are indeed some sort of inexplicable, intrinsic characteristic of mental states. Dennett (1988), for instance, thinks that "qualia are nothing but a special state of knowing and knowing that you know." Apart from that, there is nothing mysterious about them. He agrees that this is not how it seems to us but neither is this a measure for taking such seemings at face value. Mental events also do not seem to be patterns of neural firings, but that's what they are. In this view, qualia are not some kind of additional, inherently ineffable information but a figment of the imagination, a bad habit of thinking that prevents progress in the study of consciousness. He concludes that "there simply are no qualia at all" (ibid., p. 74), at least not in the sense that they are the ineffable mind-stuff people take them to be. This is an extraordinary violation of one of our fondest intuitions but, according to Dennett, it grows on you when you see the supporting evidence. Yet, despite his heroic efforts to "debunk the myth" of qualia, few people are convinced. There is no reason to suppose that the process of evolution would provide us with such a terrifically faulty insight into our own mind. And, even so, the materialist owes us an explanation why such faulty first-person seemings are part of our mental furniture. Other prominent reductionists – Francis Crick (1994), for instance – admit that qualia pose a problem for materialism. In the end, qualia remain the biggest problem for a materialist account of consciousness.

Thought experiments are a favorite contrivance in the toolkit of philosophers. They are initially designed to clarify our thinking on a particular issue but their real purpose is to lead one's philosophical opponent into an impossible theoretical position. So cornered, the opponent typically employs two tactics. First, she designs a thought experiment of her own to do the same to her rival. Second, she declares the first thought experiment either ill-conceived on the grounds that it fails to address the real problem, not to mention that it misconstrues her position, or that it is flawed and therefore absurd. Because of this, thought experiments do little to persuade opponents or clarify our thinking. They are however, heaps of fun, a sort of mental gymnastics exercise, as long as we do not take them too seriously. The issue of qualia has generated its fair share of such thought experiments and we consider two rather famous ones, to clarify our thinking of course.

The first, **Mary the color scientist**, was devised by the philosopher Frank Jackson (1982). It features Mary, who grows up to become a color scientist without ever experiencing color. At birth, her evil captors lock her up in a black-and-white room. She only has access to a black-and-white TV, her skin is bleached white, and there are no windows or mirrors to see the outside world or her own eye color. Mary lives in the future when sensory neuroscience has solved all the mysteries of vision. She has a complete understanding of how the brain does the business of perception, how surfaces reflect light, and which color goes with which object. In short, she knows *every*thing there is to know about color. Finally, her captors release her into the world. The question then is this: Does Mary learn something new that her previous knowledge did not tell her? Will she exclaim: "Oh, that's how red looks like!" Or, won't she be surprised at all? Jackson devised this scenario as an argument against materialism. According to him, nothing will ever prepare Mary for the actual experience of seeing red. As soon as she does, she gets some sort of additional information – the quale of red, the-something-that-it-is-like to see red that can only come from lived experience. Mary will have learned a fundamentally new fact about the world, one that she could not have learned from all her smart books.

It goes without saying that materialists are less-convinced of the "self-evident" conclusion that Mary is now the proud owner of a "raw feel," a "phenomenal quality" she lacked before. The strongest rebuff comes, again, from Dennett. He dismisses, in good philosophical tradition, the entire exercise on the grounds that Jackson simply fails to follow the instruction. If Mary does know *every*thing about color then she cannot possibly be surprised; this is what it means to "know all the facts." If she is surprised, she simply cannot have known everything there is about color! But Dennett (1991) goes further by adding, for good measure, his own twist to the story. He asks us to imagine that Mary's captors present her with a blue banana. Mary knows bananas are yellow; so, how will she react? Dennett argues that it makes no sense to think that she might be fooled. The sight of blue will not give her a (blue) quale that she then associates with the color yellow and proclaims: "Oh, that's what yellow looks like!" Given that she knows the reflective properties of both colors, she is likely to ask: "Who colored the banana blue?" Thus, there is no such thing as color qualia. Finally, a third, intermediate interpretation is that Mary does get to know something new but it is not some mysterious ineffable qualia; she simply learns an old fact in a new way.

A second thought experiment is the **philosophical zombie**. This one hits the same (qualia) spot but from a slightly different angle. The zombie is a creature exactly like you and me, except it lacks consciousness. Its behavior is indistinguishable from that of a sentient being but it has no qualia, or as Chalmers (1996, p. 96) put it, it's "all dark inside." The zombie has no idea of what it is like to be a zombie. The first sticking point is whether or not you think that the concept of a zombie is *logically* possible, that is, does not violate any laws of nature. It should be clear that the concession of logical possibility requires you to take consciousness itself to be something above and beyond the mere performance of mental functions. If you do you must concede that a creature could evolve whose behavior is not accompanied by experience, a creature who does everything you do, in the same way you do, but who does not share with you the same phenomenology. Searle (1992), for instance, thinks that computer systems in the future could be zombies and perform the identical functions we perform but without conscious experience. If, on the other hand, you consider consciousness an integral (meaning functional) part of the performance of mental operations, then consciousness is not something extra to behavior. Thus, consciousness cannot be selectively taken out and a zombie is not logically possible.

If you concede zombie plausibility you are forced to commit to **inessentialism**. Zombies are isomorphic twins. If they do not differ from us behaviorally, consciousness makes no difference to behavior and consciousness must be considered superfluous to causation. It is one thing to adopt dualism; it is quite another to also adopt all the consequences that go with it. Most people believe that consciousness is something outside the physical universe but can nevertheless supervene on it. Note that these are quite incompatible positions. There are, of course, ways out of this dilemma for dualism in general but in terms of zombies the matter is clear. If consciousness is to cause action, the rules of zombihood are violated; they are no longer truly functionally isomorphic. If you do away with conceivability, the whole exercise falls down. There is no point further discussing zombihood, if you take consciousness to be inseparably entangled into the system. This is what Patricia Churchland (1996, p. 404) recommends when she states that zombies are a "demonstration of the feebleness of thought experiments." Dennett (1991) takes another route. He knows of the seductiveness of the

Figure 1.1

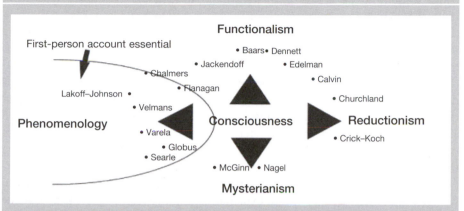

Varela (1996) made this diagram to help position prominent contemporary theories of mind in relation to one another. The placement is his own and not necessarily endorsed by the philosophers and scientists concerned. It is also purposely incomplete; for instance, quantum approaches are omitted. The diagram consists of two dimensions reflecting important directions in the study of consciousness. For the horizontal axis, phenomenology is pitted against reductionism, which roughly corresponds to the traditional dualist/materialist dichotomy. The phenomenology section has a portion cordoned off for theories that hold first-person data essential to a complete understanding of the nature of consciousness. For the vertical axis, functionalism is pitted against mysticism. This dimension can also be understood in terms of how different theories take the study of consciousness to be, with functionalism taking a decidedly practical approach.

"zombie hunch" and tries to counter it with an example of its own, the cheekily named **zimbo**. A zimbo is a creature that has evolved a little beyond the zombie and has the ability to represent its mental processes in the form of higher-order informational states. These self-monitoring systems allow the zimbo to reflect on lower-order processes and report about its own internal activities – what it is like to be in pain or to have nightmares, that sort of thing. The zimbo would have unconscious thoughts *about* its dreams and feelings and at some point it would think the unconscious thought: I am conscious! According to Dennett, this, roughly, is what happened to us during the course of evolution. Qualia are simply higher-order mental representations. With this in mind, we can appreciate the direction of Dennett's controversial statement that "we are all zombies" (ibid., p. 406).

Summary

Consciousness is the crown jewel of our existence. It is the central phenomenon of philosophy, psychology, and neuroscience and when we study it we are approaching what some might call the human essence. Despite its supreme status, defining consciousness has proven to be an exceedingly frustrating task. How could something we are so intimately familiar with be so slippery? As James (1892/1961, p. 19) put it: "its meaning we know as long as no one asks us to define it." The field of consciousness is truly interdisciplinary in nature. It asks questions that touch upon many disciplines, from physics to the humanities. Current work focuses most on the puzzle of how the brain gives rise to conscious experience.

The field of consciousness can be divided broadly into two camps. The line of demarcation is subjectivity. One camp asserts that consciousness has characteristics – the what-it's-like feel or qualia, specifically – that are inherently subjective and require a first-person frame of reference. The other asserts that consciousness has no such features and will be explicated, in time, in entirely objective terms, that is, from a third-person frame of reference. This partition overlaps significantly, but is not identical to, the traditional division of dualism versus monism. All agree that there seems to be an explanatory gap between events at the level of the brain and events in the world of psychological experience. The latter group believes this gap to be a temporary feature that will inevitably be closed by experimental research while the former believes it to be forever unbridgeable. The latest version of this gap is to divide consciousness studies into easy and hard problems. While the easy problems are those concerned with mental phenomena that can be investigated using science, the hard problem is concerned with consciousness itself and not subject to science. Opponents of this distinction claim that it creates an artificial problem that does not really exist.

Suggested reading

Chalmers, D. J. (ed.) (2002). *Philosophy of Mind: Classical and Contemporary Readings*. Oxford: Oxford University Press.
Churchland, P. M. (1988). *Matter and Consciousness*. Cambridge: MIT Press.

2 A brief history

The origins of the field

Philosophy

Historically, dualism has been the dominant theory of mind. The belief that there is more to us than our physical self, coupled with the hope that something of our essence transcends the death of the body, is deeply entrenched in the world's major religions. That consciousness is something fundamentally different from matter was, until recently, also the predominant view in philosophy. It is not surprising, then, that dualism is the most widely held view in the public at large. With the rise of science, especially the torrents of data from cognitive science and neuroscience that positively link minds to brains, the balance of power has shifted. Today, materialism has become the dominant theory of mind among scientists and philosophers, although the vast majority of the lay public remains firmly in the dual-substance camp.

Long before antiquity, in Paleolithic cave paintings and the tombs of ancient Egypt, humans left testimony to the belief in the afterlife. It was not until the Greeks, however, that dualism was made explicit and contrasted with the opposite possibility, monism. This method of contrasting opposing views was central to the way the Greeks approached philosophical problems. In ethics, good was contrasted with evil, harmony with strife, and truth with falsehood. In cosmology, the Greeks asked whether the universe is simple or complex, boundless or limited, chaotic or ordered. Finally, there were the questions regarding the essential character of man, freedom versus determinism, nature versus nurture, and, of course, mind versus matter (Russell, 1989). Many contemporary thinkers insist that this dialectic approach turned the mind-body problem into a false dichotomy that has misdirected inquiries into the nature of consciousness.

The Greeks were the first to talk about minds and souls (Hunt, 1993). **Socrates** (469–399) held the view that the soul was immortal; it is imprisoned in the body, parts in death from its physical container, only to be embodied in the next person. The concept of an immortal soul led Socrates to his **epistemology**, which is the field of philosophy that concerns itself with the origins, nature, methods, and limits of knowledge; in other words, *how* we know what we know. Earlier, several **Sophist** thinkers reasoned that we derive all knowledge from the senses. **Protagoras** (485–411) took this position to its logical conclusion. Perceptions only hold true to the perceiver, and he argued that if such a subjective starting place is our exclusive source of knowledge we can never know about absolute truth. **Democritus** (460–370) proposed further that all matter, including the soul, is made up of invisible particles he called atoms. This idea, together with the views of his contemporary **Hippocrates** (460–377), are perhaps the clearest expression of the materialist position of the mind-body problem in Greek philosophy.

Socrates took the opposite position. He argued that if Protagoras were right no opinion is better, that is, closer to the truth, than any other. Protagoras countered by pointing out that there are many criteria other than truth by which we can judge opinions, for instance heuristic value. This did not appeal to Socrates. He proposed instead that the way to knowledge and truth is through introspection – not through observation. This, he argued, leads to genuine understanding because the soul is immortal and thus already contains the truth. All we need to do is to look within ourselves. The quest for truth is essentially remembering, a view highlighted by his famous recommendations: "know thyself" and "the unexamined life is not worth living."

Plato (427–348) was perhaps the first to systematically theorize about the soul. Like his teacher Socrates, he argued for the **theory of transmigration** that envisioned the soul in alternating states of embodiment and disembodiment. When free of the body, the soul is pure; it knows the truth uncontaminated from worldly input. When it resides in a body, it interacts with it on three levels; at the highest level is thought or reason, followed by spirit or will, and, at the lowest, appetite or desire. Plato also located these faculties in the brain, chest, and abdomen, respectively. This was the first version of **dualist interactionism**, the attempt to account for the puzzle of how souls, being a substance of an immaterial nature, could interact with solid matter.

Plato also developed further Socrates' epistemology. He rejected the Protagorean concept that perception is the only source of wisdom. In *The Republic*, in what must be one of the most famous passages in all of philosophy, Plato outlined his position using the parable of the metaphysical cave. Although not originally his own and in any case not our main concern, his **theory of ideas** is inseparably intertwined with the different approaches to the study of consciousness. Briefly, he surmised that reality consists of ideas that exist in an abstract form in the soul. Material objects are only shadows of those ideas, mere appearances of the fundamental reality of ideas. The idea of beauty, for instance, is more real than the beauty we experience through the senses because worldly beauty dies, while the idea of beauty is eternal. Since reality is abstract and exists as such only in the immortal soul, the search for truth and knowledge can only proceed through deductive reasoning. In other words, knowledge is innate, and only through the power of reason and introspection can we come to understand the true nature of things. The consequence of this position is that knowledge is not only unattainable by way of perception but that perception is outright deceptive. All one can ever see are shadows of what is real. Plato argued that one is misled by looking at the universe; so studying it, to put it bluntly, is a waste of time. Considering that science is an endeavor that relies on observable data, it is not surprising that Plato has been called the greatest enemy science has ever had.

Differences in epistemology, what one accepts as sources of reliable knowledge, are also at the center of the deepest fissure in consciousness today. Recall from Chapter 1 that some philosophers assert that a subjective, first-person account is essential to the study of the mind. This approach traces its foundation to the philosophy of Socrates and Plato. It is not necessarily tied with dualism, but simply expresses the conviction that some information about the nature of consciousness, however sophisticated science might become, cannot be obtained through objective data, rendering the study of mind, fully or in part, forever beyond the reach of science. Proponents of the other view can be aligned with the philosophy of Protagoras and Democritus. They assert that introspection, however logical or systematic, is fundamentally subjective and so never constitutes a reliable source of information. Progress in consciousness cannot be made where subjectivity remains part of the equation. This modern debate can thus be dated as far back as the Greeks.

In the nearly 2,000 years that followed, inquiries into the nature of souls were virtually nonexistent. **Aristotle** (384–322) did not concern himself with the subject in the methodical manner with which he treated other topics. No doubt influenced by his teacher Plato, he was a dualist in his early writings, and claimed that the psyche – the name he gave to the thinking part of the soul – was independent of the body. Later in life, however, he came down on the side of monism and thought that the psyche is the working of the body. It cannot have escaped Aristotle what central place the issue commands in man's existence and that a nonchalant U-turn on such an important matter requires some sort of discerned treatment. But he never attended to it. It is possible that monism to Aristotle was not the position we take it to be today but rather the belief that everything contains soul, a sort of **panpsychism**.

Aristotle was a biologist of note, but, in a rather peculiar lapse, proposed that the heart is the seat of the soul. Hippocrates, who we shall meet a little later, and even Plato had been much nearer the mark. Aristotle's argument was unsound and involved the observation that damage to the brain does not cause death, while damage to the heart does. He concluded that the heart must be more important. To learn something "by heart," for instance, is a vestige of Aristotelian logic. The brain's function was merely to cool blood. The Roman physician **Galen**

(130–201) called this theory "utterly absurd." He dissected the brain of different animals and noted that all sense organs attach to the brain, not the heart.

After Aristotle, even if we allow for some breathers, the lights went out and European intellectual life was not worth the paper it was written on. This was particularly true for unsettling questions such as, for instance, the nature of souls. There was little tolerance for views other than the one that glorified God. Materialism became blasphemy, and to some, it still is. It was not until the scientific revival of the renaissance that the inquisitory way of the Greeks was restored.

René Descartes (1596–1650) formulated the modern version of Platonic dualism. Progress in the natural sciences had led to the mechanistic philosophy, a view that presupposed that the universe was set in motion by God and has operated according to immutable laws ever since. In line with the times, Descartes theorized that the body is part of this material world. He even granted reflexes and some basic behaviors to be the workings of bodily mechanics. But Descartes could not fathom that uniquely human faculties such as language or reason are part of this same mechanical system; they must be manifestations of something entirely different. This was the motive for postulating a second substance – an immortal soul that is independent of ordinary matter. Animals lack this soul substance; they are purely mechanical devices, as evidenced by their inability to reason and use language. Like Plato before him, Descartes needed to explain how this insubstantial soul-stuff interacts with the solid matter of the flesh. By sharpening further the separation between body and mind, this question became an ever more pressing issue. His famous solution involved the proposal of a rather obscure lump of tissue called the pineal gland as the liaison between body and soul. This was supposed to follow from nothing else but its special place at the midline of the brain.

Like Plato, Descartes dismissed sensory input as mere appearances. Genuine knowledge of primary qualities can only be derived through reason. But what do we take as a secure starting point from which to launch our metaphysical inquiries? The search for this place of certainty directed Descartes to a systematic doubt of everything, even mathematics, until he had to admit that he could not doubt that there was an entity that was doing the doubting. Hence his famous axiom: "I think therefore I am." The problem with this principle is that it contains the tacit assumptions that thinking is a self-conscious process and that self-reference is infallible. "I eat therefore I am" is presumably different because I could always fool myself into thinking that I am eating when I am not. But if you do away with self-consciousness, this objection also holds for the activity of thinking (Russell, 1989).

The British empiricists rejected Descartes' notion of an immortal soul. A rather practical bunch, they were not very high on metaphysics and devoted little time to pondering the nature of the mind. **Empiricism** is the heir of the Protagorean tradition; its epistemology is grounded in sense perception and its position on consciousness is vaguely leaning toward materialism. This redrawing of the mind-body line in the sand in the 1600s and 1700s was followed by another couple of centuries of relative calm. Exploration in other sciences continued, but the mind remained mysterious.

In continental Europe, philosophers remained committed to a nonscientific approach to the study of the mind. This ideology reached its peak at the turn of the century in a tradition known as **phenomenology**. Phenomenology took its cues from the epistemology of **Emmanuel Kant** (1724–1804), who argued that the knowledge we have of the world is not derived from sensory experience but is constructed by the mind. Accordingly, experience only tells us what is but not what necessarily is. Another way of saying this is that experience does not give us fundamental truths about the world; it only shows us how the world seems to be. The mind orders and comprehends experience by way of a built-in mental machinery – the **12 Kantian categories**. The phenomenologist **Edmund Husserl** (1859–1938) viewed science as a part of this process of construction and, as such, a method that distorts the nature of our experiences. He advocated going back to "the things themselves," by which he meant direct subjective experience. The essence of the mind can only be known by introspecting – without judgment or preconceptions.

In the 1970s, fueled by the new arrivals on the scene of neuroscience and cognitive science, philosophy experienced a renewal of interest in the philosophy of mind. This burst of activity was not just a commentary on the Greeks, but it generated genuinely novel positions. We will explore these positions in the next chapter.

Psychology

In psychology, consciousness has come full circle. As an independent, standalone discipline, psychology came into existence in 1879 when Wilhelm Wundt opened the Psychologisches Institut at the University of Leipzig, the first lab solely devoted to psychological research. At that time the subject matter of psychology was consciousness. When behaviorism took over as the reigning paradigm, even if we allow for the Gestalt movement and Freud, consciousness was swept under the rug and disappeared altogether. Its comeback into mainstream psychology started in the 1960s and today it again occupies its rightful central position.

Mental phenomena belonged traditionally to the domain of philosophy, but by the middle of the nineteenth century, advances in physiology made it possible to tackle some of them empirically. This endeavor started with investigations into sensory organs and how they give rise to perception, which inexorably made contact with the age-old questions of epistemology and the nature of minds. Germany was the center of **psychophysics**, as this field is known. **Johannes Müller** (1801–58) was the first modern physiologist in this tradition. He is best remembered for his **doctrine of specific nerve energies**. Müller knew that all nerves conduct only one type of message – electrical impulses – which brought to the fore the question why eyes always see and ears always hear. How does the same basic information give rise to different perceptions? Müller reasoned that the code must be location, that is, the electrical activity occurs in specific nerves that are set to interpret impulses in only one way. We know today that it is not the nerve but the brain region that gives meaning to neural activity, but Müller's work meant that the brain must be functionally divided and, importantly, that such divisions can be probed scientifically. While he dispensed with air tubes and the like, giving physiology a solid scientific foundation, he was not committed to a materialistic account of the mind. He thought humans were endowed with a vital force of a nonmaterial nature that breathed life into the mechanical machinery of the body, a position known as vitalism.

Further, **Ernst Weber** (1795–1878) demonstrated that any sensory experience can be altered in a predictable manner by changing the intensity of the stimulus. This is known as **Weber's law** and it represented the first statement of its kind: a clear relationship between the physical and the mental world. **Theodore Fechner** (1801–87), who is considered the father of psychophysics, did most of the work on Weber's law and it ought to be really called Fechner's law, but it was he who opted to name it after his teacher, Weber. The most prominent member of this group of physiologists was **Herman von Helmholtz** (1821–94). A fierce experimentalist, his work encompassed, among a good deal else, contributions to color vision, blindness, depth perception, and audition. He also determined the speed of nerve pulse conduction, jokingly known as the velocity of thought. Apart from experimental physiology, Helmholtz is of historical importance to the study of consciousness because he was the most influential member of the **Berlin Physical Society**, a scientific organization utterly committed to a mechanistic conception of mental processes. The society's motto was best stated by Du Bois-Raymond: "No forces other than the common physical-chemical ones are active within the organism." This position was, of course, not new, but when a scientist of such impeccable and prominent standing as Helmholtz put his weight behind an idea, people, at the very least, tend to listen. But it also wasn't just his authority and influence. His trichromatic theory of color vision, for instance, supplied fresh and clear evidence that an experience – color, in this case – has physical causes – different receptors in the retina. It was nevertheless a tough stand during a period when everyone else was still heavily into animal magnetism, vital forces, holy spirits, and other departures from common sense.

This set the stage for **Wilhelm Wundt** (1832–1920) to merge the new physiology with the venerable topics of philosophy. He studied under Müller and Bois-Raymond and became a lab assistant to Helmholtz. Despite this schooling, he disliked the mechanistic approach. He objected to the dismissal of introspection by these physiologists on the grounds that it did away with mental life and reduced psychology to studying the relationship between physiology and matter. Wundt was convinced that introspection could be modified with proper training so as to yield objective data. This, he felt, opened the way to study mental processes experimentally. His research program was aimed at identifying and measuring the fundamental elements of experience in the hope of uncovering the basic structure of the mind in a way similar to what Mendeleyev did a little earlier for chemistry when he proposed the periodic table. This is why his approach is identified as **structuralism**. While Wundt temporarily restored interest in consciousness it became rapidly clear that his modified version of introspection did nothing to eliminate the inherent subjectivity, and his research program fell flat.

William James (1842–1910) was a contemporary of Wundt and even studied in his lab for two years. He also regarded consciousness to be the principal subject matter of psychology; but his approach could not have been more different. James focused on the functions of the mind, not its structure, and studied what the mind *does*, rather than what it *is*. Hence the label **functionalism**. This approach was informed by the theory of evolution. Mental processes have evolved for the adaptive advantage of the organism and it is for this reason that they exist. When he returned to the USA after his stint in Europe, he became professor of psychology at Harvard University, the first such professor anywhere. He is famously quoted as saying: "the first lecture in psychology I ever heard was the first I ever gave" (James, 1890), though he must surely have heard Wundt lecture in Leipzig. He introduced America to experimental psychology and advocated the empirical study of the mind. Incongruously, he did little research of his own, so his main contributions to psychology and consciousness remain theoretical in nature.

James admitted that introspection is inherently faulty but thought that it was still a useful tool in the search for self-knowledge. Indeed, if a case is to be made for anyone that a keen sense of introspection (not theorizing) can advance science he may be that case. For James was a brilliant synthesizer of information, perhaps without equal in the history of psychology before or since. In 1890, he published *Principles of Psychology*, a textbook that gathered the available evidence and summarized the state of affairs at the time. It helped that he was fluent in German and had thus first-hand knowledge of the work of the German physiologists. In 1894, he was also the first in America to talk about a then obscure Viennese physician by the name of Sigmund Freud, who at that time was still struggling to be somebody, even in Vienna.

James understood well the evidence the German physiologists were cranking out, especially the work of Fechner. But he could not share their enthusiasm for materialism. He was raised in a home that emphasized humanistic and spiritual values. In the *Principles* we can see him struggling mightily but luminously with the mind-body problem and other knotty subjects. In the end he did not like any solution on the nature of the mind and recommended the question to be dropped from psychology. Privately, he sided with dualism.

When James is mentioned one thinks at once of the **stream of consciousness**. The concept of consciousness as a continual flow of experiences, rather than a series of discrete steps linked together, was a product of his functionalist position; the mind is a process, not a thing. Sleep, then, is not consciousness interrupted but a transient change along a natural continuum. This notion was widely adopted and exerted an influence beyond psychology. In literature, for instance, authors like Proust and Joyce started to write in stream style. James was also the first to theorize about the unconscious mind, a notion that did not really exist before him. But he did not pursue the notion further because information, to him, never leaves consciousness, so that all events that take place in the mind are, by definition, conscious. This was the prevailing view at the time. It was inconceivable that thinking could happen in the mind without consciousness. It would seem to leave morality to forces outside the control of free will. So when James introduced unconscious processes in the mind he meant that they were responsible for executing automatic movements, such as reflexes or walking.

While James preceded Freud with the unconscious mind, **Sigmund Freud** (1856–1939) developed it in a different direction. Like an iceberg that hides mostly underwater, the unconscious mind not only contains information, but the vast majority of it besides. Freud speculated that we repress into the unconscious events and experiences that are anxiety-provoking and socially unacceptable. This, however, does not rid us of them; they continue to determine behavior ominously, only now without our explicit knowledge. We need not here consider the arguments of his framework in detail. They were not very sound as arguments, though they did raise interesting questions about the internal operations of the mind. Freud's influence has declined sharply over the past few decades and, with the exception of clinical psychology, has virtually disappeared from mainstream psychology.

In contrast, James's influence is still felt today, particularly in the study of consciousness. With his astute insights and ever lucid writing style, he put his finger on the key sticking point of many issues. He disentangled consciousness from the closely related subjects of attention and memory in a manner that is remarkably close in its gross outline to the modern interpretation. He also foreshadowed the notion of a dual memory system, devised with the physiologist Carl Lange the influential James–Lange theory of emotion, and wrote extensively on the concept of the self, an issue of central importance to the study of consciousness.

By the 1910s, psychology had become a new field of study with independent departments in most major universities. But it had not become scientific. The reliance upon introspection by the pivotal early figures, Wundt, James, and Freud, produced little in the way of objective data. Against this backdrop, **behaviorism** rose to prominence, largely fueled by the desire to make psychology a scientific field. To do this, behaviorists like **John Watson** (1878–1958) proposed to study observable behaviors that were operationally defined and thus measurable and quantifiable. The behaviorist research program was spectacularly successful in building the knowledge base of psychology, a fact that is often overlooked these days. But the approach also meant that questions about the mind, consciousness, or specific mental processes must be dropped from psychology because they were unobservable and thus intractable by the methods of science. Behaviorists did not deny the existence of the mind; they simply proposed that it cannot be studied in a scientific manner. While some maintained that this is a temporary restriction that might ameliorate in time, others proposed that the mind has no causal role and can be bracketed for good. This latter position is known as **radical behaviorism** and its principal proponent, **B. F. Skinner** (1904–90), believed that studying the contingencies in the environment provides a complete account of the causes of human behavior.

The behaviorist philosophy, borne of necessity or conviction, effectively banished consciousness from psychology. The mind became not just indescribably low key, but the mere mentioning of it conjured up images of unscientific hogwash, which hung over psychology like the sword of Damocles. But by the mid-1950s, people grew dissatisfied. Behaviorism was not addressing matters that were obviously part, if not central, to a complete understanding of human behavior. As a paradigm for the whole of psychology, it could serve no longer. Several influences from within and outside psychology catalyzed this development. **Noam Chomsky** transformed the study of language, making clear in the process that language cannot be understood in the framework of learning paradigms. The theories of **John von Neumann** (1903–57) led to the invention of the computer, and pioneers like **Herbert Simon** (1916–2001) and **Marvin Minsky** produced the first software programs that simulated cognitive processes. Artificial intelligence was born. Neuroscientists were also probing the mind in new ways, such as, for instance, the work of **David Hubel** and **Torsten Wiesel** on vision using single-cell electrophysiology. **George Miller** founded the Cognitive Science Center at Harvard University and gave cognitive psychology academic legitimacy. The new paradigm caught on rapidly, largely because these developments made it possible to study higher mental functions scientifically and avoid the pitfalls of introspection that plagued the early psychologists. Today, psychology is defined as the study of behavior and mental processes, and consciousness is back on everybody's mind.

Neuroscience

In the last few decades, consciousness has been buried under a mountain of neuroscience. It is becoming increasingly difficult to tunnel into this mountain for people not completely fluent in brainspeak. What's more, scientific advances that relate to consciousness continue to flow out of neuroscience labs at an ever more breathtaking pace. We have reached a critical junction. Just as other once purely philosophical problems like the origin of life or the nature of matter have become the subjects of the independent scientific fields of biology and physics, the mind – and its faculties – is being reassigned to the field of neuroscience. It is understandable that some dislike this takeover attitude of neural science but, at the very least, the time is past when an *informed* contribution to consciousness can be made by people who are unfamiliar with the nuts and bolts of brains.

Neuroscience is totally invested in materialism. It is not uncommon to find neuroscientists treating dualism with polite derision. The gospel of modern brain research is, of course, that the mind *is* the brain. The historical roots of this position can also be traced to the Greeks. The physician Hippocrates is widely regarded as the father of modern medicine because he divorced medicine from religion by advocating that diseases have natural causes. In an often quoted passage from his book *On the sacred disease* (by which he meant epilepsy) he wrote:

> Men ought to know that from the brain, and from the brain only, arise our pleasures, joys, laughter, and jests, as well as our sorrows, pains, grief, and tears. And by this we acquire wisdom and knowledge, and see and hear and know what are foul and what are fair, what are bad and what are good . . . And by the same organ we become mad and delirious, and fears and terrors assail us . . . All

these things we endure from the brain when it is not healthy but becomes abnormally hot, cold, moist or dry. (Hippocrates, 1952, p. 159).

This passage could have been written by a contemporary neuroscientist – minus the hot and moist part. What this illustrates is that the history of the brain story of consciousness is best told as a series of steps toward an ever greater understanding of the inner workings of the brain. And this story is best organized around what is known as the doctrine of localization of function, the belief that brain functions are localizable in particular bits and pieces of neural tissue.

Francis Gall (1757–1824) was among the first to attempt to map mental functions onto brain areas. He reasoned that a person's strengths and weaknesses would be reflected in the size of the respective brain region. This idea gave rise to the pseudoscience of **phrenology**. If the brain is formed according to talents and flaws the skull must be shaped likewise. By examining the skull, a phrenologist could then determine a man's character. Needless to say, this effort to localize function backfired badly as neither the functional map nor the conjecture that this affects skull shape had any empirical basis. Ambrose Bierce (1911/2000) quipped that phrenology is "the science of picking a man's pocket through the scalp."

The task of debunking phrenology fell to **Pierre Flourens** (1794–1867). He pioneered a technique called **experimental ablation**, which explores brain function by removing circumscribed areas of brains and observing what the animal can no longer do. The control of the disrupted behavior is then attributed to the ablated region. Flourens's method quickly disposed of phrenology. For instance, Gall ascribed amativeness to the cerebellum, but when Flourens removed it he found nothing of the sort missing. Instead, Flourens grew increasingly skeptical of the notion that higher mental faculties are localized at all. While his own work showed him that subcortical regions, such as the cerebellum or certain nuclei in the medulla, do have specific roles, he was less enthusiastic about the idea that cortical regions are similarly compartmentalized with respect to processes such as language and memory. No matter where in the cortex he placed a lesion, he failed to find a neat correspondence between anatomy and function. He eventually concluded that mental faculties are distributed in the cortex, a view that was a decisive factor for Müller to opt for specific nerve energies rather than specific brain areas.

The pendulum soon swung back to the localizationist's camp in 1861 when the surgeon **Paul Broca** (1824–80) reported the case of a stroke patient who lost his ability to speak. The patient's name was Monsieur Leborgne but he is also famously known as Tan because this was the only word he could still utter. Broca examined Tan thoroughly and found no additional disability; Tan possessed normal intelligence, healthy vocal apparatus, and no deficit in understanding language. Six days after his initial visit Tan died. Broca's autopsy showed that the stroke damaged a region in the left inferior frontal cortex. Because Broca had obtained a cognitive profile of Tan, he was in the unique position to use the rationale of experimental ablation on humans and infer a specific higher cognitive function – language production – to a specific cortical region, known ever since as **Broca's area**. Soon after Broca's discovery a similar event happened to the neurologist **Karl Wernicke** (1848–1904), only this time the deficit involved language comprehension and the focal lesion occurred in the left temporal cortex, a region known ever since as **Wernicke's area**. Wernicke's aphasia, as this disorder is called, is a striking phenomenon because it does not affect the ability to speak, so that the individual fluently speaks utter nonsense. The two cases provided seemingly indisputable evidence that language had a precise locale in the brain.

In the eighteenth century, **Luigi Galvani** (1737–98) had convinced everyone that nerves contract muscles by way of electrical impulses. In the 1870s, shortly after Broca and Wernicke identified the brain's language regions, two physiologists, **Gustav Fritsch** (1838–1907) and **Eduard Hitzig** (1838–1927), used electrical stimulation in an effort to pinpoint other functions. They exposed the surface of dog brains and applied their electrodes to the primary motor cortex. When they passed a weak current through specific regions of this cortex, specific muscles on the contralateral side of the body contracted. Here, then, was more evidence for the localization viewpoint; the brain has a region responsible for controlling voluntary movement.

Recall that Fechner and Helmholtz published their work at around the same time. The explosion of research on the nervous system in the late nineteenth century, to say nothing of **Charles Darwin's** (1809–92) publication of the theory of evolution in 1859, reached a critical mass that could sustain, for the first time, a credible materialistic position on the nature of consciousness. Neuroscience never looked back and with every subsequent discovery the mind-equals-brain position was ever more solidified.

The next great leap forward occurred in the cellular realm. The conception that the human body is composed of cells had only just recently been proposed by **Theodore Schwann** (1810–82). Shortly thereafter **Johannes Purkyně** (1787–1869) described the first cell in the nervous system. But as far as neurons go, the brain was terra incognita. This changed abruptly when the anatomist **Camillo Golgi** (1843–1926) discovered serendipitously how to make neurons visible. The famous **Golgi stain** is based on silver impregnation, and the method highlights neurons pitch black against a pale, yellowish background. While Golgi used it to study neurons in greater detail, describing axons, dendrites, and the morphology of different types of neurons in the process, he failed to see with his beloved technique the larger picture of how neurons are organized to make brains. He thought that neurons form a seamlessly interconnected network with the brain as a whole, being a single, continuous entity. **Santiago Ramón y Cajal** (1852–1934), considered by many the greatest neuroanatomist, disagreed. He proposed instead that neurons are discrete units that form a network broken up by small gaps. This view became known as the **neuron doctrine**. Ironically, Ramón y Cajal used Golgi's own stain to come to this opposing conclusion. The debate, which was more of a battle at times, raged for years and was not conclusively settled in favor of the neuron doctrine until **Charles Sherrington** (1865–1940) showed the existence of this gap in the 1930s and gave it the name by which we know it today – the

Figure 2.1

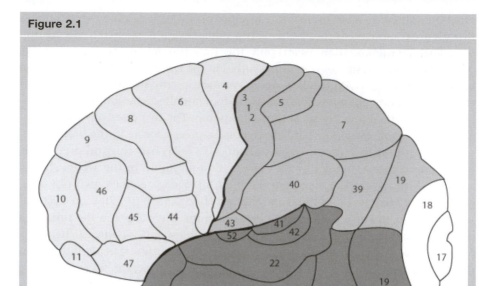

Divisions of the cerebral cortex by cytoarchitechtonics, after Korbinian Brodmann's famous map of 1909.

synapse. Golgi and Ramón y Cajal received the Nobel Prize for their contributions in 1906, but Golgi never acknowledged his error.

The upshot of this intense struggle was a careful classification of different neuronal subtypes. These data led to a major effort to characterize cortical regions on the basis of cell structure and arrangement, or **cytoarchitecture.** The working assumption was, of course, that anatomical boundaries would reflect functional divisions. The anatomist **Korbinian Brodmann** (1869–1918) mapped the cerebral cortex by this cellular organization and divided it into 52 distinct areas. Brodmann's numbers are still in use. For instance, BA (Brodmann Area) 17 is the primary visual cortex, while BA 41 is the primary auditory cortex.

In the 1940s, the experimental psychologist **Karl Lashley** (1890–1958) entered the localization debate and swung the pendulum back again toward a more holistic view of cortical function. He systematically removed sections of cortex in rats and observed their ability to learn various mazes. What he found was contrary to expectation. No matter where the lesion was, it did not correlate with a specific deficit. All he found was that the amount of damage was associated with the severity of the deficit. From this he formulated two principles: **mass action** – the larger the lesion, irrespective of location, the poorer the performance – and **equipotentiality** – the idea that all regions of the cerebral cortex are equally likely to take on any function.

But didn't this contradict the findings of nearly a hundred years of research since Broca? Let us examine a few points in more detail, because they remain instructive today, particularly when interpreting modern neuroimaging data. For one thing, considerable individual differences exist in the anatomy of the human brain and everybody utilizes slightly different cortical regions to implement the same behavior. Often this is no more than a matter of millimeters but can also be as drastic as the contralateral side of the brain, as is the case in hemispheric language dominance. For instance, Broca's aphasia may be due to lesions outside Broca's area, while lesions to Broca's area may not lead to Broca's aphasia. Speech production is still localized, just not in the exact same cortex for everyone. A similar drawback confounded Lashley's conclusions. A maze is a complex task that can be solved using a variety of strategies. A rat may navigate by using visual *and* olfactory clues. If one system is ablated, the rat may compensate for the loss with the other system and show no deficit. Should we then conclude that spatial memory is not localized? While such arguments against localization are not sound, globalists pointed out a potentially troublesome flaw inherent in the rationale of experimental ablation. A lesioned brain does not operate like a non-lesioned brain minus one part. The brain is a dynamic system. Damage to one structure produces not only trauma in others but also affects the way all other structures interact. How, then, do we know whether the observed deficit is due to the missing part rather than the result of disrupted interaction in the remaining parts?

Eventually, though, localizationists prevailed. Progress on two fronts proved decisive. First, single-cell recordings in the 1950s started to reveal detailed functional maps that correlated the behavior of individual neurons with specific mental processes. Second, the appearance of neuroimaging techniques in the 1980s provided the capability to study healthy, living brains and diminished the reliance on experimental ablation. However, while both tools supplied overpowering evidence for the view that higher cognitive functions are localized, they also substantially changed the traditional notion of what, exactly, is localized. Consider memory. As we shall see, memory is a distributed function. Many individual processes are coordinated to form the memory of, say, your grandmother. Some areas contribute specific visual features; others provide different visual features; while still others add auditory elements or contain information about your past interactions with her. Like the internet, your grandmother is not implemented in a single location; however, single processes that combine to make your grandmother – like the computers that enable the internet – *are* localized. This is important to remember when looking at pretty neuroimaging pictures of the brain that seem to show the neural "center" for, say, love, God, or consciousness. There are no such things. If we disregard the lessons of the past, brain imaging is in danger of becoming the new phrenology. The search for the neural basis of consciousness would be nothing more than the search for a substitute pineal gland.

Artificial intelligence

The field of artificial intelligence (AI) is the latest addition to the growing effort to understand the nature of the mind. The notion of an artificial device mimicking some aspect of human behavior goes back to antiquity, but it was not until the seventeenth century that **Blaise Pascal** (1623–62) built the first calculating machine. It was a mechanical device that operated on rotating cylinders and performed basic transformations such as addition, subtraction, and multiplication. **Gottfried von Leibniz** (1646–1716) later improved the design to make it more practical.

The functions of these first digital calculators were fixed. The mathematician **Charles Babbage** (1792–1871) is often credited with ushering in the modern era when he conceived of the first multipurpose device. The innards of his **Analytical Engine** consisted of a series of interlocking cogs and wheels – the hardware – which formed a (central) processing unit. The operation of this unit could be controlled by punch cards – the software. At the heart of Babbage's invention was the idea that these punch cards were exchangeable. The pattern of punched holes on each card was coded for a particular mathematical function that determined the operation performed by the processing unit. By swapping the punched cards, the device could execute any logical function. That is, the machine was programmable and flexible, the first version, in principle, of the modern digital computer. Babbage got the idea of punch cards from the textile industry. A series of innovations in loom design prior to the 1830s culminated in the Jacquard loom, which automated the weaving of intricate patterns into fabrics with the use of these punched cards. Babbage never had the chance to build his brainchild, however. It is acknowledged that the schematics would have worked, but the machine was simply too complex to be built at the time. The first functional general-purpose computing devices were built during World War II – over a hundred years after Babbage – to decipher encrypted code. The engineering feat involved in those early thinking machines was still prohibitive. The computing power that comfortably fits onto today's microchips took the space of basements filled with diodes, vacuum tubes, switches, and cables.

While there was little progress on the hardware side, mathematicians and logicians made progress on the software side. AI can only simulate systems that are formalized, that is, given a definite shape or form that specifies the composition of the system in terms of the statements that make it up and the permissible transformation rules that manipulate the statements. Once these elements are known we have a **formal system**, which is the representation of a system in abstract, symbolic language. What was needed to precisely explicate a system in such a manner was a solid understanding of formal logic (i.e., the properties of propositions, the logic of numbers and classes, etc.) and the foundation of mathematics in logic, that is, the underlying logical structure of geometry, algebra, and arithmetic. This was to be eventually accomplished by the mathematicians Bertrand Russell and Alfred Whitehead, who revolutionized formal logic with their publication *Principia Mathematica* between 1910 and 1913.

An important, early step towards this was made by the mathematician **George Boole** (1815–64), who found a way to express the problems of logic in terms of algebraic equations. **Boolean algebra** laid the theoretical groundwork for formal automata theory and computing, developed in the 1930s and 1940s by the mathematicians **John von Neumann, Alonzo Church**, and **Alan Turing**, because it restated logical relationships in a way that made them solvable mathematically. At the same time, the engineer and founder of information theory, **Claude Shannon**, applied Boolean algebra to electrical circuits. Just as the symbols and rules of algebra can be expressed in a binary code using 1s and 0s, the switches and relays in electronics operate in a binary fashion, "on" and "off." By using Boolean algebra to describe the behavior of these switches and relays, logical problems could be translated into formal systems and then manipulated systematically. Shannon called one unit of information a "bit," which is short for "binary digit." In the 1940s, von Neumann, building on these ideas, designed the basic computing architecture that now bears his name.

This paved the way for any system, including human cognitive processes, to be embodied in a machine. By the 1950s, engineers built computers that had the power required to handle more complex formal systems. What was needed, then, was to formalize human cognition. But that was just it; after half a century of behaviorism, psychologists had next to no idea of what was involved in mental phenomena. But even before psychology shifted, in the 1960, to a cognitive perspective to address this bottleneck, people started working on simulating mental processes in computers. The first such programs in the 1950s were the "Logic Theorist," followed by the "General Problem Solver," which were designed to solve problems of logic, such as proving theorems or playing chess (Newell & Simon, 1972). In 1956, Marvin Minsky and John McCarthy organized the famous Darthmouth conference on artificial intelligence and coined the term AI. This event, attended by all major players of the day, is considered to be the birth of AI. Since then, the coevolution of ever more powerful computers that could accommodate increasingly sophisticated software programs has proven to be among the most impressive scientific and technological achievements in the last half of the twentieth century. Any formal system can, in principle, be automated and the advent of extraordinarily powerful computers makes it possible to run very complex formal systems, such as higher cognitive functions or, why not, human consciousness. This is the research program of AI.

Summary

This chapter reviewed the history of the four main disciplines that make up the contemporary field of consciousness. Consciousness is among the oldest problems in philosophy. The Greeks discussed it in form of the mind-body problem and identified the basic positions. Subsequent philosophers elaborated on these views but added little in the way of new theories or solutions. However, in the 1970s, fueled by scientific progress in psychology and neuroscience, philosophers started to put forth entirely new proposals that the Greeks did not and could not have anticipated. As a result, we have today a much clearer understanding of the issues facing a science of consciousness. In psychology, consciousness has been through a rollercoaster ride. In the opening of the first general textbook in psychology, James (1890) defined psychology as the "science of mental life, both of its phenomena and of their conditions." In other words, the subject matter of psychology was consciousness. The problem with this was that psychology needed to establish itself as an empirical science but consciousness could not yet be tackled in a scientific manner. So psychologists tackled observable behaviors instead until a number of developments made it possible to study conscious mental processes empirically and return to the roots of psychology.

Until recently, consciousness was also beyond the reach of neuroscience. For centuries, advances in our knowledge of the brain did not make contact with higher mental functions and consciousness. This has changed dramatically. For the past few decades, neuroscientific data relevant to the study of the mind has been appearing at a dizzying pace. The exciting prospects provided by neuro-science are largely responsible for revitalizing interest in consciousness. Nowadays, the popular media covers aspects of the biological basis of the mind on a weekly basis and there is a real buzz among people working in the field that tangible breakthroughs on this age-old problem lay just ahead. Finally, the prob-lem of consciousness is also attacked from the perspective of artificial intelligence. The goal of AI is to embody logical operations, including mental phenomena, in a machine. Before this could occur, the technological capability to make the machinery – the hardware – and the theoretical knowledge to adequately charac-terize formal systems – the software – needed to be developed. Once in place, by about the 1950s, work in AI started in earnest when the first software programs that simulated human cognitive functions were run on computers that had the computing power to handle their execution.

Suggested reading

Finger, S. (1994). *Origins of Neuroscience*. New York: Oxford University Press.
Hunt, M. (1993). *The Story of Psychology*. New York: Anchor Books.
Russell, B. (1989). *Wisdom of the West*. New York: Crescent Books.

3 Basic positions

Classical dualism

Cartesian dualism

Descartes awakened the mind-body problem from centuries of slumber. The intellectual climate at that time was a vague mixture of **panpsychism**, a relic from Aristotle, and **pantheism**, decreed by the Church in no uncertain terms. But the slumber was not to last. Science was steadily pressing forward and by the time Descartes entered the picture ever more bits and pieces of the natural world had been explicated. It became plain that the universe, including the human body, was subject to natural laws. But what about the mind? Surely, it couldn't also be a mechanical device that fell under the purview of this new science! Mechanical philosophy was at odds with pantheism. Descartes found a way out of the imminent clash by slicing the world into two kinds of substances. Ordinary matter, or *res extensa*, is a substance that extends in space and its behavior can be described in mechanical terms. In contrast, the mind, or *res cogitans*, is a substance of a different kind – a nonphysical entity with no extension in space, and, significantly, immortal, which catapults it straight outside the fold of objective science. It is for this reason that the Cartesian framework is also called **substance dualism** (Churchland, 1984). The philosopher Gilbert Ryle (1949) called this mockingly the "ghost in the machine" view of the mind-body problem, a phrase that has entered common parlance.

By incorporating science into one side of the mind-body equation, while placing it forever off-limits to the other, Descartes sharpened the division between mind and matter. At the time, this tidy separation "saved" the soul from science and science from religion. It freed scientists from Church interference in their pursuit of natural explanations in the physical sciences, while preempting any attempt of empirical progress on consciousness – a high cost indeed.

The arguments in favor of the Cartesian philosophy are straightforward. The most persuasive is undoubtedly its intuitive appeal. Mental processes are so obviously different from solid matter that they must emanate from a different medium. For how can thoughts and feelings come from activity in a cantaloupe-sized heap of cells crackling with electricity? How can meat, however arranged, hope for the best, rethink a decision, or suffer from writer's block? Materialism seems such a remote possibility that many people simply find it outrageously at odds with common wisdom. Cartesian dualism appeals to many for the further reason that it resonates with religious beliefs. How else can the immortal soul go to heaven or hell or – in the case of reincarnation – attach itself to the next physical host? It is impossible it seems, in one and the same breath, to hold a materialistic theory of the mind and a belief in a spiritual afterlife. Given this, it is no surprise that the dual-substance conception is the most commonly held view in the public at large. Indeed, the combination of instinctive charm and spiritual comfort has also proved to be a potent mix for modern brain scientists such as Charles Sherrington, Wilder Penfield, and most recently, the last of the Cartesian purists, John Eccles.

The argument from intuition is certainly easy enough to follow but amounts to little more than a teddy bear for grownups. The problem is that ordinary experience is submitted as empirical evidence. If history is any guide, this is not prudent. Introspection has never been a reliable guide to expose how things really are and there is no reason to believe that this is different for consciousness. The fact that mental events do not seem like a coordinated firing pattern of a complex network of neurons is no grounds for dismissing it as far-fetched. To the point, introspection does not reveal ontology.

A second argument for dualism is irreducibility. Here the case is made not by appeal to religious orthodoxy or common sense but by postulating that mental events have an intrinsic quality that cannot be reduced to brain events. This claim is underscored by the fact that neuroscience, in spite of all its might, has yet to account for one iota of what it is like to have experiences. We should therefore stop trying to fit square pegs into round holes and accept that consciousness is inherently subjective. This argument is more forceful for, indeed, pretty images from brain scanners and electromicroscopes do not seem to provide such what-it's-like information. Yet, care must be taken here. Attempts to halt science by erecting an insurmountable barrier – however sensible it seems at the time – have a sorry history. It has backfired often enough to make one deeply suspect of this stance. Descartes argued for language and reasoning, which he proclaimed to be forever safe from reductionist explanations. With the advent of computers, this has fallen by the wayside. So what motivates the current proposal that qualia could not possibly be reduced to the interaction of bits of matter? Here the dualist account is largely disappointing. Instead of offering a positive justification, the dualist advances a negative one, namely that science has thus far failed. This defeatist approach is not very convincing, especially when bearing in mind the putative practice that the burden of proof rests on the person making the claim. However, recent attempts to justify irreducibility on more positive grounds have been made and we shall return to them in a later section.

Problems with classical dualism

Arguments against Cartesian dualism can be grouped into five headings; violation of neural dependence, explanatory impotence, parsimony, interactionism, and function. In its purest form, substance dualism asserts that brains are unnecessary for consciousness, a claim that stands in plain **violation of neural dependence**. How, then, do insults to the brain – disease or injury – alter consciousness? How can a few milligrams of drug X, say, fluoexetine (Prozac), make you feel wonderful? The fact that a chemical can change your belief system clearly suggests that beliefs depend on chemistry. This borders on outright refutation of substance dualism!

Explanatory impotence refers to the charge that dualism does little explanatory work. Dualist explanations often require explanations themselves. What is this thinking substance composed of? How does it do the thinking? Dualism gives no positive characterization of consciousness that addresses those inquiries. This is the more troubling because positive evidence to justify a special substance is entirely lacking. To base a dual universe on the trust-me-on-this defense is understandably unsatisfying. The lack of specifics also saves dualism from close scrutiny, making it impossible to falsify. As fatal as this critique already is, the consequence of this explanatory impotence is even worse, because it means that the failure to genuinely explain the phenomenon instills little hope that adopting it will bring about much progress in the future. Taken together, this amounts to stonewalling! In contrast, materialism runs a full-steam research program that provides many specific proposals for its claim, which, on the one hand, opens it up to criticism, but on the other brings the potential for real progress. Closely related to this objection is the issue of **parsimony**. Parsimony is the idea that a good theory should make the least number of assumptions possible. Adherence to this principle guarantees that we minimize the introduction of unknowns. Of two competing theories, *ceteris paribus*, we should favor the one that is simpler, that is, the one that accounts for the observed phenomenon with fewer conjectures. In contrast to materialism, which requires one kind of substance, dualism makes additional assumptions. It is thus less parsimonious. The dualist answers this charge by claiming that all else is not equal and that the very problem with materialism is that it cannot account for the observable phenomena, especially subjectivity. Materialism is thus inadequate and the additional assumptions are indispensable. It's the familiar logical shelling game, which results in the costumary standoff.

A third problem is **interactionism**. How does consciousness, being the separate and immaterial entity it allegedly is, cause the body to move about? How does sensory input leave impressions in the mind? At its center, this problem deals with causation. Plato had already recognized the difficulty but it became an ever more pressing problem when Descartes sharpened the split between body and soul. In the end, any form of dualism must include a proposal of how, exactly, this interaction is supposed to be accomplished. Descartes's infamous solution is now a running joke among people fluent in brainspeak. He thought that a rather obscure lump of tissue in the forebrain called the pineal gland is the soul's port of entry into the material world. The idea has little appeal and utterly fails to address the conundrum. It does not tell us anything about the mechanism of how the two interact! Even in Descartes's time, this proposal was treated with polite neglect by some and outright derision by others. In recent years, the biologist-turned-philosopher John Eccles (1994) has stuck his neck out in a similar fashion and championed another, equally obscure neural region called the supplementary motor area as the liaison between body and soul. As for the specifics regarding traffic rules, he goes on to update the neuroscience, but the theory is essentially identical to that of Descartes. His critics, who include just about everyone, regard the idea as nothing more than a warmed-over pineal gland. In sum, interaction remains a crippling problem for dualism.

Finally, there is the problem of **function**. In accordance with the principles of evolution, theorists generally agree that consciousness must have some sort of function and be adaptive, otherwise it would not have evolved. Naturally, there is less consensus on which function this would be. To see how function represents a special problem for dualism, consider a sampler of troublesome questions: How does a nonmaterial substance evolve? Given that brains have evolved, did consciousness evolve with them? At the same rate? If yes, what mechanism could account for such parallel evolution? If not, which was more evolved in our hominoid ancestors, consciousness or brain? The problem of function is tied to interactionism. If consciousness has a function, say, to cause motion through the exercise of free will, how does it do it? The alternative is that it does not have a function. This is epiphenomenalism, which raises its own set of puzzling questions.

Modern dualism

Property dualism

The Cartesian model splits the universe in a way that makes it difficult to put it back together. Cartesian dualism does not work; in at least this much there is agreement among philosophers and scientists. Faced with the deeply unsettling alternative of materialism, theorists searched for better ways to make dualism work. The upshot is a collection of theories that best fits under the headings of **property dualism** or **dual-aspect theory**. This category is also the best home for theories of **emergentism**, to which we shall turn in a separate section below, and – to the confusion of nearly everyone – **neutral monism**. In its basic form, property dualism is not a new approach. Benedict Spinoza (1632–77) proposed a version of it that envisioned mind and matter as two aspects of a more fundamental reality that is in itself neither mind nor matter.

The central thesis of property dualism is that consciousness is a special property or set of properties. The idea collapses the universe back into one kind of substance only to partition it again into two kinds of properties, mental ones and physical ones. The mental properties are held to be nonphysical in the sense that they cannot be reduced to physical properties. It is therefore a form of dualism that splits the universe in two, only here the duality is not in terms of substance but property. A dual-property model of the universe immediately prompts the question as to the sort of properties that are irreducibly mental. To address this, contemporary theorists typically point to qualia or the what-it's-likeness of experience. Take, for example, pain. Pain has attributes that can best be described in terms of physical properties, such as nocioceptor activation, neurotransmitter release, brain activity, and behavior. But pain also has attributes that can best be described in terms of mental properties, such as what it feels like to be in pain. According to property dualism, these properties are complementary, like the different sides of a coin, and neither description alone is sufficient to capture the essence of the phenomenon. In philosophical jargon, this is **ontological monism** combined with **epistemological dualism** (Metzinger, 2003).

From here, differences among theories under the heading of property dualism emerge. We can distinguish three variants. The first – held, for example, by Spinoza – understands mind and matter as different arrangements of a more elementary reality – a third kind of stuff, if you like. In its most extreme form, this view leads to panpsychism. The remaining two variants accept physical matter as the fundamental stuff of the universe, but propose that it gives rise not only to physical but also to mental events. The difference between the latter two variants is this. One ascribes associated mental properties to all matter – be it arranged in the form of quasars, toasters, or brains. This leads also to panpsychism, as consciousness must be understood as a fundamental building block of the universe. Most people find conscious toasters a difficult thing to contemplate, but there are defenders of this view in modern philosophy. The other variant restricts associated mental properties to brains. By denying the mental set of properties to other forms of matter, consciousness becomes a phenomenon that arises only in brains – and in its most radical form – complex brains of the sort only we humans carry around. For instance, according to Max Velmans (1991) and Thomas Nagel (1986), consciousness and neural firing are simply two aspects of the same process, but one cannot be reduced to the other.

To avoid the "heresy" of dualism some theorists prefer to call this approach **neutral monism**. The rationale is twofold. One, they accept that brains are the basis of consciousness, hence the label monism. Two, they claim that brains are a neutral kind of stuff in the sense that they give rise equally to the mental and the physical. This was the view held by the psychologist William James, the philosopher Bertrand Russell, and the physicist Ernst Mach (Velmans, 2000). The term, however, remains misleading. It makes no sense to speak of monism in a universe that is partitioned into two constituents when such constituents are irreducible. This is dualism insofar as the phenomenal world and the physical world remain entities of a different kind. The additional problem arises that if brains are truly neutral their associated mental and physical properties must be equally elementary. What, then, is the mechanism that so precisely links them to each other? As you can see, any step in that direction inches you closer to the problem of interactionism.

A modern example of property dualism comes from the philosopher David Chalmers (1996). His theory, which he calls naturalistic dualism, is a form of panpsychism. In a nutshell, he proposes that consciousness is a fundamental property of the universe. We should stop trying to reduce consciousness to something that it is not and accept its irreducibility. This, he argues, happens regularly in science. In physics notions such as mass, space, and time are considered irreducible in the sense that physicists do not try to account for them with some other thing or process; they are elementary units of physics. By admitting consciousness to this elusive club of irreducibles, Chalmers moves consciousness into the category of fundamental building blocks of the natural order alongside charge and gravity. In this view, consciousness is nothing mysterious but an entirely natural event governed by natural laws. The aim of a science of consciousness should be to uncover the principles determining the interaction between this new member of the family of fundamentals and the other forces of nature we already know. Chalmers's nonreductive theory has ties to functionalism, a philosophy of mind we shall discuss below. According to Chalmers, what is important are the interactions between the basic constituents of the universe. Consciousness occurs whenever an exchange of information takes place. Any type of chatter, say, between a boson and a fermion carries a bit of consciousness. The world, then, is inherently sentient. Not only brains but the stockmarket and the internet are entities that have experiences. According to Chalmers this proposal solves the problem of why mental processes are accompanied by experience; they just come with it, naturally, as a matter of course. Critics of Chalmers's approach argue that this theory is impossible to disprove and thus, in a way, arcane pontification. It neither explains consciousness nor does it come with a research program to attack the problem. Critics are even less convinced by the move to grant consciousness the same fundamental status as mass or space-time. Dennett, for instance, points out that physicists cite independent evidence to support basic categories in physics, while Chalmers has no independent grounds to add experience to this list, other than his belief in the irreducibility of consciousness. Dennett (1996a, p. 4) draws a parallel to cuteness. "Some things are just plain cute," and there is really no other way to describe it. Cutism, then, is irreducible and should be elevated to the status of fundamental property.

Problems with property dualism

Property dualism avoids some of the problems caused by the Cartesian division. For starters, it nullifies the criticism of violating neural dependence by offering a more plausible account for why mental events are so closely related to matter. It also dodges the mess of interactionism by rejecting a second substance and along with it the need for any interaction. For some dual-aspect theories, the neutral, underlying stuff of reality causes the occurrence of both, mind and matter. This solution, however, leads to determinism. One can avert this conclusion by proposing that free will can still somehow supervene on matter, but this leads straight back to interactionism. It's tough picking; fixing the problem of interaction this way entails epiphenomenalism. The property dualist's solution to dual interactionism is not only devastating to causation but also damaging to function. What is left of function, one might reasonably ask, if consciousness is without power to influence behavior? To see that a fatal blow to causal interaction must not be a *fatal* blow to function one only has to envision functions of consciousness other than causation. Proposals by property dualists for such functions include the enhancement of information processing or the role as a feedback mechanism.

The problems of explanatory impotence and parsimony retain much of their force with property dualism. To answer the charge of impotence, the property dualist is in the position to make some progress and point to the what-it's-likeness of experience. While it is true that this represents a step toward a more positive characterization of consciousness, it shifts the problem only slightly. Like the Cartesian model, dual-aspect theories are burdened with the inability to generate testable hypotheses, which are, after all, the bread and butter of genuine progress. The powerlessness to get a research program off the ground is a colossal fiasco for the dualist camp. In addressing this deficiency, contemporary theorists who hold phenomenalist views, such as Chalmers or Velmans, attack the problem head-on and call for a radically new kind of science. The rationale is this. Given that there are two very different aspects to the universe, we must also have two very different approaches to the study of each. Because an exclusively third-person science cannot discover phenomenology, we must add a first-person science capable of producing psychological data to get an understanding of consciousness in all its glory. The problem with this call for action is twofold. First, it lacks even the most rudimentary information as to what, exactly, a first-person science should entail.

Figure 3.1

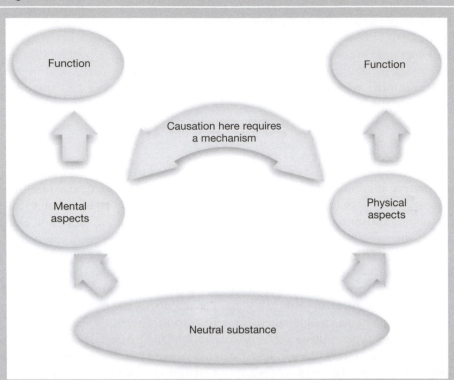

Consciousness and brain events are interdependent. If mind and matter emanate from different substances, as proposed by the Cartesian framework, this correspondence poses a problem. To better account for this, dual-aspect theory proposes a neutral substance that gives rise equally to mental and physical properties. This solution, however, leads to epiphenomenalism. The problem arises as follows. Mental properties are held to be nonphysical, that is, irreducible to physical ones. This implies that they cannot cause change in the physical properties. If you also want causation, to give consciousness the power to supervene on matter, you must also come up with a mechanism of how this is supposed to work. This brings you straight back to the problem of interactionism. The problem of causation need not apply to function. Both mental and physical aspects can serve different purposes, irrespective of their nature.

What, for instance, are its methods? In what way can it be a science, as delineated by Popperian falsification? In addition, no one, including the people calling for it, is currently getting their hands dirty developing such a science, let alone getting reliable data. At this point, it very much looks like a nonstarter.

A common tactic among philosophers to gather support for one's position is by exposing inconsistencies in rival ones. When done with finesse, a philosopher can typically manage to let alternative positions look like theoretical duds. This move is then swiftly followed by the recommendation to the reader to adopt the author's own theory on the grounds that it is the only theory left standing and thus obviously the most sensible of the options. Needless to say, this strategy is also employed by the philosopher who happens to hold the opposing position. By showing the thesis of others to be utterly absurd, philosophers often avert the pain of having to substantiate their own theories directly. One of countless examples of such intellectual stonewalling is the charge by property dualists that materialists fall prey to an obvious fallacy. The proclaimed goal of materialism is to find the neural causes or correlates of consciousness. Once found, the materialist believes herself to be in the position to establish consciousness to be nothing more than a state of the brain. Put another way, the materialist hopes to establish ontological identity between mind and brain by identifying the neural substrates of mental states. Dualists are quick to defeat the goal by interjecting that neither causation nor correlation can establish the identity of two things or events. This argument is built around **Leibniz's law**, which is concerned with the conditions required for numerical identity. For A to be identical to B, all properties of A must be properties of B, and vice versa. Thus, ontological identity is symmetrical; if A is identical to B the same must be true in reverse. In contrast, causation and correlation do not obey Leibniz's law. Correlation is symmetrical, that is, the degree to which A correlates with B is the degree with which B correlates with A, but the two variables can have very different properties. Height correlates with weight but it does not follow that height is the same as weight, even if the correlation were to be perfect. Causation is in worse shape. It is neither symmetrical, that is, if A causes B, B cannot cause A, nor obeys Leibniz's law. Lightning and thunder have different properties. The dualist concludes that the neuroscience research program is doomed to failure because finding the brain states that cause or correlate with mind states won't establish them to be the same thing (Velmans, 2000). In defense, the materialist dismisses the entire line of reasoning as irrelevant by citing historical parallels. Mass and energy also did not seem to share the same properties but they were eventually found to be identical. The same was true for molecular kinetic energy and heat. In those and many other cases, a research program based on causation and correlation succeeded in establishing the identity of these phenomena. Just because the mind seems to have properties, say, qualia not shared by the brain and the brain seems to have properties, say, spatial extension not shared by the mind does not mean these properties are indeed not shared. Dualists are typically not impressed by such parallels from other sciences and argue that equating mind and brain requires numerical identity of a phenomenon that has a first-person ontology with one that has a third-person one, which is to establish ontological identity of a very different kind. Note that this argument presupposes that consciousness has an inherently first-person mode of existence. And there it is again, the standoff.

Emergentism

Emergentism is a difficult position to classify. To see why, let's consider its key claim and main consequences. The central idea is that consciousness is an emergent property. Emergent properties are those that arise when elements or systems are combined. They are held to be emergent in the sense that they are not part of the constituent elements or systems alone. They exist only as a result of **entanglement**. Take the example of water. Water is wet but wetness (or liquidity) is not a property of either hydrogen or oxygen; it emerges from their union (Searle 1992). In a similar manner, consciousness emerges from the interplay of billions of nerve cells; it is not a property of individual neurons or brain structures but is generated in their interaction.

The idea that consciousness is more than the sum of its (brain) parts is initially appealing, but to fully evaluate this approach we must also appreciate its consequences. The main difference to mainstream property dualism is that the property of consciousness is not just irreducible but emerging. The difference is crucial. Property dualism leaves open the theoretical possibility for consciousness to be causal. One could imagine a scenario in which a neutral substance and its mental aspects exert mutual effects on each other. If this alters the constitution or operation of the neutral substance, the other, physical aspects of the neutral substance might be changed as well. This circuitous route allows for consciousness to cause actions. Although this view is problematic for the simple reason that it reintroduces the need for a mechanism, it is nevertheless plausible. But once a property is truly emergent this theoretical option vanishes. The idea of emergence excludes the prospect of feedback. Thus, emergentism implies epiphenomenalism. This demotes consciousness to being nothing but a glitzy sideshow, an inconsequential byproduct of brain activity, a cruel joke, without the power to influence physical events. It is ironic that dualism is a position largely motivated by the desire to construct an account of consciousness that does not violate intuition or ordinary experience only to wind up as a position that does so violently.

As might be expected, proponents of emergentism and property dualism have put forth several proposals to hold off the "monster" of epiphenomenalism, while others have accepted it as an inevitable consequence of their position. From a theoretical point of view, there is nothing that prevents us from accepting epiphenomenalism. It is consistent with the laws of science, as the physical universe appears indeed to be causally closed, leaving no room for consciousness to intervene. The philosopher John Searle (1992) has proposed a type of emergentism he calls physicalism or biological naturalism. He is among those arguing for **emergent interactionism**, which is designed to prevent consciousness from riding above the fray. In his view, emerging conscious phenomena feed back at the level of the neural constituents. The neuroscientist Roger Sperry has developed a similar approach in which emergent properties have the capacity to govern the behavior of the system from which they emerge. As to how, exactly, this might happen neither provides a detailed description, nor any evidence. Not surprisingly, few people find the case for downward causation persuasive. The wetness of water also does not alter the structure of hydrogen or oxygen. One might also question the rationale for labeling consciousness "emergent" if it is a property that is also "submergent." Why not simply consider it a manifestation or aspect of matter without the added fanciness of emergence?

Figure 3.2

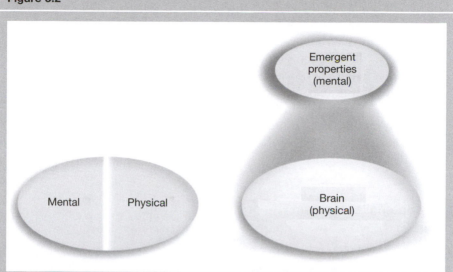

In property dualism, the mental and the physical are irreducible aspects of the same substance. In contrast, emergentism is the contention that mental events are emerging properties of brain processes. The idea behind labeling mental aspects "emergent" is to avoid a dual-property universe while at the same time holding on to the idea that mental events are somehow different from physical events after all. This move, however, makes it nearly impossible to hold off epiphenomenalism. Once held to be truly emergent, properties must be considered irreducible, otherwise there is little use in calling them emergent. How, then, being irreducible and thus different in kind, are emergent mental properties to exert downward causation? The attempt to avoid duality and determinism at the same time has not been convincing.

Searle (2002) engages in some delicate maneuvering to stay clear of dualism. He rejects property dualism because "brains cause minds" and consciousness is an emergent property that is not over and above its neural basis. In other words, the emergence of consciousness is a neurobiological process that depends entirely on the physical brain. At the same time, however, he maintains that the emergent property of consciousness contains a subjective component that cannot be known from third-person data. Experience, then, is a higher-order feature of brains but this feature has a first-person mode of existence. We may object that this first-person ontology makes the conscious mind something that does not exist in the physical world – otherwise it ought to be reducible to it. So consciousness becomes by definition something above and beyond the activity of neurons. Searle completes the theoretical backflip when he also rejects materialism. This he does because materialism denies the subjective nature of phenomenal consciousness and he thinks that the study of the conscious mind will never be complete without it.

Like Searle, Sperry (1969) classified his approach as strictly monist. But if taken all the way, emergent consciousness must be regarded as something other than the physical activity of the brain; if this weren't so, what would be the point of calling it "emergent"? It is for this reason that emergentism is best classified as a form of property dualism. By striking a bargain between seeing consciousness as an integral part of the brain's modus operanti while claiming it to be something different from it, both Searle and Sperry are aiming for duality without dualism. Indeed, emergentism may owe some of its popularity to being falsely billed as a softer version of materialism. So, against their own documented objection we shall classify this position as property dualism. The apparent lesson to be taken from this effort is that it tells us the extent to which dualism has become an unde-sirable label.

Non-materialist monism

Idealism

The collapse of dualism into monism can be made in two directions. Most theo-ries concern themselves with the reduction of mind to matter. This is **material-ism**. There are several forms of materialism but they all share the view that consciousness is nothing above and beyond the physical universe and thus the canon of science. Matter is all there is and mind is nothing but a particular – perhaps peculiar – arrangement of that matter. This is the dominant mind-set among scientists and philosophers. Before we examine those positions, we must back up and briefly consider the other possibility of collapsing the duality in the opposite direction. Here, the unity of mind and matter is achieved with a reduc-tion of matter to mind. This is called **idealism**.

When idealism is mentioned in connection with the mind-body problem one thinks at once of George Berkeley (1685–1753). Berkeley offered a unique twist to monism by arguing that the fundamental substance of the universe is mind, not matter. The consequences of this view range from provocative to absurd. With ontological primacy placed on the mental, objects in the world no longer have an independent physical existence; they exist only as ideas in the mind. Taken to the extreme, the theory, which has its roots in the Platonian theory of ideas, denies that there is an objective reality. Tables, chairs, and toasters materialize, as it were, only when they are perceived. According to Berkeley, *esse est percipi* – to be is to be perceived. This dependence of the material world on perception is captured by the famous conundrum that asks whether or not a tree falling in the forest would make a sound when no one is there to hear it. But the world does not disappear when no one looks, does it? As Velmans (2000, p. 28) put it: "if you bring an egg to the boil, then leave the kitchen for 3½ minutes, you get a soft-boiled egg whether you are watching or not." To Berkeley, an Irish bishop – which, inciden-tally, is not the theory's problem – the solution to this dilemma was God. As the eternal perceiver, She guarantees that the world continues to be. This notion renders the world the product of God's mind, a mere divine dream with nò more of a real existence than our own dreams. This is a real humdinger of an argument and, in good philosophical tradition, irrefutable. Although in principle plausible, its fantastic unfalsifiability makes it little helpful and we shall put it aside without dismissing it.

Functionalism

Functionalism has its roots in the writings of Aristotle and in its modern version goes back to William James. In consciousness, functionalism refers to the idea that the mind and its faculties are activities that can be defined in terms of their functional roles. Consciousness is neither a substance – of any kind – nor a set of special properties. Each type of mental state is specified by its causal relations to three events: stimulus input, other mental states, and behavioral output. This is better understood by taking an example. Pain is caused by some noxious stimulus; it causes other mental events, such as distress or the wish to seek relief; and it causes overt manifestations, such as crying or avoidance behavior. According to functionalism, the mind is a system organized into a network of operations in which each mental state is one element performing a specific causal function. What matters here is the function. Any mental state that bears the exact same causal relationships and carries out the same role is, by definition, pain.

The difference to **behaviorism** lies in the use of other mental states as a defining characteristic. Behaviorism defines mental states solely in terms of stimulus-response contingencies. To a behaviorist, not eating for a while causes the mental state of "hunger" as well as the actual eating. So, the mental state "being hungry" does not cause eating; the not-eating-for-while does. Mental states are epiphenomena; to understand eating behavior, one only needs to know a person's eating history; the mental state itself is not needed. This is just as well for the behaviorist because "being hungry" cannot be observed anyway. So, why then does it arise, this feeling of hunger? Behaviorists contend that mental states are shorthand for describing dispositions to behave. Indeed, it would make for long and convoluted sentences if we were to express our wish to eat by specifying the details of our previous meals. Mental states are nothing else than **dispositional states**. To say that I am hungry is to say that I am likely to seek out food and eat it, if given the opportunity. The functionalist argues that this account will not do. Perhaps the person is on a diet; perhaps he is depressed and does not feel like eating, despite being hungry. According to functionalism, these mental states – self-image and depression, in this case – enter into a causal relationship with hunger and are required for an adequate characterization of mental states.

Although some refuse to classify functionalism as either dualist or materialist (Fodor, 1975), most take it to be a materialist position. The ambiguity arises because the functionalist is not bound to insist that the brain must be the physical structure that implements the mind. In principle, any system that has the same functional organization has a mind. This means that, in its strongest form, functionalism allows for the possibility of sentient machines. The functionalist is led to this position by making a fundamental distinction between *role* and *occupant*. By defining consciousness in terms of the role it plays within the system rather than as a thing, entity, or property, functionalism emphasizes the operations that take place, not the underlying material that realizes the operations. A brain is not a necessity for the mind; consciousness can equally well occur in a silicon brain, or an alien one for that matter, as long as its role is the result of computations bearing the same causal relationships to input, other internal computations, and output. The distinction between role and occupant is better known as the distinction between software, a program that runs on a computer, and hardware, the physical stuff that executes the program. By analogy, human consciousness is a program that runs on brains.

Given this, it is not surprising that functionalism went over well in cognitive science. Adopting it gave researchers in AI a clear rationale for abstracting information processing from brains. Nature must surely have more than one way of making mentality. A great deal of scientific evidence, let alone technology, demonstrates that artificial simulations of human behavior can contribute meaningfully to the study of the mind. Functionalism has also had a good run in cognitive psychology. Just as the "Search" operation of the program Excel can be understood without knowledge of electrical engineering, cognitive psychologists believed that mental operations can be understood without bothering about the wetware of brains (Dennett, 1991). Some functionalists have gone so far as to call for the total autonomy of psychology (Fodor, 1975). There is less support for this extreme view among today's cognitive scientists. The state of the art in neuroscience a few decades ago may have necessitated the position that reducing minds to brains is not the way to proceed. Functionalism was also attractive, and still is, because it presented a middle ground on which to avoid materialism without having to embrace some kind of duality. However, increasingly more cognitive scientists have taken the position that partial reduction is both possible and useful. Consciousness, then, is a process that involves, but is not the same as, brain states. Another way of saying this is that conscious states are produced by patterns of neural activity but it is the activity not the neurons themselves that do the trick. This preserves the functionalist thesis while accomodating the mounting evidence in favor of the neural dependence of consciousness.

Contemporary functionalism also comes in fully reductionist versions. Here functionalism is simply seen as a temporary bridge until neuroscience has fully matured. It is a common occurrence in science that phenomena are first described in functional terms until such descriptions are replaced by underlying physical mechanisms. Before 1953, evolution was forced to rely on a functional account of heredity, but with the discovery of DNA genetics was able to provide a better account. Proponents of this view hold that the reductionist strategy is likely to succeed but until that time we are better off bracketing the intractable parts of the problem and seeing how far we can get. In contrast, other functionalists, most prominently Daniel Dennett, remain convinced that neuroscience is largely a waste of time as far as consciousness is concerned. It is *function* all the way down.

Functionalism is the philosophical foundation for cognitive science and represents a prominent force in the philosophy of the mind. Cognitive models of consciousness are, essentially, functional models in that they treat consciousness as a process composed of several functional components, such as attention, perception, or working memory. The best-known theory of consciousness of this kind is the global workspace theory proposed by the psychologist Bernard Baars, which we shall meet in Chapter 6.

Problems with functionalism

Arguments against functionalism take three forms: neural autonomy, sentient computers, and qualia. **Neural autonomy** refers to the notion that minds can be understood without reference to brains. This deems the study of the nervous system *ir*relevant, a claim that is looking rather dubious at this point. The idea is based on the role–occupant or software–hardware distinction. But such a distinction makes no sense for brains. Brains operate on multiple levels – from molecules to global networks – that are several orders of magnitude apart in scale. At each level, computations are performed that analyze events at that level. This means that there is no such thing as *the* hardware level. The same is true for mental events; there simply isn't anything that corresponds to *the* software level. There is no basis in reality to abstract minds from brains. Rather mind and brain form an entangled unit. Further, engineers have long known that the physical character-istics of a system place constraints on the kind of operations that can be carried out by the system. This means that in the quest to understand consciousness, cognitive science is ill advised to ignore our neurobiology (Churchland, 2002). The extreme position that studying the brain is unnecessary was more seductive in the mid-1980s but has been deflated significantly by the explosion of knowl-edge in neuroscience.

The claim that the process is what makes the mind forces the functionalist to endorse the possibility of **sentient computers**. Machine consciousness has always drawn sharp criticisms for the reason that it violates deep-seated intuitions about human nature and because machines have so far failed to show any signs what-soever of mimicking conscious processes. It has become clear that the type of material and the way it is wired up matters when it comes to consciousness. It is not simply a matter of increased complexity or computational power. Artificial minds seem to represent a different type of intelligence than the one possessed by humans. A different raw material, such as silicon, may simply give rise to different kinds of minds. Whether or not those minds will have anything remotely resembling human subjective states is highly questionable at this point. But it is this that needs to be explained in the study of consciousness. With respect to conscious computers, many people find they cannot go all the way with functionalism.

While the first two objections to functionalism come from the materialist camp, the third, qualia, is raised by dualists. The best illustration of it is the **inverted spectrum thought experiment** (Palmer, 1999; Shoemaker, 1982). Imagine that an evil neurosurgeon inverted your color spectrum while you were asleep. Everything that used to appear red to you now appears green. This did not alter your ability to function in any way; color discrimination is just as easy as it was before. You'd even say that tomatoes are red because this is the word you'd use to describe the sensation of green. What you are really seeing, though, is green. Neither you nor anyone else could tell the difference. You are functionally isomorphic to your former self, yet your experience is no longer the same. The implication of this exercise is that functionalism cannot handle phenomenal consciousness. Why are mental states associated with qualia if they do not make a difference in functional terms? Put another way, a functional account of consciousness will always be deficient for the simple reason that consciousness is a first-person phenomena and a third-person account, functional or not, cannot discover whether or not consciousness is present in a system. To really know, you'd have to *be* that system. A close cousin of this objection, the **absent qualia thought experiment**, takes aim at the same weakness, that is, the inability of functionalism to account for subjective experience in situations where it does not seem to alter behavioral output. The most famous version of the absent qualia problem is the Chinese room thought experiment, to which we shall return in Chapter 5. Again, the argument from qualia hinges on the assumption that qualia exist. If you deny that they are real, this objection evaporates.

Materialism

Identity theory

According to materialism, mind *is* matter. This declaration is the central dictum of modern brain research and presently the most dominant theory of mind among scientists in the field of consciousness. It owes its popularity largely to two factors. First, it does away with a number of problems that have plagued the various forms of dualism. Indeed, if mind is nothing but an arrangement of matter most of the fundamental issues regarding the nature of consciousness would be solved. Second, the breathtaking success of neuroscience in elucidating the neural basis of mental processes has, for the first time, nourished the hope that we may be heading toward dry land.

Materialism comes in two basic forms, **identity theory**, also known as **reductive materialism**, and **eliminativism**, also known as **eliminative materialism**. The difference is subtle. Identity theory holds that consciousness and qualia exist but both will turn out, in the fullness of time, to be identical to states of the brain. Eliminativism holds that consciousness and qualia do not exist and both concepts will be gradually replaced by explanations that are expressed purely in terms of neurobiology; that is, they will be eliminated in due course from our understanding of the issue. Clearly, the latter version of materialism is more radical than the former.

Because both theories are based on the validity of **reductionism**, a look at this concept might be helpful. Reductionism is the bread and butter of science. As a strategy it has proven hugely successful in all branches of science. The aim is to express macrophenomena as a function of the dynamics and interactions of its constituent elements. If the resulting new conceptual framework explains the phenomena at a deeper, more penetrating level of reality, the biggest prize of all awaits, the ability to predict. Some of science's finest hours are macro-to-micro explanations of this sort. Prototypical examples include the structure of DNA, the periodic table, or $E=MC^2$. Accordingly, psychology stands to gain from reductions to biology, which, in turn, benefits from reduction to chemistry. Chemistry is to be reduced to physics and, as the saying goes, physicists only answer to mathematicians, and mathematicians talk directly to God.

Is it the case, then, that neurobiology will unlock the secrets of the mind, reducing consciousness ultimately to a few mathematical equations that a neuroscientist can proudly wear on a T-shirt? Aside from quantum physics and chaos theory, consciousness has become the biggest challenge to this conception of science. This is not to say that scientists are converting to holism; the reductionist strategy will remain the mainstay of laboratory work. Rather, it shows that reductionism, if carried to the extreme, yields meaningless statements.

With this in mind, let's first consider the case for identity theory. By equating consciousness and matter, identity theory makes the claim that mental states (or processes) and brain states (or processes) are one and the same. For every state of consciousness there is a brain state that corresponds exactly, that is, is numerically identical to it (Churchland, 1984). The mistake is commonly made that materialism holds that brains cause consciousness, but it is important to understand that it takes the additional, and far more radical stance that they are identical. Thus, brains do not cause minds, but rather, as Minsky (1986) put it, "minds are simply what brains do."

To show how easy it is to confuse the claim of brain *equals* mind with the claim of brain *causes* mind, the philosopher husband-and-wife team Paul and Patricia Churchland (Churchland, 1994) use a nifty analogy that ponders the question: what causes heat? A typical answer might run like this. Molecules move, and the more they move the more they bump into one another. This causes friction and, as everybody knows, friction causes heat. This sounds like a reasonably good answer except of course, as any physicist will readily tell you, it is false. The explanation assumes that heat is something other than molecular motion. But it isn't. Temperature and mean molecular kinetic energy are identical concepts. One reduces perfectly to the other. Therefore, molecular motion does not cause heat; it *is* heat; Similarly, electricity is "not caused by moving electrons, it *is* moving electrons" (ibid., p. 106). And light is not a phenomenon caused by electromagnetic radiation; that's what light *is* (P. M. Churchland, 1996).

Identity theory applies the same rationale to the nature of consciousness. It would be absurd to demand an explanation of how molecular kinetic energy could possibly *cause* heat. It is equally absurd to ask how brains give rise to minds. Even neuroscientists frequently display this sort of residual dualism when they proclaim that memory activates such-and-such parts of the brain. This already betrays a commitment to duality, as if they are two events occurring: thing A, the memory, which comes before and causes separate thing B, the brain activity.

According to identity theory, this is factually mistaken. No doubt, the temptation to fall back on dualism is lurking everywhere.

Arguments for identity theory fall under five headings; parsimony, analogy, evidence of neural dependence, evolution, and a mighty, all-out research program. The first two, **parsimony** and **analogy**, have already been highlighted. Identity theory has the elegant touch of simplicity. Indeed, the equivalence of mind states and brain states is simplicity *an sich*. It does away, in one stroke, with the problems of qualia, explanatory gap, interaction, causation, and so on. Analogies, on the other hand, are not decisive arguments. However, they do provide us with good reason to pause next time we ponder the contention of irreducibility. By deliberately constructing analogies from other branches of science in which phenomena from seemingly different areas turned out to be isomorphic, identity theory has built a strong case, albeit circumstantial, that the closure of the explanatory gap is not so inconceivable after all. Given the neckbreaking fast-forward mode which with neuroscience unlocks the biological basis of mental phenomena, who would bet their fortune against the progress of neuroscience?

Evidence for the **neural dependence** of mental processes, including consciousness, on brain processes is overwhelming. Neuroscientists have made one impressive breakthrough after another, discovering centers for speech, memory, emotion, movement, perception, and dreams. Data is added on a daily basis. It's nearly enough to make one wonder when a team of scientists is going to schedule a press conference and announce that consciousness has been identified in the reverberating circuitry in some unpronounceable neuroanatomical location.

Neural dependence coheres with the take-no-prisoner **research program**, with which cognitive science and neuroscience steamroll the theoretical landscape. To appreciate the full weight of this overwhelming mass of evidence, one must delve into the meat-and-potatoes business of neurons and networks, which we shall do in Part III. Studying facts and understanding their consequences helps immeasurably with conceivability. Finally, there is the argument from **evolution**. The record indicates that the evolution of complex brains goes hand in hand with the development of mental phenomena indicative of consciousness, such as self-reflection. This observation only makes sense in light of the hypothesis that the mind is the brain, that is, they coevolved because they are one and the same thing. We will defer the arguments against identity theory to the end of this chapter and combine them with those raised against eliminativism.

Eliminativism

According to its leading advocate, Patricia Churchland (1994, p. 99), eliminativism "refers to the hypothesis that (1) materialism is most probably true and (2) many traditional aspects of explanations of human behavior are probably not adequate to the reality of the etiology of behavior." In other words, this approach to consciousness couples the considerable evidence pointing at a brain-based nature of souls with the hunch that our commonsense notions of mental phenomena are likely to be mistaken. The so-called "folk psychology" understanding we have developed to explain our everyday experience is undoubtedly primitive and will, according to this view, go the way of other folk wisdoms once thought to be self-evident. Intuition once told us that water is an element, that the earth is flat, and that a vital force breathes life into organic matter. These intuitions fell out of being intuitions and disappeared from the edifice of knowledge. Note that these are not examples of reductions, but eliminations; the old framework simply exploded. It would be miraculous if from all our ancient folk wisdoms we got it right when it comes to human behavior. In consequence, the fate of our folk knowledge of the mental will probably be a casualty of a maturing science of the mind. This is what makes eliminativism eliminative. This is incidentally also the reason why the eliminativist doubts that we are going to find psychological events being nicely coextensive with the theoretical framework of neuroscience. Thus, the eliminativist calls for nothing other than a full-blown paradigm shift – a revolution in psychology that will also establish an entirely new (intuitive) way of thinking about consciousness.

It follows that consciousness, as currently conceived, does not refer to anything that is likely to be real. Consciousness is an illusion in the sense that it seems to have qualities that it may not have. It is only because we hold those qualities to be absolutely true that we find it difficult to reconcile materialism with experience. If we simply change our conception of consciousness, this disparity will turn out to be a pseudoproblem. Once we reconceptualize the mind into a new framework, based on neurobiological data, it will no longer appear to us the way it appears to us now – just as the earth no longer feels flat when you look at the horizon.

Problems with materialism

Objections to materialism fall into five headings: intuition, category error, lack of precise matches, blind positivism, and multiple realizability. If you stand back and look at it, materialism is an extraordinary claim. It seems to undercut our fondest **intuitions** about being created in God's image, self-determination, and the meaning of life. Ordinary experience seems to defeat materialism easily, and when the matter turns to religion, shrieks of outrage inevitably follow. That the belief in Santa Claus is no different in kind than, say, a yellow Porsche 911 is rank nonsense. Again, as outlined earlier, this argument amounts to little more than a psychological talisman and evaporates on closer inspection. But intuition is seductive and always the hardest to defeat. It remains a persuasive argument until the materialist camp can convincingly show otherwise. It must be clear that it is the materialist here who is laden with the burden of proof.

A related objection, but one that arises from a different source, is what is known in philosophy as a **category error**. The materialist is charged with committing this error when equating phenomena of different ontological origin. Consciousness is a first-person phenomenon that has a subjective component, while brain activity is a third-person phenomenon that has an exhaustively objective mode of existence. It seems obvious that fear of intimacy is not in the same class of phenomena as fluctuating sodium–potassium currents. Because the category "mental" is something different from the category "physical," consciousness and action potentials cannot refer to something identical. When seen in this way, the aim of reducing mind to brain is an exercise of sheer conceptual misdirection. This argument is related to Leibniz's law regarding ontological identity considered earlier.

The materialist will have none of this. The charge of categorical absurdity comes down to the tacit assumption that subjectivity *just is* an irreducible characteristic of consciousness. The history of science is full of examples in which two phenomena seemingly belonging to separate categories turned out to be identical (Hardcastle, 1996). As Churchland (1984, p. 30) illustrates: "The claim that warmth is measured in kilogram x meter^2/seconds^2 would have seemed semantically perverse before we understood that temperature is mean molecular kinetic energy." We categorize the world as it seems to us but this does not necessarily reflect treal category boundaries. The eliminativist might even add that this begs the very question at issue, for it is exactly those conceptions of categories that require genuine replacement.

Opponents have no difficulty in showing that this will not do. The above cases are analogies in which one third-person perspective was reduced to another. What the materialist needs to show is a reduction from a first-person perspective to a third-person one. The reduction of the macrophenomena of consciousness to neural activity is entirely different in that it means a redescription of the phenomena, not in terms of the same methodological framework, but into a framework in which it has, as far as we can tell, no relevance. Unlike hypothetical concepts in other sciences that were successfully reduced or eliminated, such as the caloric fluid invoked to explain heat, there is nothing hypothetical about consciousness. We have direct access to our experiences and to say that it is an illusion literally means that we should wait for neuroscience to tell us how we should really feel about our experiences. This is absurd. Experience is not a hypothetical entity requiring reconceptualization. Thus, denying its existence is to deny the obvious. Reference to analogous reductionist success stories such as light, heat, or vitalism are intellectually beguiling but not indicative of what might lie in store for consciousness. As Velmans (2000, p. 35) put it: "With deeper insight we might be able to improve our theories about what we experience but this would not replace, or necessarily improve, the experiences themselves."

Identity theory has a different problem. It calls for neat, **one-to-one match-ups** of brain activity to experience. Opponents rightfully insist on seeing the data that back up this glaring claim. Researchers have compiled catalogs of facts on brain function but a one-to-one hit has so far eluded them. That the mind is in the brain has become an almost self-evident statement, but the claim that consciousness is nested in the convoluted labyrinth of the neocortex has turned out to be far harder to prove than the existence of the elusive dark matter. Decades of exploration in the rarefied realm of immunohistochemistry, electrophysiology, and nuclear neuroimaging have brought us no closer to catching *in flagrante* the qualities of experiential states, let alone neat correspondence. Thus, critics charge that identity theory requires a leap of faith, a maneuver not too terribly popular among scientists. Perhaps we should admit that the enterprise is doomed and that there are no reductions to be had, let alone one-to-one match-ups. Yet, a massive exodus from materialism is unlikely to materialize, if you'll forgive the pun. It is true that we cannot understand phenomenology by looking at pictures from brain scanners, but neither can we explain yet how the brain pole-vaults; however, few people are willing to claim that pole-vaulting is not an act performed by the brain (Churchland, 1994). The science of the mind is still in its infancy and it is too early to jump on the naysaying side. We may not have many answers yet but research can already give an account that makes material-ism much less startling. Note that this objection is less of a problem for elimina-tivism because it does not assume that the old framework will make contact seamlessly with the new.

A fourth objection is what might be called **blind positivism**, a near total faith in the inevitability of scientific progress. Western science worships the God of causality and materialists fall prey to the overly optimistic hope that there are no limits to this endeavor; that eventually the phenomena of consciousness will succumb to the omnipotent methods of empirical research and be admitted into the enlightened kingdom of science. This is a tall order and an expectation that goes well beyond what is supported by currently available evidence. There are plenty of subjects that will remain forever unfalsifiable and thus outside the realm of science, such as art, music, religion, or ethics. Perhaps this is the fate of consciousness.

A final weakness, particularly for identity theory, is **multiple realizability**. This concept refers to the fact that a function or process can seemingly be implemented in multiple ways. The same mind state can take the form of a vari-ety of very different brain states. Accordingly, neuroscience will not reduce or eliminate consciousness to specific brain events. In addition, we have good reason to believe that the plasticity of the brain allows for considerable indi-vidual differences. Indeed, complex cognitive functions, such as language, can be realized in either cerebral hemisphere. Computational functionalists have demonstrated that multiple realizability means that brains are not even neces-sary for some cognitive operations. If computations mimicking mental phenomena can be run as virtual programs on an information processor made from stuff other than carbon, how can the materialist claim that the mind is the brain? But the materialist does not have to insist on the specifics. Few working members of the Society for Neuroscience harbor the expectation of reducing a quale, say, the taste of milk chocolate to a specific, coordinated pattern of neural activity in a distributed network consisting of exactly 5,642 neurons in the parietal cortex. This is not to say that the taste of milk chocolate is not a neurobiological event but that, because of the nonlinear nature of complex biological systems, it cannot be pinned down. With the advent of quantum mechanics and chaos theory, people have accepted that indeterminism sets limits to reductionism. This deflates the strength of this neither-here-nor-there objection considerably.

Box 3.1   Public opinion poll

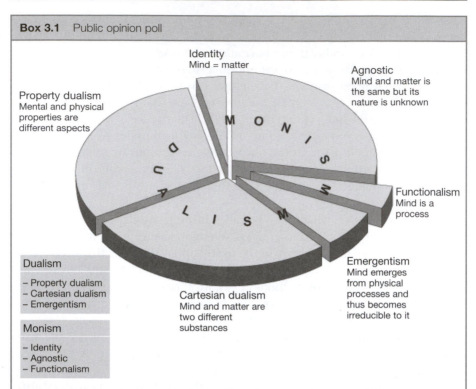

Identity
Mind = matter

Agnostic
Mind and matter is
the same but its
nature is unknown

Property dualism
Mental and physical
properties are
different aspects

Functionalism
Mind is a
process

Emergentism
Mind emerges
from physical
processes and
thus becomes
irreducible to it

Cartesian dualism
Mind and matter are
two different
substances

Dualism
– Property dualism
– Cartesian dualism
– Emergentism

Monism
– Identity
– Agnostic
– Functionalism

In philosophy, consciousness is a big problem. But like most big problems in philosophy, it isn't a problem at all to anyone who isn't a philosopher. A survey of popular opinion on the mind–body problem yields a picture that is decidedly different from the one that polls the opinion of philosophers and scientists. The most obvious disparity is the low percentage of people giving their vote to functionalism and identity theory. According to another poll, 90 percent of Americans and 76 percent of Britons believe in a spiritual dimension (based on Carter, 2002).

Summary

Dualist theories come in two main versions. One, Cartesian dualism, splits the universe into two different substances, mind and matter. This division has problems beyond repair. Most importantly, the obvious dependence of mental events on the physical brain requires the proposal of a mechanism on how, exactly, two substances so fundamentally different in kind are supposed to interact. So far no sound mechanistic explanation has been proposed. The other, property dualism or dual-aspect theory, divides the universe into two sets of properties, mental and physical. This version solves some problems while deepening others. Specifically, property dualism leads to epiphenomenalism. Nevertheless, property dualism is the only vital form of dualism today. Emergentism tries to naturalize dualism. It differs from property dualism in that it postulates mental phenomena to emerge from brain events. Because these emergent properties are irreducible to physical properties, emergentism is committed to a dual universe. A consequence of holding mental phenomena "emergent" is that epiphenomenalism becomes fully inescapable.

The principal problem of all dualist accounts is the utter lack of a research program. In the end, dualism always seems to require some sort of magic to make it work. This severely curtails its explanatory power. In addition, the lack of prospect for this to change in the future renders dualism an unconstructive, negative position. As Dennett (1991, p. 37) put it: "This fundamental antiscientific stance of dualism is, in my mind, its most disqualifying feature . . . accepting dualism is giving up." Dualism, most say, is sadly dated and the progress of neuroscience is making it look like an "outdated curiosity" (Churchland, 2002). In light of these grave – if not fatal – flaws, philosophers and scientists are turning in increasing numbers to materialism.

Monism comprises a group of theories that share the position that mind and matter are one and the same. Idealism achieves this unity not by reducing mind to matter but by reducing matter to mind. By postulating a world filled with nothing but consciousness, idealism has the drawback of being unfalsifiable, and hence useless. Functionalism makes mental states equal to functional states. Some take functionalism to be a form of materialism while others prefer not to classify it this way. By making a fundamental distinction between function and structure, functionalism has become the philosophical foundation for cognitive science and one of the most popular philosophies of mind. For all its success in contributing to the study of consciousness, its main limitation remains the inability to adequately account for phenomenal content.

Materialism comes in two versions. Identity theory makes mental states equal to physical states. This move nullifies most of the problems associated with a dual universe; however, it also raises several problems of its own. Eliminativism maintains that the apparent discrepancy between neuroscience and experience, the explanatory gap, is rooted in a poor understanding of experience. Thus, our current conception of consciousness does not refer to anything real and the task of neuroscience is not to bridge the gap but to eliminate the inadequate folk psychology and replace it with a theory informed by neurobiology. The popularity of materialism is largely fueled by a torrent of empirical data coupled with the hope of further scientific progress. However, many people find that accepting all the consequences of a materialist position is a tough pill to swallow.

Suggested reading

Chalmers, D. J. (1996). *The Conscious Mind: In Search of a Fundamental Theory*. New York: Oxford University Press.

Churchland, P. S. (2002). *Brain-wise: Studies in Neurophilosophy*. Cambridge, MA: MIT Press.

Searle, J. (1992). *The Rediscovery of the Mind*. Cambridge, MA: MIT Press.

Velmans, M. (2000). *Understanding Consciousness*. London: Routledge.

PART II

The mechanism of consciousness

PART II

4 Physical mechanisms

Neurophysiological approaches

Neural correlates of consciousness

This chapter is devoted to the most influential physical mechanisms – from neurobiology to quantum mechanics – that have been proposed to explain consciousness. Approaches falling into this rather diverse category are motivated primarily by the aspiration to account for the unity of consciousness. The puzzle arises because the brain is not a monolithic entity but a massive parallel-processing system. Yet consciousness is a serial phenomenon. We experience the world, including ourselves, as an unified whole, not composed of bits and pieces. In the first part of this chapter, we describe neurophysiological models based on neuronal competition. Here the aim is to tackle the so-called binding problem by studying perceptual phenomena, such as binocular rivalry, that allows one to identify the neural correlates of consciousness. In the second part, we outline approaches based on quantum physics and chaos theories. Here the aim is to explain the unity of consciousness by drawing a parallel to other physical systems that accomplish global coherence from the disparate activities of individual units.

Few neuroscientists declare frankly that consciousness is their main research interest. If asked, the majority would tell you that they study, say, synaptic transmission, memory processes, or neurological diseases. This is not to say they endorse the existence of some hard problem but rather that they pursue different goals in the lab. A selected bunch, however, have made it their explicit mission to conduct research that addresses consciousness head-on. This is not an easy task; let's remember that we are dealing with a supposedly unobservable phenomenon. So, to do this they have turned to the study of perceptual processes, one branch of the brain sciences that has always been recognized to have profound implications for the mind-body problem.

By studying one element of consciousness, sensory experience, the hope is to tackle consciousness empirically. The most successful research strategy to employ this rationale has exploited our detailed knowledge of the visual system. The basic experimental design is deceptively simple. Of all the light-borne information falling on the retina at any moment, only a tiny speck of it ends up in consciousness; the rest remains unconscious. One might reasonably ask, then, what is the critical difference between those two types of processing, given that the visual scene does not change? There must be, for all we know, some sort of a distinct and discernible marker in the brain. But what might this be? Does it involve a particular set of neurons, a special pattern of firing, or a critical intensity threshold? Could it be mediated by molecular mechanisms, certain neurochemicals, or a special type of cell? The possibilities are numerous and, given the profound difference in phenomenology, conscious processing is likely to be different at many levels of neural organization, from molecules to global networks. Francis Crick, a passionate advocate of the direct approach, casts this into a specific hypothesis. The **Crick hypothesis**, as we might call it, is this: If a person is presented with a stimulus, a difference in neural activity must exist for the following two conditions: (1) the subject is aware of it and (2) the subject is not aware of it.

What scientists are after here are the **neural correlates of consciousness**, or NCC for short (Metzinger, 2000). By contrasting conscious with unconscious processing, searching for the NCC is an approach unapologetically aimed at finding underlying mechanisms subserving consciousness. Such a correspondence, if it were to be found, does not, by itself, constitute a reductive neurobiological explanation of consciousness, but it certainly would go a long way in the direction of one. In the same way that DNA is a molecule that encodes information, finding the NCC would constitute a structural embodiment of information, in this case conscious experience.

Box 4.1 provides a highly oversimplified overview of the things we do know about the NCC. Much of the evidence supporting this model will be covered in Part III of this book. Beyond this minimal standard view, there is little agreement.

Modern neuroscience conceptualizes brain function as hierarchically ordered. This approach extends to consciousness. By dividing consciousness into various attributes – self-reflection, attention, memory, emotion, perception, arousal – and ordering these into a functional hierarchy we can link anatomy and function. In

Box 4.1   Locating consciousness

In a framework that conceptualizes consciousness as hierarchically ordered cognitive function, no single neural structure is necessary and sufficient for consciousness. Yet, not all areas of the brain contribute equally to consciousness. The major structures purported to play key roles in the NCC are:

Brainstem: The brainstem is the source of massive pathways that activate higher brain centers. They are the core of the basic arousal mechanism, the on/off switch of consciousness.

Thalamus: Sensory information passes through the thalamus on its way to the cortex. In this pivotal position, the thalamus is thought to be critical for the binding process, which unifies experience by linking mental representations that are scattered widely in the cortex.

Amygdala: Basic emotions seem to be generated by subcortical, automatic, and unconscious processes. The amygdala computes the basic emotion of fear. When activated by a threatening stimulus, it coordinates countermeasures and retrospectively informs consciousness about it.

Hippocampus: The consolidation of life's experiences into long-term memories requires the restructuring of neural networks. Because this process is complicated, involving, among many other things, the association between perceptions dispersed over numerous cortical areas, a separate structure devoted to this task has evolved. This is the domain of the hippocampus.

TOP: The **t**emporal, **o**ccipital, and **p**arietal cortices are devoted to perception and memory. They decode sensory information and store it as long-term memory. The parietal cortex also seems to compute the map of the physical dimensions of the self.

Ventromedial PFC: The VMPFC contributes complex emotions to the content of awareness. It also converts basic emotions into feelings by making them conscious.

Dorsolateral PFC: The DLPFC is involved in executive functions. It provides the computational infrastructure to make possible the higher-order representations that so dramatically increase our cognitive flexibility. Full-fledged consciousness requires the engagement of this zenithal higher-order structure.

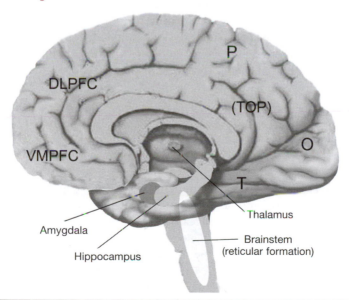

this model, the brainstem occupies the bottom of the totem pole, providing the basic arousal mechanism without which the higher brain regions cannot operate. Not surprisingly, damage to the brainstem typically results in coma, wiping out consciousness altogether. The highest level at which this kind of absolute change to consciousness can occur is apparently the thalamus (Bogen, 1995a), a structure crucial for binding together experiences (Crick, 1994; Llinás & Paré, 1991). It is generally agreed that all stages of processing beyond the thalamus provide some form of content. Among the higher brain centers, there is also a hierarchy. Limbic system structures contribute rather basic phenomenal content. For instance, damage to the amygdala eradicates a basic emotion, fear, from consciousness while damage to the hippocampus produces anterograde amnesia. A little higher up, in the posterior regions of the cortex, more integrative functions are implemented. Damage in these regions typically results in more selective alterations to the content of consciousness. For instance, patients with unilateral neglect or blindsight, neurological conditions we shall explore in later chapters, lack very specific information in consciousness. The top layers of consciousness are enabled by the prefrontal cortex. Here damage eliminates higher-order features of experience such as self-reflection or creativity (Dietrich, 2003).

Binocular rivalry

The Crick hypothesis is stated such that it becomes feasible to test it with the right experimental paradigm. One paradigm that has proven particularly useful in this regard is **binocular rivalry**. When two different images are presented, one exclusively to each eye, we do not merge them into one image but experience what psychologists call a bistable or **multistable perception**. As in the ambiguous Necker cube, we switch the two competing perceptions to and fro. For instance, if a face is presented to the right eye and a sunburst to the left, we see one or the other, alternating between them every one to ten seconds or so (Leopold & Logothetis, 1999). What makes binocular rivalry such an obvious candidate for the Crick hypothesis is that the visual stimulus is always present before the eyes while the interpretation of what is consciously seen changes back and forth. In a series of clever experiments of this sort, the psychologist Nikos Logothetis and his colleagues explored what happens in the brain of macaque monkeys when confronted with such a multistable perception (Sheinberg & Logothetis, 1997). Using the face/sunburst pair of stimuli, macaques were first trained on a nonrivalrous paradigm in which each stimulus was presented alone to both eyes. They learned to press the left button when they saw the face and the right when they saw the sunburst. Following acquisition, both images were projected simultaneously under conditions of binocular rivalry, one to each eye, and, as the multistable perception flip-flopped in their minds, the macaques did what they learned, press one of two buttons to indicate which picture was being perceived. Evidently, the macaques' behavior was driven by the perceptual experience – not by the visual stimulus itself, because this never changed. Recordings from neurons were then made that allowed Logothetis to determine which neurons mirrored what the animal saw.

The findings were highly informative. The primary visual cortex, or V1, is the first cortical relay station for visual information. Single-cell recordings from this area showed that less than 20 percent of the neurons changed their activity when the monkey experienced a perceptual switch. This meant that the behavior of V1 neurons is determined by the stimulus condition; they decode information irrespective of whether or not it eventually enters awareness. The obvious conclusion is that the bottleneck of selecting for consciousness must occur after V1, in neurons higher up the chain of the visual system. From this and other data, the Crick/Koch team (1995, p. 121) concluded that we are not "aware of neural activity in primary visual cortex." And, indeed, the higher up the visual information-processing hierarchy Logothetis looked, the higher was the percentage of active neurons that corresponded to what the monkeys were supposedly seeing. The activity of 33 percent of the neurons in MT, a cortical area responsible for motion detection, fluctuated as a function of what was being perceived. Finally, there was a corresponding change for 90 percent of the neurons in the superior temporal sulcus, a cortical area in the inferior temporal region that is one of the two end stations of the visual system (ibid.).

This tight correlation in the inferior temporal cortex between neuronal activity and conscious perception indicates that this cortex plays a critical role in visual consciousness. There are additional data to support this conclusion. Most noticeably, damage to this region produces visual agnosia, the inability to recognize forms and shapes (see Chapter 7). Such converging evidence has led some to label those regions "the visual consciousness areas" (Ffytche, 2000), the place where "it all comes together" (Taylor, 2001), or the site of "awareness neurons" (Crick, 1994). On rather different grounds, the philosopher Ray Jackendoff (1987) argued that it is in these intermediate-level cortices (intermediate in the sense of in between V1 and the frontal cortex) that qualia emerge. As tempting as such conclusions may be, we are well advised to be cautious about locating visual awareness in the inferior temporal cortex. For one thing, we cannot be sure that the monkey reported what it is actually saw, or, for that matter, that it perceived the stimuli in the same conscious way we do. For it is entirely possible that macaques do not use conscious experience to solve the binocular paradigm. This rather palpable objection is reinforced by the observation that the macaques' learning curve suggests that they acquired the task by trial and error, over time, rather than by insight. If they were really guided by conscious perception, one would expect a different learning curve, one in which a period of random responding is followed by a sudden shift in performance perfectly matching the conscious perception to behavior. Perhaps the macaques respond to other cues, a plausible alternative explanation, especially in light of the fact that humans also solve some visual tasks without being aware of the stimulus. Despite this critique, the implications of Logothetis' research for the processing of conscious visual information is generally taken as solid, especially since research on humans using the same binocular rivalry paradigm has produced fMRI data that mesh nicely with those of the macaques (Lumer et al., 1998).

At this early stage in the hunt for the NCC, the important insight taken from such now-you-see-it-now-you-don't studies is not so much the data itself, though certainly eye-opening, but the knowledge that the Crick hypothesis is a useful guide to research. By monitoring brain activity while subjects perform ingeniously devised perceptual experiments, researchers have indeed discovered that only a subset of neurons differentiates conscious from silent information processing. These data represent the first steps, no doubt, in a long program of empirical research aimed at identifying the NCC. This direct approach to studying consciousness is likely to gain considerably in strength in the future, as the still primitive status of neurotechnology improves in sophistication and our probably still faulty characterization of consciousness is sharpened in focus.

The binding problem

The brain operates on the conquer-and-divide principle. In visual perception, this translates into a small army of specialized modules, each devoted to analyzing a particular aspect of the visual scene. Consider seeing a clown. To decode her kazillion lines, shapes, colors, and motions is beyond the computational capacity of any single network. So the visual system tackles this staggering complexity by dividing up the task among many distinct regions of cortex. All told, there are some thirty of these cortical areas for vision, each processing only one of the clown's features. The clown is then assembled into the coherent view we see in front of our eyes by the simultaneous activity in countless cortical modules. But how so? There must be some kind of mechanism that links together the distributed activities of these spatially separated modules. For we do not see the clown as composed of bits and pieces – lines, shapes, colors, and so on; she comes as a unified, indivisible whole. Let's ask the question this way. Given that experience is integrated, how does this unity arise from the activity of neurons located in all four corners of the brain? Somehow, the autonomous activity of distinct regions of cortex must be pooled into a coordinated firing pattern, a state of **global coherence**, so that the various components of a common stimulus appear in unity in consciousness. This, in a nutshell, is known as **the binding problem**. It arises whenever information computed in separate areas of the brain must be combined, be it for visual experience or across the senses.

Possible solutions to the binding problem range the gamut from quantum states involving global holism to dualist accounts positing a supervenient mind. The most promising explanations, however, are based on neurophysiological mechanisms for the simple reason that they build on available evidence in neuroscience. Given that elements of a common stimulus are parceled out spatially in the brain, one attractive candidate for a binding mechanism is temporal coding; that is, neurons that code a common event fire in unison. In the mid-1980s, the neuroscientist von der Malsberg (1986) proposed that perception is associated with the synchronous firing of large assemblies of cells. Soon thereafter, researchers recorded the activity of neurons from different regions of cats' visual systems and found that neurons in different regions oscillate in such a way as to pull each other into synchrony (Gray et al., 1989). Their firing rate became locked in phase at a frequency of about 40 hertz. Von der Malsberg realized that when the oscillatory activity of neurons is entrenched, distant regions of the brain could be brought on-line at the same time. He was the first to suggest that the timing of neuronal discharge may hold the key to the binding problem. This dancing to the same rhythmical beat is a physiological solution to global coherence. As we shall see in the next part of this chapter, there are other proposals of how complex systems can exhibit large-scale synchrony from the behavior of individual units.

To better understand what these 40 cycles/second mean, let's consider the rhythmicity of neurons in general in terms of EEG spectral components. Cortical neurons can fire anywhere from 1 Hz to 250 Hz (Connors and Gutnick, 1990), which is a rather large range. Typically, the rate of firing is a good index of a cell's level of activity. Thus, rates lower than a neuron's intrinsic baseline rate indicate deactivation while frequencies higher than the norm are generally interpreted as activation. At the low end of the scale is delta activity, which is a quite regular, low-amplitude wave of 1–5 Hz. At this inhibited rate, there is no room for the high-level processing needed to sustain conscious states. It is not surprising, then, to find delta rhythm during deep sleep, a time not associated with experiences. Theta activity is a medium-amplitude, medium-frequency rhythm of 5–8 Hz. This frequency is also too low for full consciousness and a person exhibiting this rhythm reports feeling drowsy. Alpha activity is a fairly regular pattern between 8 and 12 Hz. It is prominent when a person is minimally aroused – awake but relaxed. Alpha-band activity is still interpreted as a state of cortical *de*activation because as soon as the person is given a cognitive task it gives way to beta activity, which is an irregular pattern between 12 and 30 Hz that occurs during alertness and active thinking. As you can see, the higher the frequency/activity the more lucid is the person. In comparison, oscillations around the 40-Hz mark, the so-called gamma band, really stand out against the electrical background of the rest of the brain. They must make for intensive activity; just the sort of thing one might suspect is needed for the unity of consciousness. The idea of 40-Hz oscillations underlying binding is strengthened further by studies showing that oscillations in the gamma frequency appear in regions of the brain that are actively engaged in the processing of information. This effect is particularly striking for attentional tasks. The neuroscientist Rudolfo Llinás (2001) reported that he also found the gamma rhythm in subjects during REM, the state of sleep associated with dreams and thus experiences, while it was absent during deep sleep. All this pointed to the possible importance of this 40-Hz frequency for conscious processing.

Early on, the Crick/Koch team (1990) suggested, perhaps a bit hastily, that the gamma-rate oscillations at the 40-Hz mark *is* the neural correlate of consciousness. The neuroscientist Wolfgang Singer (2000) made the case for a temporal code even stronger when he showed that the activity of independent neural assemblies can produce global coherence without the need to base their mutual entrainment on oscillations. But several observations have since cast doubt on the straightfor-ward conclusion that 40-Hz flutters are the NCC. One is that this frequency was recorded from the visual cortex of anesthetized cats whose eyes are popped open (Crick, 1994). Similar mixed results have come from recordings of monkey visual cortex. Another is that it occurs in humans during anesthesia. In one study, a researcher played a recording of *Robinson Crusoe* to subjects undergoing an unrelated surgical procedure and recorded gamma activity from the primary auditory cortex. The verbal stimulus must have reached the auditory cortex, but apparently not consciousness, as none of the subjects could recall the event after waking up (Schwender et al., 1994). This study refutes the notion that these oscillations signal conscious mental processes and, indeed, Crick and Koch (2003) no longer maintain their earlier position. But if it isn't the signature of consciousness, what then is the significance of this rhythm? There is no consensus on this but, given the sex appeal of the idea, many prominent scientists maintain that this gamma activity plays a key role in consciousness. For instance, the cognitive psychologist Anne Treisman (2003) emphasizes that binding is an essential component of conscious experience and thinks that the temporal code represented by gamma oscillations is a prerequisite for information processing that has the potential to become conscious. Thinking along similar lines, Singer (2000) believes that gamma activity is the first step to higher-order representational states. In either case, the 40-Hz activity is regarded as a necessary but not sufficient condition for consciousness. Amid all this theorizing, we do well to remind ourselves that the hard experimental evidence pointing to gamma oscillations as the underlying mechanism of binding remains rather thin.

Neurological conditions can also throw light on the binding problem. One might reasonably suspect, for instance, that schizophrenics, split-brain patients, and people suffering from dissociative identity disorder or epilepsy perceive the world in a fragmented or disjointed manner. But this does not seem to be the case. Even in altered states of consciousness, perceptions and memories are not choped into their components. One phenomenon that might offer more clues is **synesthesia**. Synesthesia is a case of multisensory integration gone awry. It occurs when stimulation of one sensory modality leads to perceptual experience in another. Colored hearing is the most common multisensory blending but, in addition to hearing sounds in color, all other crossover experiences have been reported; a synesthete might see colors in touch, scent smells in sounds and taste shapes. The condition is generally considered a genuine perceptual effect that can be distinguished from mere imagination, metaphors, or "deliberate artistic contrivances" (Cytowic, 1993). According to the neurologist Richard Cytowic (1993), synesthesia appears to be mediated by the left hemisphere and depends primarily on subcortical structures, such as the hippocampus. Others believe that it is the result of spreading activation across cortical areas (Ramachandran and Hubbard, 2001). More recent research still has shown that neurons in primary cortices are not fully specialized for one sense. They only show a strong preference and can possibly be excited by input from a different sensory system. Synesthesia is a rare capacity occurring, depending on definition criteria, in far less than 1 percent of people (Baron-Cohen & Harrison, 1997). The trait is familial, favors females and left-handers, and occurs most frequently in infants, presumably because their brain has yet to differentiate enough to clearly separate the ten or so sensory modalities adults have. The psychologist Alexander Luria (1968) reported what is probably the most famous case of synesthesia, Solomon Shereshevskii (see Chapter 7). The case highlighted characteristics of the synesthesic experience that have since been confirmed several times. That is, synesthesia is associated with improved memory capacity and, more significantly, the sensory crossover follows a specific and systematic pattern. For instance, the sound of a particular frequency does not conjure up just any color or shape but produces specific visual experiences that might even hold constant from one person to another. Synesthesia, then, is some sort of superunity of consciousness, which only deepens the puzzle of the binding problem.

Competitive models

The aim of this section is to set out the central ideas of two prominent theories of mind, one by the neurobiologist Gerald Edelman and the other by the Crick/Koch team. Both have developed ideas along broadly similar lines with respect to the "where" and "how" of consciousness. First, they reject, at times rather dismissively, that answers are to be found in philosophical pontification, quantum effects, or computer simulations. Consciousness is, in essence, a biological problem and the foundation of any successful theory must be rooted in the functional architecture of the brain. Second, both models are largely motivated by the search for a solution to the notorious binding problem and thus use as their starting point the biological basis of perception. Finally, both acknowledge the reality of qualia and aim to reconcile the more difficult aspects of phenomenology with what we know about neurons and their interactions. The models also differ. For instance, they disagree on the brain areas that are involved and whether or not there is a need to postulate special cellular properties.

In exploring these two models, we first must acquaint ourselves with a few key concepts of how neurons go about doing their business, in particular how they wire themselves up to build stable neural networks. Our knowledge of this process is much informed by Edelman's (1993) **theory of neuronal group selection**, or **neural Darwinism**, a theory that has since become a basic building block of our understanding of brain function. Clearly, neural networks in the brain are not hardwired. According to Edelman, they are shaped by a variation-selection process that resembles evolution. During growth and development in infancy – the variation phase – neurons cluster into groups and establish a profusely interconnected set of networks. But not all of these patterns turn out to be functional. Variation is then followed by a selection phase in which some neuronal patterns are reinforced by experience while others are not and thus pruned away. The infant brain produces an excess of neurons which, from the start, enter into a fight for survival against one another. Each neuron tries, in order to prevent elimination, to establish synaptic links that are useful to the organism. The whole of the brain, then, develops and operates through competitive interactions among neuronal populations.

This theory demands from us that we give up the notion of the brain as a single, monolithic entity. Instead we must envisage it as a diverse society comprised of trillions of individual member neurons, each trying to beat the other in the same game, that is, to gain access either to consciousness or the right to move muscles. The notion of an anarchic society of selfish neurons inside your head is initially a bit counterintuitive, not to mention discomforting, but it grows on you once you see how it enlightens some otherwise puzzling phenomena. The idea was first mooted by Oliver Selfridge (1959) in his **pandemonium model**, a computer program in which hordes of demons are locked into an internal struggle for supremacy. Like Charles Sherrington, who envisaged the brain as "a million-fold democracy whose each unit is a cell," Crick and Koch (2003) prefer to liken the brain's internal dynamics to a parliamentary democracy. To gain access to power, individuals in a democracy must garner support for their cause. So they form groups and broader coalitions. A winning coalition eventually emerges and forms, temporarily, the next government. In principle, the case is similar for neurons, except that the brain probably isn't so much a democracy with orderly elections but rather a sort of gangster war ruled by law of the street.

Neurons group together into assemblies. To make their computation heard in consciousness, each coalition must campaign for a larger support base. By recruiting other neurons along the way, they form transient coalitions to better compete against others. Temporal synchronization may play a key role here, as mutual entrainment can be a way of altering the effectiveness of coalitions without increasing the firing rate of its individual neurons (Singer & Gray, 1995). Crick and Koch (2003) believe that the 40-Hz waveforms discussed earlier can build the internal strength of a coalition. The top dog is ultimately determined on the basis of a competitive process, with the victorious coalition, the one with the largest backing, having its computation sustained long enough to either become conscious or contribute to the organism's next move. It's the quest for the proverbial 15 minutes of fame that drives neurons. Note how the concept of competing cell-assemblies does away with the homunculus, the infinite regress of an entity watching the happenings in the brain, because the dynamics are governed by a bottom-up process. Although the competition is likely to be strongly biased by attention, via a top-down process (Desimone & Duncan, 1995), attention is not meant to substitute for some kind of Cartesian king appointing the next government.

This large-scale selectionist theory of brain development and function offers new perspectives on the binding problem. We can ask, for instance, how neurons in a transient coalition know that they belong together. How does a single neuron know, at any one time, what its allegiance is? How are coalitions coded and how do they give way without giving us the sense of experience disintegrating along with them? Neuronal group selection also provides us with a way to think about the multistable perceptions we described earlier. How does the concept of neural competition help us understand their two main effects; first, why is just one object being perceived at a time; and second, why does it flip-flop? Given their input into different eyes, each display is represented by a different group of cell-assemblies. This sets them up for a head-to-head competition for access to consciousness. The conflict is resolved, it seems, in playoff fashion, with a winner-takes-it-all strategy that leaves no room for a loser or powerful semifinalist that might compromise the integrity of the winning perception. In other words, the unity of consciousness is achieved by way of an atrocious elimination tournament that sees only the last man standing – not much of a democracy, is it?

This view makes the NCC a moving target, a shifting supercluster of strongly interacting neuronal populations. Gerald Edelman and his collaborator Giulio Tononi (2000) postulate that these circuits constitute a **dynamic core** that generates raw perceptual experience or primary consciousness. The dynamic core is held together by reentrant connections among the participating neuronal assemblies, particularly in regions of the neocortex and the thalamus. These reentry loops that hail from the various neuronal groups and feed back into the thalamocortical dynamic core are a key element of the model for it is they that unify the brain's dispersed processing streams into the continuity and coherence of experience. Exactly how this works, however, they do not specify. Also, it is unclear how these reentrant connections are relevant to qualia and the what-it's-likeness of conscious experience. Edelman thinks that, given that we share this basic wiring diagram with other animals, we must also share primary consciousness with them. Secondary or higher consciousness, however, requires reentrant projections arising from higher-order cortical areas, such as those involved in language and abstract thinking. In consequence, secondary consciousness is unique to humans.

Figure 4.1

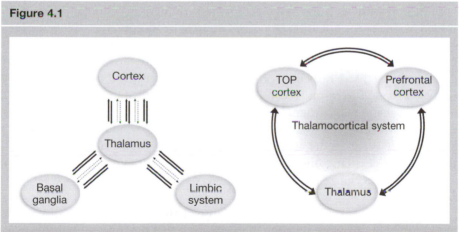

The models by Edelman (left) and the Crick/Koch team (right) share many features. They are both interactive, built around the notion of competing neuronal coalitions. The NCC is a moving target but regions of the thalamus and neocortex are thought to play key roles. The main difference between them is that in Edelman's thinking the unity consciousness arises through reentrant connections into a dynamic core, while in the Crick/Koch model global coherence is achieved by the 40-Hz synchronous firing pattern in large areas of the cortex.

In contrast to Edelman, Crick maintains that specific cell types and cortical regions are critical to the phenomenon of consciousness. His model gives the thalamus a central role in this process. By virtue of its position at the crossroad of the sensory pathways, the thalamus is responsible for selecting which aspects of sensory experience are bound together. Specifically, the NCC is sustained by reverberating circuits originating in the pyramidal cells of cortical layer 5, the principal output layer of the cortex. These cells connect with neurons in layer 6 to send signals to the thalamus, which are then linked together and sent back to cortical layer 4, the principal input layer of the cortex, and layer 6 (Crick, 1994). Similar to the dynamic core model, consciousness arises from the intense interaction among shifting coalitions, except that here the critical feature is that coherence is achieved by a synchronous firing pattern at 40 Hz coordinated by the thalamus. Both models avoid the problem of a single locale, a modern-day pineal gland, as the sole site where consciousness happens.

Physics and the mind

The quantum mind

Quantum theories of the mind represent a daunting and fascinating possibility. To understand their allure we must also make our way through a bit of quantum physics. This allow us, albeit in a very cursory and wholly conceptual manner, to explore how the imponderable paradoxes of quantum theory may relate to consciousness and to what extent, if any, this paradigm is to be taken seriously.

Let's start with everyone's favorite quantum thought experiment. It was envisioned by one of the quantum pioneers, **Edwin Schrödinger**, specifically to elucidate the strange happenings of the quantum world. **Schrödinger's cat**, as it is known, is a quantum cat that lives in a quantum box, in which a radioactive decay-powered food dispenser provides randomly either food or poison. To common sense, the cat must consequently be either alive or dead. But this is a quantum cat and in quantumland all possible realities coexist concurrently. Thus, the cat is alive *and* dead. Yet, when we open the box we would find the cat either alive *or* dead. What's more, whatever we find depends on how and when we open the box. This illustrates one of the fundamental absurdities of quantum mechanics. We must recognize ourselves, by the very act of observation, as creators of reality.

This taking-a-peek is known as the **collapse of the wave function**. Introduced by Schrödinger, the wave function is an equation that describes all possible realities a quantum system can assume – even contradictory ones – and assigns a probability to each. When the system is observed, this equation collapses and the sea of potentialities gives way to a single actuality. The cat is, then, either dead or alive. The reason for the collapse is unknown, luring some physicists to propose some rather esoteric but entirely plausible explanations. The first is called the **Wigner interpretation**. Eugene Wigner proposed that any measuring device is also a quantum entity and thus cannot bring about the collapse of the wave function. Something nonphysical must do the trick which, according to Wigner, is human consciousness. In other words, an observing mind induces any eventuality and creates – quite literally – reality. Reality is not a feature of the quantum realm, which only contains potentialities. Only by measuring the quantum system does reality emerge, and the way we decide to measure it determines what we will see. The second interpretation is called the **many-worlds theory** and seems almost deliberately designed to short-circuit the rational mind. It denies that there is a difference between actuality and potentiality. The wave function never does collapse. Rather, all possible worlds are actual worlds. Each time a measurement is taken, a whole new world branches off, complete with the observer.

So what does all this mean for consciousness? Some say nothing. For others, however, quantum physics and consciousness are weird in similar ways – similar enough to take the quantum mind seriously. The debate over quantum minds comes down to whether or not quantum effects manifest themselves in the brain. Quantum events happen at the level of subatomic particles and to have them act up on larger-scale systems like the brain, they need to stretch further in space-time. The problem is that they cancel out – even at the level of molecules – which is the very reason why mechanistic explanations of the world worked so well for so long. Quantum phenomena cannot be applied directly to higher levels of organization, a mistake frequently made with **Heisenberg's uncertainty principle**.

At present, the quantum mind is an entirely theoretical entity. There is no empirical evidence for quantum phenomena in the brain. But a quantum field across a neural network or structure is not an inconceivable occurrence. There are a few quantum events in which an astronomical number of particles join up in the same energy state and collectively make a splashy appearance in the human-scale world. These events are known as **Bose–Einstein condensations**. The best known are superconductors.

Unfortunately, the brain does not condense Bose–Einstein style but perhaps there are other circumstances not yet discovered that would allow a quantum field to be active at the length of the brain. As seen earlier, classical models of consciousness struggle with explaining the binding problem; the fact that mental events are spatially distributed but nevertheless produce unified experience. Quantum entanglement is the only other phenomenon known to science in which a distributed system shows such **global coherence**. The idea that quantum effects may apply to living creatures is not new. In biology, the conceptual analogue to Bose–Einstein condensations are known as **Fröhlich systems**. These systems are examples of self-organization that reach higher orders of magnitude and act at the length of cells or organs. Fröhlich systems help explain how certain life processes are coordinated beyond the short-range interactions of their individual components.

So, could the occurrence of a quantum field across the brain underlie consciousness? Consider, as an example, **quantum holism**. The idea is that systems have emerging properties that are not present in their individual parts or their relations. Indeed, all quantum phenomena are emerging; spin, velocity, momentum, or even particles do not exist in the system until they get measured. Prior to observation, they are mere potentialities, Indeed, which quantum reality moves from potentiality to actuality is in itself an emerging property, one in relation to the measuring method. Because a quantum foundation lurks underneath all matter, everything, from jelly beans to churches, is, strictly speaking, an emerging property. Moreover, when quantum systems meet, their potentialities are superimposed. This newly intertwined system brings out emerging properties that do not exist prior to the entanglement. This is known as quantum holism. It is ironic that reductionistic science showed us that the world is not fully comprehensible by dissecting everything. Reductionism has eventually led to holism!

By analogy, there are mental events that seem to be good candidates for emergent properties – creative insights, mystical experiences, consciousness – to name but a few. In the same way that quantum particles become entangled, some have argued that neurons can be joined in a state of similar entanglement and give rise to psychological events. Consider another analogy. The uncertainty principle states that two quantum events (i.e., position and momentum) cannot be determined with certitude. If you nail one, the other becomes indeterminate, or as Douglas Adams put it: "If you know exactly how fast you are driving, you must be lost." Quantumland is inherently fuzzy and a physicist must choose what she wants to know with certainty and be content that this makes other aspects of the system unknowable. Attention has an analogous restriction. We can focus on a specific object but this prevents us from seeing the big picture. If, however, we zoom out and take in the grand view the details become hazy. "We can't be both, involved participant and detached observer" (Marshall & Zohar, 1997, p. 183). The same choice confronts us in some perceptual phenomena. For instance, we cannot see both versions of the orientation-flipping Necker cube at the same time. To most neuroscientists such analogies sound rather kooky but they nevertheless often acknowledge that the quantum paradigm can help conceptualize aspects of the mind that cannot readily be handled by mechanistic models.

The Penrose–Hameroff proposal

Quantum theories of the mind tend to be rather vague, like the flag-waving analogies described above, but the concept of quantum consciousness was given a more definite form by the mathematician Roger Penrose and the anesthesiologist Stuart Hameroff. Their proposal focuses on subcelluar structures known as **microtubules**, which are, according to them, of about the right size and constitution to support coherent quantum states (Hameroff & Penrose, 1996). The idea is motivated by Penrose's (1989) claim that our ability to understand complex phenomena defies computational proof. Some mental events are, in his words, **"non-computable."** As a primary example, he cites mathematical knowledge, which he considers of such complexity that it cannot be realized by the kind of computation done by neurons or networks. He writes: "Mathematical ideas have an existence of their own, and inhabit an ideal Platonic world, which is accessible via the intellect only. When one 'sees' a mathematical truth, one's consciousness breaks through into this world of ideas, and makes contact with it" (ibid., p. 428).

In other words, creative insights, or – even more fundamental than that – consciousness, are emergent properties that, he believes, go beyond mere algorithmic computation. Penrose is no dualist; he simply doubts that conventional computational models of the mind can capture the essence of conscious phenomena. He underscores this doubt with **Gödel's Incompleteness Theorem**. The mathematician **Kurt Gödel** (1906–78) proved that in any finite, formal system there are statements or phenomena that cannot be proved or disproved from within the system. This is typically interpreted to mean that brains contain truths that may never be knowable to the brains themselves. It follows that we can never fully know our own mind (Hofstadter, 1979). What is required, then, is a different kind of mechanism, one that possesses the capacity to "see" such complex mental phenomena. This, Penrose thinks, is **quantum gravity**.

So, what motivates the proposal to locate quantum gravitational effects in microtubules? Microtubules are elongated strands of proteins that form part of the cytoskeleton. They are present in all cells – not just neurons – and provide, among rather many other things, a firm structure to the cell, rather like what the spinal column does to vertebrates. According to the model, microtubules have several properties that make them prime candidates for supporting subatomic effects. The details are highly technical but, briefly, involve the following observations. Coherent quantum states must be isolated from the environment to be sustained. Microtubules are essentially hollow tubes and so form a space that is protected from the buzzing madhouse of organelles that also swim around in the cytoplasm. In addition, Penrose and Hameroff list several other structural characteristics, such as the spiral organization of their walls, that may be conducive to quantum computation. Finally, Hameroff believes that microtubules are susceptible to hydrophobic anesthetic compounds and theorizes that the loss of consciousness under anesthesia may involve changes mediated by microtubules.

Gush and Churchland (1995) gave quantum approaches, including the Penrose–Hameroff proposal, a thorough shakedown. Their critique was aimed at several key points. Logicians generally disagree with Penrose's conclusion regarding the relevance of Gödel's theroem to human information-processing (see Chapter 5). What's more, many find the claim of noncomputability theoretically myopic. Others have pointed out that the insides of microtubules are not as protected as is required and the inherent heat and noise of the brain would preclude quantum mechanical effects. Likewise, anesthesiologists generally disagree with Hameroff's suggestion that microtubules play a role in the mechanism of action of anesthetics. Finally, there is currently not a shred of evidence supporting microtubules as sites for quantum effects. Quite apart from these technical difficulties, the central question remains of how could quantum phenomena in the brain – if they were to exist – address the puzzles facing the study of consciousness? How, exactly, is quantum holism related to the unity of perception? In sum, Gush and Churchland argue that the main problems of quantum theories of consciousness are the lack of explanatory power and the absence of a research program that could change this. Churchland (2002, p. 197), in one of her characteristically blunt dismissals of all theories not based on sound neurobiological evidence, concludes: "Pixie dust in the synapses is about as explanatorily powerful as quantum coherence in microtubules." At this point, quantum theories of mind are wonderful brain-teasers, but they may well turn out to be empirical duds. Until we find some hard evidence for quantum weirdness in brain cells, we must be content with their entertainment value.

Chaos theories

The neuron is the fundamental unit of the brain. A cell biologist will tell you that it is more than just a bag of enzymes humming with electrical sparks, but seen from a systems level, a neuron isn't too smart. It can really do only one thing: make a crisp, clear-cut, on/off, yes/no choice about some electrical potential. What, then, is so special when a bunch of these simpletons get together and start talking to one another? How can a hundred-billion-plus mindless units make a mind?

Under the microscope, the inside of a neuron looks like a madhouse of activity. How can this mayhem of apparent randomness produce encyclopedic dictionaries, symphonies, and lunar probes? How do all these wonderful patterns emerge from all this noise? At some higher level, something must get organized somehow. Welcome to **chaos theory**! Now a couple of decades into its reign as the best mathematical portrayal of anything that moves, oscillates, explodes, and materializes out of thin air, chaos theory has given order a new look.

Life is nonlinear, unpredictable, and openly chaotic. The behavior of molecules, patterns of firing neurons, yearly fluctuations of ant populations, dating habits of college students – all inherently dynamic systems. At the microlevel, there is always noise in the system which, if cranked up high enough, trips a system into chaos. Scientists use the term **complexity** to describe this state between regularity and randomness. It's the point chaos connoisseurs study: the edge of chaos. Fluids turn turbulent, volcanoes erupt, hearts fibrillate, metals snap, couples fight, balloons explode. To the untrained eye this appears totally random but there is order in chaos. Such systems settle to what is known by the beautifully enigmatic name **strange attractor**. What is so strange about this attractor? A linear system is not strange because it makes for perfectly regular and predictable patterns. In a chaotic system, however, units behave irregularly and rhythms become uncoupled. As nature descends into disorder, clouds form, sunspots appear, and infectious diseases break out.

Green slime may not seem like the object of a mathematician's daydream but chaos lurks in odd places, even in still water. Slime molds are amoebae that gorge on bacteria. When food is short, this simplest of creatures undergoes what must be one of the most spectacular spontaneous self-organizations in nature. Individual amoebas cluster into colonies and metamorphize into one big, continuous sheet of slime. Then, in a radical transformation, those colonies differentiate into different functional components so that the newly restructured slime mold will behave as if it is a single, larger animal. Self-organization from chaos to order! The late chemist Ilya Prigogine has coined the term **dissipative structures** for such living systems that spontaneously come to order.

From above, the new slime animal looks stable and coordinated. But under this macrostructure is slime mayhem. The closer you zoom in, the more radical individual amoebas' behavior bifurcate until, in the close-ups of an electron microscope, a higher-order stability seems totally out of the question. But there it is: differentiated slime. What would an alien watching from outer space make of New York City with its differentiated boroughs, morning rush hour, Sunday emptiness, and August exodus? How can a highly organized pattern emerge from the very disorderly and unpredictable behavior of individual New Yorkers? Well, like slime, New Yorkers settle to a strange attractor, say, making money or having fun, moving the city to stability. Order out of chaos, as long as you look at it standing back, way back. With this in mind it is easier to ponder the earlier question of how a hundred-billion-plus mindless units can make a mind. Note that this is a form of global coherence emerging from distributed components. Such binding of individual activities into stable, large-scale phenomena occurs frequently in nature and can be explained without recourse to quantum weirdness. Neurons are organized into assemblies, which, in turn, are organized into networks. The unity of consciousness may simply arise naturally from the fact that the brain is a nonlinear system.

A nonlinear system is also inherently unpredictable. Once it reaches a critical value and plunges into chaos, its behavior and future course are highly dependent on initial conditions. Tiny fluctuations at the edge of chaos are critical and can lead the system down the opposite path. This sensitivity to the initial setting is known as the **butterfly effect**; the flutter of a butterfly's wings in Beirut can change the cloud formation in Berlin.

The brain is a dynamic, nonlinear information processor – full of noise. If it weren't so, we would be linear input–output devices, entirely predetermined and predictable. This fact has important consequences for neuroscience and consciousness. Consider, for instance, the butterfly effect. If a single neuron fires at a critical time, could this force the brain, after different swirls upon swirls and wiggles upon wiggles, toward an entirely different mental state? What's more, we can neither determine the initial brain state nor do we know the nature of the strange attractors. And, even if we did, it would not help us plot the path of the system because it is inherently nonlinear. All this is more bad news for the identity theorist. Chaos theory clearly exposes the naïve thesis of nailing down to the dot the neural correlates of consciousness. This, of course, does not mean that the mind is not in the brain – just that it is impossible to exactly pin down. Apart from such theoretical limitations, this new mathematical approach to complex biological systems also has ramifications for the way neuroscience studies consciousness. It is still common practice to treat the brain as if it were a linear system. To get a clear signal, the inherent noisiness at the neuronal level is routinely filtered out by averaging many data points. However, this linearizing, as the practice is known in the trade, wipes out potentially critical details that, if amplified, might spin the system in an alternative direction – a different conscious state. Finally, chaos theories of the mind also add to our understanding of consciousness by asking different kinds of questions. For instance, how do neurons self-organize into a higher functional level? Does consciousness act as a strange attractor for organizing the chaos at the level of neurons into meaning at the level of minds? The study of consciousness has a lot to gain from a dynamic approach.

Box 4.2   The holographic hind

And what if the mind is a hologram? A holographic image is not just a fancy gig of the local science museum but nature's most efficient way to store information. It is a three-dimensional image projected into apparent nothingness by bouncing light off a few mirrors. Briefly, the trick works as follows: A coherent light source, usually a laser beam, carries information about an object, say, the mask of Tutankhamun. The light beam is then split into two by a mirror so that each continues to carry a full image of the Egyptian king. Each beam is then scattered by a different lens. One beam, called the reference beam, travels directly to the photographic paper and is a faithful reproduction of the original object. The other, the deflected beam, gets bounced around by any number of mirrors until it bumps into the reference beam again and is then reflected onto the photographic paper. Superimposing both images creates interference patterns, like ripples in a pond. When you then aim a reconstruction beam on the photographic paper, a very real looking, 3D Tutankhamun is projected into midair.

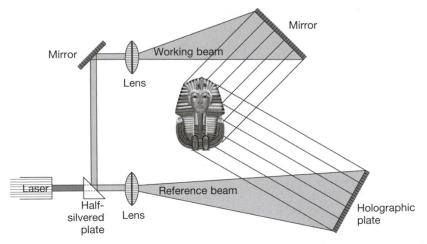

A hologram has some very spooky properties. Information in a holographic image is stored in a fully distributed manner so that every section of it contains information about the entire image. Just as every cell in the human body contains the complete genetic code to reconstruct the entire organism, every part of a hologram contains the complete information to reconstruct the whole image. As long as the reconstruction beam encounters a section – any section – of the hologram, Tutankhamun appears in full glory. A hologram is also suspended; it occupies no space, knows no time, and possesses no boundaries, and can thus store an infinite amount of information in no space at all. As absurd as this sounds, the image is everywhere and nowhere at the same time.

Box 4.2   *continued*

Could the mind be a hologram suspended in the brain, like a ghost in the machine? This would certainly make for yet another headache if you are a reductionist. The idea was popularized in the 1970s by the neuroscientist Karl Pribram (1985), not so much as a serious theory but as a neat way to conceptualize some of the hard-to-pin-down properties of the mind. He even built a holographic-like brain called the multiplex hologram that he used to model neurons in the visual cortex.

As an example, consider how a hologram might help with the problem of object constancy. To recognize a yellow Porsche, we must compare a current perception to a reference – a mental representation. But how does the brain solve the problem of recognition for a nearly infinite number of viewpoints? How does it keep perception of an object constant when the angle changes? If the brain had a mental representation for all possible angles for all objects it would be cluttered with inordinate amounts of information. But in a hologram, storage space is not at a premium. If the yellow Porsche were stored holographically, a reconstruction beam from any angle would result in interference patterns with all units of stored knowledge. So, the "reconstruction beam of consciousness" could readily produce a match. We know, of course, that this is not true. The brain is not a holographic storage device and knowledge does not dangle above neural networks. Memory is certainly highly distributed but occupies nevertheless a definite piece of the brain's real estate.

But what if, as proposed by the physicist David Bohm (1980), the whole of the universe is a gigantic hologram? Then the cosmos would possess a kind of collective consciousness suspended within space-time – above ordinary matter. What's more, each one of us would be part of this universal hologram of consciousness, with each single brain containing information about, well, everything. For one, mystical experiences would take on a whole new meaning. If the universe holds information in a holographic fashion, a special reconstruction beam could unite a mind with the Universal Mind.

The mind-as-hologram idea sounds rather strange, and probably is. Given that neuroscientists are not keen on suspending the mind in mid-tissue, the idea never caught on much. The main problem is that there is no evidence that neurons store information using Fourier waveforms, the underlying mathematical language of the holographic code. But then again, there also isn't any evidence for any other code the brain uses to create mental representation either.

Summary

This chapter dealt with the quest for the neural correlates of consciousness and surveyed a variety of physical mechanisms to account for the unity of experience. A skeleton model of the NCC exists that closely associates consciousness with the hierarchical organization of brain function. To add to this knowledge base, some neuroscientists advocate a direct approach. By contrasting experimental conditions in which subjects are either conscious or unconscious of a visual stimulus, as is the case in binocular rivalry, and combining this with brain imaging techniques, we can narrow the search for the neural basis of conscious mental representations. An important motivating theme for both neurophysiological and quantum approaches is the unity of consciousness. Information processing in the brain is divided among many highly specialized modules. This modularity raises the question of how the activity of this vast number of individual units is bound together to generate globally coherent states, which presumably must underlie the unity to consciousness. Proposals to account for this binding include the suggestion of a temporal code, primarily the synchronous firing of large arrays of neurons at around 40 Hz, and the concept of an integrative, dynamic core, a shifting coalition of strongly interacting cell-assemblies held together by reentrant connections.

The lure of quantum theories of mind comes largely from the apparent similar strangeness that characterizes both subatomic physics and conscious experience. Some inherent features of quantum mechanics, such as global coherence, makes it easier, albeit at a conceptual level, to think of how a physical system could possibly account for some of the more mercurial features of consciousness that, at the present time, elude a classical description. Quantum models of consciousness are, as of yet, unsupported by empirical evidence and may prove to be irrelevant if quantum effects indeed cancel out, as many suspect, at the level of neurons. Beyond their attractiveness in exploring theoretical puzzles, quantum consciousness remains science fiction. The same cannot be said for chaos theories of mind. Given that the brain is a chaotic system, the principles regulating nonlinear, dynamic structures, (i.e., unpredictability, strange attractors, or sensitivity to initial conditions) are undoubtedly relevant to mental phenomena. For instance, the critical insight of spontaneous self-organization in such complex systems is instructive in understanding how the brain, which is composed of billions of individual bits, produces unity at higher levels of organization, such as, perhaps, the unity of perceptual experience.

Suggested reading

Crick, F. (1994). *The Astonishing Hypothesis*. New York: Scribner.

Edelman, G. M., and Tononi, G. (2000). *A Universe of Consciousness*. New York: Basic Books.

Metzinger, T., ed. (2000). *Neural Correlates of Consciousness*. Cambridge, MA: MIT Press.

Penrose, R. (1994). *Shadows of the Mind*. Oxford: Oxford University Press.

5 Artificial minds

Dennett explained

Demolishing the Cartesian theater

We start this chapter by describing what we take to be Daniel Dennett's central position. As perhaps the leading contemporary philosopher working on consciousness, Dennett's corpus is both highly controversial and highly influential. His work is so intensely counterintuitive that it should not come as a surprise that he has been consistently and systematically misunderstood. Because Dennett's thesis is an uncompromisingly functionalist one, it meshes well with the second part of the chapter, where we highlight the contributions of artificial intelligence to the study of the mind. Principally, we examine six nested arguments against robot consciousness. Collectively, they unveil, on both sides of the vast mind–brain divide, the deeply-rooted beliefs that fuel the current debate on the nature of consciousness.

A creator must first be a destroyer. For few people is this as true as it is for Dennett. Before we turn our attention to his theory of mind, we must first consider his total demolition of the Cartesian theater. Reflecting on his own work, Dennett recently remarked: "I think, oddly enough, perhaps my most important or influential contribution was showing people that materialism was harder than they thought – that it was more counterintuitive than they thought" (in

Blackmore, 2006, p. 84). Clearly, it is one thing to commit oneself to a material-ist view; it is quite another to accept all the inevitable consequences such a view brings with it. For a thoroughgoing account of materialism, says Dennett, one has to give up many more of one's cherished intuitions about consciousness.

The cherished intuition we must abandon, above all else, goes something like this: I experience myself as being somewhere inside my own head. I look out at the world through the peepholes that are my eyes, catching the sights that are out there. Information enters through my senses and is built up, by my brain, into mental representations that are then displayed in their full glory on a virtual mental screen, or some kind of theatrical stage, for me, the audience, to see and appreciate. From my little cranial command post, the place inside where "I" am, I can order my brain to move my body. So put, and unduly sharpened, this is how having a mind feels to us, isn't it? But this implies that there is a special place – a stage or screen – that is brightly lit, where information is displayed for the Mind to be acted upon. This is what Dennett calls the **Cartesian theater**!

But none of this exists. There is no central place anywhere in the brain; no show reeling off specially selected (conscious) information; and no Cartesian homunculus, another Dennett term, who inhabits the brain and to whom consciousness happens. The theater, the whole lot, says Dennett, has to be demolished.

Before we consider why this demolition is so critical, let's look at this intuition from yet another angle. Sensory information comes in and motor commands go out. There must be a middle, mustn't there, a place or time in between, where information – however briefly – enters and exits consciousness. This is the classic sandwich conception in which consciousness occurs between sensory and motor processes. But if we carefully trace sensory input through the brain all the way until we arrive at a motor neuron, we find that there is no middle, no special place or time somewhere along the way, where *in*bound information is pooled and cata-pulted into the magic spotlight of consciousness for the benefit of a commander in-chief, who then generates *out*bound information. As Dennett (1991, p. 29) puts it: "The trouble with brains, it seems, is that when you look in them, you discover that there's nobody home."

Apart from the dualism inherent in this view, what's the danger, for material-ists, of clinging onto this convenient metaphor? Well, for one thing, neuroscien-tists agree that there is no such pivotal place in the brain where it all comes together. Nor is there a Central Experiencer, an Ego or Self, separate from the hubbub in the brain. The brain is a massive, parallel processing system. Its activ-ity is distributed in multiple, independent streams of processing, that are, at no time, synthesized, in one central location, into a coherent image for mind's eye. So, at the minimum, the Cartesian theater is factually mistaken. Materialists know this, of course, and waste no time explicitly renouncing it. Implicitly, though, perhaps due to a lack of a metaphor with similar intuitive sex appeal, they hang on to it. Dennett (1991, p. 144) dubs this **Cartesian materialism**, describing it as "the view that nobody espouses but almost everybody tends to think in terms of." He admits that this fossil trace from Descartes is nearly impossible to shake off, but we must try because it is not a benign allegory but a pernicious fallacy that, as long as we keep it, traps us in the impossibilities of Cartesian contradictions.

To see the predicament in full, consider this. Once you enter the Cartesian theater and re-represent the data that has been already completely analyzed, you must also conjure up a fully conscious **homunculus**, a little man inside the head, who marvels at the show, controls the consoles and gauges, and ultimately pulls the strings. But then you are stuck explaining the inner workings of this homunculus and an infinite regress immediately looms. But worse, the homunculus – conveniently enough – just happens to have the right kind of powers and abilities to explain what needs to be explained in the first place. The homunculus, then, does the very job that a theory of consciousness is supposed to do. This is the trap! You make some progress for a while, explaining this and that aspect of conscious experience, and right when the going gets tough you flee into the comfort of the Cartesian theater by inventing an internal agent who handles the bits that are still missing. The trouble is that this seduces you into thinking that you've done the job, that you can stop, when, in fact, you have solved nothing. You are no better off resorting to miracles on the tenth step than – like Descartes – on the first. Once the ghost is in the machine, you are tangled up in the cul-de-sac of dualism. The telltale signs of Cartesian materialism are when you explain the workings of the brain and end your exposition by declaring that the information "reaches" or "enters" consciousness. Unless this is carefully fleshed out, this typically signals that you have succumbed to the powerful seduction that there must be some other, further place where the mind is. Dennett's forte is to be consequent with applying materialism all the way down. And it is there that even otherwise good materialists tend to cringe at the full realization that there really is nobody home.

Naturally, this leaves open the burning question of how else we should think about the mind. Clearly, information is either "in" or "out" of consciousness, isn't it? There has to be a difference, a place that marks the middle, a crucial moment in time when the information changes its status from unconscious to conscious, and a creature who confers the meaning. Knowing that none of this really exists helps little with ridding ourselves of the fallacy. How, then, can we kick this bad habit and really understand, at an intuitive level, what's going on?

Skyhooks or cranes?

If you want to give Dennett a fair hearing you must try – no matter how difficult – to relinquish the Cartesian legacy. It might help to remind yourself that the idea must be wrong. Once you are clear about this, all you need is to keep an open mind and be vigilant, as we march on, of the allure of residual dualism.

First, Dennett stops **homuncularism** in the way an infinite regress is usually stopped in philosophy – right at the beginning. The underlying mistake is that we think that it takes a big fancy thing to make a less fancy thing. By this reasoning, we are forced, sooner or later, to appeal to a **skyhook**, Dennett's term for a miracle. Before Darwin, people could not imagine how design comes to be without a designer. Biologists needed a skyhook, namely God. The great inversion of reasoning Darwin made was that a big fancy thing – like us – can be the result of a mindless, purposeless process. Given sufficient time, **cranes**, Dennett's term for a bottom-up process like evolution, can do the work just fine (Dennett, 1995). Science has never accomplished anything by resorting to a skyhook when things got messy. But without an inversion of reasoning, you set yourself up for needing one. By assuming that a homunculus must have abilities greater than those of its host, you run headlong into a situation where the only recourse left to you is a skyhook. At that point the temptation becomes unbearable to request admission to the safe house of the Cartesian theater. The trouble with skyhooks, though, is that they don't do any explanatory work.

The infinite regress is defeated in two easy steps. First, you break down consciousness and distribute it throughout the system right at the outset. By embedding experience into the operations of the brain, you avoid building up a big mystery that, eventually, you cannot help but invoke a skyhook for. This is why Dennett believes the hard problem to be an "artifact of misguided theorizing" (1994, p. 130). Second, you make higher homunculi less conscious than their hosts and the homuncular regress becomes finite, bottoming out with homunculi so simple that you can replace the top ones with a machine, a circuit composed of neurons or silicon. Hence his controversial claim: "there can be conscious machines – us" (Dennett, 1991, p. 432).

Dennett points out that this nesting of homunculi within homunculi is difficult to vividly imagine because we have an inflated view of consciousness. We wrongly believe that we are more conscious than we are, a notion that is supported by recent research on change blindness (see Chapter 7). This illusion inflates the mystery of consciousness to the point that people feel that they will never have epistemological access to it, making appeal to the Cartesian theater the only rescue.

If these most cherished intuitions of ours do not work, how else can we envision what's going on inside? What can a materialist do, after describing a large part of the machine and then, because he failed to build the beast in, is forced to conjure up an inhabitant to observe the light-and-sound show he so neatly materialized? Here Dennett recommends asking yourself what, exactly, it is you are pointing to. Who is this "me" reading the neurological record? What you will find, he promises, is not some ineffable qualia, the what-it's-likeness of the immortal soul, a Higher Executive, but something that, upon further inspection, can itself be broken down into subcomponents and embedded into the operation of the system. In short, Dennett tells you to go back to work. If you take shelter in the Cartesian theater here you relapse into thinking that consciousness is something other than brain function. Only when consciousness is parceled out into the various functions of the brain, leaving the "I" inside with nothing left to do, have you explained what needs to be explained.

We can now see why critics charge that Dennett does not explain consciousness but rather explains it away. Dennett denies this outright. This objection is misbegotten, he says, because the cranial Supervisor itself dissolves into functions that themselves need no supervision. Here, while not repeating the argument, Dennett's attacks on qualia and zombies also come back into focus. If qualia are irreducible, and thus something extra to function, they make a curious property of brains indeed, for how could they have evolved if they do not make a difference in behavior? This problem does not arise if qualia are embedded into the system. The same argument holds for zombies. It is a Cartesian trap that prevents you from understanding how your mind could be your brain. When, during an introspective journey, you feel you are pointing at some ineffable mind-stuff – qualia or the what-it's-likeness feeling – you must ask yourself what Dennett (1991, p. 255) calls the "Hard Question: And then what happens." If you continue searching, you will find only dispositional states that can be properly subjected to functional analysis and thus third-person description. People who ask the hard question are not leaving out consciousness but they are leaving behind the Cartesian theater.

Multiple drafts

The brain is a federation of independently operating specialist modules with no dominant center or master homunculus. There are, of course, higher-order neurons providing some integration but there is nothing inherently special about them, functionally or structurally. Nor do they peak out at some organizational summit where consciousness resides. Dennett's **multiple drafts model** is explicitly based on this pandemonium model (see Chapter 4). In all its independent tracks, information is in a continual process of editing and reediting, like the revisions of a draft of a text on the internet that never reaches a final form in the way it does in the print media. So, at any time, there are multiple drafts at various stages of the revision process all being edited at once. Only when one draft is probed – by asking yourself a question or by some external event demanding your immediate attention, for instance – does it become conscious. What "conscious" means in this context is not that the information passes through some middle or is redisplayed in the Cartesian theater but simply that it has widespread effects in the brain; that is to say, it becomes available for behavior and there is a greater likelihood that it reaches your mouth or hands and controls subsequent action. That we can verbally report such information is simply because it also spreads to the language centers. Consciousness, in this view, is nothing more than capacity for behavior. In Chapter 6, you will see this idea of equating consciousness with global accessibility further developed in global workspace theory, a view that Dennett endorses.

You naturally want to ask which draft is conscious or who is doing the probing. But the mere asking of such questions is misleading because it sends you looking for the "when" and "where" of consciousness. As Dennett (1991, 113) puts it: "These spatially and temporally distributed content-fixations [probing] in the brain are precisely locatable on both space and time, but their onsets do *not* mark the onset of consciousness of their contents."

To better understand this, consider the **phi phenomenon**, which refers to the apparent motion we see when still pictures are shown in rapid succession – like in a movie. In one experiment two lights are flashed on a screen, one on the left followed by one on the right. Instead of seeing just that, we see the light moving from left to right. What's more, when the left light is red and the right one is green, we see the color change from red to green midway through the light's illusionary passage (Kolers & von Grünau, 1976). This gives us a strange dilemma. How can we see the green *before* it appears? According to Dennett, if we hold on to the erroneous idea that there is an exact arrival time in consciousness, we are left with two possible explanations, Orwellian memory-tampering and Stalinesque illusion-construction. The **Orwellian revision**, named after Orwell's novel *1984* in which the Ministry of Truth rewrites history, would work like this. The red light reaches consciousness first, followed by the blank screen and finally the green light. Realizing that this does not fit with what we know about the world, the Orwellian editor retroactively revises the event, filling in the intermediate steps, so that you never know what really happened. The **Stalinesque revision**, named after Stalin's infamous show trials, in which evidence was fabricated to fit the prescripted verdict, operates in reverse. Here the editing is proactive, before the event becomes history. Accordingly, the red light does not reach consciousness, but is held up in the preconscious editing room until the green light appears. The Stalinesque editor then scripts the events, filling in the intermediate steps, and passes it to consciousness. In either case, the record in consciousness is what the Orwellian or Stalinesque censor wants us to experience.

So which one is right? Neither, says Dennett, for the reason that invoking either model of event falsification is only necessary if we maintain the notion that there must be a clear boundary marking conscious from unconscious processing. In the macroscopic time scale of the real world, events can indeed be ordered into a neat sequence, but this does not work at the microscopic time intervals of neurological processes for the simple reason that events there are not single points but smeared across large fractions of seconds. Because of the large window through which mental representations are spread out in time, freezing time and asking what was in consciousness at any one moment is not possible. At any point in time, multiple drafts at different stages of editing are within this window so that continuously probing them yields a subjective sequence but this temporal order, reported by the person, does not reflect any real arrival time. Once the contents of one track are fixed, they become available for behavior – that is, conscious – which may be prior to fixing the contents of another track dealing with an event that actually occurred slightly earlier. Naturally, there is also no "I" doing the probing; this illusion arises from the self-organizing functional properties of the system, in which some information asserts more or less control over behavior.

If you have problems visualizing this, you are not alone. Dennett has updated his theory since, primarily to provide a better crutch for the imagination. In this update, he likens consciousness to **fame in the brain** or cerebral celebrity. When some information in the brain becomes conscious, it is famous in the sense that it is widely known among other demons in the brain. Once in the limelight, famous demons assert a greater influence over how the system, as a whole, functions. Like celebrity status in society, selection to stardom does not require a higher power, but is simply the result of a competitive, bottom-up process. The losers of the competition, the coalitions of demons that for some reason could not muster up enough clout, dissipate into oblivion never to get close to a motor neuron. Note that fame does not lead to, or is separate from, consciousness; it is the property of having influence. Dennett's theory has received its fair share of attacks with opponents mainly claiming that he produced nothing more than a theory of behavior – no phenomenal consciousness anywhere in sight (Chalmers, 1996).

But what, then, of the stream of consciousness? Isn't there a sequence of contents that is in some fact of the matter conscious? According to Dennett, this stream is nothing but a special kind of illusion. Imagine we'd have intimate access to all the behind-the-scenes mayhem of the brain. We'd go mad! Probing this multitrack system at different times and places filters the underlying mental racket into a narrative stream that acts as a decent indicator of what the organism, as a whole, is doing. Dennett prefers to call this the **center of narrative gravity** because it is less like a single, continuous, integrated stream than a series of discrete contents, sequenced together on the fly from different parallel streams, each consisting of continuously shifting coalitions of neurons. From this emerges, at the macro level, the story we tell ourselves, though this is not what's really going on underneath. When seen in this way, the mind is a sort of "benign user illusion" (Dennett, 1991, p. 311) of the vastly complex brain similar to an operating system like Windows, which is a user-friendly version of the vastly complex computer. Dennett calls the mind a **Joycean machine**, named after Joyce's stream-of-consciousness style of writing. It streamlines the myriads of parallel brain processes into a step-by-step narrative that makes the brain seems to work *as if* it were a serial process. The upshot is that we can tell others a coherent story, a quick summary of what is going on, at the level of the whole organism.

Dennett also offers his own method, **heterophenomenology** (phenomenology of another, not oneself), to study consciousness. In this approach, an anthropologist-minded experimenter collects all data available about someone else's phenomenology, including brain scans, behavior, and self-reports. Together they make up the person's heterophenomenological world, which is a third-person, scientific portrayal of what it's like, in the person's own terms, to be that person. Subjective experience, the fact that we have an inside, a point of view, turns out to be a hard thing to explain, but it does not require a revolution in science. According to Dennett, we can sneak up on it from the outside, comfortably within the folds of objective science. All that is required is that we take the **intentional stance** and treat people as rational beings, whose line of action is determined by their beliefs and desires. What needs to be explained, then, are the beliefs and desires people have. Heterophenomenology is neutral with respect to these beliefs; that is to say, it takes as authoritative the person's reports, but only, and that is critical, how things seem to that person not, owing to some magical direct access, how things really are. The difference to the traditional phenomenological approach, the personal, introspective approach advocated by some dualists, is that experimenter and subject are not the same person. In other words, heterophenomenology takes the first person seriously but only after the experiences are transcribed into third-person terms of how they seem in the first person. Dennett believes, along with the majority of scientists and philosophers, that as long as the first person is still in there, as part of the data, we do not have a theory of consciousness, because that is the part that we are supposed to explain. Dennett claims that his method leads to a complete understanding of the inner world according to the subject – not to be confused with the real world. "It leaves out no objective phenomena and no subjective phenomena of consciousness" (Dennett, 2003b, p. 20).

Artificial consciousness

Enlightened silicon

If the mind is nothing but an exquisite network of neural circuitry, why not try making one using semiconductors? Since its inception, computer science has contributed significantly to the study of the mind. Given all the ink that has been spilt over this issue, we can only hope here to sketch out a conceptual skeleton of this rich domain.

The question of machine intelligence has a long tradition. As we learned in Chapter 2, the idea was mooted by the Greeks and the first attempts to make thinking machines were realized by Pascal and Leibniz. Progress in both the hardware – Babbage's Analytical Engine – and the software – Boolean algebra – led in the 1930s to the conception of information theory. The attack on the problem of artificial minds has been relentless ever since, advancing nonstop on two parallel fronts. One broadside has come from computer scientists unremittingly increasing brute computing power, a move that has been flanked with equal gusto by cognitive scientists doing their best to formalize human cognitive processes. Any system that is formalized can be embodied in a machine. This realization, coupled with the reckless optimism following the overthrow of behaviorism, led to the belief that it is surely only a matter of time until the highest mental faculties become subject to replication in a machine. If consciousness is, as everyone in AI assumed it was, a product of computational complexity, the puzzle should have been solved in a few decades.

In the 1960s and 1970s, during the heady days of **computational functionalism**, when the business of mind construction was overflowing with frenzied enthusiasm, we appeared to hurdle towards inevitable computer domination. For instance, Marvin Minsky (1986), a trailblazer in the field, predicted then that the next generation of silicon intelligentsia would be so clever that we would "be lucky if they [would be] willing to keep us around as household pets." The rapid progress indeed left everyone gasping for air. Today, computers can do many wonderful things and you should be impressed. They calculate theorems, build your car, beat Russians at chess, look for life on Mars, monitor the local weather, and optimize your stock portfolio. Yet all but the hardiest members of the AI community now realize that the road is somewhat thornier than initially thought. While some problems were solved with ease, others turned out to be next to impossible to translate into computer code. Only brains can laugh at a joke, cry for help, be a proud citizen, have existential angst, fake an orgasm, look for itself, or do the hula-hoop.

This is now, but what of tomorrow? Clearly, AI is not putting on the brakes any time soon. Its seemingly unstoppable progress forces us, nearly every year, to redraw the line, albeit ever so slightly, of what mental faculties – if any – will forever remain off limits to AI. As for consciousness, the issue can be cast like this. Suppose in a future time, scientists will have formalized all mental processes in the super-duper program Virtual Mind 6.2. As the dust of the achievement settles, will these silicon minds be conscious? Will there be some light inside, the realization of meaning, the spark of ineffable qualia, or the feeling of what it is like to be Virtual Mind 6.2? Given the split of theorists on the nature of consciousness, two positions can be taken. Believers in the hard problem would consider Virtual Mind 6.2 all dark inside because consciousness is something extra, beyond the physical. Opponents of the hard problem would not suppose that something is left out because consciousness is embedded into the operations of the system. If Virtual Mind 6.2 can reason like us, play tennis like us, and report how its exploits make it feel, all activities that must be conceded as part of Virtual Mind 6.2 being a full replica, it must also be conscious like us. If so, this would bring out a different conundrum: How could we know?

It was the mathematician Alan Turing (1912–54) who developed the idea that a machine capable of performing a series of mechanical steps could solve algorithms (Turing, 1950). This so-called Turing machine could, in principle, be put to work on any problem that is specified by a well-defined computational procedure. The concept of a **Universal Turing Machine** goes further in that it assumes that any procedure can be realized by a device of any composition – silicon, neurons, cogs and wheels, or windmills, as long as it executes the same function. The digital computer, for instance, is one type of Universal Turing Machine. In the 1960s, this abstraction of function from structure gave rise to computational functionalism and fueled the first comparisons between mind and computer (Putnam, 1960). If the structural constitution that performs the mental operations is indeed irrelevant, as this theory of mind maintained, then the brain can be thought of as a kind of digital computer, one peculiar instance of a Universal Turing Machine, and the mind as a program that runs on it. In this view, there is nothing particularly biological about the mind; the brain just happens to be one of many possible kinds of hardware configurations that can implement minds. This notion has been the guiding assumption behind the goal of AI to design programs that exhibit genuine intelligence.

With the rise of neuroscience, and the realization that structure does matter after all, this extreme position has faded into the background in favor of a softer version. John Searle (1992) dubs these positions "strong AI" and "weak AI." **Strong AI** is the view that programs *are* minds; they do not imitate thoughts or work *as if* intelligent; they have thoughts and intelligence in the same literal sense as we do. There is nothing metaphorical about artificial minds. While strong AI is contentious, weak AI is not. Rather than making bold assertions about the ontological nature of machine operations, **weak AI** simply holds that computer programs are useful in *simulating* mental processes. Almost everyone agrees with this position.

The first 30 years of AI, what is now known as **GOFAI**, or Good Old-Fashioned AI (Haugeland, 1985), were marked by the development of increasingly complex systems. But the architecture of GOFAI systems – regardless how complex – had a major limitation. Its internal connections were fixed so that it could not adjust its performance based on feedback; it always processed information in the same exact way. This meant that it could only execute operations that were precisely specified beforehand; if it wasn't programmed in, GOFAI systems couldn't do it. Since the mid-1980s, this limitation has been addressed by **artificial neural nets**, or **ANNs**. This new generation of systems is different in that they are built on a **connectionist** architecture, in which units are connected up in ways rather like nets of neurons in the brain. In other words, they are computer models of neural networks. In these circuits, it is not necessary to fully specify operations *a priori*; these systems can be trained. This works because the architecture of these connectionist – or **PDP**, for parallel distributed processing – systems is dynamic; they change their configuration as a consequence of information processing. Briefly (and roughly), each link in the network has a particular weight that is adjusted – strengthened or weakened – as the system learns a task. Consider, for instance, how such a system acquires the ability to recognize complex patterns such as those of faces, a tricky problem for AI because faces, like speech or emotions, exhibit statistical irregularities that make their formal specification impossible. In the PDP architecture, the impasse of programming something that we cannot ourselves explain is avoided by letting the system itself learn to recognize faces. The network is given examples of faces to which it produces answers, say, whether the face is male or female. Depending on the feedback – right or wrong – the ANN gradually varies the weights of its connections until it arrives consistently at the correct answer. It does this by way of a **back-propagation algorithm**. That is, the feedback is rippled backwards through the network and those connections that contribute to a successful match are strengthened while those that do not are weakened. As training continues the error rate becomes gradually smaller until the system can categorize even novel faces with high accuracy. What really happens inside the system is that all links are adjusted so that each contributes, statistically speaking, in the right proportion to the determination of sex. The resulting architecture of the network reflects structurally, just as it does in the brain, the system's past experience. An interesting consequence of this process is that it is impossible to tell, even for the machine's makers, how, in the end, the machine manages to categorize faces correctly.

In addition to ANNs, another critical step toward systems with genuinely intelligent behavior is the concept of **embodied cognition** (Varela et al., 1991). From the start, AI has been plagued by the **grounding problem**. All programs do is abstract computation; they know nothing about the meaning of what they are computing. Calculating a trajectory that drops a nuclear bomb is no different from calculating one that delivers supplies to a population in need; it's all the same number-crunching – just ones and zeros. Their computations are not grounded in the real world. This is generally thought to be due to the fact that they are disembodied. Locked up in plastic cases, they do not interact with the environment and so cannot understand anything about the real world. Embodiment is thought to be the solution to this because it is, after all, this inter-action with our surroundings that is the very ground for the intrinsic meaning of our mental representations (Harnad, 1990). For AI, this means **robotics**. By hous-ing programs in robots, AI researchers can create entities with artificial sensors and limbs that make contact with the world they are supposed to represent in their programs. Embodiment, then, is what makes representation meaningful and the environment, in this view, provides the very constraints that allow for purposeful behavior. The realization that robots are an integral part for programs to have any type of common sense is highly relevant to theories of consciousness. Genuine intelligence and consciousness are not, as computational functionalism maintains, solely a matter of pure symbol manipulation. The total system, brain – wet or silicon – body – muscle or carbon fiber – and environment – real or virtual – must be considered. This might also shed some light on why there seems to be a nontransferable first-person perspective; conscious experience is simply embed-ded into the entire system and cannot be taken out of the context in which it developed. The notion of embodiment also lends support to the idea that we are only conscious of objects and events that offer the opportunity for action (Cotterill, 1995; O'Reagan & Noë, 2001). Ultimately, the function of brains is to move bodies adaptively and it seems rather likely that consciousness is intimately tied to this purpose.

It was not long before AI researchers started to combine this behavior-based robotics approach with the ability of ANNs to learn through experience. Could an artificial brain equipped in this way one day harbor consciousness? Projects that explore this exciting new possibility have been running in several labs for some years now. The two most remarkable attempts, perhaps, have been realized by the electrical engineer Igor Aleksander (2000) at Imperial College, London with a program called **Magnus**, and the AI researcher Rodney Brooks (2002) and his colleagues at MIT with a humanoid robot known as **Cog**. To take Cog as an exam-ple: here is a machine, built on the principles of embodied cognition and connec-tionism, equipped with an impressive hardware capacity that, according to its makers, will one day teach us a thing or two about machine consciousness and, perhaps, enlighten us about consciousness itself.

Cog's movable equipment consists of three degrees of freedom for head move-ment, allowing for human-like motion (though not for the sublime Indian head waggle), and two arms and hands (Cog has no legs). Sensory equipment includes two cameras for eyes that saccade for human-like vision, four ears (for better sound location), and heat and touch sensors, as well as a whole host of control systems that keep Cog from damaging its own delicate joints and motors. One consequence of dealing with an agent capable of independent sensory-motor integration is that Cog necessitates three huge external "kill" buttons that stop it outright for the protection of its caretakers and the volunteer visitors that spend many hours teaching it this, that, and the other. Cog has no "innate" or programmed knowledge about the world; its ANNs architecture is a tabula rasa that must learn to make its way through the world the hard way, by interacting with it. After passing through an "artificial infancy" stage, its makers hope that it will be able to display humanoid behaviors, such as speech and face recognition, rudimentary language, taking care of its own welfare, and so on. As Dennett (1998, p. 164), a member of the Cog team, describes it: "the motivating insight for the project is that by confronting and solving *actual, real-time* problems of self-protection, hand–eye coordination, and interaction with other animate beings, Cog's artificers will discover the *sufficient* conditions for higher cognitive functions in general – and maybe even for a variety of consciousness that would satisfy the skeptics." But, given the gridlock in the field of consciousness studies, it is rather unlikely that skeptics would be convinced of this by any of Cog's future feats. While members of the Cog team already start wondering about what sort of responsibilities they might have toward Cog, critics claim that its behavior will tell us nothing about whether or not there is anybody home inside. But if there is, how could we ever tell?

Alan Turing's legacy is closely tied to a would-be experimental test of machine intelligence, the famous **Turing test**. In 1950, in a seminal paper, he proposed a criterion that would serve as a benchmark to decide whether a machine truly thinks. He hazarded no metaphysical guesses as to what thinking is, nor did he discover some magical way of shining a light into the innards of machines to check for signs of inner musing. Instead, he proposed a functional test based on what machines can do. In the best tradition of functionalism, a machine is said to pass the test, and thus be granted the status of thinking creature, if it can hold up one end of a conversation with a human without being identified as a machine. In other words, the test proposes to take the intentional stance, holding machines to the same standard that we hold ourselves. The Turing test is set up as a blind review. People type questions and independent judges determine whether the typed replies originate from a human or another computer. The task for both, human and computer, is to convince the judges that they are the human. Naturally, the trick is to ask questions that would reveal the computer's true identity. The Turing test has turned out to be a very difficult one. For instance, asking the computer to compare the meaning of metaphors typically suffices to do it in (while asking a mathematical question usually does the human in). To date, no machine has come even close to passing the Turing test.

Given the functional basis of the test, the main objections of using a conversation criterion as definitive bar are the same as those leveled against functionalism in general. First and foremost, critics argue that it dismisses phenomenal content. A machine's capacity to fool people into thinking it is human merely shows its dazzling capacity to simulate thought; it isn't, however, a sufficient condition for real thoughts and real consciousness (Searle, 1980). It is one thing, runs this argument, to explain dispositions to behave and another to attribute mental processes. According to Velmans (2000, p. 86), a functional criterion does not, in any case, "explain the nature and function of phenomenal consciousness as such," regardless of how well it is fooling people. In other words, Velmans maintains that first-person criteria for the existence of silicon consciousness are required. Anticipating this objection, Turing argued that if a machine plays the imitation game and wins, there is no reason to consider it different to the human player – even in terms of phenomenology. Whatever the machine is doing inside, it evidently thinks, otherwise it couldn't pass the test. Despite the danger of beating a dead horse, you could easily see how this relates to the zombie. If you do not go for the zombie hunch, you'd side with Turing's argument; if you do, you'd be on the critic's side.

Five naysaying arguments

Everyone seems to agree that computers are not conscious. What's more, everyone seems to agree further that this isn't going to change – not tomorrow, not next year, not ever! Although many philosophers and computer scientists would beg to differ, when the suggestion that robots might some day be sentient beings is put to people outside these domains, they, no doubt, would sniff at it, declaring that humans will forever have the monopoly on consciousness. But what makes them so sure? If pressed, what are the actual arguments they'd use to justify their deep-seated belief that AI – however advanced – will never engender anything resembling private experience? Here we examine the top naysaying arguments against artificial consciousness and attempt, while playing devil's advocate, to evaluate the soundness of each.

We tackle this task by honing in on six arguments in total, five in this section and one in the next. Before we start, however, we might do well to clear the air of a few objections that are, by and large, not considered sound as far as arguments go but continue to be mooted frequently, nonetheless. The first and arguably strongest is intuition. Recall the earlier (and loud) noise we made about why introspective data is inadmissible as empirical evidence. A second, related objection is rooted in Cartesian dualism. It holds that consciousness requires a soul and since machines do not have one, they can't have subjective experiences. Again, it is hoped that no one needs reminding of why this claim falls flat.

Looking beyond those theoretical cul-de-sacs, we have **objection #1**: Computers only do what they are told. They are programmed and so possess no creativity, originality, or self-initiative. There are two problems with this objection. First, it is, certainly in principle, not true. From day one, even GOFAI systems did creative work. Consider the "Logic Theorist," a program built in the 1950s to solve logical problems (Newell & Simon, 1972). It proved 38 of the 52 theorems in Russell and Whitehead's *Principia Mathematica*, but, more significantly, offered a new and more elegant proof of one of them, Theorem 2.85. If a mathematician had done the deed, no one would have questioned the creative nature of the feat.

These days, with the upgrade to ANNs, silicon produces novel solutions all the time. On the other side of the equation, we have to ask ourselves how much of our own creativity is the result of hardwired or automatized behaviors. Consider, for instance, the Eureka effect where a creative solution just pops into your head, or an athlete, who makes a new move to get by an opponent. Such instances of creativity are examples of automatic processes as well (Dietrich, 2004a, 2004b). In other words, we are also programmed. In addition, we tend to glorify the creative process itself. Among psychologists, the prevailing theory is that creativity is essentially a Darwinian process; that is, it entails a variation-selection process (Simonton, 2003). Ideational combinations are generated automatically, but a selection process is required to determine which ideas are truly creative. This generate-test procedure is the basis of all biological creativity; for example, the different body plans in the design space of evolution. The key insight here is that creativity does not necessitate that selection is directed by a higher power; it can be the result of a mindless, bottom-up process. What, then, prevents machines from operating in this manner?

Objection #1 is actually a special case of **objection #2**: Computers will never do X. Ever since Descartes, people have felt compelled to protect the mind from scientific scrutiny. This has often taken the form of a list of mental abilities that presumably could never be, not even in principle, implemented in a machine. Descartes, for instance, nominated language and reasoning. He would have been surprised to learn that the real difficulty is not reasoning but "lower-order" processes like emotions, perception, and motion. Ironically, this list keeps on shriveling, as AI picks off from it one ability after another. This perpetual retreat alone ought to make one cautious about never-ever statements. Computers are long past being glorified adding machines and anyone making predictions as to the ultimate limitations of AI – given its success in a mere half a century – does so at his own peril. Recall that AI can simulate any system as long as it is formalized. But what if the human mind operates in a manner that defies characterization in a formal system?

If this is the direction in which you want to proceed, you may be inclined to go for a close cousin of objection #2, **objection #3**: Non-computability. One version of this is that computers operate using algorithms while brains solve problems in a non-algorithmic manner. An algorithm is a strategy that guarantees the right outcome because it proceeds by the unwavering application of a set of rigid rules. Note that this also applies to ANNs, as the learning procedure is entirely algorithmic. This, however, may not be the best way to solve complex tasks. If you were to look for your misplaced keys by searching your house methodically, square by square, it would certainly get you the keys but it might also take you a lot of time. Silicon employs this mindless method exclusively, while humans rarely, if ever, use it. Rather, we either use the trial and error method or, more commonly, heuristics, which are rules of thumb that may fail but may also produce faster solutions. Here you'd look for the keys in the most likely places first. By eliminating unlikely options, the heuristic method makes quick and dirty choices, which might have the potential of excluding the correct solution. A cheeky way of saying this is that humans make mistakes, while computers have no common sense.

Bearing in mind these first two objections, let's consider a classic example: Robots could never have emotions. As we shall see in Chapter 9, neuroscience is rapidly advancing toward a formal characterization of these mental events. Emotions are essentially value tags. They provide the organism with knowledge about what sensory information means to its well-being. Why should the concept of valence be so impossible to simulate in a machine? Couldn't a computer learn to code information with respect to how it impacts its own system's integrity (welfare)? You may want to counter here that machines do not really care about their survival or some equivalent, say, being taken off the power grid. But before we address this further objection, the central function of emotions – making value judgments according to some specified set of rules – is a process that must be conceded, in principle, to formalization.

What remains, then, is the doubt that humans may not use formal logic to compute this value tag. Emotions could be, for all we know, the result of unspecifiable, non-algorithmic computing (objection #3). Some – most prominently Roger Penrose (1989) – press a version of this objection by invoking Gödel's theorem (see Chapter 4), which, for consciousness, is typically taken to mean that brains contain information that they themselves cannot explicate. It follows that consciousness can never be fully formalized and thus implemented in an artificial mind. Turing (1950) made a similar observation, conceding that there are some functions that computers, for mathematical reasons, simply cannot do. The main problem of leaning too hard on Gödel's theorem is that it applies only to formal, logical statements and thus may not have any bearing on the human brain for the simple reason that it may not be a finite, formal system. The possibility that brains conduct their business non-algorithmically certainly undermines the applicability of Gödel's theorem to brains.

As a final consideration, even if mental processes involve non-algorithmic computing, it does not follow that they cannot exist in artificial minds. All that follows is that they cannot be formalized in an algorithmic manner. With the advent of quantum computers, a new generation of artificial minds is evolving that also operates non-algorithmically. Unlike conventional GOFAI or ANNs, quantum computing may be able to address this concern in the future.

Objection #4 comes from a quite different quarter: Consciousness requires life. Computers are, by definition, inanimate, a pile of metal, if you like, and thus cannot ever be conscious. Let's call this the carbon argument. It is reminiscent of the nineteenth-century position of vitalism, which found it necessary to postulate a life-giving force – élan vital – to explain why organic tissue has life, while objects made from metal, stone, rubber, or glass do not. This objection forces us to look closer at the stuff of life to see if consciousness might require it. Organic chemistry teaches us that life is primarily composed of four elements of the periodic table: carbon, hydrogen, nitrogen, and oxygen. In other words, unit for unit, living creatures are really made of rather dead molecules! Wet brains and computers are both information processors; the difference, in terms of constitution, is that the latter are decision-making devices that are made from a different element of the periodic table, namely silicon. This focuses objection #4 more sharply: What is so special about carbon? Does it have any intrinsic property that qualifies it as the sole host of conscious information processing? Is there any reason why consciousness could not be generated from some different arrangement of matter?

Searle, for instance, argues that minds can only exist in the right kind of stuff. He believes that there is something special about biological goo. Box 5.1 shows that this argument also holds in reverse. However, if you are committed to a materialist view and believe that mind and matter are one, you must concede that the carbon argument falls right here. There is no reason why a carbon-based information processor ought to be unique with respect to consciousness. Where would be the line, for instance, if AI researchers use the properties of lipid membranes to produce computations (Dennett,1995)?

Box 5.1   "They're made out of meat"

"They're made out of meat."

"Meat?"

"Meat. They are made out of meat."

"Meat?"

"There's no doubt about it. We picked up several from different parts of the planet, took them aboard our recon vessels, and probed them all the way through. They're completely meat."

"That's impossible. What about the radio signals? The messages to the stars?"

"They use the radio waves to talk, but the signals don't come from them. The signals are from machines."

"So who made the machines? That's who we want to contact."

"They made the machines. That's what I'm trying to tell you. Meat made the machines."

"That's ridiculous. How can meat make a machine? You're asking me to believe in sentient meat."

"I'm not asking you, I'm telling you. These creatures are the only sentient race in that sector and they're made out of meat."

"Maybe they're like the orfolei. You know, a carbon-based intelligence that goes through a meat stage."

"Nope. They're born meat and they die meat. We studied them for several of their life spans, which didn't take long. Do you have any idea what's the life span of meat?"

"Spare me. Okay, maybe they're only part meat. You know, like the weddilei. A meat head with an electron plasma brain inside."

"Nope. We thought of that, since they do have meat heads, like the weddilei. But I told you, we probed them. They're meat all the way through."

"No brain?"

"Oh, there's a brain all right. It's just that the brain is made out of meat! That's what I've been trying to tell you."

"So . . . what does the thinking?"

"You're not understanding, are you? You're refusing to deal with what I'm telling you. The brain does the thinking. The meat."

"Thinking meat! You're asking me to believe in thinking meat!"

Box 5.1	*continued*

"Yes, thinking meat! Conscious meat! Loving meat. Dreaming meat. The meat is the whole deal! Are you beginning to get the picture or do I have to start all over?"

"Omigod. You're serious then. They're made out of meat."

"Thank you. Finally. Yes. They are indeed made out of meat. And they've been trying to get in touch with us for almost a hundred of their years."

"Omigod. So what does this meat have in mind?"

"First it wants to talk to us. Then I imagine it wants to explore the Universe, contact other sentiences, swap ideas and information. The usual."

"We're supposed to talk to meat."

"That's the idea. That's the message they're sending out by radio. 'Hello. Anyone out there. Anybody home.' That sort of thing."

"They actually do talk, then. They use words, ideas, concepts."

"Oh, yes. Except they do it with meat."

"I thought you just told me they used radio."

"They do, but what do you think is on the radio? Meat sounds. You know how when you slap or flap meat, it makes a noise? They talk by flapping their meat at each other. They can even sing by squirting air through their meat."

"Omigod. Singing meat. This is altogether too much. So what do you advise?"

"Officially or unofficially?"

"Both."

"Officially, we are required to contact, welcome and log in any and all sentient races or multibeings in this quadrant of the Universe, without prejudice, fear or favor. Unofficially, I advise that we erase the records and forget the whole thing."

"I was hoping you would say that."

"It seems harsh, but there is a limit. Do we really want to make contact with meat?"

"I agree one hundred percent. What's there to say? 'Hello, meat. How's it going?' But will this work? How many planets are we dealing with here?"

"Just one. They can travel to other planets in special meat containers, but they can't live on them. And being meat, they can only travel through C space. Which limits them to the speed of light and makes the possibility of their ever making contact pretty slim. Infinitesimal, in fact."

"So we just pretend there's no one home in the Universe."

"That's it."

"Cruel. But you said it yourself, who wants to meet meat? And the ones who have been aboard our vessels, the ones you probed? You're sure they won't remember?"

"They'll be considered crackpots if they do. We went into their heads and smoothed out their meat so that we're just a dream to them."

"A dream to meat! How strangely appropriate, that we should be meat's dream."

"And we marked the entire sector unoccupied."

"Good. Agreed, officially and unofficially. Case closed. Any others? Anyone interesting on that side of the galaxy?"

"Yes, a rather shy but sweet hydrogen core cluster intelligence in a class nine star in G445 zone. Was in contact two galactic rotations ago, wants to be friendly again."

"They always come around."

"And why not? Imagine how unbearably, how unutterably cold the Universe would be if one were all alone . . ."

The End

The next thing in tow is **objection #5**: Humans evolve while computers are designed. For the evolution-versus-design argument we must ask ourselves whether there is anything unique about the process of evolution that qualifies it as the sole creator of conscious entities. But, as we shall see in the next chapter, evolution is an algorithm for change that has no such special role. It is a copying mechanism in which error produces variation that is then subjected to selection. Over the eons, this process has produced a truly exquisite network of information-processing units capable of some very special feats. It is also true that, at any level of organization, this wet brain does not remotely resemble anything like the design of current artificial networks. But the value of seeing evolution as a universal algorithm is that it can produce change in anything as long as that anything varies and is selectively copied. Since evolution is the process by which we got our minds, it might be a good idea, if our aim is to create human-like intelligence and consciousness, to subject silicon to some kind of a variation-selection process as well. But this is not a strict requirement for mindful robots – only, perhaps, for human-like, mindful robots. So, one might still hold on to the idea that evolution creates a different kind of mind than one that is designed but this is not the same as saying that artificial minds cannot exist. Perhaps in the not-so-distant future, robots will make lists of all the things humans will never ever be able to do – despite all their efforts in genetic engineering – say, envisioning the fifth dimension, solving the Riemann hypothesis, eliminating war, prejudice, and poverty, or, for that matter, understanding consciousness.

The Chinese room

A last argument against artificial consciousness is **objection #6**: Computers lack phenomenal content; they have no inner, private experience – no sense of what it's like to be something. Although at first not intended to be used that way, the standard illustration of this objection is the **Chinese room thought-experiment**. It was initally conceived by John Searle (1980) to attack the notion – held by proponents of strong AI – that computers that generate output indistinguishable from that of a human truly think. His aim was to show that computers lack semantics; they do not understand what they are doing. But from the start the Chinese room argument has doubled up as an objection against machine consciousness because, as Searle insists, it shows that something more is required for consciousness. That something, according to Searle, is intentionality and subjectivity. It is this last conclusion from the Chinese room debate that has people irremediably at loggerheads.

Before we explore what – if anything – the Chinese room shows, here is the basic setup. Searle asks us to imagine a man, who speaks only English, locked in a room containing a complete set of rules, in English, for manipulating the symbols of the Chinese script. The rules represent the equivalent of a computer program; that is, they specify what to do with the symbols in a formal, algorithmic language. The man does not speak Chinese and so does not know what the symbols mean. Nor do the rules tell him what the symbols mean. People on the outside slip questions, in Chinese, under the door. In accordance with the rules, he performs operations – running the program – producing a new set of Chinese symbols, the answers, that he slips back under the door. The exercise results in grammatically correct Chinese and the man gets so good at following the instructions that from the point of view of people on the outside he must understand Chinese. But, Searle says, he doesn't speak a word of Chinese. The man in the room does exactly what a computer program does, yet, he understands nothing.

Having laid out the scenario, Searle derives the following, to him obvious, conclusions. The man performs calculations, mindlessly and mechanically, without understanding the meaning of either the operations or the symbols. Thus, syntax, which is all a program has, is not, by itself, sufficient for semantics. And, if programs do not have semantics – lacking in meaning, that is – it follows that they do not have minds. Note that Searle does not take aim here at weak AI. He believes that programs are useful in simulating human mental processes; that is, they can act *as if* they were minds. What he claims to have refuted in the Chinese room argument is strong AI, the notion that the implementation of the right program, regardless of the physical material running it, is all there is to having a mind. Simulating thinking by mere symbol manipulation does not constitute thinking any more than the flight simulator gets you to Paris.

We can draw out this conclusion from another angle. What Searle is getting at is that non-computability – objection #3 above – concedes too much to AI; it wouldn't, in fact, make a difference if mental processes were computable. Should human artificers, in the fullness of time, formalize human cognition and run it as a program on a computer, the computational algorithm, although exactly reproducing thought, still does not constitute thought. Something more is required to make a mind than the automatized manipulation of arbitrary symbols. In consequence, functionalism is wrong and the research goal of strong AI is a pipe dream.

What, then, might we reasonably ask, makes us humans have semantics? What is this magical something that we have and they just don't? To this Searle responds that computers lack intentionality. Recall from Chapter 3 that intentionality means that conscious experience is always *about* something; that is, it makes a reference to something real. Computer programs do not have this property of "aboutness"; they do not refer to anything in the real world. We identified this earlier as the grounding problem. According to Searle, programs lack symbol grounding because it requires consciousness. And there we are again – back to square one: the standoff. Searle holds that the two defining characteristics of consciousness are intentionality and subjectivity. "Consciousness has a first-person or subjective ontology," says Searle (1997, p. 212), "and so cannot be reduced to anything that has a third-person or objective ontology. If you try to reduce or eliminate one in favor of the other [as you do if you characterize mental processes in terms of computational algorithms] you leave something out." Materialists typically object that intentionality is not a property of consciousness; it is only useful fiction, something we attribute to us, but possess no more than machines do. The Chinese room, then, is the reincarnation of the same playground fight: you've left something out – no we haven't! This begs the question for a more positive characterization of what this intentionality is and how we humans have come by it. What is included in our way of making mental representations that gives us meaning? According to Searle, consciousness also depends on the nature of the material that runs the program, the brain. "Brains cause minds" (Searle, 1992), and you cannot get consciousness, to use his memorable phrase, with "beer cans strung together with wires and powered by windmills."

The Chinese room argument has created a storm of replies over the years. Two have been in fashion the most. The first is what Searle dubs the **systems reply**. The simple version says that the thought experiment focuses on the wrong agent. The man in the room might not be conscious but the whole system, complete with the man, room, and rules is. By considering only part of the system, we are lured into thinking that the Chinese room is a valid refutation of artificial minds and functionalism. But consciousness emerges from interaction; after all, no single component of the brain is conscious either, but the brain, as a whole, is. Against this, Searle argues that if the man internalizes the whole system, for instance, by memorizing the rule book, nothing changes; he still would not understand what he is doing. As Searle put it, "he understands nothing of Chinese, and . . . neither does the system," adding that "while [the] person doesn't understand Chinese, somehow the conjunction of that person and bits of paper might" is ridiculous (Searle, 1980, p. 420).

But the systems reply isn't so easily dismissed. While Searle thinks that it is the weakest of all the replies, others consider it the decisive downfall of the thought experiment (Hofstadter & Dennett, 1981). To see why, let's consider the more complex version of the systems reply. As Dennett (1991) diagnoses it, the entire exercise is a "misdirection in imagination," with the main source of confusion stemming from the fact that Searle asks us to imagine something impossible. The clever setup guides people to a seemingly obvious truth because it ignores the all-important role of complexity. Searle claims that the man in the room is capable of passing the Turing test but the complexity required for a program to actually do so also requires layers upon layers of metaknowledge about the world. This, in turn, brings symbol grounding and intentionality with it. If it didn't, the program could not possibly hope to pass the Turing test. Simple programs might have no semantics but then neither might simple nervous systems. Complex programs of the kind that could pass the Turing test must have developed semantics. After all, this is, according to Dennett, how we human got ours, too – by adding layers of complexity over the course of evolution.

Searle counters that he addressed this by pointing out that more of the same does not turn something into something else. This reasoning is certainly intuitively appealing, and one might be tempted to think that it takes the sting out of the systems reply, but it is precisely this ignorance of what complexity does to a system that prevents people from understanding the simplification made in the Chinese room argument as a fundamental flaw. By analogy, consider the brain where Searle's reasoning holds without any accommodation. A neuron surely does not have semantics or intentionality; so how then is it possible that 10 to the power of 12 do? How does adding the same mindless units – regardless of how high the number – make a mind? This is also the line of reasoning taken by the Churchlands (1990). When programs are run on a connectionist platform, the complexity of interactions would make all the difference. The phenomena of entities being transformed in kind by complexity is evident everywhere in the natural world, be it in physics, chemistry, or biology. The dictum of holism – the whole is greater than the some of its parts – must surely apply to artificial programs as huge as those that pass the Turing criterion. As Dennett concludes: "when we factor in complexity, as we must, we really have to factor it in" (Dennett, 1991, p. 440).

Let's also consider the second critique which Searle dubs the **robot reply**. Here the view is that the problem of semantics can be removed if the program is embodied in a robot equipped with sensory and motor systems. The psychologist Stevan Harnad (1990) argues that semantics develop as a result of interactions with the environment. It follows that a program placed inside a robot would build a set of causal relationships that allow the symbols to become grounded in reality. Earlier, we learned that robotics is generally hailed as the possible solution to this grounding problem. Against this, Searle tweaks the thought experiment a little to allow the man to get input – the Chinese symbols – via a camera and produce output via artificial limbs. So embodied, the man still would not understand Chinese, Searle claims, if he continues to simply perform meaningless symbol manipulation. Adding a set of causal interaction with the outside world does not change anything. But the concept of embodied cognition and its implementation in projects such as Cog seriously challenges this naysaying position. Given that this is the way we get our meaning, grounding, or intentionality, why shouldn't they?

What shines through from underneath these yin–yang discussions are the dualistic tendencies of the thought experiment. According to Searle, nothing – not complexity, not interaction – will ever give machines genuine thought because consciousness is riding on top of the neural machinery. It has characteristics – subjectivity, intentionality, qualia – that cannot be translated into a program. Because the Chinese room argument is driven by a clear commitment to the existence of the hard problem, the basic arguments against dualism apply. Recall from Chapter 3 the parallel contention of vitalism that life must be something extra. But when dissected into layers and distributed throughout the system, the problem of life simply disappears. Like most, if not all, thought experiments in the study of consciousness, the Chinese room settles nothing. Phenomenalists stay on one side, materialists hold the other.

Summary

In a view consistent with the tenets of strong AI, Dennett's philosophy can be summarized as: Consciousness is as consciousness does. His entire opus can be seen as a sustained and disciplined demolition project to sanitize our bad habits of thinking about the mind. As an antidote to this residual dualism, he proposes his multiple drafts model, a thoroughgoing materialist account without resorting to any obfuscations or the fallacy of the Cartesian theater.

In a very short time, AI has come a very long way. Its declared goal – the building of intelligent systems – is a matter of obvious relevance to the study of consciousness. This is strictly true even if artificial minds turn out to have a kind of intelligence that is different from ours. Early work using GOFAI systems had two major limitations. Although any formal system can be embodied in a machine, it soon became clear that some mental processes do not lend themselves readily to formal specification. This led to the development of ANNs, which are built on a more brain-like connectionist architecture that learns by doing. GOFAI's second limitation has several ways of describing it: the grounding problem, the commonsense problem, and the lack of intentionality or semantics. The idea conveyed here is similar: programs have no clue what, exactly, it is they are computing. AI has been trying to overcome this with robotics. By providing programs with moveable equipment – arms, hands, legs – and sensory systems – eyes, ears, pain sensors – machines like Cog can build their knowledge through causal interaction with the external world. The Turing test, on the other hand, is a method to tell if such artificial minds are, well, minds. It proposes that if independent judges cannot tell a computer from a human in a conversation, the machine can be said to think. Making a functional criterion definitive of thinking, and by extension consciousness, is, naturally, rejected by philosophers who hold phenomenal views.

We also considered in this chapter six nested objections against the possibility of conscious machines. Upon closer inspection, though, none of them, though certainly intuitively appealing, constitutes an *a priori*, knockdown refutation that artificial minds could not, in principle, exist. Most are based on a lack of understanding of what is involved in the process whose replication by silicon is being doubted, such as creativity, emotions, dreams, life, or evolution. In addition, the noncomputability objection commits one only to the position that machines might have different minds, but not that they are impossible. The final objection, the Chinese room, was designed as an attack on strong AI. Searle claims to have refuted computational functionalism by showing that there is more to having a mind than mere computation. If programs do not understand the meaning of what they are computing, they lack intentionality and cannot be considered minds. A storm of replies ensued which charged that the Chinese room argument is incoherent. While the systems reply points to the role of complexity, the robot reply addresses the grounding problem. Searle thinks the replies fail, while the critics think that his answers to them fail.

Suggested reading

Aleksander, I. (2000). *How to Build a Mind*. London: Weidenfeld & Nicolson.
Brooks, R. A. (2002). *Flesh and Machines*. New York: Pantheon.

Dennett, D. C. (1991). *Consciousness Explained*. Boston: Little, Brown.

Dennett, D. C. (1998). *Brainchildren: Essays on Designing Minds*. Cambridge, MA: MIT Press.

Searle, J. (1980). Minds, brains, and programs. *Behavioural and Brain Sciences*, 3, 417–57. With responses of 26 specialists and Searle's reply to them.

6 Neurocognition and evolution

Cognitive neuroscience

Global workspace theory

Cognitive neuroscience is on a roll. Contrary to what one might imagine, the biology of the mind has become accessible through a combination of new technologies and ingenious psychological experiments. The result is potent. No longer is it the case that the investigation of the brain makes little contact with higher mental functions. Nor are there many psychologists and philosophers left who are prepared to defend the extreme position, fashionable during the heydays of functionalism, that we can make progress on consciousness without understanding the brain. While in Chapter 4 we examined models of consciousness pitched at the level of neurons and networks, in this chapter we review the perspective from systems neuroscience. The chapter also describes evolutionary perspectives of consciousness. Although these two approaches are not directly linked, they nicely complete our survey on the mechanisms of consciousness. The evolution of the brain is best seen as a series of steps toward increased behavioral flexibility, a development that goes hand in hand with the emergence of consciousness. Arguably, if you want to know what a thing is or does, it is useful to know where it comes from and how it got to be that way.

What's the one theory of mind you are prepared to defend? If a hypothetical poll were to put this question to scientists and philosophers in the field of consciousness, **global workspace theory**, or GWT for short, would undoubtedly be voted among the front-runners, perhaps even into pole position. GWT is a cognitive neuroscience approach to consciousness. Since its first conception by the psychologist Bernard Baars (1988) it has emerged as perhaps the standard model that unifies into a single framework philosophical, cognitive, and neuro-scientific aspects of consciousness. In 2001, Daniel Dennett surmised that "theorists are converging from quite different quarters on a version of the global neuronal workspace of consciousness" (2001a, p. 221). The core concept, according to Baars (1988, p. 42), is that consciousness is seen as a "distributed society of specialists that is equipped with a working memory, called a global workspace, whose content can be broadcast to the system as a whole."

Drawing from how the brain, as a whole, is organized, GWT is a cognitive architecture that is built for the fast and efficient exchange and dissemination of information. Recall Selfridge's pandemonium model (1959) of the brain as a society of demons, each striving, in a fierce tug of war, to attain dominance. The output of these highly specialized demons must be coordinated somehow if the organism is to have unity in its action. If, for example, two conflicting messages were to reach effector muscles unencumbered, the animal would literally tear itself apart. GWT offers a solution to this by postulating a virtual space in the brain, the global workspace, that provides the infrastructure for higher-order integration. It is a sort of blackboard where modules post their messages to make them temporarily available to the rest of the system. Similar to the models of Edelman and the Crick/Koch team, ascendancy to consciousness is determined through a competitive process. Modules must compete for access to the global workspace with the winner able to broadcast what it has to say to a large audience. This makes a large number of the brain's subsystems privy to the information, and it is this global availability, Baars says, that renders information conscious. This global access hypothesis differs from the dynamic core of competing coalitions models in that the latter models have no equivalent for this theater-like display of information (Baars, 2002).

The central idea behind GWT comes from artificial intelligence. There, distributed-processing systems rely heavily on global accessibility to spread information fast through a very large number of autonomous, individual processors. Going global this way is simply the best way to facilitate communication in a massively parallel processing system that needs to come up, in a reasonable amount of time, with a serial output decision. In sum, GWT holds consciousness to be a system that allows a "blackboard" architecture to operate in the brain for the "very rapid exchange of information" (Baars, 1988, p. 220).

An attractive feature of this theory is that the global neuronal workspace has no sharp anatomical boundaries. It is a moving target comprising a continually changing set of large, interconnected networks. The number of activation patterns that can constitute a transient global workspace is not unconstrained, however. At the very least, there is agreement that activity in the thalamocortical system is a necessary condition for the workspace. Beyond that, a consensus is growing that workspace neurons are particularly dense in regions of the prefrontal cortex (Dehaene & Naccache, 2001). This conclusion is based on the substantial body of evidence implicating the prefrontal cortex in the control of higher-cognitive functions, particularly working memory (see Chapter 8). Baars (1997), however, is careful not to make the prefrontal cortex the site for consciousness. The role of the working memory buffer in the prefrontal cortex is to broadcast information, but the information temporarily represented there is physically located in all four corners of the brain. Consciousness, then, always depends on a distributed network of neurons, not on a single, central location.

GWT meshes well with the empirical data from cognitive neuroscience. Brain recordings have shown that conscious content has a very wide distribution in the brain. Regions of the brain that compute the current content of consciousness do indeed seem to mobilize large areas of adjacent cortex, presumably for global distribution. On the other hand, critics of the approach question the relevance of GWT to consciousness, particularly with respect to subjective experience. What is so special, they ask, about the global availability of information? How, exactly, does this help solve the puzzle of qualia? It cannot simply be, they maintain, by virtue of the fact that information is globally accessible. The same processing architecture is in place in computers and we do not suppose that they are conscious, do we? By the same token, we do not consider the internet a conscious entity, though online information, no doubt, has the property of being globally accessible. You will recognize this attack as the familiar impasse between philosophies of mind that hold phenomenal views and those that do not.

Naturally, the way to get around this criticism is by denying outright that the point is at all valid. This is the route taken by Dehaene and Naccache (2001), who simply "postulate that this global availability of information through the workspace is what we subjectively experience as the conscious state." Dennett (2001a) agrees; as he writes: "The proposed consensual thesis is not that this global availability *causes* some further effect of a different sort altogether . . . but that it *is*, all by itself, a conscious state" (ibid., p. 223). The global workspace, then, is not the organizational summit of consciousness, in which a master homunculus observes the movie in the brain. Accessibility to a global workspace means that homunculi have access to *each other* and not some higher-order entity.

We see, in conclusion, that GWT is essentially a functional theory, but one that is grounded in cognitive neuroscience. It has many similarities with Dennett's multiple drafts model (see Chapter 5). However, whereas Dennett dismantles the Cartesian theater, Baars (1988) explicitly makes use of the canonical theater analogy. Conscious events in this metaphor are those that happen under the bright spot of the limelight – on stage – directed there by the focus of attention. The happenings on stage, "in the theatre of consciousness" (ibid., p. 31), are then visible to the unconscious audience, in the darkened rest of the theater. The few actors who are glamorously displayed in the spotlight correspond, roughly, to the few items that can be held in working memory, while the larger, silent audience represents the fact that the vast majority of mental activity occurs unconsciously, in the dark. The dynamics between stage and audience are governed by the competitive interactions described in the global workspace model. Baars denies, however, that the theater metaphor renders GWT a form of Cartesian materialism. He explains that there is no Cartesian director operating behind the scenes. Nor does the stage represent an endpoint, a finish line, where information "enters" or is "in" consciousness.

Split-brain research

The nineteenth-century neurologist John Hughlings-Jackson (1889) once remarked: "No better neurological work can be done than the precise investigation of epileptic paroxysms." The neuroscientists Roger Sperry and Michael Gazzaniga, two bold cartographers of inner space, took this advice to heart and built a career around studying **split-brain patients**, a small group of people who have been called the most fascinating people on earth. By the 1940s, it was known that seizures tend to spread by way of the **corpus callosum**, a large bundle of 200 million nerve fibers connecting homologue regions of the cortex. The corpus callosum puzzled early functional neuroanatomists. From its large size and strategic location, smack in the center of the brain, they expected it to control important functions. Yet when they ablated it in animals, they were dumbfounded to find only minor detrimental effects on behavior. Some even quipped that it is nothing but a set of cables holding the two cerebral hemispheres together. This curiosity, coupled with reports implicating the corpus callosum in the propagation of seizures, fermented the idea that epileptic patients might benefit from **callosotomy**, the dissection of the corpus callosum. It seemed a drastic treatment option but for patients who do not respond to drugs, the consequence of not doing it – death, for most of them – is infinitely more drastic. The first successful split-brain operations were done in the 1960s (Bogen, 1995b). By severing this interhemispheric superhighway, seizure activity was indeed prevented from reaching the other side of the brain. That was the good news! The bad news was that, because callosotomy disconnects the right brain from the left one, it also prevents other things from reaching across, things like information. In short, the surgery created people with two independent, noncommunicating symmetrical brain halves, a left hemisphere, **LH**, and a right hemisphere, **RH**.

If you were to meet a split-brain patient you'd not suspect – save for some momentary quirky behavior confined mostly to the postsurgical period – that something is special about them. But there is. When tested in skillfully contrived psychological experiments, they reveal a mental world so bizarre, it defies belief. The trick in a typical split-brain study is to present a stimulus so as to deliver the information to one hemisphere only. This is possible because the wiring diagram of the nervous system is such that each hemisphere receives information primarily from only one – the opposite – side of the body. So, for instance, a tone entering the left ear would only reach RH. The exception to this crossed representation of sensory systems is olfaction; here pathways run ipsilateral. Motor fibers also show the contralateral arrangement with LH controlling muscles on the right side of the body and RH controlling those on the left. With this in mind, consider the basic split-brain experimental design. A patient is blindfolded and asked to identify an object, say, an apple, with her right hand. Using this setup, only LH learns about the apple. When asked to name the object in her hand, she'd report without trouble, "it's an apple," for the simple reason that LH – in most people – also controls language production. It gets more interesting when the patient is asked to repeat the test with the left hand. This time the tactile information goes exclusively to RH. But since the corpus callosum is cut, information in RH cannot reach the speech areas of LH and she is unable to say what is in her left hand. If the patient is subsequently allowed to open her eyes, LH would be informed also about the apple and she'd say right away: "Oh, it's an apple." It is for this reason that a casual encounter with a split-brain patient does not reveal a split person; in the real world, sensory information is never delivered exclusively to RH.

In reality, the most common testing arrangement uses vision. Here the patient is instructed to fixate on a dot in the middle of a screen while a stimulus is briefly flashed to one side of the visual field. In one study, investigators flashed the words

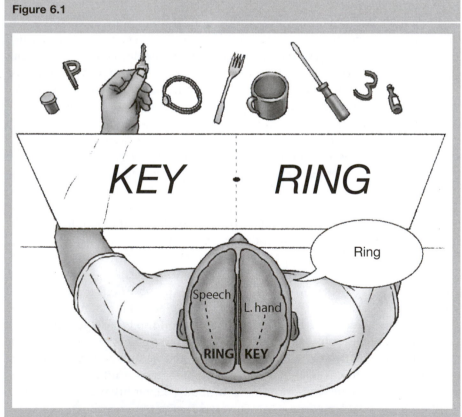

Figure 6.1

Diagram showing the basic setup used to lateralize the presentation of information to split-brain patients. See text for explanation. (From Gazzaniga et al., 1998)

"key" to the left and "ring" to the right of the fixation point (Sperry, 1966). When asked what he saw, one patient said "ring," as this was the only word the speech dominant LH knew about. But RH also saw something – namely the word "key." RH, however, cannot report its knowledge using language. So to give it an opportunity to demonstrate what it saw, the investigators showed the patient a box of objects. Naturally, he picked out the key with his RH-controlled left hand. On the other hand, as it were, his right hand was controlled by LH and therefore picked from the box what it knew, the ring. Roger Sperry, who shared the 1981 Nobel Prize for this work, and Michael Gazzaniga (1992) studied these patients extensively. The basic conclusions they drew from testing split-brain patients using this paradigm boil down to this. First, neither LH nor RH saw the combination "key ring." It follows that each hemisphere is evidently blind to what the other is seeing. Second, it seems that we become fully conscious of something, at least to the extent that we can verbalize it, only if information reaches the language-dominant LH. Full, explicit representation does not occur when knowledge exists only in RH. This is a stunning find. Not only is LH the site where full-fledged consciousness happens, but the capacity for symbolic language seems a necessary condition for it.

Given this, it is natural to wonder why split-brain patients behave coherently at all. In the end, they have, in a way, two independent minds, each one controlling the opposite side of the body. Why, then, don't they behave as if composed of two selves, each with its own will? Well, instances where the two hemispheres are at odds with one another do occur and they make for truly grotesque examples of our fascinating ability to disagree with ourselves. Upon waking up from the surgery, one of the first complaints many patients have – aside from, as one patient put it, the "splitting headache" – is that the left hand has a "mind of its own." This commonly dissipates with time but in some cases the fact that information between the hemispheres is not shared intrudes in everyday behavior. For example, in a story retold in countless popular magazines, one man found himself beating his wife with the left hand while trying to prevent it with his right (Gazzaniga, 1992). And you thought you had problems! In another case, a woman reportedly unbuttoned her blouse with one hand while buttoning it with the other. How is that for a mixed signal?

Overall, though, those stories are greatly exaggerated. The effects of the disconnection are negligible in most patients and rarely persist beyond a few months. One has to wonder, however, why that is the case. It cannot be simply explained by the fact that sensory information in the real world never enters exclusively through just one side. Just because both sides know about some event does not mean that RH might not want to do something different with it. Yet, one cannot help but wonder what this tells us about the extent to which we do react automatically to our environments. Why else would RH play ball so much with the consciousness harboring LH? One reason for this surprisingly high degree of coordination is certainly the fact that most motor behaviors – walking, chewing, clapping – are controlled by lower brain regions that are still connected across the midline. Strictly speaking, a callosotomy disconnects the right from the left *cortex*;

there are several other commissures, fiber bundles that link the two hemispheres, left intact after the surgery. With respect to emotions, Gazzaniga and LeDoux (1978) also tested whether or not the two hemispheres are incommunicado. They showed RH a film clip containing violent scenes. They found that LH is aware of the emotional computation generated in RH. The amygdalae (right and left), which mediate the response to fear (see Chapter 8), connect through the anterior commissure, one of these intact fiber bundles. So, when the right amygdala is activated in response to violence, it shares its excitement with the left amygdala. The split-brain patient is thus spared any hemispheric yin–yang when it comes to basic emotions.

Perhaps this is as good a place as any to say a word about the left-brain/right-brain craze that has taken hold in popular culture. The initial split-brain research described above sparked a flurry of studies exploring which hemisphere does what, or more accurately, which hemisphere does what better. For instance, most people process language in LH, but RH also handles some aspects of language, for instance, the rhythm and the emotional content of language. Evidently, for language to be full-flavored, we need both hemispheres. One surprising finding was that the non-language hemisphere has very poor inference skills (Gazzaniga, 1992). If a causal situation is presented to a split-brain patient so that the cause is presented exclusively to LH and the effect to RH, the association is totally lost on the person. The same is true if both, cause and effect, are presented solely to RH. Only when LH learns about both, cause and effect, does the person extract the causal relationship. This lends further support to the notion that full-blown consciousness is dependent on LH.

As more data poured in, it became clear that LH is generally more skilled at analytical tasks, such as reasoning or language. This finding raises the question: if higher-cognitive functions are controlled by LH, what does RH do? Is it stupid? It very well might be, as it happens. Michael Gazzaniga, who studied RH for decades, considers it "vastly inferior to a chimp." So what, then, should we make of the business seminar on "how to think with both sides," or the seemingly endless supply of books and magazines promising an easy step-by-step program on how to tap into your intuitive right-brain potential? In truth, there is no left-brain or right-brain person. As Gazzaniga put it, "Some scientists oversimplified the idea, and clever journalists further enhanced them. Cartoonists had a field day with it all." For anyone with normal traffic across the corpus callosum, information is fully shared. You might as well ask someone to make better use of the thalamus.

The interpreter

Split-brain research had one more surprise in store for us. In a clever series of studies, Michael Gazzaniga and his associates (Gazzaniga & LeDoux, 1978) prepared an experimental setup that permitted the simultaneous presentation of different images to different hemispheres. As shown in Figure 6.2, split brain patient P.S. sat in front of a screen that presented a chicken claw to LH and a house in a snow scene to RH. Below the display, the investigators showed an array of pictures in

Figure 6.2

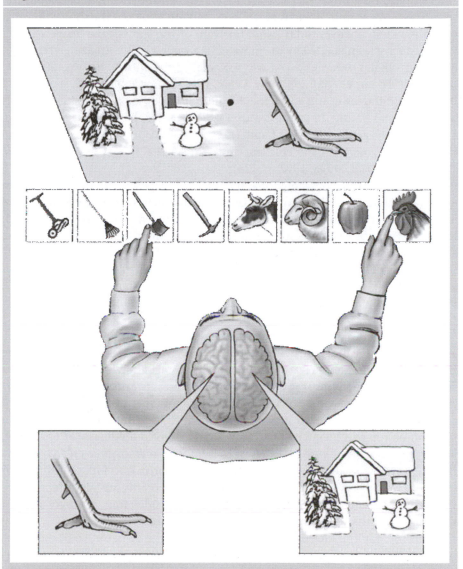

Split-brain patient P.S. saw a chicken claw with LH and a snow scene with RH. When asked to choose the picture corresponding best to what was seen, LH picked the chicken head and RH the shovel. Since the hemispheres are incommunicado, how would the linguistic LH justify the action of the silent RH? But split-brain patients always have an on-the-spot answer for their behavior, prompting Gazzaniga to suggest that LH has an interpreter module that forms "beliefs about why events occur." (From Gazzaniga et al., 1998)

plain view of both hemispheres. The task for P.S. was to match the picture that best fit what each hemisphere saw. Commanding the right hand, LH, having seen only the chicken claw, picked the chicken head. When asked why, P.S. said: "the chicken head fits to the chicken claw, easy." RH, however, only knew about the snow scene. For reasons obvious to RH, you, and me, it picked the shovel. But this action is not so obvious to LH, who, unaware of the snow-scene image seen by RH, must have been dazzled by the move of its own left hand. Amazingly, though, it wasn't. When Gazzaniga asked why P.S. picked the shovel, he was, of course, talking to LH. But LH did not know. What, then, would P.S., or LH, say? Would P.S. throw in the towel and admit that he did not have the slightest clue about his own behavior? Hardly! In fact, LH wasn't even remotely baffled and readily gave a reason for the action of his left hand. He reportedly said: "Oh, that's simple. The chicken claw goes with the chicken, and you need a shovel to clean out the chicken shed" (Gazzaniga, 1992, p. 124).

Regardless of how Gazzaniga manipulated the experiment, the results were always the same. Consider a sampler! Using headphones, Gazzaniga played a joke into the left ear so that only RH knew about it. But when asked why she laughed, it was LH that was called upon to answer. Far from admitting that it had no clue, she invented an explanation on the spot: "Oh, . . . you guys are really something!" or "you guys come up and test us every month. What a way to make a living." In another example, RH was told through the headset to stand up and walk out. When she complied, Gazzaniga inquired where she was going. Again, the answer came without hesitation: "I'm going . . . to get a Coke."

From such data, Gazzaniga hypothesized that LH has a module that formulates, as he said, "beliefs about why events occur" (ibid., p. 132). Gazzaniga called it the **interpreter** for the simple reason that LH has no direct knowledge of why the left side of the body does what it does; it must interpret its action. A module in LH that specializes in seeking explanations must be a highly evolved bit of cortical circuitry because, to do what it does, infer causal relationships, it has to occupy a position on top of a hierarchy of already highly evolved modules. For one thing, this type of computation requires access to long-term memory via a search engine that can retrieve task-relevant information at will. Further, to link causes to their effects, the interpreter requires the capacity to temporarily sustain a representation of both events in working memory. These considerations strongly support the hypothesis that the interpreter might be a prefrontal module.

From the way the interpreter weaves "the story line or narrative of our lives" (ibid., p. 130), there is good reason to assume that the process of drawing inferences is inherently structured. That is, we are predisposed to retrieve knowledge that is consistent with our worldview and past experience and tend to combine it, using rather straightforward, simple logic (e.g., A causes B), under the assumption that events in nature are indeed meaningfully connected in this way.

Consider, for instance, this eye-opening experiment demonstrating brilliantly the difficulty the interpreter has in dealing with randomness and probability. Gazzaniga and his co-workers (Wolford et al., 2000) showed that the interpreter might be so obsessed with identifying causal relationships and meaningfulness that it keeps looking for them even if there are none. In this study, subjects are given a simple task. Two dots are flashed on a screen, one at the top and one at the bottom. The top dot appears 80 percent of the time while the bottom one comes into view 20 percent of the time, but – and that's the key – in a random sequence. Subjects are asked to predict where the next dot is going to appear and quickly notice that the top one occurs more often. They start desperately trying to discover a logical pattern and deeply believe not only that there is a meaningful sequence governing this "game" but also that they can find it. This conviction results in a 68 percent hit rate when simply choosing the top dot would maximize their performance at 80 percent. You may not think this is a big deal if it weren't for two facts. First, in an adapted fashion, the same experiment poses no problem to the average lab rat. Even mice come in at an 80 percent hit rate within the hour. Second, the experiment also does not overstretch the intelligence of RH. When the experiment is repeated with split-brain patients, RH, dim as it supposedly is, has no problem responding optimally. LH, however, does the 68 percent thing, probably while scratching his head, with the right hand, of course.

In these experimental setups we can see the misattribution taking place because we control the feed into RH. But in normal brains the interpreter also does not have direct access to the backroom processing of the brain. We are only aware of the end product, the resulting thought or emotion, but not what produces the product. So here, too, the interpreter must shoot from the hip when trying to explain behavior. You could say the interpreter is the brain's press agent. In daily life, we constantly confabulate plausible reasons for what we think and do while being oblivious to the fact that these are all inferences. Introspective misadventures inevitably result. Many of our actions are caused by accidental associations or random mental noise rather than meaningful antecedents, but the interpreter is not inclined to consider such possibilities in its ad hoc logical reasoning. As Gazzaniga (ibid., p., 126) notes, the patient never said: "Well, I chose this because I have a split brain, and the information went to the right, nonverbal hemisphere." The lesson learned from split-brain patients is yet another salvo against the blind trust we often place in introspection and intuition. Consider, for instance, how we put a rational structure on the bizarre contents of our dreams after waking up. The interpreter, suddenly back "on-line," and in charge with 20/20 hindsight, brings meaning to the random brainstem-generated images while it never even so much as considers the possibility that they might be the result of arbitrary neural firing (see Chapter 12).

What do split-brain patients tell us about consciousness? At first, one is tempted, almost compelled even, to espouse the position that split-brain patients have their self split in two; two conscious people in the same head. Along with dissociative identity disorder, fugues, or cases of depersonalization, split-brain patients, then, represent further evidence that selves are countable entities and the normal number of them per brain is exactly one. To have two, something must have gone wrong, as in the aforementioned cases. This is the view taken by Sperry (1969). He believes that a callosotomy creates two selves, each complete with its own coherent stream of thought. Given the evidence, he is prepared to

---

Box 6.1   HOT models

Thoughts, feelings, and perceptions are mental representations that occur in one of two states, conscious and unconscious. The million-dollar question is, of course, this: What's the magical difference? According to the **higher-order thought**, or HOT, theory of consciousness, held most notably by the philosopher David Rosenthal (1993, 2004), the answer is simple. A conscious state is one in which the individual is aware of being in that state; that is, for a mental state to be conscious, it has to be the object of a higher-order thought directed at it. Thus, we are conscious of a thought or feeling when we have a thought about that thought or feeling. Conversely, a mental state is unconscious when we do not have a HOT about it. HOT theories presuppose that the second-order representation is a thought, not a perception. There are also higher-order perception, or HOP, theories, in which we perceive the first-order mental states.

As an example, consider being hungry. You can be entirely unconscious of having this mental state until you direct a thought at it, at which point you become cognizant of your desire to eat. Another way of saying this is that a thought or feeling becomes conscious when we think about it. It is this "doubling up" of knowledge that defines consciousness; knowledge itself becomes the item of a representation.

This proposed explanation does not require that the HOT itself be conscious. When the mental state of hunger is accompanied by a HOT, we are conscious of being hungry but no more. It does not mean that we are also conscious of the fact that we are aware of being hungry. This would require a second HOT, a HOT about the HOT. Rosenthal thinks, however, that this is exactly what happens when we engage in introspection. What we in fact do in our exploratory voyages through mental hyperspace is to direct thoughts at our own mental states. So, if HOTs give rise to consciousness, then HOTs about HOTs give rise to self-consciousness. The position that HOTs themselves are not conscious is important for stopping the looming infinite regress. If HOTs were necessarily conscious, we'd have homunculi ad infinitum.

One commonly raised objection to HOT theories is that they demote animals to be unconscious automata. Making HOTs is presumably the ability of complex brains. Animals that lack the resources to represent their own knowledge in a higher-order format must therefore lack consciousness, at least the self-reflexive kind. While some HOT theorists reject this conclusion (Gennaro, 1996), others accept it as a necessary corollary (Carruthers, 2000). Equally, and more disturbingly, the argument can be made that HOT theories plunge infants and people with mental retardation into zombihood. Another objection is that HOT theories have trouble explaining mental states, such as meditation and other ASC, whose defining characteristic is the very absence of HOTs; after all, a meditator is hardly unconscious. Finally, one concern that is often mooted against HOT theories is that they fail to account for the subjective quality of experience. As always, this objection hinges on the concept of consciousness as inherently subjective. Rosenthal defends his theory against this criticism by suggesting that a HOT is a meta-representation and, as such, contains information about the first-order representation, including the subjective feel of qualia.

On the plus side, Rosenthal (2004) argues that HOT theories are well substantiated by reaction time data, as it takes time to build a HOT. He also points out that they explain well phenomena of consciousness, such as blindsight or the data from Libet's famous free-will experiment, both of which we shall discuss later in this book. Another attractive feature is that HOT theories require no place, no threshold, and no theater; they simply propose a mechanism that makes mental representations about mental representations. There is some empirical evidence that suggests that HOTs occurring by themselves are not enough for consciousness. The lower-order representation on which the HOT is based must also be active at the same time (Pascual-Leone & Walsh, 2001).

grant LH a dominant status but insists that RH sustains a distinctly human kind of consciousness and so is not an unconscious zombie system. As we will discuss in Chapter 10, this position is an example of an ego theory, the idea that the self is a stable and persistent entity. Ego theories can be contrasted with bundle theories, the idea that there is no such thing as a self that unifies experience, an entity that has experiences; rather, the self *is* the stream of mental activities. In consequence, counting the number of selves in a split-brain patient is futile. As Parfit (1987) maintains, the number of selves in a brain, irrespective of the brain's integrity, is exactly none. Perhaps influenced by his mentor, Gazzaniga initially took Sperry's position but quickly found himself forced to reconsider. It was his discovery of the interpreter that changed his mind. RH, he thinks, is not capable of full consciousness and thus unable to compute a self-system. There is no stream of consciousness in RH. This view falls in line with the canonical position that verbalizability is a defining criterion of conscious information. Language, then, is an important feature of full-fledged consciousness, a position that has strong implications for animal minds.

Evolutionary perspectives

Brain evolution

Brains do not fossilize. Nor, as a matter of consequence, do mental processes. How, then, are we to reconstruct the evolution of complex brains and their package of cognitive talents, including consciousness? Clearly, pursuing questions of consciousness from an evolutionary perspective provides more than its fair share of challenges. The evidence, as it so happens in evolutionary biology, is indirect: skull size, footprints, ancient tools, paraphernalia of burial sites, cave paintings, and so on. Despite these obstacles, the study of human behavior by way of our evolutionary past has recently spawned a new discipline, **evolutionary psychology**, which is fast becoming a major force in psychology.

Leaving aside for the moment the position that consciousness is not a property of brains or somehow did not evolve like other mental abilities, there are several instructive ways in which we can shed light on the **evolution of consciousness**. One is **comparative anatomy**. Given our current knowledge of the NCC, we can examine the extent to which we share with other animals the anatomical structures that support consciousness. Another is **comparative psychology**. Here we can examine the extent to which we share with other animals the cognitive functions that form the basis of consciousness, such as language, ToM, and the ability to empathize or deceive. Combining both lines of research not only holds clues as to "when" and "why" subjective experience evolved but also helps to address the puzzle of animal consciousness itself. Recall that the brain is a loose federation of neural systems, a patchwork of add-ons, with each previous version only fit to handle the evolutionary pressures of its time. Brain evolution, then, is a series of steps toward greater cognitive flexibility or, more pointedly, intelligence (not in a strict teleological sense, however, as the modern understanding of the evolution by natural selection grants no direction to evolution). From the onset, this makes all but certain that the appearance of consciousness was a gradual process. We have good reason to reject the notion of consciousness as an all-or-none phenomenon. Evidently, the question is not whether or not animals are conscious or which animal has it and which one does not. Nor is there any use in asking at which exact point in the evolutionary history brain complexity crossed some magical threshold to support conscious processing. We are obviously dealing with a continuum here, not a dichotomy.

The standard model of brain evolution was devised by the neuroscientist Paul MacLean (1949). Although this **triune brain theory** has undergone substantial revisions since its first formulation more than half a century ago, it remains, in its overall structure, a useful, if rough, guide to understanding the rise of complex brains. The central thesis is that the human brain consists of three brains, one stacked on top of another, in a hierarchy with the brainstem at the bottom and the cerebral cortex representing the latest in neural innovation. MacLean's anatomical divisions are functional in nature. Accordingly, the most basic piece of hardware, the brainstem, is responsible for elementary behaviors, such as walking, orientation reflexes, and foraging. An alligator is a prototypical, present-day example of an animal equipped with this, in MacLean language, reptilian brain. It's a basic input/output device with little intermediate computation to allow for flexibility. More sophisticated circuitry evolved atop the reptilian brain to remedy this situation. This limbic brain added the advantage of basic learning and memory processes, including emotional behaviors. Finally, a third brain, represented by the neocortex, evolved, particularly in mammals. This neomammalian brain implemented higher cognitive functions, providing even more flexibility. To assert its dominance, this new brain inhibited the two more primitive brains on which it was built. Reflexes and "animalistic" emotions then were simply failures to control the functions of these more ancient brains. In this way, MacLean reconciled the triune brain theory with the long philosophical tradition – started by the Greeks – that the hallmark of humanity is our ability to think rationally. As we shall see in later chapters, this view has disappeared in the neurosciences.

So how far, then, does consciousness reach down the tree of life? Adopting the putative position that mental functions, including conscious processes, are closely tied to brain complexity, it would be reasonable to look for clues in brain size. But **absolute brain size** turns out to be a poor indicator of biological intelligence. If it were so, cows, for instance, would be smarter than monkeys. Another possible index might be the **brain-to-body ratio**, but this, too, does not give an accurate reading. Besides, it forces one to endorse the absurd corollary that a diet would make a person smarter. The best index – which in any case must be the one in which we Homo sapiens are featured on the top spot – seems to be the ratio of the size of the cerebral cortex to the rest of the brain. Still better than the **cortex-to-brain ratio** is the relative size of the prefrontal cortex. Deacon (1990) estimated that the human PFC is about 200 percent larger in size compared to that of other primates, while other cortical regions do not show such a large disproportionate increase.

This comparative analysis allows one to make some tentative observations. Theorists often divide consciousness into two types, a core or primary kind of consciousness and an extended or secondary type. Baars (2005) points out that primary consciousness depends on brain structures – brainstem, thalamus, etc. – that are phylogenetically ancient. It is likely, therefore, that many animals possess a substantial amount of this type of consciousness. As for extended consciousness, several theorists have emphasized the importance of the thalamocortical system. Given that this structure, too, is well developed in many mammals, especially in the great apes, there is a tendency to credit them with at least some form of subjective experience. The question, then, is rather over how much lucidity is present in the minds of other animals. For a large part of that answer we must turn to studies in comparative psychology. By testing animals for higher cognitive functions we can estimate the level of higher-order understanding they have of the environment. Before we do this, however, we summarize the proposals that have been put forward to explain why consciousness might have evolved.

The mind's big bang

We cannot even hope here to begin to cover the story of human evolution, but recalling a few key milestones may facilitate the discussion that follows. Human evolution is marked by five great transitions. About 6 million years ago our **hominin** ancestors split from the chimpanzee line (Corballis, 1999) and started walking, on two legs, onto the open savannah. More than 4 million years ago, they were making stone tools and began to consume a diet heavy in meat, which caused their brain size to increase. By 1.5 million years ago, in the third transition, they were making hand axes and the technological record became denser. About half a million years ago, they mastered the use of fire. In the final transition, 50,000 years ago, they left the first signs of truly modern minds. It is this last transition, the mind's big bang, which interests us the most.

At two million years ago, the first hominins started to leave Africa. As hunters and gatherers, **Homo neanderthalensis** migrated to Europe and **Homo erectus** settled across Asia. However, the weight of the archeological and genetic evidence suggests that none of these early hominins evolved into us. They all became extinct. Modern humans, **Homo sapiens**, appeared in Africa around 60,000 years ago. They had evolved a revolutionary way of life and behaved in truly modern ways. In a second wave of migration, these Homo sapiens also left Africa spreading, by about 35,000 years ago, to Southeast Asia and Western Europe. Eventually, they outcompeted the other hominin species already living there so that today Homo sapiens is the only species of hominins left today. It should be noted that not everyone adopts this "**out-of-Africa**" model of human evolution. Other scholars maintain that Neanderthals and Homo erectus evolved independently into Homo sapiens, a model known as **multiregionalism**. Genetic evidence, however, seems to favor the out-of-Africa hypothesis, suggesting

Figure 6.3

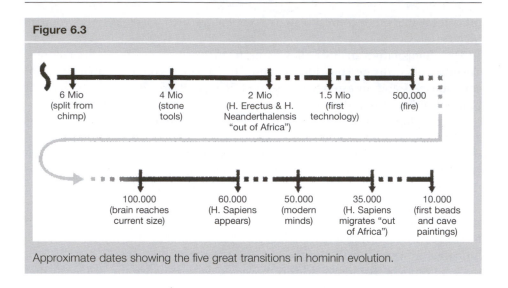

Approximate dates showing the five great transitions in hominin evolution.

further the far more radical position that we might all have descended from only a small group of individuals, perhaps no more than a few thousand.

Be that as it may, the archeological record of this period, the upper Paleolithic, holds a wealth of information showing that modern humans behaved in ways no other hominin species had ever behaved before. Clearly, they had more on their minds than mere survival. They made a large variety of beads and used them as ornaments, suggesting that, for the first time, they felt the need to say something about themselves using artifacts. The first signs of culture appeared in the form of material expression of social identity and social relationship. This period also marked the beginning of symbolic life, clearly seen in the way early modern humans buried their dead or by the things they painted on cave walls.

Evolution moves at a glacial pace. But this revolution occurred very rapidly. Some 100,000 years ago, early hominins probably did not act very differently from the way chimps act today. A mere 50,000 years later or so they had burst, from seemingly nowhere, into a new realm of sophistication. This explosion begs the question: How did this change come about? Some paleontologists think that a brain change gave birth to this radically new mind. It is unlikely, however, that this change was one of mere size, as our brain had reached its current size by about 100,000 years ago, before the mind's big bang. Thus, some argue that the answer is to be found in the wiring of the brain. Irrespective of this, the essential question is left unresolved. What drove this neurological change? What selection pressures in the environment made our ancestors truly human, forced them to develop language, a battery of cognitive skills, and complex social lives? What sort of advantage did consciousness confer upon us?

In the last few decades, several exciting new answers to these questions have been proposed. We shall first highlight two less prominent ones before we focus, in the next section, on the theory that currently seems to have the most support among biologists and psychologists. The first idea is a consequence of neural Darwinism. It proposes that the function of consciousness is to settle competition among neural assemblies. As bigger brains developed and regions in the brain became ever more specialized, the need for integration and coherence became ever more pressing. So the brain evolved a single system, capable of temporarily buffering multiple representations so that the organism can examine them before it acts. According to this view, the purpose of consciousness is not so much to unify perception but to unify action. A complex organism – composed of many subunits each doing a different thing – must still have singleness of action if its motion is to be purposeful (Cotterill, 1995).

The second idea is offered here primarily for completeness sake. Though few philosophers and scientists entertain the idea seriously, it must be acknowledged that inner experience might be a *by*product of evolution, an inconsequential free-bie that hitched a ride on the back of other mental abilities that did have an adaptive function. Note that this possibility does not violate the principles of evolution. The paleontologist Stephen Jay Gould (1997) dubbed the idea that everything must have evolved for a reason "**pan adaptationism.**" He points out that there are plenty of examples of nonadaptive traits – exaptation, as he calls them – that have evolved on the side. These bonus traits, once there, may then have either turned out to be valuable in some other context or insufficient selection pressure failed to eliminate them. If this is the case with consciousness, experience would be a mere spandrel of other processes, a quirky sidekick of evolution. Note also that this position is different from epiphenomenalism, in which consciousness is said to have no function at all, irrespective of whether or not it evolved as a footnote. As for philosophers holding onto the concept of zombies, the evolutionary perspective presents a particularly messy situation. Recall that a zombie is behaviorally indistinguishable from a sentient being. But how, then, could the process of evolution, working through natural selection, favor one over the other? How could a mutation that inches an individual toward the conscious processing of information influence reproductive success if that mutation does not make a behavioral difference? The problem of zombie evolution underscores the difficulty with the concept of zombies and the distinction between easy and hard problems of consciousness.

Box 6.2   Memes

Biological evolution has been the primary engine of change. By around 50,000 years ago, it had even created human culture. An explosion of new ideas and technologies followed that would radically transform our lifestyle. This cultural outburst proved so potent that it turned the tables and soon altered the course of genetic evolution. To illustrate this, one merely has to take account of the last 4,000 years. In an evolutionary flash, we went from cave dwellers to our high-tech world of skyscrapers, telecommunications, and genetic engineering. Biological evolution, operating at a glacial pace manifold slower than this, had little, if anything, to do with this. A new kind of evolutionary process, **cultural evolution**, has taken over as the primary engine of change. By way of books, songs, or movies, humans can transmit and accumulate information nongenetically. In other words, culture itself evolves.

Box 6.2 *continued*

As the zoologist Richard Dawkins (1989) has pointed out, the principles of evolution say nothing specific about genes, life, or natural selection. Instead, evolution is a process that takes place whenever three conditions are met: (1) **replication**: there must exist a unit capable of making copies of itself; (2) **variation**, which occurs when error creeps in the copying mechanism; and (3) **selection**, which determines the differential fitness of the variant copies. Whenever a replicator makes copies that vary and a selection process affects their differential survival, you must get, inevitably, evolution. Evolution, then, is a general algorithm for change (Dennett, 1995), which implies that other kinds of evolutionary processes – not based on genetic mutation and natural selection – could exist, just so long as there is something, anything, that replicates with variation and selection. This is what Dawkins (1989) calls **universal Darwinism**.

Dawkins goes on to suggest that the theory of evolution – first generate, then test – applies to culture. Our thoughts, he notes, have surprisingly similar gene-like properties. They can be seen as virus-like chunks of information that are copied in a variation-selection process, as they are passed from person to person. Dawkins dubbed these units of cultural replication "**memes**," a word derived from "mimeme" meaning "that which is imitated," and shorted to meme to link it phonetically to gene. If units of culture replicate themselves in the same way as DNA molecules replicate themselves, then we are dealing with memetic evolution and the differential survival of memes. Memes are any unit of cultural transmission – images, jokes, ideas, technologies, songs, skills, stories, and so on. Just as the fitness of genes is determined by their success, so the fitness of memes is determined by how well they multiply and spread through a culture. For that, memes do not have to be superior in any intellectual way; all they need to flourish is to be superior at getting themselves copied. Consider, for instance, the magnificently useless song from the Village People, "YMCA." By definition, this meme is as successful as the meme of gravity. Furthermore, a "memeplex" (Blackmore, 1999) forms whenever memes can propagate themselves better as part of a group. Excellent examples are religions, scientific theories, or the notion of democracy.

Susan Blackmore (1999) has taken the meme meme further and suggests that all of culture is the product of the brain infested by memes. She envisions us as "meme machines" in which ideas renew themselves only to be sent out again. Accordingly, language has evolved for the sake of memes, not genes. Likewise, we may think we invented the internet but another way of looking at it is that the internet was the doing of memes; simply to create a more efficient copying mechanism for themselves. The idea of memes as replicating entities that thrive in brains is a new way of looking at culture and the direction in which culture evolves, but taking the meme's-eye view, as Dawkins and Blackmore do, forces us to ask the question of who is in charge. According to Dennett (1991, p. 210), it isn't us as "human consciousness is itself a huge complex of memes."

Social intelligence

If consciousness is a natural product of the physical brain, like all other biological phenomena, it must have evolved over time. But why? What advantage did it bestow upon us? The answer to what might have triggered the evolution of consciousness may be surprising. The conventional view has it that consciousness boosted our ability for rational thought and strategic planning, making us smarter hunters and more creative problem solvers. Recently, however, several independent lines of inquiry have started to converge on the possibility that the origins of the human mind may have their roots in the social life of our ancestors.

The great apes – chimps, bonobos, gorillas, orangutans – live in societies in which individuals are very sensitive to social relations. To attain and preserve their social standing, they must detect the interactions among other members of the group and be able to manipulate this knowledge to their own advantage. Like humans, they are keenly aware of the shifting realities of their social world. Unlike humans, however, they must impose their place in the pecking order by either force or the threat of force; that is, they must be physically present to control the behavior of others. They have no means by which to communicate symbolically and transcend space or time. For a chimp, out of sight is out of mind. What's more, they only understand the meaning of social relationships in terms of its threat to their own social rank, and not in some more global context.

Primatologists have based these conclusions on studies of animal consciousness that test for the existence of **ToM**. The acronym stands for the somewhat scary phrase "**theory of mind**," a concept coined by psychologist David Premack (Premack & Woodruff, 1978). Mental states such as desires, intentions, and beliefs are not visible, but since they make for excellent predictors of the behavior of others, it is highly beneficial to know about them. Humans appear to have evolved a specialized system or module to infer the mental states of others. According to Premack and Woodruff (ibid., p. 515), the ability to represent the mental states of others "may properly be viewed as a theory because such states are not directly observable, and the system can be used to make predictions about the behavior of others." Another way of saying this is that ToM refers to the ability to understand that others have a mind, separate from one's own, and that this other mind represents thoughts and feelings that are different from one's own.

Three-year-old humans do not seem to yet have a ToM. A simple experiment, known as the **mountain range test**, illustrates that young children cannot understand that their own mind is an entity separate from the rest of the world and that their views are not everyone's views. They are shown a drawing depicting a little girl and a doll on either side of a mountain range and asked whether or not the little girl in the drawing can see the doll. Children under the age of three typically say yes, demonstrating that they operate under the premise: "if I can see it, so can everyone else." They are not yet able to see the world from another person's perspective. By age 4, this task presents little trouble for them.

By 4 years of age, children discover a profound truth about the world. Beliefs are mental states that represent, but are not the same as, the real world. This distinction between mind and world is perhaps seen most clearly when the mind misrepresents reality. The ability to understand the notion of a **false belief** is the standard test for theory-of-mind capabilities. Consider this series of ingenious studies by Daniel Povinelli (Povinelli & de Bois, 1992; Povinelli & Eddy, 1996). Under the child's watchful eyes, one experimenter, the guesser, leaves the room while another, the knower, hides some food under one of several cups. The guesser then returns and both experimenters point to different cups. Needless to say, the correct response is to pick the cup identified by the knower. This response would indicate that the child understands that seeing leads to a privileged state of knowledge. In other words, the child must infer the existence of a mental state in another person's mind, namely the state of knowing. Four-year-olds take the "advice" of the knower right away while 3-year-olds choose randomly. Importantly, chimps also choose randomly on the first few trials. Only with a little practice do they come to pick the cup the knower points to. The fact that perfect performance develops over trials is an indication that they are using an alternative strategy (e.g., pick the person who stayed in the room) rather than base their selection on an inference about the knower's mental state. Chimps do not seem to understand the perceptual basis for knowledge, that is, the link between seeing and knowing. If they do not understand how knowledge arises in the first place, how much more difficult, then, to understand the notion of a false belief. Consider, for instance, a chimp catching how another sees an event that it knows is atypical. Does this chimp understand that the other must have a distorted view of reality as a result of it? Would this chimp prevent the other from making a mistake based on the fact that it knows that the other holds a false belief? Povinelli's data suggest that this is rather unlikely. The existence of a ToM in humans is readily demonstrated in a children's play when the villain plans to harm the hero and the children in the audience try to warn the hero about it. The plot would be lost on the average chimp.

A second study explores the link between seeing and knowing further. A chimp is trained to ask for food from one of two experimenters. One of them is blind-folded and so cannot see the chimp while the other has her mouth covered with an identical piece of cloth. Obviously, the chimp would do well to ask the seeing person for the food, but that is not what it does. It responds randomly, indicating that it has no clue that the eyes are for seeing. This is even the case when one experimenter wears a bucket over their head. In comparison, a human can solve this task before the age of 3 (Povinelli & Eddy, 1996). Clearly, the subjective experience of chimps is quite different from that of humans.

Another clever way to tease out the extent to which animals might consciously represent the world is to study their ability to recognize themselves in the mirror. The mirror test is a simple way to check for the presence of a self-concept. It was first systematically used by the psychologist Gordon Gallup (1970), who reported that chimps initially treated their reflection as just another chimp but soon learned to use the mirror in ways humans would. For instance, they picked spots off their back or examined parts of their body they could not see, such as the teeth. Bonobos and orangutans also pass the spot-test, albeit after some time, but gorillas, with the notable exception of the language-trained Koko, do not. By contrast, human infants recognize themselves in the mirror by 18 months of age. Thus, apart from us, some great apes may indeed be capable of self-recognition.

In a complex society, the best way to outcompete others, get better access to resources and mates, is to understand what they are likely up to next. For any input, humans can generate a nearly infinite number of outputs. While this flex-ibility is the basis for our unrivaled adaptability, it also renders our behavior difficult to predict. The ToM module evolved to counteract this problem, to filter out infinity, as it were. Like the turn signal of a car, it indicates the intention of others. This specialized module has probably arisen from the ability to represent one's own mental states. In other words, mind reading emerged from introspection and the capacity to attribute one's own actions to mental representations (Humphrey, 1978). Thus, by getting a feeling of what we would do next in a given situation, we can get into the mind of others and, being one step ahead, outsmart them.

According to the evolutionary psychologist Nicholas Humphrey (1978, 2002), consciousness arose as follows. Social competence requires that brains evolve the capacity to monitor their own internal states. Understanding one's own intentions made it possible, by extrapolation, to predict the behavior of others. Individuals with a knack for this had a distinct competitive advantage and thrived. Social complexity, then, begot greater social intelligence, which triggered an even greater social complexity in an escalating upward spiral that left us with full-fledged conscious experience. It was the complex social environment of Homo sapiens, Humphrey argues, that provided the evolutionary pressures to bring about the emergence of consciousness. Consciousness, then, developed as a tool to promote social standing.

It is generally agreed that language played a key role in fueling this positive feedback loop. Indeed, some people, Daniel Dennett most prominent among them, believe that language was *the* most important component triggering the extraordinary explosion of human creativity. As he wrote: "Perhaps the kind of mind you get when you add language to it is so different from the kind of mind you can have without language that calling them both minds is a mistake" (1996b, p. 17). We do not know when precisely human language evolved in its modern form but all indications point to a date about 50,000 years ago, around the time of the mind's big bang. The primatologist Robin Dunbar (1996) believes that the primary purpose of language was not, as commonly thought, to transmit technical information – location of food, how to make a spear, and so on – but to regulate social relationships. In short, to gossip. Dunbar goes on to argue that the function of language is to hold big groups together. By about 100,000 years ago, group size reached 150 individuals. Primates typically maintain social bonds through grooming, which works well for the smaller groups in which they live. But grooming takes a lot of time and using it as a social currency to maintain social cohesion is impractical in groups with 150 members. Dunbar (1992) showed that group size is the single best predictor of neocortical volume; that is, primates living in larger groups had bigger cortices. This data corroborates the theory that big brains are the result of a complex social environment and that language was a critical factor in permitting these larger, more complex societies to form. Language eliminated the biggest problem of monkey society; it allowed for displacement, the symbolic representation of the past, present, and future and in a linguistic environment, the ones most gifted at language would be the ones that prospered.

Summary

Cognitive neuroscience has made some of the most important contributions to the study of consciousness. One model based on this perspective, the global work-space theory, has emerged as the industry standard. The principal idea is that a massive, parallel processing system composed of distributed and highly special-ized processors, such as a brain, requires, for the sake of unity, a central informa-tion exchange that makes accessible the message of individual modules to the rest of the system. Selection to this global neuronal workspace is a competitive, reso-nance phenomenon. Thus, according to GWT, consciousness is the result of the wide broadcasting of information that renders the content of the global work-space the information that we are conscious of at any time.

Split-brain research is another cognitive neuroscience approach that has thrown much light on consciousness. Split-brain patients are perfect subjects to study the laterality of cognitive functions. Research on this population has shown that information is only fully conscious if it reaches the language-dominant LH. What's more, Michael Gazzaniga discovered that LH has an interpreter module, a specialized module that formulates, as he says, "beliefs about why events occur." Thus, the presentation of information to RH may cause behavior to which LH has no direct access. But instead of being dumbfounded, LH provides a ready-to-go explanation, which further suggests that the invention of intentions is a routine event even for healthy people, as we never really have direct access to the causes of our behaviors.

The evolutionary perspective tries to shed light on the whys and hows of consciousness. It is generally agreed that consciousness, like all biological phenomena, evolved over time. This provides the rationale for evolutionary psychology, using comparative neuroanatomy combined with a comparative approach to the study of higher mental functions, such as self-recognition, theory of mind, or language, to reconstruct the origins of consciousness and the extent to which we share this extraordinary capacity with other animals. The evidence to date most strongly offers support for the notion that consciousness is a continuum. While primary consciousness is likely to be a feature of other animals with complex brains, higher-order consciousness seems to be unique to humans. Clearly, when it comes to consciousness, we are not just slightly better chimps.

As for why consciousness evolved, the predominant view is that consciousness is an adaptation to the social environment of early hominins. About 50,000 years ago, social groups grew complex enough that further social intelligence could only come from the explicit knowledge of one's own mental states. This develop-ment, many think, is also what necessitated the evolution of language. As the abil-ity to introspect increased the social intelligence of early Homo sapiens, it transformed society into even more complexity, which, in a self-sustaining process, required ever more explicit representation of information.

Suggested reading

Baars, B. (1997). *In the Theater of Consciousness: The Workspace of the Mind.* New York: Oxford University Press.

Dawkins, R. (1989). *The Selfish Gene.* Oxford: Oxford University Press.

Dunbar, R. I. M. (1996). *Grooming, Gossip, and the Evolution of Language.* Cambridge, MA: Harvard University Press.

Gazzaniga, M. S. (1992). *Nature's Mind.* New York: Basic Books.

Humphrey, N. (2002). *The Mind Made Flesh: Frontiers of Psychology and Evolution.* Oxford: Oxford University Press.

PART III

The content of consciousness

7 Perception

The visual system

Basic concepts in vision

This chapter is divided into three major sections. The first considers visual awareness because vision is the best-known perceptual system and the target of several empirical approaches to the study of consciousness. In tracing information through the visual sense, we explore how this system gives rise to normal and abnormal visual experience. The second describes the sense of pain, including phenomena such as phantom limb pain and anesthesia, which bear directly on the study of consciousness. Finally, the third explores broader issues concerning perceptual awareness, specifically Libet's famous half-second delay and the fascinating topic of subliminal perception.

A cardinal rule in psychology is that perception is not physics. We do not see the world in the same way a camera does. A camera takes a snapshot that faithfully reproduces objective reality – pixel by pixel. In contrast, the visual system is analytical. That is, it first dissects the world into its components, processes these elements in several different subsystems, and then reassembles the lot into a coherent picture. Because this reconstruction process is guided by a variety of schemas, the resulting mental representation is not a faithful reproduction at all but a personalized interpretation of the world. For instance, the reality of illusions, as it were, can only be understood in the context of this reconstruction. This is counterintuitive, to say the least, because we do not perceive the world deconstructed into umpteen million bits and pieces, but as a unified whole. The insight that visual processing is analytical in nature is perhaps the single most important concept in visual science. It is also the reason why vision demands such a prominent role in the study of consciousness.

Visual consciousness is often debated without the necessary background in the nuts and bolts of the visual system. Some details are critical, however, not only to understand the phenomena themselves but also to address their implications on the study of consciousness. So, before we get into the thick of things, let's trace how information is processed in the visual sense. In the retina light strikes first an inner, light-sensitive photoreceptor cell layer containing the rods and cones. It is then relayed by a bipolar cell layer to a ganglion cell layer. Axons of retinal ganglion cells form the optic nerve that leaves the back of the eye at the optic disc. This region contains no **photoreceptors**, creating the well-known **blind spot**. So why don't we experience a blank dot in the visual field? This is partly due to the fact that we are binocular. But even with one eye closed we do not perceive a hole in the world. The reason for this is explored later in the chapter.

About 90 percent of optic nerve fibers travel to the **lateral geniculate nucleus** (LGN) of the thalamus in a well-organized manner that preserves the topographical map of retina. The other 10 percent project to the pulvinar, also a thalamic nuclei, then on to the **superior colliculus**. This pathway is responsible for the control of eye movements and plays a critical role in blindsight, a phenomenon we will also return to later in this chapter. The projection area of the LGN is the **primary visual cortex**, located in the occipital cortex. This region is also known by several synonymous terms – striate cortex, area 17 – but today most people refer to it as **V1**. The way neurons in V1 process visual information was discovered in a monumental single-cell mapping expedition begun in the 1960s by two Harvard physiologists, David Hubel and Torsten Wiesel (1977, 1979), who received the Nobel Prize for this work in 1981. They showed that cortical neurons do not respond to dots of light but to features, such as a line in a particular orientation. Yet others responded best to movement, spatial frequency, texture, retinal disparity, or color. Hubel and Wiesel dubbed them **feature detectors**. V1 is organized in columns or modules, the basic functional unit of the cortex. Each of these modules contains 150,000 neurons and is devoted to the analysis of all features in a small portion of visual space. A total of 2,500 modules combine to map the entire visual field, a cortical retina, if you will. Hubel and Wiesel called these columns **hypercolumns** and a repetitive matrix of them extracts and segregates all visual information from the field of vision. At this stage, a scene is in a million bits and pieces and must now be put back together, a task performed by the extrastriate cortex.

The overarching theme in **visual association cortices** is *integration* and *convergence*. There are more than thirty of these extrastriate areas – denoted V2, V3, V4, V5, etc. – each making a distinctive contribution. The reason for this high number of distinct visual processing areas is that vision is analytical. The visual scene in V1 is like a jigsaw puzzle fresh out of the box, a hodgepodge of lines, edges, and a host of other features. They must now be rebuilt into a coherent picture. Because this is an extraordinary feat of biological computing, each extrastriate area can only analyze one type of information. Some areas may deal with color while others have feature detectors specialized for motion. To that end, the organization of **extrastriate cortex** is hierarchical, with successive cortical areas performing ever higher perceptual functions. An important aspect of this is convergence. Throughout the visual pathway, information is combined so that ever larger and more complex features can be detected.

From V1, information is processed along two routes that weave themselves through the extrastriate cortex. The dorsal stream passes through several areas, including V5 (known also as MT), and terminates in regions of the **posterior parietal cortex**. The ventral stream flows through V3 and V4 and has its end points in the **inferior temporal cortex**. This wiring led to the notion that each stream handles a distinct aspect of vision, the so-called what and where (or how) systems (Zeki, 1993). The **dorsal stream** (where or how) specializes in special perception and extracts information about movement and location. The **ventral stream** (what) deals with object recognition and decodes form and shape (Ungerleider & Mishkin, 1982).

Form perception in the inferior temporal cortex is highly specialized. Output from visual cortices converges on inferotemporal neurons that respond to very complex stimuli, such as hands or faces. But this specificity has limits. There exists no place or region where the whole picture comes together. The hypothesis of a "pontifical neuron," to use James's (1890) memorable phrase, selective for, say, your grandmother has been replaced by the notion of **ensemble coding**. A final percept still requires the simultaneous activation of an army of feature detectors, each contributing specific features to the process. Recognition, then, is due to the collective activity of higher-order neurons firing in parallel. Ensemble coding also appears to be the modus operandi for how information from different senses is integrated. Again, no central place exists where everything comes together. Representations of sight, sound, or smell remain distributed in their respective, specialized regions but evidence suggests that they can be brought online at the same time.

What we know about the process of vision comes as much from empirical work as it does from the careful examination of people with brain damage. Naturally, lesions anywhere along the primary visual pathway, from the retina to V1, result in blindness. Damage to association areas, however, causes very selective feature detection deficits. For instance, **agnosia** is a peculiar deficit that results from lesion to the inferotemporal cortex, the end station of the ventral stream. Agnosia is a failure of object recognition. Patients may look at an object but do not recognize what it is they are looking at. This is not the

Figure 7.1

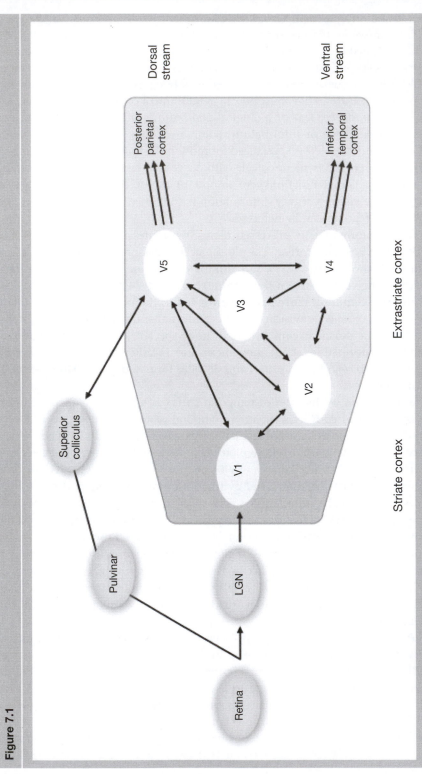

A simplified schematic wiring diagram of the interconnections in the extrastriate cortex. The dorsal stream is the "where" system and terminates in the posterior parietal cortex. The ventral stream corresponds to the "what" system and terminates in the inferior temporal cortex.

same as blindness; their perception of the object is mostly normal and they are often able to accurately describe its features. Agnosia is also not a memory problem. If information about the object enters via a different sensory system, say, the smell of soap or the ringing of the phone, they can identify it immediately. They often know what to do with the object or can tell which of two objects is heavier or colder, which makes agnosia a higher-level perceptual deficit that is best described in terms of integrating parts to a whole (Warrington, 1985). This can get erringly specific as, for instance, in cases where the agnosia is stronger for living than nonliving things (Warrington & Shallice, 1984). A special type of this is **prosopagnosia**, the inability to recognize faces. Prosopagnosiacs have often normal vision but cannot identify faces, not even when looking at a picture of their own. Again, they may describe facial features in detail but fail to integrate them into a whole face. Because this disorder may occur independent of other agnosias, some say that we might have a separate neural system for faces, a hypothesis that makes sense from an evolutionary perspective (Kanwisher, 2000).

Deficits also arise when the dorsal stream is disrupted. One odd example is the selective loss of motion perception. In monkeys, V5, located in the lateral occipital lobe, contains neurons that respond best to moving objects. Lesions, however, do not normally compromise motion perception because the superior colliculus can partly compensate for the loss. But what if this secondary system is also damaged? This seems to be the case for one elderly woman living in Munich, Germany, known as L.M. in the literature (Zihl et al., 1983). She has selective bilateral lesions in the middle temporal gyrus and V5 and cannot perceive any motion at all, a condition termed akinetopsia. She sees cars or people but she cannot see them moving. This is difficult to imagine but she describes her visual world as successive still pictures or freeze frames with large gaps in them. She is the only reported case of this kind, a truly unique phenomenological subtraction. The important conclusion for the content of consciousness is that these deficits do not alter the overall capacity for consciousness. What they do is eliminate a particular type of information from phenomenology.

Blindsight and neglect

The analytical nature of the visual system makes it the ideal target for what many see as the key question in consciousness. Where or when in the perceptual process does awareness enter the picture? Several strange phenomena of vision have proven useful in the quest for an answer. The best known is probably **blindsight**, which was for a time one of the most debated topics in consciousness.

Because V1 is organized as a retinotopic map, circumscribed damage to it produces blindness in a corresponding spot in the visual field. In World War I, the Scottish neurologist George Riddoch (1917) first noticed that despite such scotomas some blind soldiers would still mysteriously dodge bullets. Lawrence Weiskrantz, professor emeritus of psychology at Oxford, who gave the phenomena its fittingly oxymoronic name, studied blindsight extensively. In 1974, he reported the case of patient D.B., who was blind in the left hemisfield. When Weiskrantz presented him with stimuli in the blind area, D.B. reported, as expected, no visual experience. He then asked D.B. to make guesses about the stimuli anyway. Both were surprised to see the guesses to be mostly correct (Weiskrantz, 1997). Blindsight abilities in patients with cortical blindness are now well documented. Patients can tell horizontal stripes from vertical ones, discriminate color, grasp objects, even open their hands to accommodate the size of the object, slip an envelope through a slit, and, in the case of the star blindsighter Graham Young, distinguish different facial expressions (Barbur et al., 1993; Heywood & Kentridge, 2000). It has even been demonstrated in monkeys (Stoerig & Cowey, 1997). What makes blindsight so interesting to consciousness is the fact that patients report seeing nothing at all.

At first pass, blindsight seems to be perception without consciousness. This would undermine functionalism because consciousness does not seem to be necessary to successfully navigate the world. Zombies could exist and qualia would be "real extras" in terms of knowledge and behavioral performance. But straightforward conclusions such as these are nearly always tricky. Blindsight has been abducted to support just about every conceivable position on the dualism–materialism divide. Consider one alternative explanation form Dennett (1991). He points out that blindsighters do not act normally at all; they must be prompted to act. They also receive no visual feedback for their action. But what would training do to their behavior and phenomenology? According to Dennett, a blindsighter would only need to learn to regularly prompt himself to act and use the feedback to gain confidence about his guesses. Over time, he would become a "superblindsighter," who not only performs on par with normal sighters but would also develop a feel for it. Superblindsight and normal vision are, then, one and the same.

In neuroscience the debate has centered on a possible mechanism for blindsight. Although the details are still somewhat contentious, a clearer picture has now emerged. Recall that 10 percent of optic nerve fibers project to the superior colliculus. Lesions to V1 leave intact this secondary, more ancient visual system, which probably first evolved in our ancestors to detect fast motion of high-contrast objects, like a bear running at you at full speed. It still performs this function today; dodging bullets remains the job of the superior colliculus whether you are a blindsighter or a normalsighter. This also explains why blindsight is so crude; as a forerunner of the cortical system, this mechanism does not possess the sophistication to compute detail. Current thinking is that blindsight is sight that bypasses V1 with a considerable loss of detail along with a corresponding loss of awareness.

In light of this anatomical picture, more pointed questions about consciousness can be asked. Why, exactly, is blindsight blind? Three possibilities have been explored. Is blindsight blind because subcortical structures such as the superior colliculus do not have the omph for consciousness? Or is it blind because primary sensory areas such as V1 are necessary for consciousness? Or, does consciousness depend perhaps on activity within the ventral stream of the extrastriate cortex?

All three candidates have pros and cons but most investigators of the phenomenon seem to lean toward one or a combination of them.

According to Milner and Goodale (1995), blindsight is not perception without consciousness but simply the activation of visuomotor responses that do not require full awareness to be performed successfully. Upon closer inspection, blindsight might not be so special after all. As you will see in the next chapters, the amygdala, indeed the entire implicit system, operates in much the same manner. Full higher-order representation is not necessary for many behaviors, which does not preclude the possibility that consciousness is an indispensable element for other behaviors – rather than some added fun factor. Consciousness, in this view, comes along with higher mental function. "Blindsight is paradoxical only if one regards vision as a unitary process" (ibid., p. 86). Consciousness occurs on a need-to-know basis and it does not need to know about everything or else everything would take too much time. What can be done without it will be done without it.

Another condition closely impinging on the study of consciousness is **neglect**. It occurs most often to stroke victims who suffered damage to the right inferior parietal cortex, leaving them without the ability to map spatial relationships on the left side of personal space (Bisiach, 1992). As a result, they ignore everything on the left side of the world. They fail to put on makeup or shave the left side of their face, do not acknowledge people approaching from the left side, and may even deny ownership of their left bodily extremities. Even their imagination is affected. Asked to describe a famous Milan cathedral from one end of the piazza, one patient omitted the left side; asked to describe it from the other end, he again neglected everything to the left of his mental image (Bisiach & Luzzatti, 1978). On an imaginary journey from England to Scotland, one woman ignored all towns to the west while on the way back down failed to mention the ones to the east (Marshall et al., 1993). The problem is that people with unilateral neglect do not form any mental representations of spatial relationships in that part of space. So it is not that they cannot see the left hemisfield – as if blind – but rather that they do not know that there is anything to be seen. In the same way we do not know that there is information to be had in the infrared, they no longer attend to information on the left because they no longer encode it. As in blindsight, this does not impede their functioning much. They continue to successfully navigate the left side of their environment. They avoid obstacles and discriminate emotional stimuli (Berti & Rizzolatti, 1992; Marshall & Halligan, 1991), presumably because these functions are handled by lower, automatic processes.

Vision as a grand illusion

We experience sight as a flow of images, rich in detail and continuous in time and space. The conventional way to explain this experience is that we thoroughly analyze each scene – line by line, color by color – and rebuild them as images in the mind much like Disneyworld rebuilds pristine miniature replicas of, say, the city of London. Sight becomes the result of a meticulous and continual bottom-up process that decodes and reassembles light-borne information. At some level of complexity, qualia are added *et voilà*, the visual experience is complete. Although this movie-in-the-brain conception of vision is intuitively appealing, "an almost irresistible model of the end product of visual perception," in the words of Dennett (1991, p. 52), there are good reasons to be skeptical about it. Phenomena such as inattentional blindness, change blindness and filling-in have all but make it clear that the continuity and apparent detail of visual consciousness are figments of the imagination, so much so that vision has been called the grand illusion (Thompson et al., 1999).

But wait – vision a grand illusion? Before we can appreciate such a seemingly extreme position we must be clear what is meant by an illusion. Unlike a hallucination, which is an event that does not exist, an illusion is merely an event that does not appear to be what it is. Vision is illusionary insofar as it is not what we think it is. To see how this is possible we must know a little bit about how our eyes scan the world. We think we smoothly glide our eyes across the expanse of the visual field, taking in along the way all the glorious details it contains. But that is not the case! We traverse visual space in a series of ballistic jumps, so-called eye **saccades**. We can make up to five of these saccades per second. After each one, we focus on a particular spot of visual space, which is then scrutinized in more detail before the next saccade takes us to another fixation point. That is, we do not scan the world like a photocopier scans a document. Rather, we sporadically sample what is in front of our eyes. This is easily shown with eye-tracking devices, which monitor eye movements and reveal where and for how long the eyes come to rest.

Figure 7.2

THE PAOMNNEHAL PWEOR OF THE HMUAN MNID

I cdnuolt blveiee taht I cluod aulaclty uesdnatnrd waht I was rdgnieg. Aoccdrnig to a rscheearch at Cmabrigde Uinervtisy, it deosn't mttaer in waht oredr the ltteers in a wrod are, the olny tihng is taht the frist and lsat ltteer be in the rghit pclae. The rset can be a taotl mses and you can sitll raed it wouthit porbelm. This is bcuseae the huamn mnid deos not raed ervey lteter by istlef, but the wrod as a wlohe. Amzanighuh?

This text does not give you any trouble, does it? It drives home the message that we do not smoothly move our eyes across a visual scene. We use saccades to scan the world, jumping from place to place, and fill in the rest.

When people fitted with an eye tracker are asked to look at a picture, the saccadic sampling shows that we see clearly only a few spots. The majority of the picture is never foveated. This sampling mechanism has probably evolved to efficiently extract relevant information from the deluge of data contained in a scene, so the visual stream of consciousness is not a stream at all. Vision is actually discontinuous in time and space. Why, then, don't we see any gaps?

Psychologists have found several ways to confirm that vision is indeed a sharp-shoot and pause affair. Two phenomena, **inattentional blindness**, which exploits the fact that we see little detail and **change blindness**, which exploits the existence of temporal gaps, leave little doubt that the unity of visual consciousness is an illusion. There is no better way to illustrate inattentional blindness than with the clever little film clip *Gorillas in our Midst*. Simons and Chabris (1999) had subjects watch a movie featuring students playing an impromptu basketball game and asked them to keep track of the number of passes. Then, someone in a gorilla suit (!) walks right through the playing students, stops in the middle of the screen, turns to the camera, thumps its chest and walks off to the other side. You'd think it is impossible to overlook such an event but half of the subjects never registered the gorilla! What happens is that the task of counting passes biases the locations of an observer's fixation points and the slow-walking gorilla is never foveated. This shows how little detail we really extract from a scene.

While inattentional blindness exposes the patchiness of vision, change blindness demonstrates that large-scale changes can go unnoticed even if they occur in the focus of attention. All what is required is that those changes take place during a saccade, in which case the effect is like a brief mudsplash on the windshield of a car (O'Reagan et al., 1999). When change blindness was first discovered it baffled experimenters. In one study, subjects were asked to read a text while an eye tracker analyzed the start and length of each saccade. Then, in mid-saccade, the researchers changed the to-be-foveated text. If the new text was not discontinuous in meaning, subjects did not register the change and experienced the text as solid as any other (McConkie & Zola, 1979). If such a change took place during a fixation, the switching was noticed instantly. When two pictures that are identical except for one central change are flashed on a screen in succession separated by a delay that coincides with a saccade, it can take many alterations to detect it (Rensink et al., 1997). Using this flicker method, entire buildings can disappear from pictures without anyone noticing (Grimes, 1996).

Change blindness is so odd that a person change occurring right in front of our eyes may go undetected. In one study, students entered a room to report for an experiment and were met by a young man who handed them a consent form. As they filled it out, the man briefly stepped out and someone else took his place. This second actor was not a twin but a man with different hair color wearing a different colored shirt. Most students never detected the substitution (Mack & Rock, 1998). What appears to happen in change blindness is this. Because a saccade causes a brief but full-blown blur, we have to rely on memory for visual integration across saccades. But we already know from inattentional blindness that we see little detail as it is during fixations, especially for events that transpire in the peripheral field of vision. This makes trans-saccadic memory very poor and explains how it is possible to miss someone in a gorilla suit. However, this is rarely a problem outside the lab, as gorillas simply do not pop up and disappear in a blink of an eye. But the modern world has created situations where change blindness can be a life-or-death matter, as, for instance, for air-traffic controllers or pilots!

Although vision seems to us as stable, complete, and uninterrupted, the underlying mechanism is changeable, spotty, and broken. Knowing this capriciousness, we should ask: why don't we see gaps and jumps? Why doesn't the world appear jerky to us like a Hollywood movie from the 1920s? Does the brain edit out the gaps? If so, how does consciousness know what to fill them with? For these questions we turn our attention to the blind spot.

Recall that the blind spot is the result of a hole in the retina. With no light decoded from that area of visual space, we should see a blank spot. But we don't!

Figure 7.3

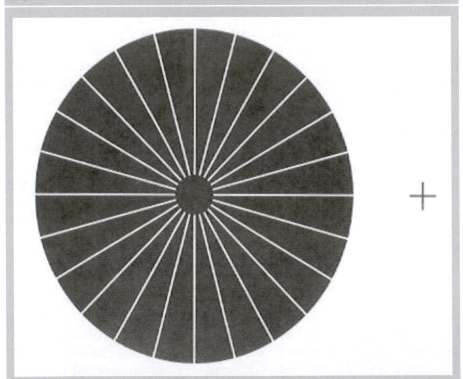

Close the right eye, focus on the cross, and move the book until the middle of the circle falls on the blind spot. What do you see instead of the black patch? Do you see the lines completed? Most people do. Since no light-borne information is decoded from this area, your experience cannot be a bottom-up result of neuronal activity. Do we fill the blind spot with qualia? (From Ramachandran, 1992)

So what appears in its place? To shed light on this question, Vilayanur Ramachandran, professor of psychology at the University of California San Diego and Susan Blakeslee (1998) performed a series of experiments. They presented subjects with two vertical lines, one above and the other below the blind spot, which they promptly connected in their minds to a single, continuous line that bridged the blind spot. They even lined up and joined two vertical lines that were slightly offset. Importantly, they did not join horizontal lines in that way. Ramachandran also tested people with circumscribed scotomas, who typically do not see anything missing if the blinded area is small. One patient also connected two vertical lines – but in his case across the scotoma. Initially he did see a gap between the lines but after a few seconds the gap closed and he saw one continuous line.

It is tempting to conclude from such studies that there are indeed gaps and that those gaps are not experienced because the brain fills them with a continuation of the surrounding area. But conclusions in the field of consciousness are rarely this simple. Dennett (1991), for instance, dismisses the possibility of gaps altogether and with it the need for any filling in. He thinks that the notion of supplying the missing bits to complete the picture is a regression to Cartesian thinking, because it presupposes the existence of a place where conscious perceptions come together. He offers an alternative interpretation based on the fact that vision is necessarily deficient because our limited processing capacity does not allow us to capture every detail contained in a scene. This deficiency is not the same as having gaps; for gaps to exist, we would need the ability to perceive that there is an absence of information. This, in turn, would require the ability to see all the details, which, however, we do not have. In the same way that you cannot tell that there is anything stolen from a house you do not know well, you cannot ascertain that there is anything missing from a scene you do not fully decode. He argues that our impoverished vision lacks the sharpness for even registering that there are gaps. Consequently, no filling in takes place. But how then do we get a rich, panoramic view from a visual process that actually should rather give us a largely blurred view with a small sharp center spot that would be, to top it off, periodically interrupted – due to saccades – by complete haziness? Dennett explains that the *impression* of seeing detail does not mean that we really form a mental representation of any detail, either as a result of actually seeing it or filling it in. It only means that we represent *that* there is detail. This is captured in his statement: "the detail is in the world not in your head" (ibid., p. 355). Dennett accounts instead for the unity of visual consciousness with brain mechanisms that mask our ignorance, not by flashing out that ignorance with educated guesses of what should be there, but by *labeling* it as having features that we know from experiences should be there, a sort of painting by numbers, if you like.

To many this explanation falls short of accounting for all the empirical data. Why, for instance, did subjects connect vertical but not horizontal lines across the blind spot? Similarly, cortically blind patients joined up some stimuli across the scotoma but not others. In one study, Ramachandran and Blakeslee even managed to create a stimulus that appeared at the blind spot – but instead of just filling it by perpetuating the background, it stood out against it. How can the blind spot be made to contain information more salient than the surrounding area if the sense of seeing detail, as Dennett claims, is a matter of ignoring a lack of information? Ramachandran thinks instead that consciousness actively fills in the unnoticed gaps with content or, in his words, qualia.

It is clear that visual experience cannot be explained by a neat bottom-up process, in which activity in retinal and cortical neurons is built up into representational images that are passed in front of the mind's eye. This realization led to the formulation of other theoretical models that give a greater role to top-down processes. One leading departure from this movie-in-the-brain conception of vision was formulated by the psychologist Kevin O'Reagan and the philosopher Alva Noë (2001). In their sensorimotor theory of vision, there is no need to build mental representations. In fact, we do not have the neural resources to represent the world as images in our minds. Recall that we can only make use of a small portion of visual information. Since we do not know in advance what is useful to us, we would have to build a detailed representation only to discard most of it. This would be like cooking a lavish seven-course meal for someone who only eats one thing. O'Reagan and Noë's proposal is radically different. To them, we see an object, not because we represent that object, but because we visually manipulate it at that moment. Objects we do not actively manipulate, we also do not see. How, exactly, is object representation different from visual manipulation, you might ask? First, in the O'Reagan and Noë theory, we do not convert the world into representational images: we keep visual information where it is – in the world. We only extract what is useful for us at the time. What is meant here by visually manipulating an object is that we actively explore what we can do with it. The nature of visual representation is not of objects themselves – that information is kept out there like an external memory buffer – but of knowledge that explores our abilities to make use of it. That is, it is our interaction with the object that makes us perceive and experience it. Seen in this way, sight is limited to only those aspects of visual information that are currently useful to us. To understand this better, think of vision as you do about touch. We only have tactile information of objects we are currently in contact with and can directly explore. All other objects we do not sense. But if you do not explore the object, touch itself is of little use. For instance, we cannot tell an apple purely by touch; we must run our hand all over it to identify it. Sight is similar in that it requires a kind of reaching out, which intimately involves the motor system in perception.

So how does this theory account for the phenomenal experience of seeing more than just the part you actively manipulate? Like Dennett, O'Reagan and Noë assert that we represent *that* there is more detail in the world but we do not actually build a representation of it that is seen by some mental eye. Then, when we decide to look (visually reaching out), it is actually there – just as we expected. The fact that information is available on demand reinforces the sense that we have seen it all along. O'Reagan (1992) likens seeing to being rich. A wealthy man knows he has millions in the bank although he does not constantly feel them. Still he acts as though he does. Every time he reaches for his credit card he finds out directly that he is indeed rich. This is what qualia are like: as soon as you check whether you have them, well, you just have them. It is rather like the light–fridge conundrum. Every time we open the door and decide to look inside the fridge, the light is on. The difference is that the movie-in-the-brain theory assumes that the light is indeed always on and when we look we see it as such. The sensorimotor theory assumes that we see the light on only when – actually because – we opened the door.

Finally consider someone with **Anton's delusion**. In this scurrile disorder people become blind but believe that they can still see. Oliver Sacks (1992) reported one such individual who said he enjoyed watching TV. This is a form of anosagnosia, the not knowing (*a-gnosis*) of having a disease (*nosos*). They construct an entire visual world from memory and, naturally, run into many objects that exist in the real world. But normal sight is also mostly illusionary. The difference between theirs and normal vision is that their visual consciousness is wholly constructed while ours is only partly so. We also bump into things, just not that often. Yet, the experience is the same. Vision, then, is part sight, part dream.

Somatosensation

Phantoms in the brain

Many principles of visual perception – hierarchical organization, convergence, feature detection – apply also to somatosensation. This system provides information about the body and includes several submodalities, such as touch and kinesthesia. Several pathways relay this information to the brain. Generally speaking, afferent signals travel to the ventral posterior nuclei of the thalamus, then on to the **primary somatosensory cortex** or **SMI**, located in the parietal cortex, and finally to secondary association cortices for further processing. Projections from there inform the posterior parietal cortex about body location and position, information that it uses as a central reference point for spatial perception. We understand all space in relation to our bodies and the brain seems to divide space into three areas, personal space, reaching space, and far space. For instance, there are so-called near-space neurons that respond only to objects that are within an animal's reach but not when they are in personal or far space.

Like V1, SMI is organized in columns, which together form a map of the body, the so-called **sensory homunculus** discovered by the pioneering work of the neurosurgeon Wilder Penfield in the 1940s (Penfield & Jasper, 1954). This neural map reflects functional neural processing – not actual body surface – magnifying areas, such as the hands or lips, to represent extra detail. This cortical map is not hardwired but also reflects experience. For instance, the area for fingers is enlarged in musicians who play string instruments (Elbert et al., 1995). Likewise, when amputation of a limb denervates the input into the cortical area responsible for that limb, the map undergoes functional changes. The newly "freed" cortical space is then taken over, in part, by the adjacent cortex and will now respond to the new body part (Kaas, 1995; Merzenich & Jenkins, 1995). How this adaptation gives rise to changes in conscious experience was explored by Ramachandran (1993) in the interesting case of a young man who had his left arm amputated. In the cortex, the hand area is adjacent to the face area. Ramachandran reasoned that stimulation of the face might evoke sensations of being touched on the hand. This is exactly what he found. Similar cortical cross-wiring may result in odd juxtapositions that can explain other phenomena. For instance, the genital and foot areas are neighbors on the neural body map and, given what we know about cortical plasticity, it is perhaps not surprising that the foot fetish is the most common of all fetishes.

Functional reorganization of neural maps due to learning or amputation has its limits. Consider **phantom limbs** and phantom limb pain. Over 70 percent of amputees feel that their missing limb still exists and they move consistent with this feeling, avoiding, for instance, bumping it into objects. People report all sorts of conscious sensations in the phantom limb (Melzack, 1992). This would be but a curiosity if one of them were not excruciating pain. A knee or elbow may itch or ache incessantly and legs may feel as though they are locked into an impossibly twisted position. The phenomenon was first noticed by the physician Silas Weir Mitchell during the American Civil War, which produced amputees by the droves. So, what causes a phantom pain? Initially, it was thought that the distal end of nerves still responds to stimulation, but attempts to alleviate the pain through surgery on the stump proved ineffective. Melzack thinks that the feeling of pain is inherent in the organization of somatosenory cortices because people born with missing limbs also report phantom sensations. The pain, he thinks, is caused by activation of the brain's maps that decode the missing body part.

So how does one treat pain in a body part that no longer exists? One solution is as weird as it is amazing, but it underscores the central importance of consciousness in pain perception. Ramachandran (Ramachandran & Blakeslee, 1998) thought of it when he applied models of motor predictions to the problem (see Chapter 11). For some, the pain involves the excessive clenching of the fist so that their phantom fingernails dig deeply into their phantom palm. Ramachandran built a "mirror box" that would provide them with sensory feedback. We typically stop motion, such as making a fist, when kinesthetic and visual feedback tells us to. But neither type of feedback is available to them. The mirror box is divided by a mirror into two compartments, one for each hand. The patient slides the normal and phantom hand into the compartments and, because the contraption is open at the top, now sees the phantom hand, except that this image is a reflection of the normal hand. The illusion is real because the phantom hand is exactly in the place where the patient feels it. The patient now makes a fist and releases it, creating the impression that the phantom fist is unclenched. This ingenious procedure has given some relief to patients with this type of pain and prompted Ramachandran to claim to be the first to amputate a phantom limb.

Pain

It is worth considering pain in more detail because there are several particularities that make it a very interesting sensory system for consciousness. The pain system of the body is unique; that is, it is not simply the excessive activity of the same system that conveys normal sensation. Thus, like all senses, the ability to feel pain can be selectively lost, a condition known as **congenital insensitivity syndrome**. There are few such cases reported in the literature, but the fact that sufferers do not live long, as they ignore even the most minor injuries, underscores the importance of the sense of pain as an alarm signal. One odd fact about pain perception is that it is poorly related to the amount of tissue damage and can even occur without any outside stimulation. Pain is also a private event and people vary greatly in how they experience it, depending heavily on mood, stress, or prior learning. Yet another oddity is that pain can be temporarily eradicated without (**analgesia**) or with (**anesthesia**) the loss of consciousness. But perhaps pain's most unique feature is its sensitivity to rather peculiar manipulations, such as hypnosis, acupuncture, meditation, and other altered states of consciousness, not to mention beliefs and convictions. The guru walking barefoot over 20 yards of white-hot charcoal while yodeling the Marseillaise is a testament to this as much as the placebo effect. Finally, pain has the unique ability to totally dominate the content of consciousness like no other sensory input.

To account for these particularities, two neuroscientists, Ronald Melzack and Patrick Wall (1965), formulated the **gate control theory**. The general idea is that incoming sensory information must pass through a gate in the spinal cord before entering the brain. Acupuncture works, for instance, by temporarily closing certain gates so that the pain no longer reaches consciousness. But how does the gate control theory handle the fact that willpower can block the feeling of pain? This is where top-down meets bottom-up. The activity of each gate is also influenced by descending tracts hailing from the brain. The brain can control, to some degree, the amount of pain it wishes to receive. It does this – not by convincing itself that it does not feel pain – but by preventing the signal from reaching the brain in the first place.

Like all sensory systems, pain is best thought of as a functional hierarchy in which higher-order structures compute ever more sophisticated features. The distressing, emotional component of pain is a higher-order representation and is not added to the signal until it reaches the emotional centers of the brain. In the same way that eyes don't see and ears don't hear (sight and sound happen in higher brain regions), the body does not feel pain – what it does is transmit signals about tissue damage. It is in the brain where the conscious feeling of pain happens. Under local anesthesia, we can feel the cutting of the skin but the unpleasantness is dissociated from it. So at which level, then, do pain-qualia come in?

This is not only an academic problem but one that carries tremendous implications for the ethical treatment of animals. Any mammal shows the outward signs of distress but do they *feel* pain the same way we do? How about the risk of administering anesthesia to infants undergoing surgery? Do you risk the possibility of complications from the anesthetic, or trust that the infant has not yet fully developed the higher brain structures that encode the conscious feeling of pain? To see how tricky this debate is, consider how we misattribute the causes of pain-related behavior to pain itself. When you touch a hot stove, nocioceptors in your hand transmit the signal into the spinal cord where it synapses on motor neurons, which send a signal down the same spinal nerve to retract the hand. The round trip – from sensory input to motor output – happens in a lightning-fast 20 to 40 milliseconds. Once in the CNS, the signal is also sent up to the brain in a meandering path involving several relays until it reaches the cortex, at which point we become aware of it. This journey takes a little longer – actually ten times as long – or 200 to 500 milliseconds (Hardcastle, 1999). Yet, if you asked people why they withdraw the hand they answer: "because it hurt." It should be obvious that this explanation is false. Pain is not the reason for the behavior because the feeling of hurting comes a full order of magnitude later. The cause is a speedy, fully automatic reflex that carries in it no flicker of emotion whatsoever. Consciousness is not necessary for simple avoidance learning and we avoid or escape most dangers without prior thought or emotion. This, then, raises the menace of epiphenomenalism again; but only superficially. It is easy to think of more hidden dangers that can only be identified through thought processes, giving consciousness its adaptiveness back.

It is common practice in behavioral neuroscience to study function by its absence. People or animals with brain injury allow us to deduce the function of the missing brain area by examining what they can no longer do. This technique, however, has not proven useful with consciousness. Coma and anesthesia – cases of life without consciousness – eliminate nearly all functions along with it. For anesthesia, there is little consensus on how it might temporarily abolish consciousness. There are many different drugs with widely different mechanisms of action and no drug exists that is selective for consciousness. The few attempts to find a common underlying mechanism such as NMDA receptors or microtubules (Flohr, 2000; Hameroff & Penrose, 1996) have not been adopted in anesthesiology. There is also no consensus on which brain areas are involved (Alkire et al. 1998), but it is believed by many that the brainstem and the thalamus must play vital roles. Anesthetics may ultimately work by interfering with the thalamocortical system, perhaps preventing the thalamus from relaying any signals to the cortex (perhaps disrupting the 40Hz cycle). Finally, there are reports that some people retain memories of horrific pain while under anesthesia. The reasons for this are unknown but do not seem simply attributable to insufficient dosage. The phenomenon is reminiscent of the hidden observer in hypnosis (see Chapter 13) and it must be a frightful experience to feel the pain of an operation while not being able to do anything about it.

Box 7.1 Sensory deprivation

The point of brains is to handle input to produce output. But what if there is no input? Would they still have experiences? Most people thought that they would go blank, like a TV unplugged from the cable, but in the 1950s, a NIMH scientist by the name of John Lilly turned his attention to this classic question and found the opposite; without input, brains have a fantastic life of their own. Lilly constructed the first sensory deprivation tank. No light, sound, or smell breaks through and by floating suspended in 34°C salt water a person feels no touch or gravity either. But instead of the weightless, tranquil, womblike void some had predicted, Lilly's brain went into overdrive with visions of the Universal Vibration, OBEs, and mystical revelations. He later combined his tanking adventures with the chemical nirvanas of LSD and ketamine, trips he recounted in *The Deep Self*, which is undoubtedly the most break-through-to-the-other-side book ever written. Sensory deprivation does not readily produce hallucinations. For instance, the winner of the Nobel Prize for physics, Richard Feynman, took many trips to Lilly's tank before he visited other dimensions (Feynman, 1985).

At the same time the psychologist Donald Hebb at McGill University also experimented with sensory deprivation. He found that short bouts in such chambers can be relaxing but that extended periods produce unpleasant effects. People became disoriented and anxious, exhibited antisocial behavior, and could no longer distinguish sleep from waking. After only a few hours most wanted to break the monotony for any kind of stimulation, a phenomenon known as **stimulus hunger**. Hebb even offered $20 (good money in the 1950s) for every day subjects stayed longer but most pressed the panic button after just two days, with the longest lasting five (Hebb, 1958). Other studies found that people are very susceptible to persuasive messages or any type of propaganda during sensory deprivation. Not surprisingly, prolonged sensory deprivation has been used as an interrogation method and is generally recognized as a form of torture (Storr, 1971).

Perception and consciousness

Libet's half-second delay

From the time sense organs transduce a stimulus until it is perceived consciously, the brain must do an astronomical amount of computational work. Naturally, this number crunching takes time. But how much? In a series of experiments carried out in the 1970s by Benjamin Libet, professor of neuroscience at the University of California at San Francisco, this time-lag turned out to be, on average, half a second. Given what we know about the brain's internal workings, Libet's half-second delay – as it became famously known – might not surprise you. But what should surprise you is why we do not feel the delay. In the end, we do not experience life as trailing behind by half a second, do we? The results Libet obtained in his experiments suggest that the brain subjectively refers perception back in time by about the same 0.5 seconds, to the time it actually occurred (Freeman, 2000), creating the illusion that consciousness is immediate.

For his studies Libet (1982) took advantage of the fact that some brain surgeries require the patient to stay awake during the operation. During such operations, he stimulated the hand area of the exposed primary somatosensory cortex (SMI), which patients reported as a tingly touch sensation to the hand about half a second later. Libet quickly found that the intensity and duration of the stimulation was important (Libet et al., 1979). If the intensity was below a certain threshold it never resulted in a conscious perception, regardless of its duration. Above that threshold, however, it must last for about 0.5 seconds to elicit a reportable experience. He called this the **neuronal adequacy**, which meant that a stimulus, say, a touch to the skin, must induce half a second of continuous cortical activity in SMI, even if the actual touch was much shorter in duration. When Libet also stimulated the hand itself, he found the same half-second delay. Although this finding was unexpected at the time, it makes sense in the present light. The speed of nerve conduction is quite fast and the distance between the hand and SMI is too short to make a noticeable difference. What causes the 0.5 seconds is not travel time to the brain but the computational work performed by the unconscious brain to convert the sensation into a complex, conscious mental representation.

By the time we are conscious of an event, it's already half a second old. What is so extraordinary about that? Due to their light-years of distance from us, we also see the stars as they were in the past. If everyone perceives the world this way, no one should notice. The problem here is that motion does not lag behind by a half-second. We consciously know of our own actions at the time they occur. If perception is tardy but motion immediate, we should experience any conversation as we do an overseas phone call that has an annoying split-second delay in it. Obviously, we do not experience life offset in this way. So what is going on? How does consciousness make us feel as though perception is instantaneous?

To get to the bottom of this, Libet performed more experiments with the aim of clarifying what was happening between the stimulus onset and the subjective arrival time. He stimulated both, the hand and SMI, and asked his subjects which they felt first. To his surprise, they felt the skin stimulus first, even if it came after the cortical stimulation by as much as 200 milliseconds. This was certainly puzzling. If the skin stimulus occurred 200 msec later one might also expect that we would sense it 200 msec later. By varying the order and times of both stimuli, Libet could establish that our conscious perception of a stimulus coincided most closely with the moment it was first picked up by the sense organs. Mind you, to the outside observer the reportable experience still occurs half a second after the stimulus; only in the first-person perspective do they occur at the same time. According to Libet, what seems to happen, then, is this. Incoming sensory signals must build up about 0.5 seconds of continuous activity in SMI. If they do not we also do not experience them consciously. But once this neuronal adequacy is achieved, we slide them back in time so that they do not appear out of tune with other happenings. It is unclear how consciousness manages to backdate itself to just the right time but it is conceivable that the brain might have a mechanism that tags the incoming sensory information with an arrival time that is later used as a reference point.

Naturally, Libet's findings caused a stir. But as is often the case when empirical data are injected into questions relating to consciousness, the results do not provide definitive answers but instead are interpreted to support whichever position one holds on the mind-body spectrum. Dualists such as Popper and Eccles (1977) see the results as evidence that there are conscious processes that cannot be accounted for by neural activity. Libet's own interpretation of "subjective referral of sensory experience backwards in time" (1982, p. 235) gives consciousness power beyond brain activity. Materialists, such as Churchland (1981) and Dennett (1991), reject such interpretations. Dennett argues that the whole discussion is futile because it depends on the faulty assumption that there is a moment in time when events "enter" consciousness (Dennett & Kinsbourne, 1992). To him, the idea that information is built up in order to enter the special spotlight of consciousness – the Cartesian theater – is a bad habit of thinking. Since there is no place or time for information to achieve the special status of qualia, the subjective experience of which came first, the skin or the cortical stimulus, has nothing to do with any actual priority. Thus, consciousness does not need to intervene and backdate anything to a specific time in order to preserve any temporal order.

Consider also this illusion, which, on the face of it, seems for all the world like precognition. It is called the cutaneous rabbit (Geldard & Sherrick, 1972). A person closes his eyes and is tapped on his stretched out arm with a pencil at equal intervals five times at the wrist, three times at the elbow, and twice on the biceps. Instead of feeling just that, the person feels as though the taps are running up his arm. How is that possible? How can he know ahead of time where taps 2, 3, and 4 are going to be when the first elbow tap is yet to come? (For a possible explanation, see Dennett's Orwellian and Stalinesque revisionism in Chaper 5.)

Subliminal perception

The idea of **subliminal perception** has had a long and confused history. It came out of nineteenth-century classical psychophysics when several German physiologists began to study sensory thresholds. Natually, if we present a stimulus below an absolute threshold, we can ask whether or not we still somehow detect it and to what extent it might affect behavior – two entirely different issues, actually, that became immediately mixed up. The issue was not helped by a hoax at a New Jersey movie theater in 1957 when James Vicary, a marketing executive, inserted the words "Eat popcorn" and "Drink Coke" into some films. No one reported seeing the messages but Vicary claimed more popcorn and Coke were sold during these films. Vicary later admitted that he tampered with the results to increase sales, but this nevertheless started a thriving business with hidden messages on audio tapes to help you relax, be more assertive, or learn Spanish, to say nothing of satanic verses in rock music played backwards and erotic images embedded in cracker boxes. Lab experiments have never found any evidence that those messages influence complex behavior (Merikle, 2000). It took a while to sort out the good, the bad, and the ugly of subliminal perception.

Before we explore this, we should mention that classical psychophysics has been superseded by **signal detection theory** (SDT), which has done away with absolute thresholds altogether. In this paradigm, perception is not solely determined by a person's sensitivity but also by his response criterion. In a way, SDT put the psychology back into psychophysics by recognizing that decisions about the presence of a stimulus are made by humans and depend, in addition to sensory thresholds, on a host of subjective variables, such as mood or prior experience.

Early research on subliminal perception used semantic priming in a force-choice paradigm. In a typical setup, a word, say, "doctor" is flashed on a screen at subliminal intensity followed by the presentation of two words above the threshold, say, "nurse" and "dog." The subject is forced to choose between them and tends to pick the one that is semantically linked. This preference is also accompanied by a feeling of "nurse" popping into the head. This effect was not reliably replicated until it was realized that there are two subliminal thresholds with some studies measuring the first and others the second (Cheesman & Merikle, 1986). Below the **objective threshold** a subject responds truly by chance but there is also a **subjective threshold** above which a subject becomes conscious of the stimulus. Priming works in the narrow range between these two thresholds. Moreover, the more complex the stimulus and the further it is below the subjective threshold the less likely it is that priming occurs (Kihlstrom, 1996).

An exciting area of research in the cognitive sciences is the intersection between subliminal perception and implicit learning. As we shall see in Chapter 8, implicit learning "takes place largely independently of conscious attempts to learn and largely in the absence of explicit knowledge about what was acquired" (Reber, 1993, p. 5). For instance, we learn our native language without conscious effort and we speak it without exactly knowing the rules. The difference between subliminal perception and implicit learning is the time delay between stimulus presentation and the testing for any retained knowledge (Kihlstrom, 1996). Priming is lost when the second display is delayed. This let people speculate that the effect might be due to a temporary sensory buffer that represents the first stimulus at an unconscious level for just long enough to bias an immediate conscious decision forced by the second display. In contrast, implicit learning occurs when stimuli are presented clearly above the threshold. This leads to a representation that is also unconscious but one that can influence motor output for a much longer time. Note that this account of subliminal perception is a form of Cartesian materialism that presumes that information is either unequivocally "in" or "out" of consciousness. Again, the alternative view is to reject all forms of Cartesian thinking and question whether perceptions have to cross any type of threshold to reach consciousness (Dennett, 1991).

Summary

A popular way to study consciousness empirically is to investigate how perceptual processes give rise to experience. Two sensory systems, vision and pain, are exploited most often. The visual system is fundamentally analytical and processes information by deconstructing the world into its basic components only to reconstruct it again along a functional hierarchy that reflects reality as much as it does current need and past experience. What we see in front of our eyes is not a faithful reproduction but a personal view, custom-built to specification. Although seeing does not feel this way, this insight is the basis for understanding normal and abnormal visual experience. Phenomena such as agnosia and neglect are the result of selective damage that eliminates specific information from consciousness. In blindsight all visual consciousness is lost, but patients can still respond to elementary stimulation showing that the vision is a multilayered system that processes some information unconsciously.

The surround cinemascope experience of visual consciousness is even more perplexing when considering the cursory process by which we extract information from the world. Our eyes do not scan the world in a systematic, algorithmic fashion but skim over it in a way that should leave large gaps and jumps. That these holes exist is powerfully demonstrated by change and inattentional blindness, which expose the continuity and completeness of vision as a grand illusion. But how then does consciousness create, out of the sporadic sampling, the impression of an unbroken stream of detailed panoramas? And with what does it fill the gaps? While some claim that such questions are ill-conceived because no filling in is necessary to explain what we see, others claim to have found evidence, by studying the nothingness of the blind spot, that consciousness does actively fill in the missing bits. A third way to explain what we see is to give up on the concept of mental representations altogether and think of vision as an interactive system that only extracts from the environment what it currently requires to function.

Pain has also been used to study consciousness. The brain contains a neural map of the body which changes with experience. When these changes are radical, such as the amputation of a limb, they alter the way we perceive our body, showing that consciousness of tactile information occurs at the level of the neural map, not the body itself. This is why it is so difficult to treat phantom limb pain although some methods, informed by the role of feedback in shaping consciousness, have provided some relief. The feeling of pain is also interesting because it can be altered by consciousness itself, as is the case in hypnosis or the placebo effect.

Research by Libet has shown that the immediacy of all perception appears to be an illusion. A stimulus must achieve neuronal adequacy, that is, induce 500 msec of continuous neural activity in SMI, before it is perceived consciously. Since we do not experience a half-second delay, Libet interpreted those findings by suggesting that consciousness backdates events to the time they occur. Finally, we considered in this chapter subliminal perception. The topic has been plagued by many misconceptions and several false starts but it is now clear that a stimulus presented between the objective and the subjective threshold can for a brief duration bias our behavior without itself becoming conscious. It is also clear that this is limited to simple stimuli and simple behaviors.

Suggested reading

Hardcastle, V. G. (1999). *The Myth of Pain*. Cambridge, MA: MIT Press.

O'Reagan, J. K. & Noë, A. (2001). A sensorimotor account of vision and visual consciousness. *Behavioural and Brain Sciences*, 24, 883–917.

Ramachandran, V. S., & Blakeslee, S. (1998). *Phantoms in the Brain: Probing the Mysteries of the Human Mind*. New York: Morrow.

Weiskrantz, L. (1997). *Consciousness Lost and Found*. Oxford: Oxford University Press.

8 Memory

The explicit system

Concepts in memory

The brain has developed several anatomically and functionally separate systems to handle the acquisition, storage, transformation, and usage of knowledge. Perceptual processes described in the previous chapter are used to extract two broad classes of information from the world. The emotional system, which will be the focus of the next chapter, appraises the information for its value to the organism. The cognitive system, which is the focus of this chapter, performs a detailed analysis of the information which serves as the basis of all kinds of thought processes and motor skills.

The cognitive system can be subdivided further into two systems that are distinct in anatomy and function. A mountain of research has shown that each cognitive system handles its own encoding, consolidation, retrieval, and forgetting of knowledge (Schacter & Bruckner, 1998; Squire, 1992). The **explicit system** is rule-based, its content can be expressed by verbal communication, and it is tied to conscious awareness. In contrast, the **implicit system** is skill- or experience-based, its content is not verbalizable and can only be conveyed through task

Figure 8.1

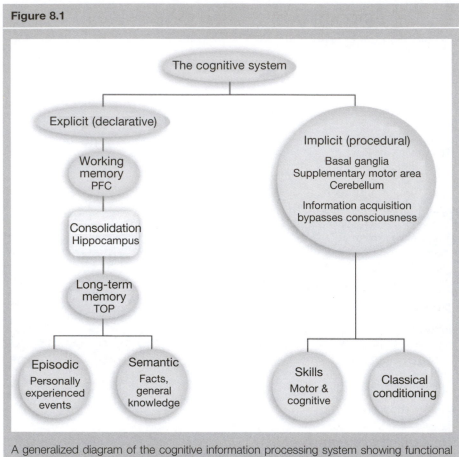

A generalized diagram of the cognitive information processing system showing functional processes and related brain structures. Later, the emotional system will be added, which is yet another separate system in terms of anatomy and process modularity.

performance, and it is inaccessible to conscious awareness (Dienes & Perner, 1999). We will flesh out these notions throughout the present chapter.

The explicit system is a phylogenetically recent, highly evolved, and complex system. It consists of three components, each corresponding to a different process and set of brain structures. The first component is **working memory**, which is primarily enabled by the dorsolateral prefrontal cortex (Ashby & Casale, 2002). The second component is the **consolidation of memory**, which is critically dependent on the hippocampus and other medial temporal lobe structures (Poldrack & Packard, 2003). The third component is **long-term memory**, which is primarily stored in **TOP** (temporal, occipital, and parietal) regions of the neocortex (Gilbert, 2001). In contrast, the implicit system is an evolutionarily ancient and comparatively simple system. There is no evidence pointing to several structural components; instead, brain structures such as the basal ganglia or cerebellum handle all information-processing stages: acquisition, consolidation, storage, retrieval, and forgetting. There are several types of learning that are managed by the implicit system, such as procedural (motor and cognitive) skills, priming, conditioning, and habituation (Mishkin et al., 1984; Tulving, 1995).

The first section of this chapter examines the various components of the explicit system, while the second section describes the implicit system, largely by contrasting it with the explicit system. Solely for the sake of convenience, we will adopt here the view that some anatomical and/or physiological differences exist between unconscious and conscious representation and information is either "in" or "out" of consciousness. Accordingly, information encoded in the implicit system is "inaccessible" to consciousness and must cross over to the explicit system to "reach" consciousness. This should not be taken literally! It is not our intention to promote here a form of Cartesian materialism (see Chapter 5), tacitly presuming that consciousness is something extra, an additional step beyond the brain function; it is simply a convention to avoid cumbersome and long-winded sentences.

To start, we should clarify a few conceptions about memory. No single model of memory can account for all the available data (Tulving, 1997). Historically, the **three-stage model**, proposed in its first form by Atkinson and Shiffrin (1968), has had the most support among cognitive psychologists. It describes the process of memory formation in three stages that mainly differ in duration and capacity: **sensory memory**, **short-term memory** (STM), and **long-term memory** (LTM). Sensory memory has a large capacity but holds information for only a fleeting moment. It is a snapshot of reality. STM has a short duration (up to 30 seconds), a limited capacity, and functions as a temporary buffer that allows for the active manipulation of information. LTM has an endless duration, an unlimited capacity, and functions as a general holding tank for all knowledge. A critical component of the model is that the individual is actively involved in the flow of information through the various stages. Information is moved from sensory memory to STM by attentional processes and reaches LTM by effortful rehearsal. Information that is not attended to or rehearsed is lost or forgotten.

This model continues to dominate the popular conception of memory. It stems from the early days of cognitive psychology when the computer analogy served as the general paradigm for human information processing. Although the straightforward version of this analogy has been abandoned for some time now, it lingers on as a convenient but pernicious conceptualization of human memory. Human memory is not stored in the same sense as it is in a computer. Life's experiences structurally alter the very fabric of the brain and the resulting memories affect every act of perception, feeling, thinking, and performance at every moment. Memories are not stored apart in some box to be retrieved whenever needed but are fully interlaced into the brain's tissue. This is the reason why we cannot have selective amnesia for, say, the years between 1975 and 1990 or all words starting with the letter D. In contrast, articifial memory is independent of the structures that do the processing; it is a filing cabinet located apart from other system components. Items can be selectively altered without affecting the rest of the system. In the brain memory *is* the processing.

For the study of consciousness, the critical question is how these systems inter-act to determine the content of consciousness. The computational infrastructure of one particular system, namely the explicit system, enables full-fledged consciousness, making knowledge contained in the explicit system readily acces-sible to consciousness. Knowledge contained in the implicit system has to be transferred to the explicit system first before we can be fully conscious of it.

Working memory

The term **working memory** has largely replaced the older term short-term memory; however, both terms refer to essentially the same concept. Working memory describes the ability to process information online. It is a monitoring system of ongoing events that temporarily keeps in mind information that is rele-vant to the situation, so that one can "work" with it. It is in working memory that you are holding the information you read in the beginning of this sentence so that the end of this sentence still makes sense to you. There is a growing accep-tance in cognitive science and neuroscience for the view that the information that is temporarily buffered in working memory *is* the content of consciousness (Courtney et al., 1998; Dehaene & Naccache, 2001). This is not to say that work-ing memory is the seat of consciousness but that information must be represented in working memory to be fully conscious. In other words, our immediate conscious experience of the here and now is made possible by the sustained buffering of information in working memory. In this section, we will concentrate on the cognitive aspects of working memory while in Chapter 10 we will explore its neural underpinnings.

Cognitive research has shown that working memory is severely limited in capacity, either in storage, processing, or both (Baddeley, 2000; Cowan, 2001). In one of the most cited papers in all of psychology, George Miller (1956) argued that this **capacity limit** stands at seven items, plus minus two. Take, for instance, the ability to look up a seven-digit number in the telephone book, briefly memorize it, and turn to the phone to dial it. Most people can perform this task successfully because the number of items in working memory does not exceed seven. However, if it were an international number – with country and area code – most people cannot perform the task because 12 items busts the capacity limit. Equally, if they are interrupted during the dialing process by someone asking for, say, the time, working memory needs to hold additional items to answer the query and must push the phone number out of its buffer, leaving them with the frustration of having to look it up again.

If a task exceeds the capacity limit we must evoke **executive processes**, which are mental operations that actively manipulate the information. One type of exec-utive process is **rehearsal**. Rehearsing information activates long-term memory processes, which frees storage capacity in working memory. Items in working memory are subject to gross forgetting if they are not rehearsed. Another executive process is **chunking**. The capacity limit restricts the content to 7±2 *independent* items but each item itself can contain an unlimited amount of information. For instance, try to memorize the following string of letters: F K D T G M T O P S D S. Now, try to memorize this string of letters: U S A C I A F B I K G B. The first string contains 12 items, while the second contains only 4 because we are able to group the 12 letters into 4 chunks. Sweller (1993) illustrated this concept nicely with a problem that most people find very frustrating: Try to solve it: *"Suppose five days after the day before yesterday is Friday. What day of the week is tomorrow?"* The complexity presented in the problem is such that it cannot be solved in one go. It is necessary to collapse it into separate chunks, which are then solved in a serial manner, chunk by chunk. This makes clear that working memory limitations are the key to understanding the bottleneck of consciousness.

The cognitive psychologist Nelson Cowan (2001) has shown that the limited capacity actually caps the amount of information that can be held accessible in the focus of attention, and thus working memory, to four independent items or chunks. Carefully controlled experiments in which subjects are completely prevented from rehearsing or chunking support only this lower capacity limit. Miller's famous 7±2 is already a compound estimate of the capacity limit that allows for some executive processes but is thought to be more typical of real-world situations. Also, this capacity limit of four chunks is valid only if the chunks are part of a coherent scene. If two chunks are logically inconsistent or mutually exclusive to common sense, the capacity limit is even more narrow (Baars, 1988). In those instances, humans appear to be able to process only one single item. This is nicely illustrated by the amount of time it typically takes to combine two seemingly conflicting ideas into a single concept, for instance, the fact that electromagnetic radiation is a wavicle, a wave and a particle.

Box 8.1   The mnemonist

There have been many reported cases of individuals with extraordinary memory but none quite like the one of Solomon V. Shereshevskii. Shereshevskii was born in Russia in about 1886 but his surreal memory was not discovered until 1905 when he was working as a journalist for a Moscow newspaper. His editor noticed that he never took notes during meetings and, assuming a lack of professionalism, questioned him about it. Shereshevskii replied by proceeding to recall their last meeting with astonishing accuracy. Shereshevskii was a shy man and did not realize how amazing this feat was, although he did wonder why everyone else needed to take notes. The editor recognized Shereshevskii's talent and referred him to the famous psychologist Aleksandr Luria. Luria studied S., as he is known in the literature, in a semi-clinical fashion for the better part of the next 30 years and reported the case in a book that has become a classic: *The Mind of a Mnemonist* (1968).

S. could reproduce up to 70 digits accurately after only a single hearing! Compare this to the norm of seven plus or minus two. He could also recall long lists of words, nonsense syllabus, musical motifs, or complex scientific formulas. Over the years Luria gave S. countless lists to memorize and he unerringly repeated each one of them flawlessly, even after a delay of 20 years. Luria told of one instance in which S. recalled a 50-word list without a single error after hearing it only once 15 years earlier. Indeed, Luria found that S. had not forgotten a single list he had given him.

S.'s remarkable memory was accompanied by extreme synesthesia. As we learned in Chapter 4, synesthesiacs experience sensory-specific information in more than one modality.

Box 8.1   *continued*

Colored hearing is the most common form of synesthesia but S.'s case was unusual in that he coded all information in almost all sensory modalities. Luria noted S.'s synesthesic condition one day when S. told one of Luria's colleagues "what a crumbly yellow voice" he had. One could think of S.'s images as a sort of mental hologram, which was undoubtedly the basis of his seemingly inexhaustible memory. How could anyone forget a person whose voice sounded as "though a flame with fibers protruding from it [her mouth] was advancing towards me?" In addition to his intense sensory experiences, S. also used his capacity for direct visualization to help him fix objects in virtual space. For instance, he would place items along an imaginary walk from Pushkin Square to Gorky Park and retrace his virtual walk during recall. Sometimes S. would not be able to recall an item, not because he forgot it, but because he could no longer see it, as was the case when he placed an egg against a white surface.

S.'s memory was so phenomenal that forgetting became a problem for him. His mind became so cluttered with meaningless details that he frequently felt distressed, particularly late in life. For instance, he could not appreciate poetry because it contained metaphors that evoked images that clashed in his mind. S. went so far as to try various proactive methods to forget. One method that Luria suggested involved writing items on a piece of imaginary paper and throwing them into the trash. Although he could not forget that he trashed certain items, he did sometimes succeed in forgetting the items themselves. He also tried to forget items by imagining that they were covered up by a great canvas. Because his memory depended on rich mental imagery, these methods proved useful at times.

Memory consolidation

Neuroscientists agree that long-term memory requires structural changes to the brain. Incoming information must alter brain physiology, chemistry, and anatomy; otherwise it cannot possibly affect behavior. For the explicit system, the synaptic processes that consolidate life's experiences into LTM occur in the hippocampus. In recent years, the hippocampus has become almost synonymous with memory but it must be stressed that the role of the hippocampus in memory is confined to the **consolidation of explicit memory**. The hippocampus neither stores memory nor is it involved in the formation of implicit memory.

The functions of the hippocampus started to unravel in 1953 following one of the most famous cases in medical history. H.M. was a man of 27 who suffered from untreatable, life-threatening epileptic seizures. To save his life, William Scolville, a New York neurosurgeon, removed large parts of the medial temporal lobe that included the hippocampus (Ogden & Corkin, 1991). Although the treatment greatly ameliorated H.M.'s epilepsy, the surgery produced **anterograde amnesia**, the inability to form new memories.

For the most part, the surgery did not produce **retrograde amnesia**, the loss of already existing memories. H.M. could remember much of his childhood – his parents, his own name, and where he went to school – and thus retained his sense of identity. H.M.'s short-term memory was also largely unaffected. He could hold a normal amount of information in working memory and carry on a short conversation. In his ephemeral existence, he could laugh at the same jokes day after day and reportedly spent much time watching reruns of old television shows. H.M. was fully conscious of his deficit and was greatly distressed by the fact that every moment of his life was erased as soon as it had passed. H.M. and other cases like his demonstrated that the hippocampus plays a critical role in converting temporarily buffered information into long-term memory.

H.M.'s anterograde amnesia was remarkably pure, which helped reveal another important fact about memory. Psychologist Brenda Milner (1970) spent several decades studying H.M. and discovered early on that the consolidation deficit was restricted to explicit memory. He had no trouble learning motor tasks or acquiring knowledge through conditioning procedures; he just could not consciously remember ever having learned them. This provided the first solid evidence for multiple memory systems in the brain.

A massive effort is currently underway to understand the biological basis of memory. This effort focuses on discovering the cellular mechanisms that gradually produce a stable, enduring memory trace. An in-depth treatment of this field is wholly beyond the scope of this book and we restrict ourselves here to a conceptual treatment of hippocampal function.

Compared to the implicit system, which represents only simple relationships, the explicit system forms higher-order representation, which requires the brain to code a barrage of complex relationships. This is where the hippocampus comes in. It links information that is physically located in different areas of TOP (Squire & Kandel, 1999). When we try to recall a recent event, the hippocampus is asked to supply the codes, which are then used to re-create the firing patterns across TOP cortices that occurred during the actual event, which is, in effect, the neural equivalent of a memory. H.M., then, did not lack the ability to form new memories in the cerebral cortex but the ability to code the relationship among them. Like trying to find information on, say, the American Civil War in the Library of Congress without the aid of a catalog system, H.M. could not consciously recall events that were parceled out all over TOP; he did not have the codes. The cortex might still form memories but their components would dangle in isolation.

This leaves open the question of why H.M. kept his existing long-term memories. How does LTM become independent of the hippocampus over time? Perhaps the hippocampus, in a way, does to memory what Leonard Bernstein does to music (Carlson, 2004). In the same way a conductor of a philharmonic orchestra does not play any instruments the hippocampus does not contain any memory. A conductor keeps the codes to the music like the hippocampus keeps the codes to the memory. These codes are vital if the orchestra performs a symphony for the first time; however, if the orchestra plays a symphony for the nth time, the codes slowly become embedded into the procedure of playing the music itself. Although this can surely be argued, an orchestra can play a repertoire piece reasonably well without a conductor, with each musician taking cues from others in a kind of spreading activation. Likewise, over time, the codes for a particular event become intrinsic to the memory and thus independent of the hippocampus.

The hippocampus is also involved in **infantile amnesia**. If you are like most people, the first events you remember are mostly trivial and fall between 3 and 6 years of age, with perhaps a few unsharp images prior to this age. All other experiences, important or not, are simply lost. This is likely due to the fact that neither the hippocampus (Nadel & Zola-Morgan, 1984) nor the cerebral cortex (Goldman-Rakic, 1992) are sufficiently developed to perform the complex task of laying down explicit memories. Thus, in contrast to the unsubstantiated but popular belief that we repress childhood memories, our inability to recall early childhood events is caused by a mechanism similar to that of H.M.'s amnesia, highlighting further that the content of consciousness is critically dependent on how the brain accomplishes the formation of memory.

Representation of knowledge

For the study of consciousness, there are three central questions regarding the long-term storage of information: (1) How is long-term memory organized? (2) How is information from this vast databank pulled into the focus of consciousness? (3) How accurate is the memory once it becomes (again) the content of consciousness?

For the explicit system, long-term memory is the realm of the cerebral cortex. Explicit LTM is subdivided further into episodic (events) and semantic (facts) memory (Tulving, 1997). **Episodic memory** refers to events in your life, for instance, a beautiful vacation in Paris. **Semantic memory** refers to general knowledge, facts, names, abstract concepts, rules, and the fact that Paris is the capital of France. Episodic memory contains a self-reference and we typically encode the time, place, and context of the memory acquired. Semantic memory contains no self-reference and we typically do not store its when and how – or do you remember when and where you learned that Paris is the capital of France?

One of the central questions of long-term memory research concerns its structure and organization. For instance, what did you do on October 18, 1999? How would you go about looking for this information in the convoluted vaults of your cortex? Cognitive theorists have proposed several general models of knowledge representation but all agree that knowledge is organized in clusters or categories and connected by associations that link items either in time, space, or semantic meaning. All models make clear that our general knowledge is not organized like a database that can be searched with different keywords from different angles. This can be easily seen by the difficulty of retrieving information that cuts across clusters or categories, for instance, recalling the months of the year in alphabetical order or listing all the animals that are green. While there are several models that emphasize categorization, network models emphasize interrelation between items. Since network models better account for the available evidence, they have become the paradigm of this field of cognitive science.

The first and best-known network model is the **semantic network model** proposed by the cognitive psychologists Collins and Loftus (1975). We will use it to highlight the basic tenets of network models although it has been superseded

Figure 8.2

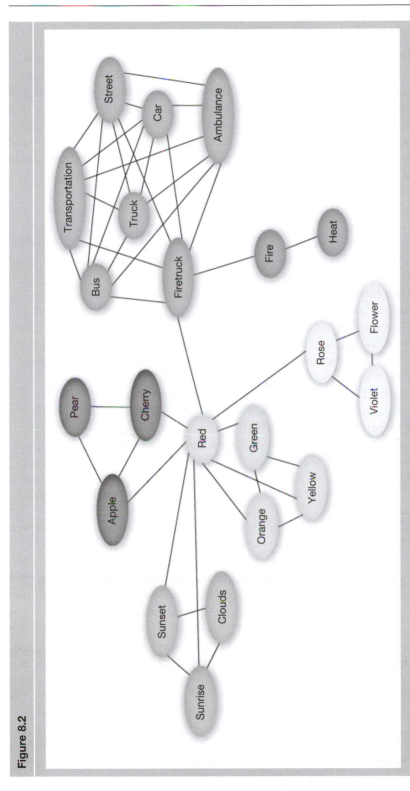

The semantic network mode proposes that knowledge is organized in terms of concepts that are connected together in a network-like structure. Activation of the concept "red" will spread through the semantic network according to the stength with which other concepts in the network are connected to it. (Adapted from Collins & Loftus, 1975)

by more sophisticated models, namely the parallel distributed processing or PDP approach (McClelland, 1995), which also goes under the names connectionism or neural network model, and the adaptive control of thought or ACT theory (Anderson, 1996). The semantic network model is based on the idea that knowledge consists of concepts that are interconnected in a network-like structure. The model represents concepts as nodes, which are linked to each other in a way that takes into account the strength of their associations. Thus, when we retrieve information, or activate a concept, the activation will spread to other concepts and eventually throughout the network. This process, appropriately called **spreading activation**, proceeds by favoring a path along the strongest semantic connections – like lightning favoring the path of least resistance.

The second question of how information shifts in status from unconscious to conscious has received much less attention. One way to think about it is in terms of top-down or bottom-up processes. While top-down involves effortful, deliberate retrieval of knowledge; bottom-up refers to the spontaneous representation of information in consciousness. Several proposals have been put forward with respect to how knowledge might shift unprompted from a dormant, inactive to a conscious, active status but one possibility that might predict the likelihood of retrieval of a given stored item is the spreading activation through a knowledge-based or semantic network. We shall explore these processes and their consequences for the content of consciousness in more detail in the next section and in later chapters.

The third question addresses the accuracy of memory. One of the most profound insights from cognitive psychology is that memory is an active and reconstructive process. Perception and cognition are strongly dependent upon a preconceived mental structure. Psychologists use the term **schema** to refer to such preset compartmentalization of knowledge. Schemas facilitate the efficient encoding and storage of knowledge; however, during retrieval they are also sources of potential errors. Because we reconstruct memory consistent with our schemas, it becomes vulnerable to distortions, which is true for semantic, episodic, and autobiographical memory.

Consider, for instance, research on eyewitness testimony. In a classic experiment, Elizabeth Loftus asked students to view a film of a car accident. In an immediate follow-up questionnaire, students were asked to describe, in writing, what they saw. She divided the students into five groups. All students were given the same questions except for one which was presented in five different versions, one for each group. In one version, the question read: "About how fast were the cars going when they contacted each other?" The other four versions contained just one minor change, namely the word *contacted* was changed to *bumped*, *hit*, *collided*, and *smashed*, respectively. As a first result, the groups differed in their estimate of the speed of the cars. In ascending order, the *contacted* group gave an estimate of 32 mph, the *bumped* group of 34 mph, the *hit* group of 38 mph, the *collided* group of 39 mph, and the *smashed* group of 41 mph, clearly demonstrating how a leading question can influence memory formation. The more surprising result occurred when the students were brought back into the lab in a one-week follow-up. Although there was no broken glass in the film, when asked about it, 60 percent of the *smashed* group responded with yes, while only 30 percent in the *contacted* group did so (Loftus & Palmer, 1974). Note that this is different from forgetting or not remembering owing to a lack of attention. It is a false memory. It suggests that the content of consciousness based on the retrieval of memory is as unreliable and subjective as that based on perception.

Box 8.2   Flashbulb memory

Where were you on September 11, 2001 at about 11 o'clock EST? Do you recall what day of the week it was? How about other impressions of the moment you first heard the news about the attacks on the World Trade Center? Most people have a very clear and vivid memory of this day. But, do you also remember what you did on September 11, 1999?

Flashbulb memory is the term used for a vivid memory that is formed during surprising, unusual, or traumatic events or situations (Brown & Kulik, 1977). The more unexpected, extraordinary, or bizarre the event, the more likely it is to be retrieved from long-term storage (Hunt & Ellis, 1998). We all form flashbulb memories for important personal events such as our wedding day or our first day in college. However, we also form flashbulb memories of significant historical events that eventually become part of a sort of collective consciousness. For older generations, the assassination of John F. Kennedy or the moon landing are perhaps the best examples. However, since 9/11, we all share a new flashbulb memory.

Cognitive psychologists agree that traumatic events are better remembered but research has shown that, contrary to popular conception, flashbulb memories are neither immune to forgetting nor more accurate than other memories. Many studies of flashbulb memories such as the O. J. Simpson trial (Schmolck et al., 2000) or the attempted assassination of the American President Ronald Reagan (Pillemer, 1984) have substantiated this conclusion. For instance, one of the pioneers of cognitive psychology, Ulric Neisser, asked college students about the explosion of the space shuttle *Challenger* a day after the event and again after three-years. The results showed significant lapses in memory (Neisser & Harsch, 1992). About one-third of the respondents were flatly mistaken about the event itself or how and where they heard the news. But here is the rub. When Neisser confronted them with their inconsistencies by showing them their own handwritten recollection from the day after the event, the students had such extreme confidence in the accuracy of their memory that they suggested that their own, handwritten recollection might be wrong!

The events of September 11 prompted several labs to collaborate on a comprehensive study of flashbulb memory. With time of the essence, a detailed questionnaire was hurriedly developed and distributed between September 17 and 24 to all geographical regions of the USA as well as to special demographic groups, such as the elderly. A one-year follow-up has been completed and the group is likely to publish its findings soon after a longer follow-up has been completed. Other less ambitious surveys have already produced some results. Kathy Pezdek (2003) surveyed 690 people about the events and found significant memory distortions just seven weeks after September 11. For instance, 75 percent of the respondents remembered seeing the first plane crash into the tower on television on 11 September when, in fact, this footage was not aired until the next day. Subjects also estimated that the time interval between the first plane crash and the collapse of the second tower was about 1 hour when, in fact, the two events were separated by a full 2 hours. Research on flashbulb memory demonstrates most clearly that the content of our consciousness is never a faithful reflection of the reality, even for events that allegedly are unforgettable in all their detail.

The implicit system

Implicit learning

Unlike the explicit system, the implicit system is a simple all-in-one system as one structure handles all information-processing stages. For reasons that will become clear in this section, implicit knowledge is not verbalizable and remains inaccessible to consciousness. The explicit system with its working memory buffer can only know of the existence of implicit knowledge through task performance. This leads to the curious but common situation that we often cannot explain why we do what we do or how we know what we know. For example, a good typist is fluent on the keyboard but is typically unable to recite the letters of the alphabet that make up the middle row of a keyboard. Can you explain, without the use of hands, how to tie shoelaces? In this section, we focus on procedural memory to illustrate the functions of the implicit system and its significance to the study of consciousness.

Although probably uncommon, information can be acquired exclusively by either the implicit or explicit system. Implicit learning "takes place largely independently of conscious attempts to learn and largely in the absence of explicit knowledge about what was acquired" (Reber, 1993, p. 5). A prototypical example is language acquisition in children but implicit learning can readily be demonstrated in adults (Schacter & Bruckner, 1998). For instance, the Tower of Hanoi is a game in which three rings that are stacked according to size on a pole have to be moved, one by one, over an intermediate pole to a third pole without ever putting a larger ring on top of a smaller one. The optimal solution involves seven steps and students learn it readily. Yet, it is virtually impossible for those students to give an accurate account of how they did it. If their verbal account is translated into a computer program the machine is unable to repeat it (Gazzaniga et al., 1998). In contrast, explicit learning is, as we have seen, not "learning-by-doing," but proceeds through the conscious application of rules. In the process, the explicit system forms a mental representation that includes not only the actual information but also knowledge about what and the fact that it was acquired. A prototypical example might be the acquisition of a second language in adulthood.

A more common scenario, however, is that learning engages both systems simultaneously. Studies suggest that a typical learning situation results in the formation of two distinct mental representations, one explicit and one implicit (Milner et al., 1968; Schacter, 1987). Because each system subserves different functions, it is unlikely that either representation alone is a complete characterization of the learned task. While some information may be represented in both systems, other information may reside in only one. For instance, cooking a multi-course dinner requires some tasks that are explicit, such as mixing ingredients according to instruction, while a variety of other tasks, such as deciding when the vegetables are done, are implicit.

The degree to which either system has a complete representation depends on the amount of practice and the nature of the task. Consider a person's native language, which is entirely learned and largely represented in the implicit system, but with considerable study, the explicit system can develop its own representation of the phonology, semantics, and grammar. This is not easy, as any English major will tell you, yet it is a paramount requirement to be able teach a native language to others. In contrast, a second language learned in adulthood is acquired painstakingly by the explicit system with no "feel" or intuitive understanding for it. Yet, with extensive practice, often nothing short of total immersion, the knowledge can also become represented in the implicit system. Building a representation in the implicit system is referred to as "internalizing" or becoming "second nature" in colloquial speech. Either case would result in two complete and independent mental representations, which is almost certainly a defining characteristic that qualifies a person as a true expert. Thus, knowledge can be explicit and/or implicit, but is mostly represented in varying, partially overlapping degrees of each.

The nature of the task appears to determine the initial degree of explicitness and implicitness. From an evolutionary perspective, the existence of two distinct systems for knowledge representation indicates that each must be specialized in some way. Thus, each system is likely to be predisposed to handle certain tasks or certain task features. For instance, tasks that are either one-dimensional, i.e., can be described by a single rule, or tasks that have relatively few conjunctive (sequential) rules are easily learned by the explicit system. An example is the **Wisconsin Card Sorting Task** (WCST), in which cards are sorted by one of three characteristics: color, number, or shape. The person is asked to discover the sorting rule empirically using only feedback from the examiner. When the sorting rule is changed, the person is to adapt to the new rule. Subjects have no problem accurately describing the rule(s) verbally. However, as the task complexity increases and the optimal rule is either multidimensional, i.e., requires the integration of several rules, or is probabilistic in nature, the task is notoriously difficult to describe explicitly. This is nicely illustrated in a categorization experiment by Waldron and Ashby (2001). The experimenters created 16 stimulus cards that could vary in four dimensions: background color (blue or yellow), embedded symbol color (green or red), symbol number (1 or 2), and symbol shape (square or circle). The two levels of each dimension were coded in a binary fashion as either +1 or 0. In addition, one dimension was arbitrarily selected to be irrelevant. The subject was presented with a stimulus consisting of a combination of eight of these cards and was asked to decide empirically whether the stimulus belonged to category A or B. The implicit rule that determined category membership was: "The stimulus belongs to category A if the sum of the values on the relevant dimensions > 1.5; Otherwise it belongs to category B." The interesting result of the study was that virtually all subjects achieved perfect performance; however, no one was able to describe the rule. In other words, tasks that have less salient rules are more readily imprinted in the implicit system.

This raises the question, given that one-dimensional and multidimensional tasks are coded implicitly, why the explicit system exists at all. This is, of course,

Figure 8.3

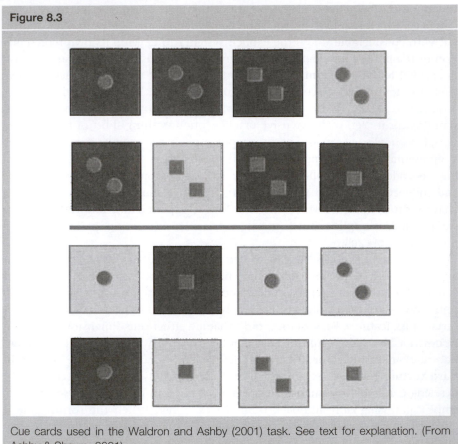

Cue cards used in the Waldron and Ashby (2001) task. See text for explanation. (From Ashby & Shawn, 2001)

part of the larger question of the evolutionary significance of consciousness. Anticipating a discussion in the next section, a simple solution has been offered by Crick and Koch (1998). A frog responds stereotypically, zombie-like if you will, to visual input, that is, to small, preylike objects by snapping, and to large, looming objects by jumping. These responses are controlled by rigid and reflexive but fast-responding systems. As the number of reflexive systems must grow to handle increased complexity, such an organization becomes inefficient. A more advantageous solution is to evolve a single system capable of temporarily buffering and sustaining multiple representations, so that the organism can examine them before making an output decision. This is particularly useful when two or more of the organism's systems generate conflicting plans of action. This is also the concept behind the higher-order thought (HOT) models of consciousness (Chapter 6). Thus, implicit knowledge can be thought of as task-specific, that is, inaccessible to other parts of the system and thus less versatile (Karmiloff-Smith, 1992). Explicit knowledge, on the other hand, can dramatically increase behavioral flexibility, because it can be broadcast to a global workspace (Baars, 1997), which allows us to test conflicting hypotheses and to integrate seemingly counterintuitive notions about the world. Nearly all scientific knowledge is not intuitive and the implicit system would have never learned that the earth is round, that it has a molten core, or that it is at the outer arm of some small galaxy, to say nothing of eleven-dimensional string theory.

The flexibility/efficiency trade-off

Why are multidimensional tasks, such as the one used by Waldron and Ashby, more likely embedded implicitly? The answer to this question can be found in the capacity limit of working memory. In contrast to the explicit system, the implicit system is not capacity limited. Take, for instance, a motor task such as a tennis serve. Anybody who has tried it can tell you that more is involved than tossing the ball straight in the air, swinging the racket in an arc, hitting the ball as it descends, and following the motion through. Consider, for instance, what it would take to write a computer program that specifies each muscle twitch in the correct order and intensity to make a world-class tennis serve. The computational difficulty of complex motion is enormous, a fact that is readily recognized by the AI community. The amount of information that must be held concurrently in working memory far surpasses the capacity limit. A complex motion is either learned by observation or, if learned through explicit instruction, by breaking it up into smaller components, each of which cannot contain more than four independent pieces of information. Once these are morphed into a single chunk, larger chunks can be combined to acquire intricate motion.

To further illustrate, consider how we learn to drive a car. Using the explicit instructions of the person in the passenger seat, our explicit system forms a mental representation of the task requirements and recruits the premotor cortex and primary motor cortex to execute it (Jenkins et al., 1994). This effortful process takes time because the capacity limit restricts the number of items that can be amalgamated at a time to smooth out motion. As a result of this working memory cap, the frontal attentional network is fully engaged, making it impossible to attend to anything else, such as listening to the radio or daydreaming. Neuroimaging studies have shown that skill acquisition activates the prefrontal cortex, the premotor cortex, and the parietal cortex, as well as the cerebellum (ibid.). It is thought that during this acquisition process the basal ganglia acts as a passive observer. However, studies have also shown that shifts in neural control occur as a function of practice so that the details of a motor task become gradually controlled by the basal ganglia (Mishkin et al., 1984) in a circuit that also includes the supplementary motor cortex, the motor thalamus, and the hippocampus (Jenkins et al., 1994). Put another way, the implicit system builds its own mental representation, which is the equivalent of what is known conversationally by the unfortunate misnomer "muscle memory." This results in an internalized motor pattern controlled entirely by the basal ganglia circuit and little prefrontal activity is required during its routine execution. This is the brain's conquer-and-divide principle: as the basal ganglia and supplementary motor cortex drive the car, aided by perceptual input from the parietal cortex, working memory is no longer tied up, allowing executive attention to fill its premium computational space with other content such as listening to the radio or reloading a favorite daydream scenario. In other words, performance of implicit skills can fully bypass consciousness.

Evidently, the main advantage of the implicit systems is its efficiency. The mechanism(s) by which knowledge shifts from an unconscious state to a conscious state is one of the most fundamental questions of cognitive science and lies at the heart of consciousness research (Cleeremans & Jiménez, 2002; Dulany, 1996). From a theoretical point of view, this boundary is not sharp and several steps might occur before knowledge is fully accessible to consciousness (Karmiloff-Smith, 1992). Take the example provided by Dienes & Perner (2002): "I know that this is a cat." This information has three elements: (1) the content (this is a cat), (2) the attitude (knowing, as opposed to a different attitude, for instance, wishing), and (3) the holder (I – rather than you). At the lowest level, the content (this is a cat) is part of the information-processing system and can be put to use, i.e., run away if the system is a mouse brain. This is the level of procedural knowledge and it leaves the elements of attitude and holder implicit. At the next level, the system represents the attitude explicitly, that is, the system *predicates* the information to be knowledge (rather than a wish). The system now not only possesses and uses the information but also represents what it is that it possesses and uses. In other words, it labels it as knowledge. This is a higher-order thought (HOT) or meta-representation that makes the information usable for other parts of the system. However, this leaves implicit whether or not the information is a fact. Information can be false, and the ability to engage in hypothesis testing necessitates that we can distinguish between true and false, which requires the validity of the information be made explicit in a higher-order representation. Thus, at the next level, the system represents content, predication, and factivity but leaves implicit the holder. Only if the holder also becomes a higher-order representation can we speak of information as fully explicit or fully conscious (Kihlstrom, 1996). Also, it is only then that we can verbally communicate the knowledge.

This makes clear why procedural knowledge is so limited in its usability. Because it is impossible for the implicit system to determine whether or not something is a fact (implicit knowledge treats all events as true), it cannot represent the knowledge as a hypothetical possibility, and this makes it inflexible and idiosyncratic (Dienes & Perner, 2002). It is, however, this very inflexibility that explains why procedural knowledge is more efficient. Higher-order representations exponentially increase computational complexity. Given the mind-boggling complexity of even the simplest of motor skills, the explication of this knowledge would become a serious resource issue. Indeed, it would be impossible given the capacity limit of our highest-order computational space, working memory. Instead, procedural knowledge is contained in the application of the procedure and need not be extracted from general rules that are represented at a higher-order level and then applied to a specific example in real time. Motor skills are more efficient because they leave implicit predication, factivity, and the reference to self.

It has been suggested that implicit knowledge holds the key to *what it is like* to be something. Recall that the what-it's-likeness – the qualitative content of experiential states – is considered by many the defining characteristic of consciousness and lies at the center of the raging debate whether or not consciousness is inherently subjective. For some, qualia have a mode of existence – a first-person mode – that cannot be redescribed in third-person, objective terms. But others have argued that qualia are simply embedded, implicit knowledge (Cleeremans, 1997). The fact that implicit information is not accessible to other parts of the system would explain why qualia seem to defy description. What's more, implicit information can very easily be simulated by connectionist models (ibid.). On the one hand, this suggests that qualia, if they indeed were embedded as implicit knowledge, are not ineffable after all, although they certainly seem like it. On the other hand, the ability to model information does not automatically mean that it is also reducible to a third-person perspective.

Computational issues in skill performance

If information is part of the explicit *and* implicit knowledge base, as is the case with driving a car, the neural control of its execution can be transferred from one system to the other. However, a skilled behavior that is largely acquired implicitly would have to be explicated first. This must proceed though the induction of inference processes (e.g., Dienes & Perner, 2002; Frensch et al., 2002). Naturally, the skill is performed by a conscious person and is thus *accompanied* by conscious experience. This allows the explicit system to observe the behavior and extract the skill's critical elements. It should be clear that this is an educated guessing game that is imperfect. Note that fully (predication and factivity) implicit knowledge cannot *cause* explicit knowledge through a bottom-up process. The implicit system cannot label the information itself as knowledge and thus cannot broadcast it to the system. Only through the circuitous route involving actual behavior can the explicit system come to embody an implicitly learned skill. This is exemplified when trying to retrieve a phone number that is temporarily inaccessible. We typically solve that problem by dialing the number on an imaginary phone dial, using the execution of implicit knowledge to trigger explicit representation. In contrast, knowledge in the explicit system can be accessed internally, through a top-down process. As we mentioned earlier, the fact that the implicit system cannot tell the explicit system directly what it does and why it does it leads to the exceedingly curious situation that we often cannot explain why we do what we do, leaving us little choice but to exclaim that the behavior was guided by intuition. This is a particularly common experience when trying to explain a motor skill to others.

Two studies further illustrate the way the explicit and implicit systems interact in skill performance. In a series of experiments by Bridgeman and colleagues (1991; Bridgeman et al., 1997) the motion of a rectangular frame across a computer screen created the apparent motion of a stationary dot placed inside the frame moving in the opposite direction. Subjects were briefly exposed to the visual illusion and then asked to either indicate verbally which of five marked spots best described the last location of the dot or to point to that location using their hands. The verbal condition would engage the explicit system while the implicit system would control the steering of the finger. The results showed that all verbal subjects were highly susceptible to the illusion, whereas half the subjects in the pointing condition could accurately specify the location of the dot. These results indicate that procedural knowledge is not only fast and efficient but also more accurate in real-time sensory-motor integration. A famous Austrian down-hill skier apparently hit the nail on the head when he said: "You can't win a thing by thinking." This blunt statement is backed by a study reporting that 95 percent of athletes believe that thinking hinders performance (Ravizza, 1977). Interestingly, when the subjects in both conditions were asked to withhold their response for 8 seconds, all were susceptible to the Roelofs effect, as it is called. This indicates that visually guided movement leaves time (along with predication and factivity) implicit; procedural memory is thus inflexible and only useful in the here and now.

A similar insight can be obtained from another study by Castiello and colleagues (1991). Subjects were seated in front of three candle-sized rods and were asked to grasp one of the rods as soon as it was illuminated. On some trials a rod was illuminated, but after the subject had already started a visually guided movement to that target, the target was changed by illuminating a different rod. Not surprisingly, this resulted in a smooth and very rapid correction of the hand's trajectory. The subjects were also asked to give a vocal indication as soon as they were aware of the switch. The experiment produced numerous instances in which a subject had already grasped the new target before they were aware of it.

Compare this to the lightning-fast escape maneuvers of a squirrel. Lacking an overall strategy or plan, the squirrel gets to safety entirely by relying on moment-to-moment adjustments. Such smooth feedback-driven sensory-motor integration can produce extremely complex movement patterns that can serve an overall and/or higher goal (safety), yet requires no more than the reaction to immediately preceding input. Now consider how an outfielder catches a flyball. Starting with only a vague idea as to the ball's ultimate location, the player progressively approximates that location by continuously adjusting his movements based on updates of the ball's trajectory and speed as it approaches (McLeod et al., 2001). Because these are fluid situations occurring in real time, they require, first and foremost, efficiency. A system is most efficient if it represents knowledge in a fully implicit manner; that is, it codes the application of the knowledge within the procedure and refrains from buffering any other property (e.g., predication, factivity, or time) of the information in a higher-order representation. On the flip side, this setup is the reason why motor behavior must progress stepwise from immediately preceding input. The lack of meta-representation precludes the system from calculating hypothetical future scenarios that would enable it to anticipate several steps in advance.

Figure 8.4

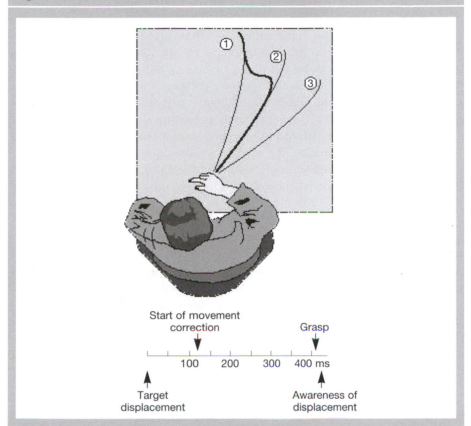

Start of movement correction

Grasp

100   200   300   400 ms

Target displacement

Awareness of displacement

Subjects in the Castiello et al. (1991) study were asked to grasp one of three rods as soon as it was illuminated. In some trials, the illumination was switched to a different rod after the subjects had already started a visually guided movement to the first target. Subjects adjusted smoothly, demonstrating the efficiency of the implicit system. Subjects were also asked to report the change verbally as soon as they were aware of it. Many subjects noticed the change after they had already made the adjustment, showing that the explicit system is inefficient and slower for the performance of skilled action. (Reprinted from Frith et al., 1999)

Framed in computational terms, it becomes clear why such meta-representation is unattainable for movement. Even for squirrels, the number of possible next moves is so astronomically high that future projections would quickly bifurcate to infinity. Such a nonlinear system is unpredictable, rendering the calculation of hypothetical future scenarios useless. Accordingly, the complexity and speed requirement of purposeful motion makes explication not only prohibitively costly but impossible. Such a nonlinear, dynamic system is unpredictable but it is not random and might settle to a strange attractor (see Chapter 4). For instance, a tennis match is a dynamic system with two moving targets. Although it might settle to one or more strange attractors, such as one player's weak backhand, moment-to-moment events are completely unpredictable. Consequently, the explicit system is limited to representing tasks that can be solved *outside* real time and that can be broken up into less than four chunks. Since this is not the case for movement, the only viable solution is to increase either the number of reflexive systems and/or the number of response patterns within a reflexive system. This does not change the system's modularity; it is still a reflexive system, as output remains guided by the immediately preceding input, but it now has an increased number of specialized and independent response patterns.

Due to its limited capacity, the explicit system cannot handle the combinational explosion presented by multidimensional tasks such as skilled movement. This combinational potential coupled with the real-time requirement of production make it impossible for the explicit system to micro-manage purposeful motion. Because a highly practiced skill is still performed by a conscious person, it is possible for the explicit system to partake in its execution. To stay with the example of tennis, this occurs when a player buffers any part of the game (e.g., reflecting on the strokes or what it would mean to lose) in a higher-order representation and allows such analysis to guide movements. It should be obvious now that any amount of transfer of the skill from implicit to explicit control gravely affects its quality. John McEnroe apparently knew this intuitively. The story is told that when he played an opponent who was "in the zone" and could do no wrong with his, say, forehand, McEnroe would call it to his attention by praising his rival on his excellent forehand during the switching of sides.

Summary

Memory is a collection of cognitive processes organized into multiple systems that depend on many brain areas. Each memory system manages independently the acquisition, storage, and retrieval of knowledge, enabling specific skills that subserve different adaptive behaviors. For cognition, two broad systems can be delineated in terms of anatomy and function.

The explicit system is a sophisticated system that represents knowledge in a higher-order format, which permits it to broadcast its knowledge to a global workspace. The complexity involved in organizing information in propositional and abstract terms is beyond any single brain structure's computational ability. Thus, the explicit system depends on several brain structures; each specialized to perform a particular step of information processing. The effortful encoding and retrieval of information is managed by working memory processes that depend on the dorsolateral prefrontal cortex. Working memory is also the workshop of consciousness, in which explicit knowledge is buffered and manipulated in the current focus of attention. To consolidate multimodal knowledge that is parceled out over many cortical areas and several levels of abstraction, the explicit system recruits the hippocampus and other medial temporal lobe structures. Finally, long-term memory is located, fully interwoven into existing circuitry, in the various TOP cortices. The explicit system appears to treat episodic and semantic knowledge somewhat differently but both types of explicit knowledge are assumed to be stored in associative networks. The recall of explicit memory is a reconstructive process and thus prone to distortions. It follows that the content of consciousness, be it based on perceptual or memory processes, is never a faithful reflection of the physical world.

The implicit system is a more primitive and evolutionary ancient system that does not form higher-order representations. As a consequence, the explicit system, or any other functional system, does not know about knowledge imprinted in the implicit system, making it unavailable for representation in working memory, and thus consciousness. For implicit knowledge to reach consciousness it must first be explicated, which cannot proceed, due to its concrete-operational organization, through a bottom-up process. We must perform or execute implicit knowledge, which allows the explicit system to observe it and extract its essential components. Because the implicit system refrains from abstractions, it is not burdened by the computational complexity that comes with higher-order thought, and a single brain structure, such as the basal ganglia or cerebellum, can handle all information-processing steps. This makes knowledge in the system highly efficient, albeit only to its specific application. Smooth sensory-motor integration leading to purposeful motion must occur in real time and this is the domain of the implicit system, responding to environmental stimuli in a fast and accurate manner.

Suggested reading

Anderson, J. R. (1996). ACT: A simple theory of complex cognition. *American Psychologist*, *51*, 355–65.

Cowan, N. (1995). *Attention and Memory: An Integrated Framework*. Oxford Psychology Series, No. 26. New York: Oxford University Press.

French, R. M., & Cleeremans A. (2002). *Implicit Learning and Consciousness*. New York: Psychology Press.

Squire, L. R., & Kandel, E.R. (1999). *From Mind to Molecules*. New York: Scientific American Library.

9 Emotion

Basic emotions

Early roots

As a field of study, emotion has suffered from historical neglect. Neither philosophers nor scientists held it in high regard or gave it much attention. This is surprising given the central role emotions play in our lives. There is really no emotionless moment in life (McGaugh, 2002)! The affective content of consciousness is an ever-present feature of our subjective psychological experience either as enduring background music in the form of a mood or as loud and honest signals capable of completely dominating phenomenal consciousness. Today, emotions are increasingly recognized not just as a quirky little curiosity that fills our life with meaning, but as an indispensable survival mechanism and a central organizing process for consciousness.

The first section of this chapter examines basic emotions before we move on, in the second section, to describe complex emotions. Note that we will adopt here, as we did in earlier chapters, the convention of distinguishing unconscious from conscious representation. Although this implies in some way that information is either unequivocally "in" or "out" of consciousness, we simply use it here as a linguistic convenience and not as an endorsement of Cartesian materialism (see Chapter 5).

Greek philosophers – the Stoics among them most explicitly – thought of emotions as harmful. They held the distinguishing feature of man to be his **rational soul**, which endows us with the ability to think logically and, so the view goes, saves us from generally behaving like any other beast. In the quest for knowledge, truth, and morality, they placed absolute trust in reason. For the most part, Western philosophy has perpetuated this false dichotomy, always contrasting reason with passion, with the latter portrayed as primitive and, at best, a hindrance in the pursuit of noble virtues. Eminent philosophers such as René Descartes and Emmanuel Kant routinely dismissed emotions as untrustworthy and argued that man is defined by the rational mind. By the romantic period, reason was placed in the brain, while emotions were relegated to be the domain of the body.

Society has largely accepted the emotional/rational distinction, complete with its laden value judgment, perhaps because it is so intuitive. It is not difficult to think of instances in which emotions are maladaptive and get in the way of achieving our goals in life. Emotions are the source of most problems in society, be it divorce, corruption, crime, or racism. The seven deadly sins are all emotions. This way of thinking overlooks, of course, that emotions must be adaptive in general, otherwise, they would not have evolved by natural selection.

Psychologists also assigned a back seat to emotions. This is perhaps not surprising for the early days of psychology, as the field only developed into an independent discipline in the late 1870s from philosophy and psychophysics. Yet, emotions did not occupy center stage thereafter either. In the twentieth century, psychology was dominated by two paradigms, behaviorism and cognitive psychology, that treated emotions as either epiphenomenal or irrelevant. In one of the few highlights in the study of emotions from the first century of psychological science, the psychologist William James and the physiologist Carl Lange formulated a theory of emotion (James, 1884; Lange, 1887). With the exception of a few theories and classification systems, there was little information on emotions in the psychological knowledge base at the centennial birthday of the field in 1979.

Neuroscientists similarly neglected the study of emotions. To be sure, emotions are more tricky to study than, say, memory or vision, especially in animals, but this neglect was also due to the perception that emotions are rather ethereal entities, not the sort of things that lend themselves easily to scientific inquiry. Historically, the only influential advance came in the form of a one-two punch initiated by the neuroanatomist James Papez, who in 1937 published a short theoretical paper, in which he proposed that a set of structures – hippocampus, cingulum, anterior thalamus, etc. – form a functional circuit that controls emotions. It was a bold pitch, especially since he lacked any hard evidence in support of the proposal. The second punch came in 1949, when the neurophysiologist Paul MacLean added a few more structures to the collection, notably the amygdala and the septal area, bestowed the **Papez circuit** with additional evolutionary duties, and gave it the name by which it is known today: the limbic system (MacLean, 1949). The limbic system was part of MacLean's larger theory of the **triune brain** (see Chapter 6). According to the theory, the limbic system evolved prior to cortical tissue and controlled basic survival behaviors, such as emotions. The capacity for cognitive processes only developed with the subsequent evolution of the cerebral cortex. Although this new cortex superseded the limbic brain in sophistication, it was built on the base of the more primitive limbic system, which remained in control of emotions. To dominate behavioral output, the cortex inhibited the functions of the limbic system but with only partial success, making human behavior rational at times and emotional at others.

Like all theories, MacLean's theory was a result of the *Zeitgeist*, in this case the accepted convention that reason and passion indeed correspond to a strict dichotomy with the former representing the pinnacle of the human intellect. As a consequence, the theory resonated well with philosophical traditions and influenced the thinking of generations of neuroscientists. Today, neuroscientists know considerably more about the brain mechanisms underlying emotion and cognition, and a fundamental reconceptualization has taken place. First, the respective assignment of emotion to the limbic system and cognition to the cerebral cortex is false. Most limbic structures, notably the hippocampal formation, do not mediate emotions at all, but contribute instead to cognitive processes. Similarly, complex or social emotions are mediated by the cortex, notably the ventromedial prefrontal cortex, making the cortex not only the brain's thinking cap but also the brain's feeling cap. The most important conclusion of the research since the mid-1980s, however, is that emotions are neither separate nor the counterpart of rationality but rather their prerequisite. Also, from a neuroscientific perspective, there is no longer anything special or ethereal about emotions. Like any other information processing, emotions are patterns of neural firing that can be studied using the methods of neuroscience.

The road to fear

Empirical work on the neural control of emotions has focused on fear and anxiety and we now explore how those processes might give rise to the affective content of consciousness. The pioneering research explicating the brain's fear circuit was performed by Joseph LeDoux, professor of neuroscience at New York University. In a series of studies, LeDoux zoomed in on the **amygdala** as the pivotal structure mediating the emotion of fear (LeDoux, 1996). As a behavioral measure, he used the **conditioned reflex**. Recall that in a conditioned reflex, a stimulus (food) that elicits a natural response (salivation) is presented together with a neutral stimulus (a bell). If food and bell are paired together repeatedly, they are associated, and the previously neutral bell alone can trigger the flow of saliva. A **conditioned emotional response** (CER) contains a slight variation. Here, an unpleasant, negative stimulus, such as a predator, evokes a fear response.

If the negative event is associated with a neutral stimulus, such as the music from the soundtrack of *Jaws*, a strong CER occurs simply from listening to what otherwise would be a nice piece of music.

LeDoux used an experimental setup that exposed rats to a weak foot shock (negative stimulus), which was paired with a tone (neutral stimulus). In the auditory system sound travels from the ear via the eighth cranial nerve to a couple of pit stops in the brainstem, eventually arriving at the place that must be negotiated by all sensory information: the thalamus. The thalamus sends the signal to the primary auditory cortex in the temporal cortex, which decodes the signal. The standard view was that the tone had to travel the entire way to the cortex before the rat could learn to fear it. However, to everyone's surprise, a lesion to the primary auditory cortex did not affect the rat's ability to learn to fear the shock. This meant that fear, and possibly other basic emotions, can be acquired without the cortex, or to spell it out, without consciously comprehending the stimulus that caused the emotion. Consciousness requires the involvement of the cortex and LeDoux's experiment carried the far-reaching implication that basic emotions are generated outside conscious control.

If the tone does not only go to the cortex, where else does it go? LeDoux placed lesions in successive structures along the auditory pathway and could show, with the use of standard anatomical tracing methods, that the thalamus not only sends the tone up the normal chain of command to the cortex but leaks information about the tone to the amygdala besides. Thus, the amygdala is privileged to a sneak preview of the action even before the cortex gets wind of it. So when LeDoux made lesions to the amygdala and completely abolished the CER, the rats reacted as if they were deaf, dumb, and blind or, if you like, as cool as Clint Eastwood – fearless and unflappable.

From this and other findings, LeDoux worked out the sequence of events that settled a century of research and theoretical musings on the nature of fear. Suppose you walk on the proverbial path through the woods and make your encounter with a snake lying across your path. The sight of the snake is processed by the visual system and sent to the thalamus, which forwards the input along two routes. The destination of one route is the visual cortex, which conducts high-level perceptual analysis of the snake. LeDoux called this thalamo-cortical route the **High Road**. Recall from Chapter 7 that the 30-plus extrastriatal cortical areas must perform detailed feature analysis before an accurate mental representation of the environment is built. It is this computational feat that enables us to tell the snake from an ordinary stick on the ground. The tradeoff for this precision, as with anything that is done well, is that it takes appreciably more time. The destination of the other route is the central nucleus of the amygdala, which assesses the value of the incoming sensory information. LeDoux called this thalamo-amygdala route the **Low Road**. Because visual signals coming from the thalamus have not yet been subjected to sophisticated analysis, the amygdala must work with imprecise information. It is therefore unable to tell a snake from a stick, but the advantage of not waiting around for a detailed perceptual analysis is that the amygdala can act fast and furiously.

Figure 9.1

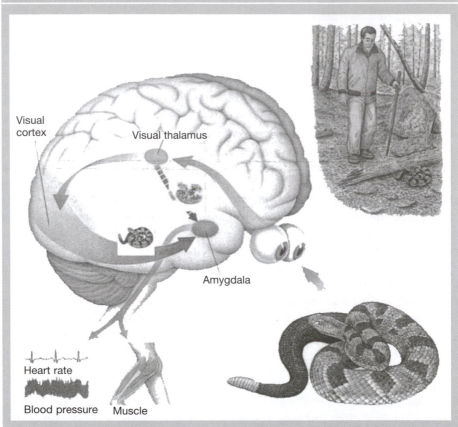

The thalamus is a waystation for sensory signals that sends information about the snake to the amygdala and visual cortex. The amygdala route is the Low Road that quickly registers the danger and initiates appropriate countermeasures. The cortical route is the High Road that constructs a conscious image of the snake, a process that takes more time. Due to the necessity of speed, a fear response is amygdala-driven and will occur regardless of whether the stimulus is indeed a snake or just an ordinary stick on the ground. (Reprinted from LeDoux 1996)

As you encounter the snake on your way through the woods, you jump away swiftly. This reaction is amygdala-driven. In the meantime, the cortex constructs a conscious image of the visual signal, which is why it takes just a split second longer to realize what it was that made you jump. If it was indeed a snake, your speedy amygdala saved the day. If, on the other hand, it was a stick, you would have jumped just the same. The amygdala is a quick and dirty system that operates under the motto: rather safe than sorry. The survival value is obvious. If you wait for conscious confirmation as to the identity of the danger, there is little hope you will contribute further to the gene pool.

Here, then, is the rub. LeDoux's research confirmed that the *formation* of basic emotions is subcortical, automatic, and unconscious, which does not preclude, of course, that their subsequent processing can make them cortical, controllable, and conscious.

The free-spirited amygdala

This leaves us with the question of how, exactly, the neural activity in the amygdala produces the emotion of fear. More pointedly, how does the amygdala accomplish the integration of what psychologists consider the three main components of emotion: the subjective experience, the physiological response, and the behavioral expression?

The amygdala is an almond-shaped structure located in the temporal lobe. It consists of several groups of nuclei that contribute to survival behaviors, including reproduction, parental care and aggression. In LeDoux's own words:

> The amygdala is like the hub of a wheel. It receives low level inputs from the sensory-specific regions of the thalamus, higher level information from the sensory-specific cortex, and still higher level (sensory independent) information about the general situation from the hippocampal formation. Through such connections, the amygdala is able to process the emotional significance of individual stimuli as well as complex situations. The amygdala is, in essence, involved in the appraisal of emotional meaning. (1996, pp. 168–9)

The principal region of the amygdala, the central nucleus, projects to the ventromedial aspect of the prefrontal cortex and various regions of the brainstem, including several nuclei of the hypothalamus. These projection systems enable the central nucleus to act as a kind of alarm-response center that coordinates the integration of the three components of fear. The upstream pathway to the VMPFC sets off a series of computations that eventually leads to the phenomenal experience of fear. Several downstream projections to the brainstem activate the various physiological and behavioral components.

The sight and sound of a threat compels the amygdala to switch to DEFCON 1 mode. Forced to act on nothing more than a hunch, the central nucleus activates three bodily systems that bring about the visible manifestations of fear. The amygdala has direct access to activating the motor system, which makes sense from an evolutionary perspective, as it evolved, at the time, to directly affect behavior. Thus, as a first countermeasure, the central nucleus activates the motor system, which may be anything from freezing to all-out sprinting. Second, the central nucleus orders its brainstem intermediaries to activate the autonomic nervous system, which serves to sustain the motor activity. Incidentally, this downstream activation is also the reason why fear is accompanied by a queasy feeling in the stomach. Third, it arranges for the activation of the endocrine system to further reinforce the autonomic response. The entire sequence of events is fully automated and not subject to oversight by the cortex. Indeed, it occurs while the TOP

Figure 9.2

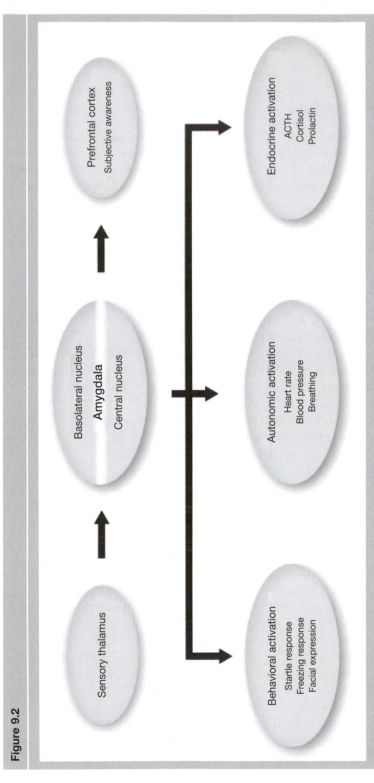

The basolateral nuclei receive inputs about the environment, which are relayed to the central nucleus. The central nucleus integrates the input and functions like a central command post. Its complex projection systems to prefrontal and brainstem regions allow it to mount a coordinated response to the threat. After lesions to the central nucleus, humans and other animals no longer show signs of fear. They cannot be bothered by a life-threatening stimulus, act generally rather tamely, show low levels of stress hormones, and have little autonomic nervous system activation. The popular bumper sticker "NO FEAR," properly neurologized, should read: "NO AMYGDALA."

cortex is still busy constructing a conscious mental representation of the threat. To fully appreciate the power of this amygdala system, consider the lightning-fast escape maneuvers of a squirrel. We can think of the amygdala as free-spirited because it acts without respect for the functional hierarchy of brain organization. Neural activity in the amygdala is primarily the result of events in the environment; not opinion or willpower.

Finally, the central nucleus also sends information about the threat to the VMPFC, which gives rise to the experience of fear. This is when we *feel* emotions. Thus, feelings and emotions are not the same; **feelings** are one aspect of emotions, and it is this one aspect of emotions in which we are likely to differ most from other animals. A dog shows similar physiological and behavioral responses to danger, but it is doubtful that it *feels* similarly afraid. The downstream pathways have been extensively road-tested by evolution but the upstream pathway is a recent addition that ends in the prefrontal cortex, a structure with unique abilities in humans, including the full capacity for the conscious representation of emotions as feelings.

Two inherent features of this amygdala-prefrontal circuitry have important ramifications for the study of consciousness. First, the transmission to the VMPFC lacks detail. The exact identity of the threat cannot be part of the upstream message because the amygdala itself cannot tell a stick from a snake. So the amygdala cannot transmit why it is activated or what activated it – only *that* it is activated. Recall from Chapter 8 that the implicit system owes its efficiency and speed to the fact that it does not form costly higher-order representation of its knowledge. In consequence, it does not know about the knowledge it has and thus cannot tell other parts of the system about it. This is why fully implicit knowledge must be explicated through the circuitous route involving actual behavior and cannot be *caused* by a bottom-up process. Basic emotions are speedy and efficient survival mechanisms that also cannot afford to be bogged down by costly higher-order representation of its knowledge. So the broadcast from the amygdala to the VMPFC cannot contain metalevel information about the stimulus. It must be a rather general message, perhaps something like: "Hey up there, I am going nuts down here." In other words, an explicit representation of what activated the amygdala cannot come from the amygdala itself but must occur through perceptual searches of the environment. In the case of a snake this should not force the person into any computational reserves but not all triggers are this obvious. As we shall see shortly, this is more so a problem because the amygdala learns by classical conditioning and can thus link two stimuli that might be totally meaningless to the rational mind.

The second feature of this circuitry is that it is primarily a one-way street. While the amygdala projects profusely to the VMPFC, the returning top-down projections are minor in comparison. This wiring limits conscious control over amygdala activity (LeDoux, 1996) and accounts for our experience that we can neither stop the generation of fear nor shut it off as long as the trigger is present. Imagine riding the elevator to the top floor of the Empire State Building and, as soon as the door opens, running straight up to the glass and looking down. There is absolutely nothing you can say to yourself during the 101-floor ride up to avoid feeling afraid. Basic emotions are bottom-up processes and the prefrontal cortex cannot stop their computation. The best option to calm the amygdala is to step away from the glass, which works because it removes the amygdala from the trigger. The amygdala is an experiential learner and must be reeducated the hard way – talking to it is useless. Amygdala neurons are a free-spirited bunch indeed.

Emotional memory

The amygdala also keeps its own memory of events. We discussed in Chapter 8 the role of the hippocampus in the consolidation of explicit memory. This process results in long-term memory stored in a metacognitive format in TOP regions. Implicit memory is consolidated without the hippocampus and results in long-term memory stored without metalevel representation in the basal ganglia and cerebellum. A real-world learning situation engages both systems, leaving separate memory traces in each. When the situation also has biological significance for the organism, an additional third record is kept. In this case, the dual cognitive system (see Figure 9.3) is complemented by the emotional system, which consolidates and represents its own version of events. To continue with the basic emotion of fear, **emotional memory** is located in the amygdala (ibid.).

This means that at least three independent but incomplete records are kept of the same event, each extracting different information for a different purpose. Suppose you drive a car on a country road and a deer suddenly jumps out of the woods. Unfortunately, your well-intended evasive maneuver sees you driving straight into the nearest tree. Suppose further that you hit the steering wheel with your head and the horn goes off. For the amygdala, the sound of the horn, formerly a neutral stimulus, now becomes associated with pain. Note that the amygdala learns this association even if you are knocked unconscious by the impact. It acquires the information via the Low Road conducting its business in the dimly-lit subcortical underground well below the conscious radar screen. A year later, you will be able to tell the story of the scar on your forehead but by then the memory of how the scar got there will be a cold fact. You will remember that pain was involved but the feeling of pain will not be experienced at that moment. The story will be a conscious memory *about an emotion*. This is different from *emotional memory*, which occurs when the amygdala is activated, generating the three components of fear. As you know by now, due to the free-spirited nature of the amygdala, this must take the route of direct experience, in this case a visit to the site of the accident or, by association, the sound of a horn. Due to limited top-down control, emotional memory is exceedingly difficult to trigger by the conscious recollection of events, especially if they occurred in the distant past. This is a neat trick of evolution, for otherwise few women would be willing to give birth twice or nobody would endure another day of stress at work. On the flip side, this is also the reason why the effects of a long vacation seem to evaporate after just a few days of being back at work.

Figure 9.3

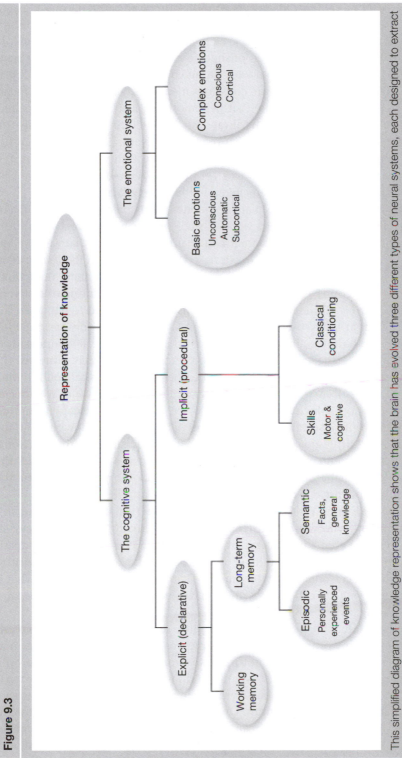

This simplified diagram of knowledge representation shows that the brain has evolved three different types of neural systems, each designed to extract a different kind of information from the environment. The two cognitive systems (explicit and implicit) extract perceptual information while the emotional system evaluates salience. Each system keeps a record of its initial decoding effort so that a complete memory of any event does not exist in any one system.

The capacity of the amygdala to acquire information without consciousness leads to the curious but common situation that we can have an emotional memory for an event for which we have no conscious memory. For a clear demonstration of this consider this little offshoot experiment by Edouard Claparede (1911/1951). It involved a woman who sustained bilateral hippocampal damage and who, like H.M., could not form conscious memories. However, her amygdala was not damaged. To demonstrate that her emotional learning was unimpaired, Claparede decided to greet her, as he always did, by extending his hand; only this time he concealed a pin in his hand that pricked her. Naturally, she withdrew her hand immediately. The next day, she had no recollection of the incident, but when Claparede extended his hand to greet her, she refused to do likewise. She could not say why. She did not remember, but her amygdala did!

Patients suffering from amnesia are not alone in this predicament. Recall also from Chapter 8 that the underdeveloped state of the hippocampus and TOP regions at birth is the likely reason for infantile amnesia, the fact that we have few memories of the early years of life. In contrast, the amygdala is fully developed at birth and emotional memories can be formed readily. Imagine, then, the following (if somewhat contrived) scenario. As a 3-year-old toddler, during one of your exploratory journeys through your parent's house, you managed to fall down the flight of stairs that led to the basement. Except for a few minor bruises, the incident turned out harmless. Imagine further that the basement was illuminated by a pale yellow light, smelled of heating oil, and the resident rat that witnessed the event squeaked violently and ran away. Remember that in classical conditioning two stimuli are associated that occur together in time, irrespective of whether or not this association is logical or meaningful. Not exactly the perceptual genius, the amygdala would associate the experience of pain with pale yellowish light, the smell of oil, and little squeaky, furry creatures. The acquisition of the emotional memory is further enhanced by the stress hormone cortisol, which excites the amygdala. At the same time, cortisol inhibits the hippocampus, suppressing the consolidation of conscious memory about the emotion.

Cut to 20 years later. While your parents might take great delight in telling this story to everyone who wants to listen, you do not actually remember any of it. However, one day your amygdala might. Perhaps when you look for a new apartment and find this gem in the middle of prime real estate. After the first visit to the house, however, something tells you to be cautious. You do not know what it is. The house is well-kept and cheap, and the pale yellowish lighting and the faint smell of heating oil can surely be changed.

It is perhaps advisable not to stretch this little illustration too far but one can easily see how many of our preferences, suspicions, and beliefs might develop in this manner. Perhaps we should not make too many decisions dependent on a funny feeling in the stomach. Also, we might do well not to overemphasize what our likes and dislikes say about ourselves, as we may owe many of them to accidental and insignificant associations. On the flip side, an interesting side note to Claparede's experiment is that a healthy person does not learn to avoid danger in a single trial the way amnesic patients do (ibid.). For a healthy person, any suspicion might be overruled by the cortex because it does not make sense to distrust the good doctor. So, to listen or not to listen to the emotional content of consciousness is somewhat of a dilemma. This discussion also warrants a note of caution on the Freudian concept of repressed childhood memories. In the above story, a memory of the factual aspects of the event was never formed in the first place. It thus cannot possibly be repressed. Nor can the nonexisting memory be pulled into consciousness by quacking on some couch. It is simply not in the system! At any rate, research to date has failed to support the notion of repressed memories (Kihlstrom, 1999).

Dysfunctions of basic emotions

What, then, does all this tell us about disorders of emotions? A great deal, as it happens. A strategic motivation to study the contribution of the amygdala to the content of consciousness stems from evidence implicating the amygdala in emotional dysfunctions, such as anxiety and stress disorders (Johanson et al., 1998; Shin et al., 1997). For instance, functional imaging has shown that the amygdala of patients suffering from phobia is activated by the presentation of a specific stimulus even when it poses no real danger. The amygdala seems to simply overreact. There is much debate over the relative importance of genetic and environmental factors for this heightened sensitivity of the amygdala. Some evidence suggests that this hyperactivity has its roots in neurochemistry, perhaps an insufficient number of $GABA_A$ receptors in the amygdala that could cause a lack of inhibition there. Alternatively, there are endogenous substances that bind to the $GABA_A$ receptor and produce the opposite effects, tension and fear. These compounds mediate amygdala activity under normal circumstances but their overproduction might be responsible for excessive anxiety. There is evidence for several such substances, for instance β–CCM or CCK (Frankland et al., 1997), which would be, if extracted and collected in a container, the equivalent of bottled fear.

The evolutionary past of the amygdala is also clearly discernible from a casual inspection of the top-ten list of the most diagnosed phobias (Seligman, 1971). The list is dominated by dangers that our Pleistocene ancestors had to face, such as snakes, lizards, and spiders; animals that produce nowadays a combined annual death toll of less than a few dozen people worldwide. In contrast, the amygdala is not prone to overreact to cars, guns, or cigarettes, which are today's common killers.

Clinicians have known for a long time that the best way to treat phobia is through a behavioral method called **systematic desensitization**. This therapy exposes the patient to progressively more realistic presentations of the trigger, while maintaining a relaxing and soothing ambience. For instance, a patient suffering from a fear of snakes might be asked to watch a documentary on snakes in the comfort of their home. After getting used to this, the next step would involve more intensity, perhaps a visit to the zoo. This forces the amygdala to associate pleasant stimuli with snakes. Systematic desensitization works because it reeducates the amygdala via a bottom-up process. The amygdala does not listen to sermons from "above."

People suffering from **post-traumatic stress disorder** (PTSD) may owe their condition to the same malfunctioning mechanism in the amygdala. The condition develops shortly after experiencing the kinds of events that are typically outside the realm of ordinary stress, such as combat or the unexpected loss of a loved one. Researchers believe that such terrifying trauma sensitizes the amygdala to react to events that were either part of or incidentally associated with the extraordinary stressor. The release of the stress hormone cortisol further enhances the acquisition of such emotional unconscious memory by exciting the amygdala. These triggers, then, cause the undue retrieval of emotional memory, forcing the person to reexperience the terror. Like all traits, the tendency to develop PTSD occurs in varying degrees, with a minority of people being highly susceptible to the condition. The traumatic experience, coupled with the genetic predisposition, can hijack a once adaptive mechanism and profoundly alter the affective content of consciousness.

In psychopaths emotions can go awry in the other direction. When a healthy individual is hooked up to neuroimaging or biofeedback tools and exposed to a sudden and loud noise, the instruments show the activation of the amygdala or a healthy shift of the recording needle into the red zone. In contrast, a true psychopath is a flatliner, who shows no such startle response or amygdala activation (Kiehl et al., 2001). When people do not display a particular function, such as fear, their phenomenological experience probably does not contain its computation. The absence of fear not only affects the content of consciousness but also produces changes in behavior. Without personal links to the emotion of fear, the psychopath lacks the capacity to empathize and shows no signs of compassion, remorse, guilt, or regret. Some investigators suspect a dysfunction in the fear-generating mechanism in the amygdala. The consideration that in some countries psychopaths often find themselves hooked up to an entirely different set of electrical instruments drives home the message of the general adaptiveness of basic emotions.

Box 9.1   Lateralization of emotions

The prefrontal cortex shows hemispheric specialization. For emotions, the left hemisphere (LH) has a tendency to compute more positive emotions, while the right hemisphere (RH) has a tendency to compute more negative ones. Functional MRI can detect this lateralization for both the recognition and expression of emotions. For instance, a cheerful person shows more activation in LH, whereas a sad person shows more activation in RH. The psychologist Richard Davidson of the University of Wisconsin, Madison, has used this difference in emotion-related processing between both hemispheres as a basis for his **theory of affective style**. According to Davidson (Davidson & Irwin, 1999), individual differences arise as a result of preferences to process emotional information in LH or RH. This theory sorts out more than people's predisposition of seeing a glass either half-full or half-empty. It honors the subtlety in the function of prefrontal circuits that are likely to account for the different emotional capabilities, talents, and temperaments observed in the normal human population. In short, the biology of personality.

Box 9.1   *continued*

As a general rule, RH is overall more emotional. For instance, the ability to recognize the emotions of others depends heavily on RH activation. Likewise, people with damage to RH have problems figuring out what others feel. Recall that RH controls the left side of the body. With this contralateral organization one would expect that the left face also expresses more emotions. This is indeed the case. Test it yourself! Take two identical photographs of yourself smiling, cut them in the middle, and put the two left sides and the two right sides together. The picture composed of the two left sides will be more expressive.

As it happens, there are two ways to make a facial expression, each controlled by a different neural system. We use one system to make voluntary facial expression, which comes in handy if your professor tells a lame joke in class and you need to fake a smile. This system's master is the left PFC, which tells the primary motor cortex to send a signal to the motor nucleus of the facial nerve (CN VII) in the brainstem, which in turn contracts the muscles of the face. Damage to the left PFC can result in a peculiar disorder called **volitional facial paresis**. People with this condition do not have voluntary control over their facial expression and thus cannot fake a smile even if the social situation desperately demands it. The strange thing about this disorder is that they can smile if the joke was actually funny; indeed, they cannot avoid smiling as this would require voluntarily control. What's more, they can yawn and cough but not act as if they yawn and cough. Clearly, this is not the best set of circumstances if your ambition is to be a successful poker player. This is because spontaneous facial expressions, those that are elicited by genuine emotions, are managed by the other neural system, which originates in both hemispheres and uses different pathways to control the motor nuclei of the facial nerve. Damage to this system can also occur (e.g., in the insular region), which results in an equally peculiar disorder called **emotional facial paresis**. People with this condition have the opposite problem; that is, they have control over voluntary facial expression but they do not make facial expression to express emotions. They can, of course, always fake a smile if the situation demands it but they cannot genuinely laugh.

Complex emotions

Lessons from brain damage

Unlike basic emotions, complex emotions are not rigid, reflexive systems. They can be talked to and shaped by beliefs and values. If you tell yourself often enough not to feel guilty about taking an extra day off work, you will eventually feel less guilty. This does not work with nail-biting fear. Likewise, jealousy depends on social norms. An Argentinian might not think twice about it but how would it make you feel seeing the love of your life dance a passionate tango with someone else? To see the difference between basic and complex emotions, let's continue with fear. Take an opening scene from a Hitchcock film that features Jenny, who is all alone in the bedroom of her house. She suddenly hears a door slammed shut downstairs and all the lights go off. Jenny grabs a tiny flashlight and yells: "Who is there?" She stumbles through the bedroom to the top of the stairs and yells again: "Is anyone there?" The creepy background music is getting louder and the audience is captivated. What will happen next? Then, another noise echoes through the house. No doubt, someone is lurking in the dark. The camera starts zooming in on Jenny until the audience sees a close-up of her frightened face. Suddenly, Jenny's cat jumps out of the dark, driving a solid jolt straight into her amygdala. Everyone in the audience jumps in their seats – no exception. Hitchcock was also a master of a more subtle type of fear sensation, the suspense. Suspense hangs over his films like the sword of Damocles. It is generated from an understanding that the villain's actions ten minutes into the film have dire consequences for Jenny towards the end of the film. That's too sophisticated for the amygdala.

Compared to the cortex, the amygdala is a rather basic piece of hardware. It detects blatant triggers that are right in front of it. The amygdala can neither read nor write and thus cannot be tickled by a threat that comes to you over email, at least not via the Low Road. It is also not triggered by a threat that is removed in time. You may watch in horror the numbers on the computer screen showing your mutual fund falling into nothingness, but it is not the amygdala that gives you the feeling – it does not comprehend the concept of retirement. The Low Road is not clever enough to inform the amygdala of the threat of cigarettes, cholesterol-dripping junk food, or nuclear war. Only the cortex possesses the computational prowess to compute the consequences of multidimensional triggers. As Bertrand Russell solemnly put it: "The mark of a civilized human is the ability to look at a column of numbers, and weep."

The amygdala remains in charge of activating the downstream physiological and behavioral components of fear. But in cases involving complex triggers, it does not make the decision; it is merely the push-button. Who, then, is ordering the amygdala around?

It was not your ordinary explosion that first gave away the secrets of the frontal lobe. In the late spring of 1848, Phineas Gage, a Vermont railroad worker, became the victim of a freak accident. Gage was responsible for detonations and one charge accidentally exploded into his face. A tamping iron the size of a baseball bat entered the left cheek bone and shot straight through the brain, exiting the cranium at the very top. Gage, now sporting a gigantic hole in the head, was shocked but oddly enough remained conscious. The examining physician John Harlow even wrote that he could pass "an index finger in its [the brain] whole length, without the least resistance, in the direction of the wound in the cheek, which received the other finger in like manner" (Harlow, 1868, p. 4). Before the accident, Gage was a serious, intelligent, and well-respected member of his community. After the accident he became profane, impulsive, rude, and vulgar. He showed no moral behavior, social inhibitions, or ability to plan for the future, and had a total lack of concern for himself and others.

Neurologists have described countless such cases since, making the prefrontal cortex the front-runner for the seat of the soul. If the damage extended into the VMPFC, the effects consistently included profound personality changes, impaired social skills, and lack of prudent judgment. So what, exactly, does the VMPFC do?

Box 9.2   Frontal lobotomy

Even for the illustrious annals of medical science, frontal lobotomies are an altogether curious story. In hindsight, it's difficult to see how anyone would ever go for the idea. How would you react to the following suggestion: "Hey, let's poke a stick into your brain and wipe out some neurons? Maybe it'll help calm you down, mmh." So, why then were they performed in the first place?

It all started in 1935 with Becky, a rather ill-tempered chimp. At the time, Becky was a subject in a memory experiment except that she wasn't terribly cooperative. Prone to rage whenever things didn't go her way, the investigators decided to remove her frontal lobes in a last-ditch attempt to eliminate the volatility. To their utter surprise, it worked. Becky calmed considerably and awaited each trial without any signs of emotional distress. In the words of Jacobson, the lead scientist, Becky seemed to have joined "the happiness cult of the Elder Micheaux." In August 1935, Jacobson reported the results of the memory experiment at the annual meeting of the International Neurological Congress (Jacobson et al., 1935, p. 10). At the end of his talk, he mentioned in passing Becky's personality changes, a sound bite that was to have far reaching consequences.

Enter Egas Moniz! The neuropsychiatrist Moniz attended the conference's all-day symposium on the frontal lobe and heard the report by Jacobson. It immediately occurred to him that this surgery might also calm his psychiatric patients. He stood up and asked Jacobson about such a possibility, who was reportedly greatly alarmed by the question. But Moniz knew that mild frontal lobe damage produced no noticeable impairment on IQ tests. He went back to his clinic and tried a modified version of the surgery, one that only severed the fibers connecting the prefrontal cortex to the thalamus. The initial reports were quite positive, especially considering the lack of a real alternative to treating symptoms of anxiety, obsessive compulsive disorder, and paranoia. Thousands of operations were subsequently performed by Moniz and others. In a move the Nobel Foundation would rather like to forget, Egas Moniz received the Nobel Prize for this work in 1949.

It took many years of careful follow-ups to see the good, the bad, and the ugly of the frontal lobotomy. The procedure did reduce psychiatric symptoms; however, it also reduced a person's ability to properly function in the world. Patients started acting irresponsibly and childishly, which made them unemployable and eventually outcasts of society. They also reported that they lost not just the unpleasant emotions, such as anxiety, but all emotions. This list of side effects is now easily diagnosed as the **frontal dysexecutive syndrome**, which was first documented in the case of Phineas Gage (although this was a more severe case). Moniz was forced to personally reconsider the impact of his brainchild when one of his own patients demonstrated just how few emotions he had left when he shot Moniz in cold blood, leaving him paralyzed for the rest of his life.

With the advent of drug therapy in the 1960s, the frontal lobotomy was eventually abandoned. But before you think it was all wrong, consider the following all but unbelievable case reported by Solyom, Turnbull, and Wilensky in 1987. It involved a young man who had enough of his obsessive compulsive disorder. He put a .22-caliber rifle in his mouth and pulled the trigger. But instead of shooting at the life-sustaining neural circuits in the medulla toward the back of the mouth, he angled straight up, hitting his frontal lobes. The miracle was not that he survived but that he managed – magically, for no one knows how – to cure himself of his obsessive compulsive handwashing without the ruinous side effects of the dysexecutive syndrome. Perhaps neurosurgeons are not made, but born.

The key insight to this question came from Antonio Damasio, professor of neurology at the University of Southern California. Damasio (1994) reported the case of Elliot, or EVR, who had damage to the VMPFC caused by the removal of a benign tumor. The surgery resulted in a highly selective deficit. At first, Elliot appeared to have no deficit at all. He outscored healthy subjects in standardized tests. Importantly, he had also no trouble assessing and judging hypothetical scenarios of complex moral and social situations, demonstrating a clear understanding of what society considers ethical and proper behavior. Despite these cognitive abilities, his personal life was soon headed south. In a manner typical of frontal patients, he behaved without regard to social norms, eventually losing his wife, his job, and his life savings in risky investment schemes. Although he apparently knew the right thing to do, a real-life situation did not trigger the execution of appropriate social behavior.

From this and similar cases, Damasio suggested that the VMPFC is critical for internalizing the values and standards of a person's culture. It is not directly involved in the comprehension of complex social situations but in assessing the personal consequences of one's behavior. This assessment, then, gives rise to appropriate feelings that are used as a basis for future decisions. Elliot's deficit was only apparent for actual social behavior because he failed to assess the emotional (personal) content of events, which is not a necessary component for solving a similar but hypothetical scenario. In a radical departure from 2000-plus years of philosophical thinking, Damasio proposed that passion and reason are not opposites and that feelings are an essential prerequisite to making logical decisions. This conclusion underscores the notion that emotions are a central player for the way we organize the content of our consciousness.

Theories of VMPFC function

Antonio Damasio proposed an influential theory that outlines a possible mechanism by which emotions influence how we make decisions. The key idea of his **somatic marker hypothesis** is that any event is tagged with a marker, which is then translated into a feeling by the VMPFC. In general, the task of the emotional brain is to attach a value tag to incoming information, which is the first step in evaluating what possible meaning the event might have for the organism. This tag can be generated by one of several mechanisms and at multiple levels of processing. According to Damasio, the marker signals are related to body states elicited by the stimulus, hence the term somatic markers. Touch, for instance, elicits physiological and behavioral reactions that are mapped in the brain's representation of the body, the somatosensory cortex. Changes in this somatic map indicate changes in the organism's physiological state, which then serves as a basis for making appraisals. Another possibility is that the amygdala generates a marker signal, for instance in cases of imminent triggers signaling danger. There is also growing neuroimaging evidence that the insula region serves as a neural substrate for the conscious experience of bodily sensations. There appear to be special pathways conveying interoceptive sensory information to the insula and anterior cingulate cortex that have the purpose of making information about the physiological state of the body available to conscious awareness (Craig, 2002; Critchley et al., 2004). A final possibility is that cortical areas in TOP generate a marker. For instance, a sophisticated trigger that is beyond the amygdala's computational capacity, such as the hint of sarcasm in someone's voice, is analyzed in cortical areas involved in language.

Irrespective of the origin of marker signals, the VMPFC translates them into feelings, a process that appears fundamental in order to effectively relate to the world. Complex social situations require the absorption of countless explicit and implicit rules and the VMPFC brings these rules to our attention in form of feeling states. If markers are either not generated or not translated by the VMPFC into feelings, we have no clue as to the significance of a stimulus. This meshes well with Elliot's reports about his own behavior. Despite his free-fall through the social order, he showed no indication of being distressed by it. He would describe his own failures with surprising indifference, as if the embarrassing events had happened to someone else. He was obviously not feeling the personal pain that comes with social decline. Nothing would make him feel anything; he was thus bound to repeat his mistakes because they did not feel like mistakes.

To test his theory that emotions play an essential role in the making of consciousness, Damasio and his colleagues devised a task known as the **Iowa Gambling Task** (Bechara et al., 1994). Players choose cards from several decks that are associated with different odds. Some decks are risky with large payoffs and payments. Other decks are conservative with milder rewards and penalties but tend to be more advantageous on average. The task is to maximize one's earnings. Healthy subjects soon discovered that the best overall strategy is to avoid the high-risk decks. In time, the mere thought of choosing from a risky deck produced an anticipatory galvanic skin response indicative of the autonomic nervous system activation accompanying anxiety. Patients with prefrontal lesions never hit on the best strategy by trial and error and did not follow it even after they were told of the odds. They might even admit how unwise their actions were and then proceed with them anyhow. They also showed no anticipatory galvanic skin response, which provided evidence for the hypothesis that it is the lack of *feeling* the possible consequences that causes irrational decisions.

To underscore the difference between complex and basic emotions, VMPFC patients show the same startle response to a loud noise as do healthy subjects, except of course, they might not *feel* afraid the same way. A loud noise is a blatant trigger and the amygdala can mark it as dangerous and initiate physiological and behavioral countermeasures. However, the *feeling* of fear is generated by the translation of this marker into a subjective experience, which depends on the VMPFC. In contrast, VMPFC patients show no affective response to complex triggers, such as emotionally disturbing images of other people's suffering. The complexity of this trigger stems from the fact that the danger is one step removed from one's own survival and thus depends on an inference. If the amygdala cannot decode it via the Low Road, the trigger must be marked as disturbing by the cortex and then translated into a relevant feeling by the VMPFC. Because this process is deficient in VMPFC patients, the person neither generates a subjective feeling state nor activates, via a top-down process, the otherwise functional amygdala.

The somatic marker hypothesis emphasizes bottom-up processing in human emotion. But the VMPFC also exerts inhibitory, top-down control over inappropriate or maladaptive behaviors and damage there also produces deficits in top-down processing. Indeed, François Lhermitte (1983; Lhermitte et al., 1986), a neurologist, documented the tendency of VMPFC patients to act without inhibitions. So in addition to having *no feel* for a situation, or perhaps because of it, they are overly dependent on immediate cues and cannot take into account the bigger picture. Lhermitte's famous and somewhat diabolic demonstrations of what he termed **utilization behaviors** involve staged situations that bring out this deficit unambiguously. In one example, a patient would be asked to wait in the hallway where he sees a table, a hammer, a nail, and a picture. The set-up also included an empty spot on the wall, which was obviously meant for the picture. While a healthy person might take into consideration that this is not a friend's house but a physician's office, Lhermitte's patients took the hammer and the nail, and secured the picture on the wall. The behavior by itself is, of course, not odd but the context makes it so. According to Lhermitte, these patients are too dependent on environmental cues to guide their behavior.

In another scenario, Lhermitte would suddenly interrupt an ongoing conversation with a patient, take a hypodermic needle from his drawer, open the cap, place it on the desk, get up, turn around, and pull down his pants. This exposed the patient (as it were) to a situation that left little to the imagination of what had to be done. Never mind that this is your physician's rear end or that they have never done this before, his patients proceeded, without hesitation, to do what the situation seemed to demand. A tightly controlled experiment, if you'll pardon the expression, must have a control condition but it is not known what Lhermitte's nonfrontal patients thought of the experiment.

His patients also showed a strong tendency to imitate inappropriate behaviors modeled by others. As Lhermitte put it: "the sight of the movement is perceived in the patient's mind as an order to imitate; the sight of an object implies the order to use it" (1983, p. 330). Without a fully functional frontal lobe, patients can utilize only immediate cues, and they fail to select behaviors based on more universal principles. Thus, the frontal lobe provides for cognitive flexibility and freedom, and it releases us from the slavery of direct environmental triggers or the memory stored in TOP.

Emotional decision making

We conclude this chapter with a final question: How, exactly, does a feeling state engendered by the VMPFC help us make decisions? A hint comes from the fact that VMPFC patients show deficits in planning or, in neuroscience speak, goal-oriented behaviors. In a telling experiment, patients were asked to complete a number of ordinary real-life tasks (Shallice & Burgess, 1991). During the course of a morning, they were to shop for everyday household items – bread, soap, newspaper – keep an appointment at a certain time, and make note of a few bits of information, such as the price of tomatoes. To avoid making this into a memory test, they were even given the list in writing. In the end, no patients successfully completed the to-do list. One patient, for instance, failed to pay for the paper while another failed to buy soap for the irrelevant reason that the store did not have her favorite brand. They also seem unable to multitask. While healthy subjects can complete several concurrent tasks, prefrontal patients concentrate on one or two and neglect the others.

The inability to plan, formulate strategies, and carry out sequential tasks requiring a step-by-step implementation of behaviors is due to the fact that the prefrontal cortex orchestrates action in accordance with internal goals (Miller & Cohen, 2001). In everyday life, pursuing subgoals while keeping in mind the main goal is a common occurrence. In contrast, standardized tests measuring IQ or scholastic aptitude have only a limited number of answers. What's more, no single answer needs to be kept in mind for the successful completion of the next item in the test. This is not to say that such tests are easier but only that they consist of disconnected questions, each with a limited solution space. This might explain the fact that VMPFC patients often show no deficit in standardized testing instruments. Elliot's case even showed that VMPFC patients can solve moral dilemmas in such test situations. With only a small number of outcome options to consider, the rational mind is able to reason through the consequences of each.

Life in real time does not grant this luxury, as choices and possible solutions quickly bifurcate into infinity. Each new step opens yet another myriad of choices and we have to decide on them quickly because, whether you like it or not, they keep on coming. It is at this point that emotions can help us make decisions. The fact that, as Robert Ornstein (1991) put it, "there has never been, nor will there ever be, enough time to be truly rational," necessitates a mechanism that quickly prescreens the options with respect to their likely impact. Damasio thinks that emotions are that mechanism. Emotions are quick and crude selection processes that give preliminary feedback about the environment in the form of a subjective bias – a feeling. This bias prioritizes choices that guide us toward beneficial responses. Another way of saying this is that emotions transform a complex social situation into a simple multiple-choice test, which can then be scrutinized in more detail. Elliot was able to solve hypothetical social scenarios because they were presented as clear-cut, binary choices that he could ponder outside real time. A real social situation, however, offers a never-ending stream of subtle alternatives for proper behavior. A VMPFC patient, it seems, is simply trapped in a whirlpool of options with no preselection mechanism to help sort through them. Like a computer, VMPFC patients are left to consider all options as if equally legitimate and equally probable to lead to successful social behavior. With the phenomenological subtraction of feelings, then, we are left only with the cognitive content of consciousness, which, alone, cannot ensure proper social conduct.

Some decisions in life are obviously based on emotions. Despite the danger of sounding terribly unromantic, falling in love is, in essence, a prescreening process that effectively eliminates a nearly infinite number of other equally valid choices.

Should you choose a mate on a severely restricted list of cold criteria – social status, religion, money, etc. – as is done in many societies, you still have to sift through countless options if you want maximum value. There are thousands of perfectly suitable mates, and if you live in a high-density population area, millions. To base your mate selection on love is a convenient biological mechanism, albeit not foolproof, as evidenced by current divorce rates.

In other decisions, emotions play a more obscure but nevertheless indispensable role. Take, for instance, the task of buying a car. We like to think that we base decisions involving large sums of money on a rational analysis. Yet this is not only unlikely but impossible. There are dozens of car manufacturers, each with dozens of models that have each hundreds of options. If you want to be fully rational about it, you have a lifetime of work to do. Even if you restrict the search to a certain price range, gas mileage, and color, you are still facing a logistic nightmare – imagine the spreadsheet tabulating all possible factorial combinations. Instead, the emotional system makes a first-round selection; quick, easy, but relatively uninformed. This computation results in a number of subjectively experienced preferences that eliminate all but a few options, which are then scrutinized in detail. Emotions narrow the playing field so that rationality can occur at all.

Chess is an instructive hybrid example. On the one hand, chess is a purely strategic game and the sharpest (logical) thinker should win. On the other hand, a typical chess game has about 35 possible moves for each turn and the average game takes about 40 moves. This yields a total of 10^{120} possible combinations (Pinker, 1999). To put this into perspective, there are only 10^{70} particles in the universe. Thus, a chess player must use emotions to filter out infinity. A computer, however, uses a fundamentally different approach; its computational resources sift through possible outcome options in a fully systematic, algorithmic manner. The sheer speed of computers and the fact that computing a few moves in advance is sufficient to beat all but the best players, makes it possible for this purely rational approach to succeed. Thus, since the historical win of IBM's Deep Blue over Gary Kasparov in 1996, the best chess player is a silicon brain. It is doubtful, however, that this approach will ever get a computer to the number one world ranking in poker, a game that relies almost exclusively on emotions!

Recall from Chapter 5 that opponents of AI pointed out that decisions calculated by computers, albeit logical, are devoid of common sense. We have seen in this chapter why this might be the case. The brain's emotional and cognitive systems can be dissociated in anatomy as well as in the way they process information (Churchland, 2002). While we have focused more on the anatomical dissociation, the process modularity of emotion and cognition, that is, whether or not they compute information in a fundamentally different way is equally important to understanding the nature of consciousness. Neuroscience research has shown that, unlike the computational mode of the cognitive system, emotions are a form of "bio-computation, i.e., *dirty, me-relevant computation*" (ibid., p. 228). Nowhere is the process modularity of emotions as evident as in AI, where "failures in programming computers to conform even roughly to common sense, or to understand what is relevant, are an indication of the nonalgorithmic, *skill-based* nature of rationality" (ibid., p. 231). As we noted in Chapter 5, however, this so-called grounding problem is being addressed in AI with the use of robotics.

Summary

The brain has developed two different types of neural systems, each designed to extract a different kind of information from its environment. On the one hand, the emotional brain is designed to represent value that allows the organism to evaluate the biological significance of an event. On the other hand, a separate and parallel line of information processing that is devoid of any salience is designed to perform detailed feature analysis. Each line contains a functional hierarchy in which increasingly higher-order structures perform progressively more sophisticated computations. Each track also keeps a record of its activity so that emotional memory is part of the emotional circuitry and perceptual and conceptual memory is part of the cognitive circuitry.

Various limbic-system structures, such as the amygdala, compute basic emotions. They are subcortical, automatic, and unconscious and get triggered directly from sensory events and before any part of the cortex is involved. Their functions are: (1) to mount a fast response to a potentially significant event and (2) to notify the cortex that something potentially significant just happened. Primary emotions are reflexes, not much more voluntary than a knee jerk.

The computational product of limbic structures is used by the next higher level of affective processing represented primarily by the ventromedial prefrontal cortex. This structure computes complex emotions by translating initial appraisals into a neural firing pattern that is experienced as a subjective feeling state. As is the case with all contents of consciousness, we are only aware of the product of emotional processing (the conscious feeling), but not what produces the product. The primary purpose of this system is to compute a rough guesstimate, in real time, of the outcome-options of multidimensional triggers, including the consequences of one's own behavior, and introduce a "felt" bias that influences the rational decision-making process.

Neuroscientific and psychological research of the past two decades has made it clear that emotions are not an epiphenomenological sidekick to the content of consciousness but a central organizing process for consciousness. The scientific study of consciousness is not complete without the study of emotions.

Suggested reading

Damasio, A. R. (1994). *Descartes' Error: Emotion, Reason, and the Human Brain*. New York: Putnam.

Ekman, P., & Davidson, R. J. (eds.) (1994). *The Nature of Emotions: Fundamental Questions*. New York: Oxford University Press.

LeDoux, J. (1996). *The Emotional Brain*. New York: Touchstone.

10 Metacognition

Computational infrastructure

Working memory

Unlike the implicit system, which is idiosyncratic and inflexible, the explicit system has evolved to form higher-order representations of its knowledge base. This metaknowledge is made possible by a computational platform that is located primarily in the prefrontal cortex and consists of three so-called executive functions: working memory, executive attention, and temporal integration. The first section of this chapter examines this computational infrastructure. The second section describes how those executive processes enable the computation of still other higher cognitive functions – mental flexibility, creative thought, sense of self, theory of mind – and so generate the cognitive content of consciousness.

In Chapter 8 we learned that working memory has a stringent capacity limit of 4±1 items. We also learned that working memory is the workshop of consciousness where explicit knowledge is buffered and manipulated in the current focus of attention. Here we build on this information and focus on the neural basis of working memory and its key role in supporting higher cognitive functions. Research on this topic has made heavy use of a task known, rather descriptively, as the **delayed non-matching-to-sample task**, which has two conditions. In the working memory condition, a monkey is placed in front of a screen and shown two objects, say, a circle and a square. By touching the screen, the monkey must select one. The objects then disappear and a delay period begins. When the two objects reappear, the monkey is rewarded for selecting the object it previously did *not* select. Monkeys typically solve this task in a few trials. Lesions to the dorsolateral prefrontal cortex (DLPFC), however, cause a deficit with the monkeys seemingly unable to remember their own initial choice. One could argue, however, that the monkeys fail the task for the simple reason that they do not remember the first presentation of the objects at all. To address this confound, the reference condition, which contains only a subtle change, is introduced. This condition starts in exactly the same way but, after the delay, one of the two objects flashed on the screen is novel. More precisely, the object selected by the monkey in the first presentation is substituted for a novel object, while the one that was not selected is reused. Again, the monkey is reinforced for selecting the object previously not selected (the reused one). Monkeys with lesions to DLPFC have little trouble with this slightly different version of the task. So they do remember the first presentation of the stimuli and it is their own behavior – what they selected – that they no longer remember. Once a second cue – novelty – is

Figure 10.1

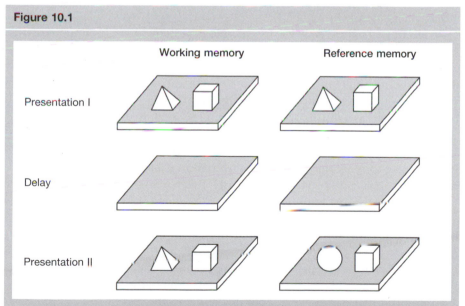

The delayed-non-matching-to-sample task is used to study working memory. In the initial presentation, the subject must select one of two stimuli. After a delay period, the two stimuli reappear in a second presentation and the subject is reinforced for selecting the one it previously did not select. The task requires the animal to temporarily remember its own behavior, a feat that recruits working memory neurons located in the DLPFC. In the reference-memory version of the task, the second presentation contains a novel stimulus. This provides an additional cue and the task no longer depends exclusively on working memory.

introduced, the task becomes one of plain recognition and the monkey can solve it easily (Goldman-Rakic, 1992). Children, whose frontal lobes are still "under construction," also have problems with the working-memory condition of the task.

The classical demonstration of how the prefrontal cortex accomplishes the feat of temporarily buffering information combines this non-matching-to-sample task with the technology of single-cell recordings (Quintana & Fuster, 1993). By measuring neuronal activity in both the visual cortex and the prefrontal cortex during task performance, one can study how each region is involved in the different stages of the task. During the initial stimulus presentation, neurons are active in both cortices. With the onset of the delay period, however, the visual stimulus is no longer present and neurons in the visual cortex promptly return to baseline activity. Neurons in the prefrontal cortex, however, are unaffected by this change and maintain the heightened firing rate. When the stimulus eventually reappears, both regions fire away again. So here is the rub. By maintaining during the delay the pattern of activity that coded the first stimulus, prefrontal neurons make it possible to directly compare it to the firing pattern created by the second one. This means that no elaborate, chemical memory consolidation process is required for working memory; a purely physiological process based on changes in activity patterns is able to, so to speak, keep information alive for a short time. If the delay period is extended indefinitely, however, prefrontal neurons also return eventually to their baseline firing rate.

In recent years, these early electrophysiological studies have been substantiated and further detailed by neuroimaging tools. This work has expanded our knowledge of the anatomical basis of working memory. It seems that working memory does not occupy a definitive piece of prefrontal real estate but consists of several spatially overlapping modules, prompting the proposal that working memory is best understood as a distributed property of prefrontal tissue.

The current paradigm in cognitive neuroscience holds that information must be represented in working memory to be fully conscious. Unless this is carefully fleshed out, this is a form of Cartesian materialism (Chapter 5) that lures one into hoping that there is a special place after all – the working-memory buffer – where information processing leads to – magically, for no one elaborates on exactly how – the additional and further step of consciousness. To prevent anyone from starting down this path, you are reminded here that the convention of treating information as if it comes in two distinct states, "in" and "out" of consciousness, is merely an expedient linguistic contraction. To further disabuse you of the seductive and simplistic proposal that the prefrontal cortex is the seat of consciousness, keep in mind that damage to it does not result in the loss of consciousness. As evidenced by, for instance, prefrontal patients, it "only" wipes out the topmost layers of conscious processing. So what role, then, does working memory play in conscious processing? Recall that in the global workspace theory (Chapter 6) working memory is the bulletin board of the brain. It is a process that allows information that is normally stored elsewhere in the brain to be also represented, albeit only briefly, in a separate, neutral locale. This makes the information accessible to all parts of the system and permits it to be superimposed with other information, which is, of course, an essential element in forming metalevel knowledge of any type. Working memory, then, makes it possible for information to become fully explicit and, thereby, enabling more mental flexibility, which is a very different assertion than suggesting it is the place where consciousness happens.

Attention

A prerequisite to an effective working-memory buffer is the ability to direct and sustain attention (Cowan, 2001). Without the ability to guide and maintain attentional focus, we would drift through mental hyperspace like a spacecraft without a rudder. The meaningful management of complex information necessitates **executive attention**. Attentional processes in the form of selective perception occur at all levels of the perceptual process, and thus areas of TOP. However, intentional control of focus and the maintenance of concentration appear to be a prefrontal lobe function (Posner, 1994).

In a passage quoted time and again, William James (1890) described attention as "the taking possession by the mind, in clear and vivid form, of one out of what seems several simultaneous possible objects or trains of thought. Focalization, concentration of consciousness are of its essence. It implies withdrawal from some things in order to deal effectively with others." Since then, much debate has centered on the relationship between attention and consciousness. Many thinkers, James among them, favored the position that consciousness can be equated with what is in the focus of attention. In this view, attention is a gatekeeper that selects what will be in consciousness; whatever is outside the focus of attention is unconscious (Cowan, 1995; Posner, 1994). But there are good reasons to avoid this move. Even if attention controls access to consciousness, a position most investigators endorse, attention is not the same as consciousness. If this were so the study of attention would be the study of consciousness and the neural basis of attention, already well studied, would constitute the NCC. But we know, from research in psychology and neuroscience, that attention is not sufficient for consciousness. That we attend to things that nevertheless fail to enter conscious awareness – think binocular rivalry (Chapter 7), for instance – is evidence that there might be a separate, further selection process at work (Lamme, 2003). A second reason to distinguish attention from consciousness comes from recent evidence that attention alters appearance (Carrasco et al., 2004). Attention, then, is more than just a selection mechanism; it also changes the properties of the stimulus itself, boosting, among other things, contrast sensitivity. Finally, we should also regard the two as different for the simple reason that consciousness can direct attention, which indeed may be one of its principal functions.

Recall from Chapter 1 that Block (1995) made a similar distinction between phenomenal and access consciousness with only the latter fully accessible to verbal report. This distinction is misbegotten, argue others, because it proposes the existence of a kind of consciousness that either divorces consciousness from its central meaning of phenomenal content (Velmans, 2000) or, given the lack of clear examples of one kind of consciousness without the other, draws a qualitative line when the evidence only supports a difference in degree. In other words, what Block considers access consciousness is simply phenomenal consciousness that is richer in detail and, as such, has greater power over motor output. That does not make it a different type of consciousness (Dennett, 1998).

Present-day psychologists classify five different types of attention. The first two types, (1) **orienteering or automatic attention** and (2) **selective attention**, appear to be fairly reflexive filtering mechanisms that allow us to efficiently process relevant information. Functionally and anatomically, these two types of attention are embedded at the level of the perceptual decoding process itself. For instance, large objects flying through the field of vision engage selective perception processes in extrastriate cortices. Excellent attention grabbers of this type are fast moving objects, attractive members of the opposite sex, Beethoven's Fifth, or, in the case of dogs, bacon strips. The next two types, (3) **focused attention** and (4) **sustained attention**, are different in function and underlying brain circuitry. Together they are also referred to as **executive attention**. They enable us to voluntarily direct our attention to a particular stimulus and maintain it in focus for a prolonged period of time. Humans have a great deal of intentional control over what they attend to and executive attention is not only a mechanism to select the content of consciousness, but also to maintain that content online long enough to engage in meaningful manipulation of information. This conceptualization does not solve, in any way, the all-important question of how, exactly, a certain tidbit of knowledge stored in TOP becomes momentarily fully conscious. Neuroimaging research has identified several prefrontal sites involved in executive attention (Sarter et al., 2001), implying that executive attention is also, like working memory, best conceptualized as a global prefrontal capacity. The fifth and final type of attention is **divided attention**. There are several factors influencing the ability to divide one's attention among several tasks, an issue that is explored in more detail in Box 10.1.

There are several cognitive models of attention. Two notions underlie all of them: (1) there is a flood of information bombarding us at any moment and (2) we have a limited information-processing capacity. As a consequence, we are forced to make choices to avoid overloading the system. The most influential model of attention is the **filter model**, which was initially proposed by Donald Broadbent (1958) and later elaborated upon by several cognitive scientists (Cowan, 1995; Treisman, 1992). The model envisions information processing as a pipeline, in which information is passed on in a serial fashion from a sensory store over a short-term store to LTM. Although there are multiple channels through which information can be processed, we cannot attend to more than one channel at a time. To avoid sensory overload, other channels must be filtered out or, at least, toned down (Treisman, 1992). We can, however, switch from one channel to another. All cognitive models of attention acknowledge that there is more information entering the system than can be assimilated; the models differ mainly in placement of bottleneck. Early selection models place the bottleneck prior to the perceptual analysis, while late selection models place it closer to

Box 10.1   The myth of multitasking

Multitasking is one of today's buzzwords. It refers to the ability to do more than one thing – actually, more than one complicated thing – at the same time. As early as the 1950s psychologists investigated the mind's potential to allocate resources to several tasks at once. The classical divided-attention experiment, performed by the psychologist Colin Cherry (1953), was inspired by the so-called **cocktail-party effect**. When engrossed in a conversation, we do not pay attention to other conversations around us unless, that is, someone incidentally mentions our name. This, for some reason, turns our heads, although we, presumably, were not following that conversation. Cherry reproduced this effect under controlled conditions by asking subjects to wear headphones and exposing each ear to different messages. He then asked them to attend to only one ear and shadow it, that is, repeat its content. This shadowing procedure has become a standard tool of attention research. The principal finding has been that the message played into the unattended ear is virtually ignored, even if it is repeated ad nauseam. This and similar findings prompted Donald Broadbent to introduce his filter model of attention, which proposed that we only have one channel open for information processing. We can switch between channels but we cannot keep two channels open at the same time.

So how, then, do we multitask? The answer lies in the brain's conquer-and-divide principle. The acquisition of a new skill, say, driving a car, requires all our attention. While we fully focus on processing the task requirements, the capacity limit of working memory makes it impossible to handle additional information – listening to the radio, for instance. But with practice the control of the behavior is transferred to the basal ganglia. As the basal ganglia drive the car, cortical resources are freed to process other information and reloading our favorite daydream scenario is no longer a problem. It is this automatizing that permits multitasking. We can consciously do two things at a time if, and only if, one requires few, if any, attentional resources.

If two tasks require executive attention, multitasking is impossible. You might think you can study and watch TV simultaneously. Wrong! If you carefully observe youself, you'll notice that you constantly switch between the two. At no point, however, do you process both streams truly in parallel. This switching, controlled experiments have shown, gives you the gist of each source, but the recall for details is very poor (Rubenstein et al., 2001). Consciousness – that much is clear – is a serial processor.

consciousness. Recent empirical work suggests that the first two types of attention, automatic attention and selective attention, occur during the early stages of sensory processing and are controlled by the **posterior attentional network** based primarily in the parietal cortex. In contrast, executive attention occurs during the later stages and is critically dependent on the **anterior attentional network** in the prefrontal cortex. Thus, attentional processes are at work throughout the entire information-processing pathway.

Executive attention appears to be a uniquely human trait, which is not surprising given its neural basis in the prefrontal cortex. We seem to be the only species that is capable of sustaining attention on a biologically *ir*relevant stimulus. Even chimpanzees, our closest relatives in the animal kingdom, are not capable of even sitting through the first minute of one of Wagner's five-hour operas from the Ring of Nibelungen. However, paying attention is a very costly and taxing mechanism

Figure 10.2

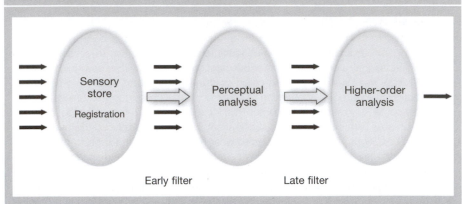

Where is the bottleneck of attention? We can process only a tiny amount of information at any one time. The filter model presumes that we have multiple channels for processing but, owing to our limited capacity, we are prevented from attending to more than one channel at once. In this one, open channel (unfilled arrow) information is passed through a series of stages to consciousness, while information in other channels is toned down or filtered out. Cognitive models of attention differ in the proposed location of the selection process (early or late), but research in cognitive neuroscience has shown that filtering takes place at all information processing stages.

that cannot be maintained indefinitely (Posner, 1994). As a consequence, we enter mental states that are marked by defocused attention or mental drifting, such as daydreaming, which are simply the inevitable result of the constant demands placed on the attentional system to selectively process information (Singer, 1978). Anecdotal evidence would suggest, however, that executive attention is a mechanism that can be trained like a muscle. On the one hand, there are meditation practitioners that appear to have gained a high level of control over their ability to select the content of consciousness and they can sustain that content almost at will. Beginners to the practice of meditation can rarely keep their minds from wandering for more than a few minutes, but they typically get better at controlling their attention with time. On the other side of the spectrum are children suffering from attention-deficit hyperactivity disorder (ADHD). Children do not have much control over executive attention to begin with, as it depends on a brain structure, the prefrontal cortex, that is yet to fully mature. However, children with ADHD seem to have an abnormally short attention span. The insight that attention can be trained suggests that behavioral measures aimed at extending attentional capabilities should be considered as viable alternatives to drug therapy.

Temporal integration

Ordinary experience teaches us that time is unidirectional. There is no reason, however, why that should be so. There certainly is no such constraint traveling back and forth in the three spatial dimensions. Why, then, should there be any for time? This is even more curious considering that except for a handful of physical phenomena – entropy, expanding universe, collapse of the wave function, and some particle effects – all fundamental laws of physics are time-reversible.

This raises the question of why it is so nearly impossible for us to think of time moving backwards. The brain, of course, models the real world and of the few time-irreversible phenomena mentioned above only one, **entropy**, manifests itself at the scale of human perception. According to the second law of thermodynamics, entropy, a measure of unavailable energy, always increases in a closed system. This increase of entropy or disorder is associated with the passage of time. We would find the sight of broken cups being spontaneously repaired strange for the simple reason that it would mean that order increases, which would give us the sense of time flowing backwards. From this we can conclude that it is entropy that hardwired the time arrow into brains.

Consciousness arranges mental representations accordingly. Throughout life we continuously time events and put them in some kind of temporal context. Consider how difficult it would be to infer cause and effect without this sense of time, without the ability to determine which event comes first. Experiences are also stored in memory relative in time to other events. This continuous timing produces a chronological record, without which we would lack any concept of past and future altogether. And without that, we would not be able to learn and adapt.

The prefrontal cortex is the master of this temporal integration of behavior (Fuster, 2000). Indeed, temporal organization of goal-directed action appears to be the overarching theme of prefrontal information processing (Fuster, 1995). Accordingly, animals with prefrontal lesions show deficits in timing ability. Many complex behavior patterns require a sequence of steps. Suppose an animal wants to build a shelter, a behavior that requires a series of actions – finding a good spot, looking for sticks, dragging in leaves, and so on. If the steps are performed out of order, as is the case with prefrontal-damaged animals, the shelter is rendered useless. Sexual courtship equally depends on proper timing. It is an elaborate ritual requiring a precisely choreographed sequence of behaviors. If a male performs the steps out of order, the female probably thinks of the male as just that, out of order. Consider an analogue human case reported by Wilder Penfield (1975). A woman, stuck in a time warp by prefrontal damage, knew all the ingredients to make the family dinner, but she could not organize the actions into the proper temporal sequence. She remembered and performed all steps of the cooking process but executed them in the wrong order!

In complex social networks like ours, impeccable timing ability is even more crucial. Consider, for instance, the following study from the annals of crosscultural psychology. Following World War II, American GIs stationed in England reported that women there were easy to get. Paradoxically, the English women said the same about the GIs. A psychologist investigating the matter asked the GIs to rank into 25 discrete steps their sense of the proper sequence of courtship. They ranked the first kiss, for instance, as number 5. The women were asked to do the same. As you can imagine, this ranking looked a little different. Kissing for them, it turned out, came much later in the game, at number 20. Suppose now a GI made it to what he thought was step 4, he would naturally proceed to step 5, the kiss. The woman must have been stunned by the move, feeling cheated out of steps 6 to 19. All of a sudden, she faced a big decision: to slap the guy or to kiss him back. Assume she did the latter; she would naturally start behaving consistent with the expectation that step 21 is next. This behavior must have stunned the GI, who was barely at step 6 at this point. Given how easily this can happen to healthy people, how difficult must proper social interaction be for prefrontal patients?

The mental flexibility provided by the prefrontal cortex liberates us from being stuck in the here and now. By manipulating the fourth dimension, we can escape the present, move backwards and forwards in time, plan for the future, and reflect on the past. Mental disorders that involve dysfunction of the prefrontal cortex – depression, schizophrenia, Alzheimer's disease – are all accompanied by time distortions in phenomenal consciousness. A sense of timelessness is also a hall-mark of altered states of consciousness (Dietrich, 2003). Be it dreaming, daydreaming, meditation, hypnosis, drug states, or voodoo dancing, the exclusive domain of existence is the here and now. In such a state, the person is simply unable to extract himself from the confines of the concrete present and consider time as a variable.

Self-reflective consciousness

Cognitive flexibility

Initial and much ensuing information processing on perception, attention, memory, and emotion occurs in other brain areas before it is further integrated in the frontal lobes (Crick & Koch, 1998; Taylor, 2001). Indeed, computation of these functions appears to be all but complete so that prefrontal patients, espe-cially those with mild damage, do not show any deficits when directly tested for them with standardized tests (Hebb, 1939). The prefrontal cortex, then, does not simply add more of the same – further detail or a more refined analysis, for instance. Instead, it utilizes this already highly processed information to enable still higher cognitive functions, such as cognitive flexibility (Lhermitte, 1983), abstract or creative thinking (Dietrich, 2004b; Rylander, 1948), self-reflection (Courtney et al., 1998), a self-construct (Vogeley et al., 1999), complex social func-tion (Damasio, 1994), strategic planning (Norman & Shallice, 1986), willed action (Frith & Dolan, 1996), and theory of mind (Povinelli & Preuss, 1995). It does so by means of its unique computational infrastructure – working memory, atten-tion, and temporal integration. Together these executive functions provide a buffer to hold and maintain information in mind and order it in space-time. It is this ability to juxtapose already sophisticated content that so exponentially increases our cognitive flexibility and enables the complex phenomenology that is the hallmark of human consciousness.

Perhaps the best way to see the lack of cognitive flexibility in patients with prefrontal damage is through their performance on the Wisconsin Card Sorting Task (WCST), a cognitive testing tool we introduced in Chapter 8. The WCST exposes nicely the tendency for **perseveration** or the inability to shift between modes of thinking (Boone, 1999). Recall that in this task a patient must find, by trial and error, the sorting rule – color, number, or shape – of a deck of cards. Once found, the rule is changed and the patient is asked to adapt to the new one. Functional neuroimaging has shown that in normal subjects this flexible shifting of cognitive sets is accompanied by prefrontal activation (Konishi et al., 1998; Monchi et al., 2001). Patients with prefrontal lesions, however, show perseverative errors. They keep sorting the cards according to the old rule, even after they see that this leads nowhere. This selective deficit is typically inter-preted as a failure of working memory because it demands that one remembers relevant past behavior. Note the similarity to the DNMTS task explained earlier, which also requires one to monitor one's own actions. Importantly, prefrontal patients have no problem learning the initial rule; they only have great diffi-culty adapting as the rule changes. Adapting to a new set of rules requires, of course, that one inhibits the well-ingrained habit of responding to the older ones. It certainly seems, then, that prefrontal integration is the essential compo-nent for this ability. Performance in the WCST also declines, in a linear fashion, as a function of age, especially this ability to adapt to changing rules (Axelrod et al., 1993). Again, the elderly have little trouble finding the first sorting rule but do not seem to be able to inhibit knowledge of this rule when it changes. What's more, they even report being aware that the old rule no longer applies but continue, just as prefrontal patients do, to emit habitual behavior nonethe-less. This shows that cognitive flexibility deteriorates as we age, depriving us of our independence from immediate environmental cues or memories stored in TOP.

A strikingly similar deficit can be produced in animals. Using a simple T-maze, an animal is trained to find food located in one of the T's arms. Once it acquires this rule, the food is placed in the other arm. After a number of such reversals, a strategy emerges that is called **win/stay lose/shift**. The animal learns that the presence of food indicates an advantage to stay put, whereas its absence signals the need for change. In other words, the animal learns the concept of shifting. As might be expected, a prefrontal lesion – indeed, just the normal process of aging for that matter – causes animals to perseverate, as they run down the same arm that always had the food (Dietrich et al., 2001; Means & Holstein, 1992).

From this data, we can conclude that the prefrontal lobe allows us to select behaviors based on more universal principles. It gives us the cognitive flexibility and freedom to reflect, however briefly, before we act. This understanding of the functions of the prefrontal cortex complements Lhermitte's notion of utilization behavior (Chapter 9). The prefrontal cortex can compute the bigger picture, with-out which we are slaves to the reactionary emotional brain or the knowledge hard-wired, through years of reinforcement, into the cognitive information-processing system.

Creative thinking

Perseveration to old knowledge, of the type discussed above, is anathema to creative thinking. Cognitive flexibility, then, as provided by the prefrontal cortex, must be regarded as the pivotal ingredient in this highest expression of human consciousness, creativity (Dietrich, 2004b). The fact that prefrontal lobe patients, even those with fairly mild damage, demonstrate an almost complete lack of creative or abstract thinking has been known for some time. Gösta Rylander (1948) showed this deficit most elegantly by asking patients before and after frontal lobotomy about the meaning of fables, metaphors, and proverbs. The results were illuminating. "People in glass houses should not throw stones," for instance, was interpreted after surgery by one patient as "otherwise they will break the walls around them." Contrast this rather concrete reading with the response given before surgery: "One should not criticize others: One can make the same mistake oneself." Or take the proverb: "Too many cooks spoil the broth." Before surgery, one patient's interpretation was: "If too many people are working with something it won't be good." After surgery, the response became: "If too many people do the cooking, the food will not be good." Evidently, they were no longer able to think abstractly or creatively.

The role played by the prefrontal cortex in creativity can be seen as a threefold process. It is key in (1) making ideational combinations occurring in the brain fully conscious, (2) assessing their likely value, and (3) ultimately implementing their creative expression (Dietrich, 2004b). We can focus here only on the first step, the creative insight. Given the view that working memory holds the content of consciousness, a novel computation becomes an insight when it is represented in working memory. The question of how it gets there, that is, in general, how information, stored somewhere in the folds of your cortex, becomes available for conscious processing, is one of the most fundamental questions in the study of consciousness. Two general mechanisms can be imagined. The first are top-down processes which rely on effortful retrieval. They require the engagement of executive attention, as evidenced by neuroimaging studies that show that the prefrontal cortex is recruited in the retrieval of memory, solving the so-called tip-of-the-tongue phenomenon and explicit categorization (Cabeza & Nyberg, 2000). Another way of saying this is that the prefrontal cortex has a kind of search engine that can pull into working memory task-relevant information from long-term storage in TOP areas. Once online – fully conscious, that is – the whole arsenal of our cognitive abilities can be brought to bear on the insight. There is good reason to assume that this effortful retrieval is inherently structured, that is, the search engine operates under a number of constraints, such as using formal logic (e.g., A causes B) or holding assumptions about meaningfulness.

The second mechanism of transferring memory from an unconscious to a conscious status are bottom-up processes. They involve the spontaneous representation of knowledge in consciousness. During the inevitable times when the attentional system is downregulated – in daydreaming, for instance – knowledge that is not guided by societal norms and not filtered by conventional wisdom becomes represented in working memory. In such a mental state, the content of consciousness is characterized by unsystematic drifting, and the sequence of thoughts manifesting itself in consciousness is more chaotic. This is not to say that all items stored in memory have the same likelihood of popping up into consciousness. Memory is organized in semantic networks and the spreading activation through such a network can lead to an orderly train of thought. Complex ideas, then, including novel ones, can be assembled unconsciously, and enter consciousness in their fully finished form. This experience of sudden understanding without intentional reasoning is often described as mysterious and indicated by such metaphors as being hit by a ton of bricks, or the proverbial light bulb turning on.

So, creative insights occur in consciousness via the deliberate or spontaneous processing mode. Anecdotal stories in the arts and sciences abound that describe the creative process as automatic and effortless. From Kekulé's daydream of whirling snakes forming a (benzene) ring to Coleridge's poem *Kubla Khan*, such flashes of insight are the very cliché of creative genius. Others have argued the opposite view, that is, that creativity is the result of methodical problem solving. From Watson and Crick's discovery of DNA to Edison's inventions and Bach's Brandenburg Concertos, it is abundantly clear that creative work can also be the result of laborious trial and error. When seen in this way, creativity can come in four flavors, the factorial combination of both modes, deliberate and spontaneous, with emotional and cognitive processing. Regardless of how the novelty is generated initially, the prefrontal cortex is the key brain structure that transforms the novelty into creative behavior by enabling its explicit representation, evaluating its appropriateness, and implementing its expression (Dietrich, 2004b).

Sense of self

The content in consciousness is accompanied by an experience of ownership. In my mind, this sense of self is undeniably real, as I experience my feelings, thoughts, and acts as just that, mine. In philosophy, however, the existence of a self as a distinct entity is a hotly debated topic. Two extreme positions can be taken, each with its strengths and weaknesses. The first conforms to introspection and maintains that there is indeed, as advertised, a self that unifies sensory experience. This experiencer is assumed to be a stable and persistent entity that prescribes perceptions, thoughts, and acts as its own. As a consequence, I feel as though there is continuity to my existence. That is, I feel the same person despite my ever-changing experiences. Although this position appeals to common sense, it raises the question of what exactly this selfhood is. If there is an experiencer what, then, is its nature? Naturally, this question does not represent a problem for dualism, as the self is simply equated with the nonphysical mind. For materialism, however, the postulation of a persisting ego-self is problematic, as it conjures up the troublesome possibility of a homunculus in the brain, a Cartesian master, and the ever-present danger of the deadly infinite regress.

Theories defending this first position are known as **ego theories**, while theories defending the second position are known as **bundle theories** (Parfit, 1987). Bundle theories maintain that the sense of a self is an illusion. This is not to say that bundle theories deny the phenomenal experience of ownership but only that this effect is not due to a single, experiencing entity called the self. The idea here is that the self is, in the words of David Hume (1739/1888), "a bundle of sensations," hence bundle theories. Accordingly, we simply construct a self model from a continuous stream of perceptions and thoughts that then are linked together by association. In this view, a sense of self is an emerging property of information processing. A position that denies the existence of a self – consciousness without a self to experience it – is hard to even contemplate but this is, of course, no measure for rejecting it. Nowadays, this position is defended most forcefully by the philosopher Daniel Dennett, but it has a long tradition in philosophy dating back to William James, David Hume, and ultimately the Sophist philosophers Protagoras and Democritus. Of the world's major religions only Buddhism can be categorized as a bundle theory. By banishing all thoughts and feelings from consciousness, the practice of meditation leads to a state of consciousness that has no content. The Buddha realized that a mental state that contains no experiences also contains no experiencer. It is for this reason that meditation is said to lead to total denial of self – a case of lights on but no one home.

Several more moderate versions of both extreme positions exist but the major critique remains the same for each. While ego theories cannot satisfactorily explain the nature of the self, bundle theories cannot account for the sensation that there seems to be a central subject who has experiences. As with many philosophical issues related to consciousness, the empirical data emerging from neuroscience and psychology are not yet sufficiently clear to favor any particular position. There are several psychiatric and neurological disorders that have significant implications for how the human brain computes a self-model. Conditions such as dissociative identity disorder, fugue or depersonalization, and split-brain operations appear, at first, to produce multiple selves, selves within selves, or severely altered selves; however, neither ego theories nor bundle theories have trouble fitting these cases into their respective paradigms.

Generally speaking, theories of the self from the domain of neuroscience tend to lean toward bundle theories, although rarely is this preference aligned explicitly with the respective philosophical tradition. This trend toward bundle theories appears to be simply a result of approaching the question of the self in the same way neuroscience approaches any other mental function, that is, as a functional hierarchy. Antonio Damasio (1999) provided a detailed account of how the self is built up at various functional neuroanatomical levels in a hierarchy of increasing complexity. The self has many subcomponents, such as representation in somatic, kinesthetic, and motor maps (Damasio, 1999), as well as experiences of ownership, body-centered spatial perceptivity, and long-term unity of beliefs (Vogeley et al., 1999). Damage to structures that process information lower on the hierarchy produces severe distortions of the self, such as unilateral neglect, which results from right parietal damage; whereas prefrontal dysfunction results in lesser

Figure 10.3

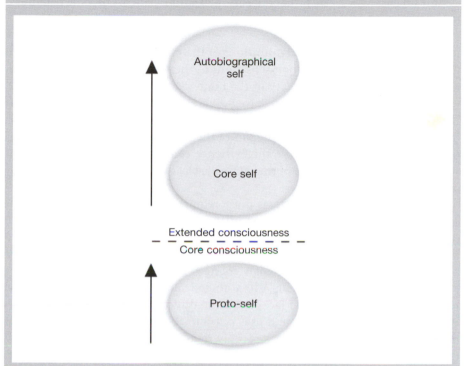

Damasio (1999) distinguishes between proto-self, core self, and autobiographical self and believes that each is implemented in a different neural system. The proto-self represents the state of the organism in a preconscious manner and is mapped in brainstem, hypo-thalamic, and basal forebrain regions as well as the insula. The core self emerges from a second-order mapping of body states represented at the level of the proto-self. It is a nonverbal but conscious kind of self that relies on second-order evaluative structures. The autobiographical self is the fully conscious sense of self that builds its records from core-self experiences. It is implemented in cortical areas. (Adapted from Damasio, 1999)

distortion of the self, such as delusions of grandeur. Research has shown – not surprisingly, at this point anyway – that the implementation of the highest-order understanding of self occurs in the prefrontal cortex (ibid.).

While meditation might lead to the only known selfless state of consciousness, there are plenty of ways the self can undergo changes. At each level of the functional hierarchy, the self-system can malfunction with unique consequences for the experience of the self. In schizophrenia the self can either expand or contract – kind of like a balloon. In some cases, schizophrenics inflate their ego to the point of thinking they are God. In others, the self shrinks and they experience their own thoughts as no longer their own. Or take the most bizarre distortion of the self imaginable: **Cotard's delusion**. In depersonalization people typically report feeling like robots, disembodied and unreal. The feeling of experiencing one's own body from a third-person perspective is not uncommon, but in Cotard's delusion, a severe form of depersonalization, patients become convinced they are dead and no amount of arguing can persuade them otherwise.

A malfunction at a more fundamental self-representational level causes phantom limb and neglect, two odd distortions of the physical self that we detailed in Chapter 7. Amputees often report sensations in their nonexisting limb. The experience is caused by neural activity in the brain's maps of the missing body part, which are, of course, not amputated. Neglect is another neurological disorder that is difficult to believe at first encounter. It results from right parietal damage, usually caused by stroke, that leaves part of the left body paralyzed. Patients with neglect fail to even acknowledge the existence of the paralyzed parts of the left side. These strange alterations of the self make clear how fragile the sense of body ownership is.

The presence of mental illness is not a requirement for changes to the sense of ownership. It can also be induced in the lab, using healthy subjects. Recall that the brain represents its body in topographical maps. A very clever experiment by Ramachandran and Blakeslee (1998) showed that distortions of these neural maps can give rise to peculiar changes in the perception of the body's physical boundary and location. A blindfolded subject is placed in a chair next to a passive collaborator, who faces the same direction. The experimenter takes the subject's left index finger and uses it to tap the nose of the collaborator. At the same time, the experimenter precisely matches this guided action with his other hand, which taps the nose of the subject. Within a few seconds, subjects often report that their nose has moved to the left to where the collaborator's nose is. The subjects even report that water dropped on their noses is felt at the "new location" of the nose. What might be going on here? Ramachandran and Blakeslee think that because the brain's motor regions provide feedback that it is tapping something, and the sensory maps report that the nose is actually being tapped in precisely this manner, the only feasible interpretations for the brain seems to be that the nose is located where the finger is doing the tapping! The illusion of displaced body parts can also be produced by several other means. Imagine a subject sitting at a table in a darkened room. Her forearms are placed in a mold to prevent them from moving and small lights are attached to the fingers. To create the same internal feedback that accompanies actual arm movement, the biceps are stimulated by a vibrating hammer. Subjects typically report that their arms are moving outward, although they are kept in place by the mold. They also report seeing the lights moving apart, which also remain stationary.

Approaching the self in terms of functional levels not only inherently challenges the notion of an experiencing entity inhabiting the brain, it also makes it considerably easier to contemplate how the brain might give rise to the illusion of such a central experiencer. We learned in Chapter 6 that chimpanzees and gorillas recognize themselves in a mirror, a display that suggests the presence of a rudimentary self-model. Unlike these great apes, we have evolved the additional ability to make inferences about this self-model, that is, we possess brain structures that represent components of the self-model, such as beliefs and attitudes, as higher-order representations. As a result, the brain not only has beliefs and attitudes but also represents *that* it has beliefs and attitudes. At the next level of explication, the brain predicates these components of the self-model to a holder, making the holder itself a higher-order thought. This metarepresentational upgrade endows brains with consciousness *of* self rather than *with* self. Consciousness and the modeling of a self are so closely related because the holder must be represented explicitly before information can be considered fully conscious (Kihlstrom, 1996). The self, then, is neither a ghost in the machine nor an illusion. Instead, the various elements of the self-system are represented at several neuroanatomical levels located in diverse regions of the brain. Breaking down the self into its constituent components eliminates the pitfall of a "mini-me" watching the movie-in-the-brain, because the self-system simply emerges from interactions with other modules computing higher-order content. According to the paradigm emerging from neuroscience research, the self is simply the outcome of the high-level representational capacities of brains.

Box 10.2   Mirror neurons

The discovery of mirror neurons has been called the "single most important unreported story" of the 1990s (Ramachandran, 2000). Using single-cell recording techniques, the neuroscientist Giaccamo Rizzolatti and his colleagues (Rizzolatti et al., 1996) found these cells in the ventral premotor cortex of monkeys and their unique response patterns might well be the underlying cellular mechanism of imitation.

It has been known for some time that the primary job of neurons in the premotor cortex is to compute motor plans. Individual premotor neurons are quite specialized in this regard. While some control, say, grasping with the hand, others might control other types of hand movements, say, holding or tearing. Mirror neurons are special in the sense that they are not only active when the monkey performs those movements, but also when it sees another monkey (or an experimenter) doing so. Mirror neurons are not visual feature detectors either because they do not respond to the sight of the other monkey's hand or the manipulated object alone. What they do, it seems, is to run virtual-reality simulations of the actions of others, which, presumably, is the cellular mechanism of understanding the intention of others.

The ventral premotor area of the monkey is the homologue of Broca's area in humans, the cortical region that controls language production. If language evolved from hand-based signs, as proposed by Rizzolatti and his colleagues (2001), the discovery of mirror neurons also carries significant implications for the evolution of language because the response characteristics of these cells would have permitted the development of hand gestures for the purpose of two-way communication. This speculation is underscored by the observation that fMRI scans show activity in the inferior left frontal lobe, a part of Broca's area, when people observe finger movements of others (Iacoboni et al., 1999). At first glance, this finding suggests that mirror neurons must play a prominent role in deaf people's ability to use sign language. More importantly, though, it suggests that the language-based concept of hand movement is a clue as to the possible origins of our extraordinary language abilities.

Theory of mind

We encountered the concept of a theory of mind (ToM) in Chapter 6. The term refers to the ability to make inferences about the mental state of others. A ToM module makes it possible to predict a person's behavior based on mental processes – beliefs, intentions, attitudes – that are otherwise unobservable. This extraordinarily sophisticated computation is likely to have evolved from the ability to reflect on one's own mental states, suggesting that a conceptual sense of self is a prerequisite and an evolutionary antecedent to theory-of-mind capacities (Povinelli & Preuss, 1995). For a species with highly complex social interactions the ability to have insight into the mental state of others – mindsight, as some call it – and anticipate their reactions has obvious implications for biological fitness. The faculty of introspection can thus be seen as a specialized cognitive function that evolved in response to the tricky problem of figuring out the ever more complex behavior patterns of others. This adaptation to the social environments has been suggested as the primary trigger for the evolution of introspective consciousness (Humphrey, 1978). In other words, the emergence of ToM capacities as well as mirror neurons (see Box 10.2) was a crucial step toward the development of self-reflective consciousness.

Like other mental processes requiring a higher-order representational format, ToM is computed in the explicit system. Studies with brain-damaged patients and healthy subjects have shown further that the ability to represent the mental state of others is implemented in areas of the prefrontal cortex (Frith & Frith, 2001). ToM dysfunction is a prominent feature of several psychiatric disorders but in autism the inability to gain insight into other minds may lie at the very heart of the disease (Stone et al., 1998). Autistic children exist in a world of their own, preferring to keep to themselves. They do not appear to mentalize, not even about their own thoughts and feelings. They act independently of the people around them and seem not to care what others might think of them or, indeed, if other people think at all. This also occurs in other disorders, such as schizophrenia, but the hypothesis that autism might be a selective dysfunction of the ToM module is based on a curious dissociation. On the one hand, the autistic child solves tasks of high-level reasoning, including those that require metarepresentations. They understand, for instance, that maps can represent the world and, more importantly, that maps can misrepresent the world. On the other hand, they fail in tasks that ask them to do the same inference for minds, that is, they do not understand how a belief can represent or misrepresent the world. This evidence led the psychologist Simon Baron-Cohen (1995) to propose that autism is not a global dysfunction of higher cognitive processes or abstract reasoning but a more selective deficit for ToM. This evidence also underscores that the ToM module is likely an independent neural system.

When ToM first evolved, humans did not have cross-cultural experiences. Because a ToM must extrapolate from a single case, namely oneself, we are much better at predicting the behavior of people that are like us. The socialization process "hardwires" cultural norms and beliefs, which differ, of course, from one society to another. Understanding people from different cultures represents a true challenge for ToM, because this kind of computation requires more than simply imagining what we would do in the same situation. Some people are quite skilled at this type of social intelligence but a little illustration makes clear how quickly we reach the limits of ToM ability. Suppose you are being air-dropped into a remote jungle location and encounter a tribe you don't know anything about. One day you happen to observe a woman getting it on with a man. The next day you see the same woman flirting with a different man. Finally, on day three, you see the two men facing each other in the village center with the woman standing between them. Now, try to predict what will happen next? Suppose further that you are told that such behavior is normal and acceptable and our three jungle characters met in the village center to celebrate their recent adventures. Despite this inside information, it remains extraordinarily difficult to truly empathize with them if you were raised in a monogamous society.

Summary

The crown jewel of consciousness is the ability to go off-line, turn inward, and reflect on our knowledge. This truly amazing feat of self-reflection is made possible by the computational infrastructure of the explicit system based in the prefrontal cortex. More pointedly, it comes courtesy of three higher-cognitive functions, working memory, executive attention, and temporal integration. Working memory provides a buffer that can temporarily hold information in mind, which allows us, among rather a lot else, to engage in complex behavior, because we can, for instance, keep track of a higher-order goal while actually pursuing a specific subgoal. Attention has received, as it were, a lot of attention in the study of consciousness. There are several types, operating at all information-processing levels, but sustained and focused attention – executive attention – appears to be unique to humans. Some have equated attention with consciousness, or, rather, equated the content of consciousness with what is in the focus of attention, but these two processes do not appear to be the same. Finally, we have seen that the ability to order behavior in time, on a very subtle scale, is a critical component for proper social interaction. It is this computational platform, composed of those three executive functions, that so dramatically increases our cognitive flexibility.

The prefrontal cortex has clearly emerged as the brain region that enables our metacognitive abilities, especially the kind of self-reflective conscious processes, such as creative thinking, that are the hallmark of human experience. However, the seductive proposal that the prefrontal cortex is the seat of consciousness should be avoided. Rather, it contributes the highest-order mental functions to the content of consciousness.

The evolution of neural modules that compute such higher-order content was a critical step in the development of the kind of consciousness we humans have. Neuroscience research has shown that the neural basis of self-representation is distributed throughout several levels of brain organization. At the highest level, in the prefrontal cortex, the ability of the human brain to monitor its own thoughts and feelings led to a conceptual understanding of a sense of self, a level that is a prerequisite for information to be fully explicit or conscious. The same capacity to map mental states as metarepresentations has also led to the development of the ToM module, which attributes mental states to others.

Suggested reading

Baron-Cohen, S. (1995). *Mindblindness*. Cambridge, MA: MIT Press.

Damasio, A. R. (1999). *The Feeling of What Happens*. New York: Harcourt.

Miller, E. K., & Cohen, J. D. (2001). An integrative theory of prefrontal cortex function. *Annual Review of Neuroscience*, 24, 167–202.

Sarter, M., Givens, B., & Bruno, J. P. (2001). The cognitive neuroscience of sustained attention: Where top-down meets bottom-up. *Brain Research Reviews*, 35, 146–60.

11 Free will

The basics of free will

Theories of free will

This chapter examines the all-time favorite problem of philosophy, free will. In recent years, those aspects of the problem concerned with the exercise and experience of volitional action have been buried under a mountain of neuroscience. Other aspects of free will remain, perhaps for good, in the realm of metaphysics. We therefore sidestep, except for a few introductory remarks, any *a priori* arguments for or against the freedom of will offered by earlier thinkers and focus instead on the mechanics and phenomenology of willed action. We describe empirical research at neural and psychological levels that influences the decision-making process. These data highlight not only the functional neuroanatomy of self-determined motor acts but also inform our understanding of the role of consciousness in free will, which is the issue at the heart of this chapter. To that end, we cover the seminal research of Benjamin Libet and some intriguing proposals that have been put forward to come to grips with his controversial findings. We then explore the mechanisms that give rise to the experience of free will as well as several neurological conditions that distort our normal sense of agency.

Few philosophers of stature have been able to resist the temptation to give their two cents' worth to the problem of free will. Whether or not we choose our actions freely (without coercion) has profound implications for the way we operate in society. The foundation of social life, our deep-seated convictions of individual freedom, responsibility, and morality, depends on the assumption that we make our own choices and cause our own actions. Reward and punishment make little sense if we take behavior to be entirely predetermined and out of our direct control. Our mental flexibility implies choice. As a result we hold people responsible for their actions. If, however, we are part of a deterministic world governed by immutable laws, the course of events is inevitable and we are not the agents of our decisions. Instead we would be mere puppets in a grander scheme equipped with the cruel addition of having the sweet illusion of free will.

The writings of David Hume (1739/1888) represent a pivotal turn in the history of thought on free will. Prior to Hume, it was common to subscribe to the notion that free will can only exist if behavior is totally uncaused. That is, there can be no prior cause, external or internal, that determines our actions. This school of thought is known as **libertarianism**. Hume exposed the basic error in this reasoning by showing that all actions are, in fact, caused by antecedents, other mental events such as desires, beliefs, preferences, and so on. This does not mean that choices are predetermined but simply that they do not pop out of nowhere. Indeed, Hume argued that libertarianism is incompatible with free will. If we engage in a behavior without apparent reason, people would question our sanity and we would not consider such behavior indicative of free will. Instead, we think of people as being in charge of their own actions when they act consistent with their stable traits, dispositions, and beliefs. To Hume, a choice is truly free only if caused by other internal events; uncaused choices are indicative of randomness. This position was endorsed later by Voltaire (1752/1924) and is nowadays defended most forcefully by thinkers such as Dennett (1984, 2003a) and Wegner (2003). It should be noted that Hume's arguments hold independently of whether one adopts a dualist or monist position.

Free will feels so real that doubting its existence seems almost silly. Despite the phenomenal fact that we act "on purpose," most philosophers have come down in favor of determinism, prompting Samuel Johnson to exclaim that "all theory is against the freedom of the will; all experience is for it." Modern positions on the issue come in several flavors.

One set of positions hinges on the assumption that the brain is a causal machine. This assumption is supported by the fact that, as yet, there is no evidence to suggest that brain events occur uncaused. Thus, at this point, the brain should be regarded as deterministic in nature. There are two ways to deal with this apparent determinism. **Non-compatibilitists** argue that determinism implies inevitability, which leaves no room for free will, while **compatibilitists** have found a variety of clever ways that accommodate free will within a deterministic universe.

Another set of positions arise from the possibility that the brain is not a causal machine. Arguably the most profound insight of twentieth-century science was the discovery that the universe is inherently acausal and indeterminate. In

Chapter 4 we learned that quantum events can change spontaneously – without prior cause. Although there is, to date, no evidence showing that the inherent randomness of quantum systems manifests itself at the scale of neural events, the possibility has given libertarianists new ammunition for the argument that free will is an uncaused and unconstrained choice. Few people find this argument convincing at this point.

Neural control of motion

For the challenging task that lies ahead it is paramount to get a brief overview of how the brain's motor system operates. Motor control is the ultimate purpose of a brain. As such, it is not surprising that a large amount of neural tissue is devoted to the planning, programming, and execution of movement. There are two key concepts that are most central for the anatomical organization of the motor system. First, the motor system consists of a number of distributed systems, each making a unique contribution to skilled action. Second, the motor system is organized in a functional hierarchy with multiple levels of control. This is a highly efficient arrangement as higher-order structures need not be concerned with the details of the execution but delegate such tasks to lower-level components of the system.

In a way, the prefrontal cortex can be viewed as the highest-order motor cortex responsible for the conception of action plans (Fuster, 1995). It sends signals to two motor association regions, the **supplementary motor area** (SMA) and the **premotor cortex** (PMC), located just adjacent to the prefrontal cortex. Broadly speaking, the functional role of SMA and PMC is to carry out the initial planning of the action based on current perceptual input and past experience. This planning stage is essential for higher-order goals as they typically require sequences of complex actions. Suppose you want to drink from the coffee cup in front of you, a goal that can be accomplished in countless different ways (left arm, right arm, feet if you are flexible, and so on). Computations in SMA and PMC select the type of movements needed to get the job done.

Box 11.1   Telekinesis through population vectors?

What would you say if we told you that monkeys can control a robotic arm by just thinking? How about playing a video game using nothing but their imagination? Wouldn't that blur the line between mind and brain for you? You may think this is some gobbledygook straight out of a science-fiction film but several labs have made this a reality and given new hope to people suffering from spinal-cord injuries and other disorders of the motor system.

The key is what is known in motor physiology as **population vectors**. Microelectrodes implanted into the motor cortex of rhesus monkeys can record the activity of single motor cells during movement. This single-unit technique shows that neuronal firing rates are strongly correlated with movement direction. For instance, while some neurons are most active when the animal moves a limb toward its body, others respond best to the opposite action. This coding scheme suggests that the behavior of motor cells can be used, in principle, to foretell the precise magnitude and direction of the planned movement. When

---

Box 11.1   *continued*

recordings are made from an entire population of neurons, each cell's preferred direction corresponds to a vector and the activity of the entire ensemble of neurons can be summed to obtain what Apostolos Georgopoulus (1995) called the population vector. Population analysis is an incredibly accurate predictor of the trajectory of forthcoming motion. During continuous recording of a dynamic movement, the population vector is recalculated every 200 msec to update the direction of the intended movement. Thus, as the motor plan unfolds, shifts in the population vector can be plotted to anticipate the moment-to-moment progression of movement.

Against this backdrop, consider this slightly Frankensteinian experiment. Miguel Nicolelis (2003) trained macaque monkeys in a simple video game that required them to manipulate a joystick to drag a cursor into a target. At the same time, he recorded spike trains from sites in cortical motor areas and showed that it is possible to translate this neuronal activity – population vectors, specifically – into motor commands in order to directly control artificial devices in real time. First, he used the population vector to drive the cursor on the screen. He then disengaged the joystick from the computer and the animal quickly learned that just thinking about the movement was sufficient to control the cursor. You have to visualize this to fully appreciate it: Here is a monkey in front of a computer screen playing a video game by pure thought alone! Second, Nicolelis showed that a robotic arm can be controlled online by the population vector. He fed the population analysis into a robotic arm in an adjacent room and managed to mimic the monkey's intended wrist movement. This research may not be easy to digest upon first encounter, but the technology of establishing a functional interface between living brain tissue and artificial limps breathes new hope into people suffering from paralysis. Neuroprosthetics are becoming a viable alternative to research solutions that focus on neural repair. This work reminds us that determining where the mind starts and the brain ends is an impossible task.

Motor association regions are late adaptations that have evolved to create a flexible response system. Subcortical structures are also intimately involved in the planning and programming necessary for purposeful actions; however, they are less concerned with the selection of motor plans but rather with their effective execution. While prefrontal regions represent goals in a highly abstract manner, for instance, the desire to drink some coffee, SMA and PMC compute motor plans to achieve this goal by specifying which muscles to use and in which sequence. The overarching theme at the subcortical level is to translate this still conceptual representation into more concrete motor commands. The main components of the subcortical motor system are the **basal ganglia** and the **cerebellum**.

The internal wiring of the basal ganglia is quite complex but its overall net effect can be described in simple terms. Cortical motor areas provide excitatory input, presumably containing contents of motor plans, which prompts the basal ganglia to send excitatory signals back, via the thalamus, to the same cortical motor areas. Current thinking regarding the functional significance of this configuration is as follows. At any time, we hope to achieve many goals, some of which may create conflicting motor plans. We settle on a particular course of action on the basis of a competitive process, that is, motor plans are mere candidates that must compete for the right to activate muscles (Rosenbaum et al., 1991). The basal ganglia are in the unique position to help resolve competition among potential responses (Berns & Sejnowski, 1996). Normally, the basal ganglia's strong inhibitory baseline serves to restrain the execution of cortical motor plans, a good measure given the frequency with which we desire socially unacceptable goals. However, as one motor plan starts getting the upper hand in the competition, this leading candidate can use the basal ganglia to its advantage. More precisely, the positive feedback circuit strengthens its winning position by removing the basal ganglia's inhibitory grip on it, while its competitors continue to be subjected to the strong inhibitory influence. So the basal ganglia promote response selection through a winner-takes-it-all strategy that leaves no powerful semifinalists that can compromise the motion. In short, the basal ganglia are critical for movement initiation – a gatekeeper for all but the optimal response. This conception is supported by disorders of the basal ganglia. Patients with Parkinson's disease have difficulty initiating movement and often look frozen in place. For instance, they might not break a fall with their hands, indicating that even obvious movements cannot be executed if the motor plan is not sufficiently disinhibited to reach motor effectors. This deficit is also apparent in task switching, which requires the termination of one motion and the initiation of another.

The cerebellum is a vast network of neurons devoted to fine motor coordination. Its principal role is to specify the details of the motor plan. This program effectively spells out direction and force each muscle must follow to achieve the grand plan. We can accurately reach for the coffee cup, lift it to the mouth, tilt back the head just enough, and drink a sip in one flowing motion, thanks to the cerebellum. So far we have emphasized the functional neuroanatomy of the motor system but the cerebellum is an ideal place to disabuse anyone of the notion that motor output is a primitive matter, a mere outlet for such noble cognitive functions as language, reasoning, or declarative memory. In computational terms, motor control is a feat of the highest order, as evidenced by the failure in artificial intelligence to produce anything that looks remotely like smooth motion, let alone robots dancing classical ballet. Indeed, this highlights how exquisitely evolved the human motor system is.

Computations from motor association areas, basal ganglia, and cerebellum converge on the primary motor cortex, which functions as the final tallying point for all the preparatory planning. The **primary motor cortex** is the main source of the **corticospinal tract** which regulates the activity of **motor neurons** in the spinal cord. There are also several other descending tracts and countless feedback loops, the most prominent of which is mediated by the cerebellum. The cerebellum receives direct input from most sensory systems and is so ideally positioned to handle real-time, sensorimotor integration tasks, such as shooting at a moving target. When a basketball player decides to make a jump shot, the cerebellum not only performs the hands-on programming of the motor plan but also adjusts it, in-flight so to speak, if a defender thwarts it.

A last note regarding the primary motor cortex concerns new insights into the nature of motor plan representation. Work in the 1930s by neurosurgeon Wilder

Figure 11.1

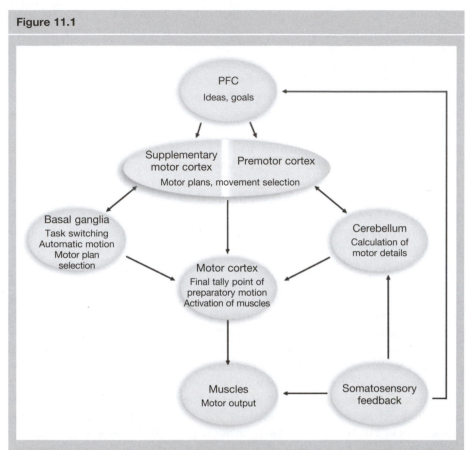

The functional architecture of the motor system reflects the fact that a number of distributed and specialized systems contribute to achieving skilled motion. The notion of hierarchical control is important. Cortical motor areas only need to represent goal states and are not bogged down with specifying detailed patterns of muscular activity. They simply issue commands to subcortical structures that then busy themselves with the execution of the motor plan.

Penfield led to the hypothesis that motor neurons contain a somatotopic map of the body, the so-called motor homunculus. But, on closer study, it has become clear that this homunculus needs to be redrawn, as primary motor neurons appear to represent "goals" of movement rather than specific muscles and joints. Graziano (2002) stimulated the motor cortex of rhesus monkeys at specific sites and found that the induced action was always a coordinated movement involving many muscles and joints. What's more, the action resulted in the same final posture, irrespective of the starting location of the limbs. This indicates that the content of motor plans specifies a goal position in the space around the body. This coding scheme aimed at achieving a final configuration is termed **endpoint control**. As explained in Box 11.1, this has profound implication for medicine.

The nature of free will

The Libet experiment

In 1985, Benjamin Libet (who also discovered the 0.5 second delay described in Chapter 7) carried out an experiment that was designed to answer no less than the eternal question of free will. As you might expect, the experiment did not settle the question but its findings had such a profound impact that one can still hear them echoing through the field of consciousness 20 years after their publication.

Libet set out to determine the sequence of events associated with an internally generated, self-paced motor act. For conscious will to be the cause of action, it obviously would have to precede the act. If, however, action is programmed by the brain prior to the intention to act conscious will cannot possibly be the cause of the action. In order to establish which comes first, the intention or the motor program, Libet timed three events, the occurrence of the will to act, the moment cortical areas start the motor sequence leading to the act, and the actual performance of the act. Libet used EMG, a method that detects muscular activity, to measure actual motion. He also knew how to determine the point in time the brain initiates the motor program. In the 1960s, when EEG became a routine tool to measure brain activity, it was discovered that voluntary movement is preceded by a so-called readiness potential or RP (Kornhuber & Deeke, 1965). RP is a slow, scalp-recorded negative shift in electrical potential that originates from the SMA and occurs up to a second (in average 400 msec) prior to a volitional act. The shift presumably measures the onset of the brain's preparatory activation of bodily motion. Automatic movements such as reflexes, which are organized at the level of the spinal cord or lower brainstem, do not show a RP. Neither do motor tics, the characteristic symptoms of Tourette's syndrome, which are also considered out of the patient's control.

The tricky part was to pin down the last time point, the moment when the will to act became conscious. Libet solved this problem in a unique way and it was this solution that enabled him to carry out his seminal experiment. He knew that relying on a verbal report of the awareness of will was not an option because language entails its own motor sequence and RP. Instead, he used the perceptual system. He set up a large analogue clock face and asked subjects to watch a light spot that made a clockwise sweep of the face every 2.56 seconds. Libet instructed his subjects to flex their wrists and fingers whenever they felt like it and indicate the location of the light on the face, say, at 20 minutes, when they became aware of the urge to act. He called this moment W for will. It took Libet 40 trials from each subject to separate the RP from noise. The timing method not only allowed Libet to determine fractions of a second but a series of preliminary studies convinced him that the procedure also yielded accurate time estimates. In this pilot work, he asked subjects to time the awareness of the motion, a moment he called M for movement. The estimate of M could be checked against the actual motion and Libet found a high correspondence between the two. Subjects also had no trouble

Figure 11.2

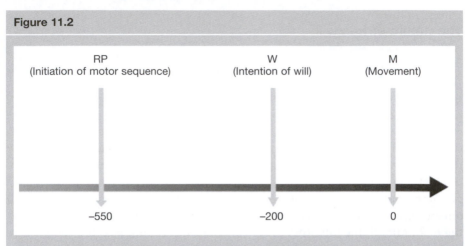

Timeline showing the correct sequence of events accociated with consciously chosen action. If we take performance as point zero the intention to act occurs 200 msec in advance of motion while the RP occurs 550 msec prior to it. If the brain is already in the midst of preparing to make a move before we even consciously decide to move what does this say, if anything, about the status of free will? (Based on Libet, 1999)

telling the difference between M and W (Libet et al., 1983). Libet's experimental design operationalized the problem of free will to this question: Which one comes first, W or RP?

The experiment left no doubt as to which came first. After averaging hundreds of trials and rechecking his data several times, a wise measure given the stakes, Libet announced his results: Conscious will occurred after the RP, by a whopping 350 miliseconds! The performance of movement followed after another 200 msec. The full sequence of events was this: −550 msec for RP, −200 msec for W, and 0 for the motion. Put another way, the intention to act occurred *after* the brain had already instigated the act. This meant, in no uncertain terms, that we start voluntary motion before we consciously decide to move. Libet's conclusion was that, as far as causation was concerned, consciousness was "out of the picture"; it simply came too late. Perhaps, then, Thomas Huxley (1910, p. 240) was right when he observed: "Consciousness would appear to be simply a by-product of the body's working, completely without power to modify that working, just as a steam whistle that accompanies the working of a locomotive is without influence upon its machinery." Libet's study was later replicated using slightly different methods with essentially the same results (Haggard et al., 1999).

For the usually calm waters of academe, a storm erupted over the findings that was fueled as much by scientific arguments as by gut feelings. Perhaps Searle (2000) expressed the mood best when he said: "if this were so it [free will] would be the biggest joke of the universe." Whatever we make of the findings, if we accepted the standard criterion that good science raises more questions than answers, Libet's experiment must count as one of the most successful empirical studies in the short history of consciousness research. This is the more puzzling as it neither settled the question of free will nor did it present dualists or materialists with trouble explaining its results.

Researchers were quick to highlight methodological limitations. Some questioned the validity of the timing procedures, particularly the method used to measure W. Others argued that subjects could only freely choose the timing of the act but not the act itself. Still others maintained that flexing fingers was too trivial a task to serve as a model for volition. Motor programs underlying complex motion, which are more characteristic of voluntary acts, might be different, perhaps involving consciousness to a greater extent. Subjects also had to pay attention to two events at the same time, the location of the light and the urge to act. Some researchers pointed out that task switching could account for the delay. Taken together, these objections warrant serious consideration because carefully controlled experiments are the bread and butter of science.

If, for a moment, we accept the validity of the methods the data make for some intriguing theorizing regarding the role of consciousness in free will. For a materialist, the finding that conscious will lags behind the RP should be entirely expected – otherwise we would be dealing with magic! Libet went a different route and felt the need to search for a remaining causal role for consciousness. Like William James, he could not bring himself to demote consciousness to the role of impotent bystander and was convinced that the phenomenal reality of free will must be part of the explanation. To rescue conscious will from the grip of inconsequential epiphenomena, he proposed that the sequence of events grants consciousness the **power of veto** (Libet, 1999). Although intention occurs too late to cause action, it does occur prior to action. The window of opportunity of 200 msec in length would be enough to veto action. In this view, consciousness may either stop an action from being executed or participate in the selection of the best action. If consciousness is policing the unconscious brain in this manner, it is perhaps more accurate to say that we have free-won'ts rather than really free will! One problem with this interpretation is that a veto should evoke its own RP and experiments in which subjects were instructed to suppress an action show that conscious movement inhibition is indeed preceded by a RP.

Latto (1985) offered yet another explanation that makes reference to backward referral. Recall that Libet also showed that a stimulus must achieve neuronal adequacy, that is, induce 500 msec of continuous neural activity in the primary sensory cortex, before it is perceived consciously. Since we do not experience a half-second delay, Libet interpreted those findings by suggesting that consciousness backdates events to the time they occur. In the present study, backward referral already occurs for the perception of the light spot, but it is not figured into W. If we refer W back in time as well, by 0.5 seconds, it would precede the RP. Libet countered this interpretation by arguing that W is not time-sensitive as is perception. It does not require backward referral because subjects can report it at their leisure.

In his characteristically narrative manner, Dennett offers yet another interpretation, focusing on the misconception that there is a precise time at which events "enter" into consciousness (Dennett & Kinsbourne, 1992). It is natural to think that information processing starts out in the unconscious hinterland of the mind and slowly rises to the headquarters of consciousness where we – the audience – experience the light spot or the conscious will. To Dennett, this is a kind of residual dualism reminiscent of the Cartesian theater (Dennett, 1991). To him, there is no place (localized or distributed) or special state of activation that propels information over some threshold to acquire the status of qualia. Only if one latches on to this idea is it even conceivable to discuss Libet's results in terms of the conscious will making judgments or vetoing actions. He argues that each event, RP and W, has its own temporal sequence and the order of subjective experience does not establish any actual priority; that is to say, the sequence "in" consciousness does not correspond to the order in which it actually occurs in the brain. Dennett (2003a) believes free will exists but not in the conventional sense. By adding randomness, as proposed by libertarians, we do not get the kind of free will, in his words, "worth wanting." To Dennett free will is an evolved capacity for weighing options, which equates the idea of free will with behavioral flexibility.

Although the nature of free will remains, in its essence, in the realm of metaphysics, Libet's research certainly has helped shift the focus of the question. If conscious will trails behind in the sequence of events, which it seems to do, why does the brain compute it in the first place? To answer this, we turn our attention to the mechanisms that give rise to the *experience* of free will and explore its possible evolutionary purpose.

Conscious will as a feeling

Hume (1739/1888) made another important observation with respect to free will. He recognized that cause and effect is an inference. Like gravity, we cannot see causality in an object; all we know is a temporal association that A is reliably followed by B. A bowling ball might seem to cause pins to fall but we cannot see a causal force in the ball itself (Wegner, 2002). We must infer cause and effect because causality is an event and not a property of the ball. Accordingly, causal attributions are a habit of the mind. Hume was clear that this also applied to conscious will. In the same way that causation is not a property of an object, it cannot be a property of a person. We cannot see a direct relationship between conscious will and behavior; we can only infer a causal link from the consistent relationship between our intentions to act and the actual behavior. The possibility that a third variable causes both always exists. Our understanding of cause and effect is a theory because it must, by definition, go beyond the evidence.

This insight, coupled with Libet's results that programming of action occurs prior to conscious will, led the psychologist Daniel Wegner (2002) to develop his **theory of apparent mental causation**. The question of why we have the experience of agency would seem pointless for someone who believes in free will but it represents somewhat of a paradox for anyone who asserts that free will is an illusion. If we do not have free will why, then, do we privatize our intentions and experience our actions as willed?

A fundamental concept in Wegner's theory is that conscious will is a feeling. Hume had realized this and defined the will as "the internal impression we feel and are conscious of, when we knowingly give rise to any new motion" (Hume, 1739/1888). Huxley (1910) stated it even more clearly: "Volition ... is an emotion *indicative* of physical changes, not a *cause* of such changes." Free will, then, is not so much a mental force but a feeling of causing one's action. We *perceive* a consistent relationship between motion and its effect and *feel* that we have caused it. In other words, free will is an ownership-of-action emotion. One consequence of this conceptualization is that the free will-versus-determinism debate is a false dichotomy. Free will is a feeling; determinism is a process (Wegner, 2002).

A second consequence of the notion that conscious will is an experience of a person who acts rather than a psychological force of a person is that experience and

Figure 11.3

	Feeling of doing	No feeling of doing
Doing	Normal voluntary action	Automatisms
Not doing	Illusions of control	Normal inaction

The experience of free will and voluntary action are separate processes that can be dislodged. The upper left quadrant represents the case of willing an action that is indeed followed by the action. The lower right quadrant depicts the case of not willing an action that is also not followed by any action. Apart from these two normal cases, there are instances in which the sense of agency shows its fragility. In the upper right quadrant is the case of not willing an action that is nevertheless executed by the motor system. Examples include hypnosis, alien hand syndrome, and unilateral neglect. Finally, in the lower left quadrant is the case of willing an action that is not followed by the action. Examples are some schizophrenic delusions and superstitious behavior. (Adapted from Wegner and Wheatley, 1999) action are two different processes mediated by different mechanisms. There are indeed several neurological conditions in which there is little or no correspondence between the two. Moreover, there is data from healthy subjects in experimental settings showing that will and motion can be dissociated.

According to Wegner, the factorial combination of will and action yields four possibilities: Will can occur with or without action and action can occur with or without will. Figure 11.3 shows a schematic representation of the four types. The upper left and lower right quadrants represent the two default cases of normal action and inaction, in which will and motion correspond according to conventional wisdom, that is, we feel that we did what we wanted to do and did not do what we did not want to do. The other two cases are trickier. The bottom left quadrant describes the illusion of control, which occurs when intentions are not followed by action but appear nevertheless executed just as we intended them. Although this may sound like a peculiar experience this is the reality for the schizophrenic suffering from delusions of grandeur. The underlying psychopathology is explained in more detail below. The illusion of control is also part of superstitious behaviors as, for instance, in the belief that my favorite team cannot lose if I watch the game.

The top right quadrant involves automatisms in which doing is not accompanied by the feeling of willing. For instance, people may feel on "autopilot" during altered states of consciousness such as hypnosis or daydreaming. Several psychiatric conditions are best characterized as disorders of volition of this type, such as schizophrenia involving symptoms of alien control or thought insertion. A particularly informative example is **alien hand syndrome**, a condition caused by damage to the left medial frontal regions, including anterior cingulate and SMA as well as the anterior corpus callosum (Spence & Frith, 1999). Patients acknowledge ownership of the contralateral right-sided hand but feel that it has a will of its own. Stereotyped and compulsive actions such as reflexive grasping are common but patients do not intend these motions and deny agency. The frontal lesion is thought to release the hand from inhibitory control and PET scans have shown corresponding excessive activity in parietal regions (Feinberg et al., 1992). This is reminiscent of utilization behaviors in which patients become slaves to environmental cues (see Chapter 9). When the lesion is confined to the anterior corpus callosum the condition can get outright arcane. Here the left hand is affected and may commit acts the person objects to. **Anarchic hand syndrome**, as the condition is known, has even produced cases of attempted self-strangulation. In another variation involving seizures in the parietal lobe a left hand may become truly alien and the patient will deny agency and ownership (Leiguardia et al., 1993).

Wegner's theory of apparent mental causation postulates that we infer causality under three conditions: A thought of will must occur prior to behavior (priority), behavior must be consistent with the thought (consistency), and behavior cannot be accompanied by alternative causes (exclusivity). When these conditions are met, we ascribe behavior to conscious will and think that its cause lies within ourselves. It is easy to imagine how the experience of causing action would be undermined if there is no prior thought or the action is inconsistent with the thought.

The mark of a good scientific theory is its heuristic value and Wegner's theorizing has spawned a number of testable hypotheses. As with the sense of self, the sense of agency can be tricked so that we feel we cause our action when in fact we do not. In one experiment, Wegner used transcranial magnetic stimulation (TMS) to fool the feeling of will (Wegner & Wheatley, 1999). TMS is a noninvasive procedure that temporarily induces a weak electrical current in a specific cortical region. If applied to the motor cortex it produces spontaneous and automatic limb movement in the subject's ipsilateral body. The subject has no control over these movements but when Wegner also instructed the subjects to move the same limb he stimulated with TMS, they reported feeling that they were causing these movements.

Ramachandran and Blakeslee (1998) went one step further and showed that the two systems can be dislodged in a truly remarkable way. In a series of simple but very clever experiments they managed to trick people into thinking that they control the movement of someone else. In one study, subjects were placed in front of a rigged mirror. The bottom half was a true mirror that reflected the subject's lower face, including the mouth. The top half of the mirror was see-through glass and a dummy face was lined up to match the subject's lower face. To strengthen the illusion, the room was darkened and two spotlights illuminated respectively the upper dummy face and the subject's own mouth. The subject was then instructed to smile or stick out their tongue while the researchers secretly moved the dummy face consistent with these movements. This trick induced in the subject the impression that they were causing the dummy's facial expressions when in fact these movements had external causes. When the dummy was pinched subjects even showed signs of pain (galvanic skin response), indicating an illusion of ownership. In another study, two subjects were placed in front of a mirror, one standing behind the other. The subject in front was asked to keep his arms out of the way while the subject at the back was situated so that his arms appeared to hang from the shoulders of the person in front. When the "back" subject was instructed over a headset to make arm movements, such as clapping, the "front" subject did not report owning the motion. However, in a slight variation of the experiment both subjects received the same instructions independently via earpieces but only the back subject was allowed to move. In this case, the front subject did get the distinct illusion that her conscious will produced the movement. This false feeling was created because the experimental setup met the terms of the theory of apparent mental causation. The subject intended the motion (priority), they saw the intended motion carried out (consistency), and there was no alternative explanation (the front subject did not know of the back subject's presence). These virtual agency studies are a testament to the changeability of the exercise and experience of free will.

According to Wegner (2003), conscious will operates like a magician who fools us into perceiving a causal sequence that does not exist. The real cause of our

Figure 11.4

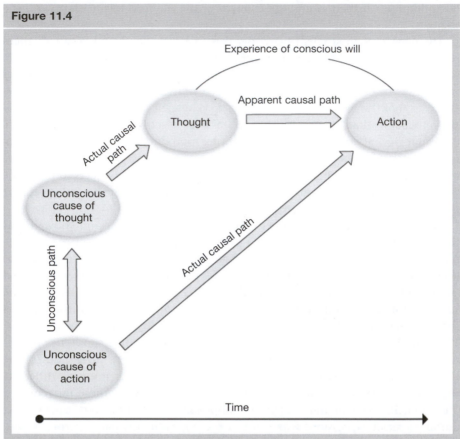

The theory of apparent mental causation proposes that unconscious brain activity causes motion, the actual causal path. At the same time, these unconscious processes also give rise to conscious thoughts about the action. When these thoughts appear in consciousness prior to the action, we infer a causal link between the will and the action, the apparent causal path. (Adapted from Wegner and Wheatley, 1999)

action lies in unconscious brain activity to which we have no access. We only become conscious of the two end-products of this activity, the thought and the motion. We link them and interpret our actions as willed. Imagine looking at a tree and by some miraculous method you know ahead of time when and how each branch of the tree moves. If the branches do move accordingly it would be quite difficult to avoid the feeling that you caused their motion. As Wegner put it, "we believe in the magic of our own causal agency" (2002, p. 89).

The mapping system

The above evidence strongly indicates that we can experience free will independent of action. We sense causing motion that we are not causing and we feel not doing motion we are doing. What mechanisms in the brain create these perverse cases? If conscious will is, as Wegner and others have proposed, the product of the same unconscious processes that also give rise to motion how, then, do these processes give rise to the sense of normal and abnormal agency? A key insight here is that we feel that we *own* our actions. This suggests that the sense of agency developed from the self system. Agency and self are not identical, however; we can feel that a particular motion is ours, such as a reflex, but not get the sense of intentionally causing it.

To see the agency system as an extension of the self system, recall that the brain represents its body in topographical maps. As we move through our environs, the brain must continuously update these maps with the body's new location and position of its movable equipment. We accomplish this by monitoring the changes in sensory input that occur as a result of the motion. The experience of our own arm moving is created by kinesthetic feedback from receptors in the muscles and by the visual feedback of seeing the arm moving. On the basis of this, we conclude retrospectively that the executed motion was ours. Because this feedback occurs for involuntary and voluntary motion it can account for the sense of ownership but it cannot account for agency. To experience ourselves as agents we must also have advance notice that our body is about to do something.

Motor plans cooked up at the highest level of the motor hierarchy take a sizable chunk of time until they activate muscles. Several cortical and subcortical structures are involved in selecting, conceptualizing, programming, and detailing the plan. It is thought that during this processing time a carbon copy of the plan is sent to consciousness, effectively providing prior knowledge of the upcoming action. Involuntary action is organized by structures lower on the motor hierarchy. These motor plans are more quickly executed, providing less time for a sneak preview.

This model of the agency system is intuitively appealing at the conceptual level but it poses a fundamental problem for neuroscience. How does consciousness interpret motor plans? To see the basic problem, consider that the motor system is designed to move muscles and represent motor instructions in terms of joint and muscle positions. However, brains understand motion in terms of perception, such as changes in spatial coordinates. Purposeful motion is motion toward some goal and an understanding of upcoming motion must be represented in terms of upcoming changes to sensory systems, not motor systems. How does the brain solve this problem? Current thinking evolves around the notion that signals from motor regions in the frontal cortex are sent to sensory regions in the posterior cortex that map current motor instructions onto sensory maps representing the body (Frith, 1992). This mapping process converts the motor plan into a representation that predicts the sensory consequences of the planned action. Central to the mechanism is that the mapping occurs to regions processing sensations so that the nature of the prediction is not what we are about to do but what we are about to experience! The phenomenal result of this representation is what we call intentions. In this view, intention is not prior

Figure 11.5

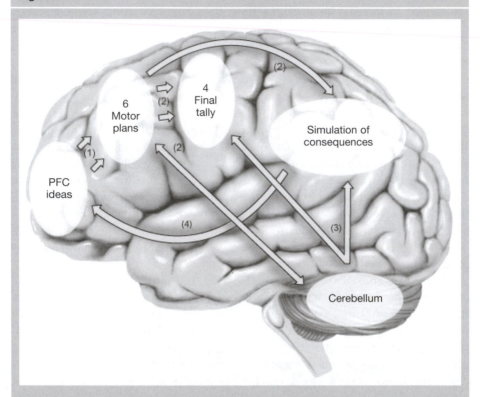

Normal agency depends on three components, a simulation of possible sensory consequences of planned motion, actual sensory feedback validating the simulation, and an interpretation by conscious thought processes of how well expectation matched reality. The process – simplified in this diagram – begins when the prefrontal cortex initiates willed action in accordance with internal goals (1). The sophistication of motor plans organized at this level of the motor hierarchy necessitates long processing times, allowing time to leak the plan to consciousness. The nature of this precipitated representation is as follows: Frontal motor regions send signals to posterior sensory regions that analyze perceptions (2); these signals convey the same instructions sent to muscles detailing how to execute the plan but when they are mapped on to sensory areas they have the effect of simulating the consequences of the plan in terms of changes to perception. Aided by additional feedback from the cerebellum (3), this mapping process effectively amounts to a prediction, buffered in working memory (4), of what we are going to see and feel, which is the neural activity we interpret as an intention. If performance of the motor plan indeed results in the anticipated changes to sensory input, we feel we intentionally caused the motion. In this view, the experience of free will is a misinterpretation of matching prediction to feedback.

knowledge of what we are going to do but an expectation of what we are going to find.

These insights into the inner workings of the agency system inform our understanding of the adaptive advantage of the experience of free will. Pressures to represent choice consciously may derive from the enhanced ability to differentiate between us as agents and other causes of change in the world. This clarifies the reason why the system that maps motor movements prior to performance is likely an extension of the system that generates the feeling of owning motion. By anticipating sensations that relate to our actions we can label actions as our own, knowledge that we can use to build a self-concept that includes what we like and do not like to do. The ability to predict how our actions will make us feel also allows us to better assess how important they might be to us, which in turn shapes the selection of future behavior. In addition, planned action mapped onto sensory areas might play a pivotal role in social interactions as theory-of-mind capacities and empathy rely on understanding the intentions of others in terms of sensory consequences. Computational scientists use the concept of **emulators** to describe this capacity of the brain to model the consequences of behavior (Gush, 1997). An advantage of emulators is that a simulation of the effects of motion provides feedback faster than actual motion; indeed, it provides feedback in the absence of motion. The power of such comparator operations lies in the brain's ability to adjust or even stop motion prior to execution. This idea is consistent with the rationale given by scientists such as Libet for why we internalize motor plans in the first place, that is, consciousness functions as a late error detector to correct motion.

According to this framework, the sense of agency is created when the prediction of the mapping system is validated by sensory feedback. Thus, agency depends on the adequate mapping of predicted movement and a confirmation report that the expected experience actually occurred. If current motor instructions are not mapped, either because the motor plan is executed too fast by the trigger-happy implicit system or because it is mapped only weakly onto sensory regions, we cannot predict what we are going to see and feel. As a result, our own motion would come as a surprise to us and we get the sense that we did not produce it intentionally. The reason why human infants and other animals do not seem to experience themselves as agents the way we do is likely due to an immature mapping system. For them all action, such as crawling or running, would appear as involuntary. In contrast, when we engage in volitional acts we do anticipate what we are going to see and feel, which makes the experience less expected and less intense. Incidentally, this is the reason why we cannot tickle ourselves (see Box 11.2). The sense of agency, in this view, is the misinterpretation of neural activity as conscious intentions when in fact it is a simulation of possible motor plan outcomes. The illusion of free will is completed when ensuing feedback matches the prediction of the simulation.

Box 11.2   Why is it impossible to tickle yourself?

New models of motor prediction, six subjects in a functional MRI camera, and a rigged robot arm have recently lifted a long-standing mystery that has baffled scientists and children alike: Why can't we tickle ourselves? Although the stimulus applied to the belly is roughly the same, being tickled by someone else evokes hysterical laughs while tickling yourself causes boredom. The standard response to the conundrum has been that much of our behavior is guided by our expectations of specific consequences. If we tickle ourselves we know what is coming and that makes just about everything less funny. The problem with that explanation is that if you were told exactly how you will be tickled it would still feel ticklish despite the fact that you knew precisely what to expect. A nifty little experiment has recently taken us one step closer to a more sound, mechanistic explanation of the puzzle.

Susan Blakemore and her colleagues used a robot arm to tickle the palm of subjects while their brains were scanned with fMRI. Subjects felt this to be ticklish and their scans revealed corresponding activation in somatosensory cortex, anterior cingulate, and the cerebellum. When subjects tickled their own palm either by using the other hand or by controlling the robot arm the stimulation did not feel ticklish and the brain activation was significantly reduced, particularly in the cerebellum. In a slight variation, the experimenters rigged the robot arm to introduce a half-second delay before the tickling action occurred. This made the sensation ticklish again despite the fact that the subjects controlled the robot arm (see Blakemore & Decety, 2001).

The mystery seems to lie in the cerebellum. Recall that the cerebellum receives direct and immediate sensory feedback for its mission to solve real-time sensorimotor integration tasks. Blakemore hypothesized that this gives the cerebellum a critical role in matching predicted motor effects to sensory feedback. If I decide to tickle myself, I generate a prediction of the likely sensory consequences. This prediction is the key to the "whodunit" question because it tells the cerebellum what to expect. The cerebellum compares this expectation to incoming sensory information and, if they match, warns other sensory areas to ignore the sensation. If someone else tickles me I do not generate such a prediction. In this case, the cerebellum does not know what to expect and cannot warn sensory cortices what is coming up. This makes the sensation more ticklish or intense, which can be seen in fMRI by greater neural activity in SMII and cingulate cortex. This model explains the reason why some schizophrenics can tickle themselves. They fail to generate a prediction and thus cannot distinguish between self-touching and other-touching. It also explains the reason why it still feels ticklish when someone else tells me exactly how I will be tickled. Only if I produce a prediction myself is the cerebellum activated. Adequate matching also depends on temporal parameters. If the tickling action is delayed by 500 msec the cerebellum concludes the motor plan had no effect and the actual sensation is novel and unrelated to the prediction. Although this research has shed some light on the issue, many questions remain unresolved, for instance, why some people are not ticklish at all.

Distortions of volition

Ideal agency is based on authentification of motor plans by sensory feedback. The derailment of this process is thought to underlie the abnormal phenomenology of action that characterizes several neurological disorders in particular schizophrenia (Frith, 1992). Schizophrenia includes both, the overexperience and underexperience of will. Current thinking implicates a faulty prediction system. In delusions of alien control or thought insertion, the patient believes that their actions are caused by others. Here the brain probably fails to generate a prediction altogether. Without the representation of prior intentions to act these patients cannot anticipate the consequences of their actions, which creates the impression of being under the direct control of other agents. Imagine how it must feel to never know what to expect from yourself! To the schizophrenic their own behavior must appear as if guided by magic and it is perhaps not surprising, then, that they tend to misattribute it to some supernatural force. Neuroimaging data support this hypothesis. Delusions of alien control are associated with underactivity in the prefrontal cortex and overactivity in the parietal cortex (Spence et al., 1997). This neural profile suggests two inferences. While the lack of prefrontal activation may prevent signals mapping current motor instructions from being sent, the excessive parietal activation may induce reflexive responses to environmental stimuli. It is perhaps not surprising, then, that they are also able to tickle themselves (see Box 11.2).

Schizophrenics also suffer from the opposite distortion, experiences of excessive control. They believe they possess Godlike powers and their direct intervention causes, say, the solar motion across the sky. These delusions of grandeur are thought to be created by an overwhelmingly strong prediction system. Fantasies of ruling the world, which we all harbor from time to time, are inadvertently run as simulations on sensory maps. A mere passing thought of the desire to influence world events may thus create the intention to rule the world. When the sun complies, the sense of control is undeniable and irresistible. Grandiose ideas of omnipotence involving predictions that are unverifiable by sensory feedback, say, the defense of Xanadu from Martian invaders, also pose no threat to the thought–action consistency necessary for experiencing agency. Even when predictions can be checked against reality, patients with schizophrenia are not deterred from inferring that their intentions have real effects. Frith thinks that this is due to a double whammy. First, motor plans are mapped onto sensory areas with such force that the simulation itself might serve as a substitute for real sensory feedback, a hypothesis that is underscored by brain imaging showing that delusions of universal power are linked to *hyper*activity in circumscribed prefrontal areas. Second, this effect is exacerbated by inactivity in the parietal cortex which makes it difficult for them to monitor the outcome of their own motion (Malenka, 1986). To the schizophrenic, denying the distinctive feeling of being the author of events around him would seem more insane than acknowledging any discrepancy between expectation and outcome, if they detect them at all.

The series of studies by Ramachandran and Blakeslee (1998) described earlier demonstrated how readily the feeling of authorship of motion, once generated, can override the problem of intentions poorly matching sensory feedback. Recall the mirror experiment in which a front subject hears instructions to make arm movements but refrains from performing them, while a back subject, whose arms appear to the front subject to hang from her shoulders, performs arm movements that correspond to these instructions. The front subject gets the sense of causing someone else's motion because she produces a prediction in response to the instructions and receives visual confirmation that the plan is carried out. The sight of an arm, albeit not her own, moving at just the right moment and in just the right way to match the internally predicted effect is sufficient to create the illusion of authorship, despite the fact that no kinesthetic feedback (except for some twitching) was registered for the action.

Models of motor prediction are also relevant to altered states of consciousness. Distortions of self and agency are common experiences in these psychological phenomena. Hypnosis, for instance, is characterized by the lack of spontaneous generation of action and feelings of being an automaton. A similar loss of volitional control occurs in daydreaming. When we drive a car on a familiar route we switch to autopilot and get to our destination realizing that we did not actively supervise, moment by moment, our actions. Most striking perhaps is the total loss of willed action in non-lucid dreaming. We experience dream motion as entirely involuntary and do not direct the script of our personal film noir. Evidence is accruing that mild to moderate alterations to consciousness involve transient downward shifts in prefrontal activation (Dietrich, 2003). A state of prefrontal hypofunction would, presumably, affect the mapping system. In the dream state, the hypofrontality is accompanied by strong motor inhibition down the spinal cord, which renders the body paralyzed (Hobson et al., 2000). What seems to happen, then, is this. The underactivity in prefrontal regions suggests that a rather weak mapping process is at work, which results in little or no prediction as to what we are about to experience. Notice that this mechanism for explaining the absence of intentions is the same put forward for schizophrenia. However, the reason why the underexperience of will in dreams does not result in the feeling of being controlled by alien forces, as it does in schizophrenia, is because there is also no actual motion in dreams and thus no need for such a desperate explanation. Dream motion is simply due to activity in lower-order motor structures that occurs in response to dream images. Recall that ownership of motion is an interpretation that relies on sensory feedback. Dream motion feels ontologically compelling, despite the paralysis, because the sole sensory input during dreams comes from the self-generated images that construct the dreamworld, which are entirely consistent with the motion. In contrast, hypnosis is associated with the downregulation of the entire frontal cortex, including motor cortices (Gruzelier, 2000). This can account for the two most prominent features of hypnosis, the lack of initiative and the perceived involuntariness of action. While the former may have its roots in the relative inactivity in motor regions, the latter may be caused by reduced prefrontal activity, which prevents the mapping of predicted motion.

Summary

Free will is perhaps the oldest and most discussed topic in all of philosophy. The question at the heart of the matter is determinism, and early theorists can be divided into those who believe that free will is a totally uncaused choice, a position known as libertarianism, and those who are convinced by Hume's proposal that actions are caused by antecedents, such as thoughts and beliefs. Many aspects of free will have become part of the realm of science and investigators have started to delineate the neural and cognitive events that constitute choice. These developments provide the backdrop for examining free will using the framework of neuroscience.

The exercise of free will depends on the brain's motor system. The functional architecture of the system reflects the fact that its organization is hierarchical and that a number of distributed and specialized systems contribute to achieving willed action. In his seminal free-will experiment, Libet used this knowledge to measure the moment when the motor system initiates a voluntary motor act and compared it to the moment when the person became aware of the will to act. The result – the famous delay of 350 msec between RP and W – indicated that we start to move before we consciously decide to move. Taken at face value, this suggests that the conscious will cannot cause action because it simply comes too late in the sequence of events. A variety of explanations have been offered to account for the implications, the most famous perhaps being Libet's own. Since the conscious will does occur prior to the actual action, Libet suggested that consciousness has the power to veto action.

The basis of Wegner's theory of apparent mental causation is that free will is not a mental force but the feeling of causing action. In thinking of free will in this manner we can see that will and action are two different processes. Will can occur without action and action can occur without will, so that the experience of volitional control of motion depends on a proper intention–action synchrony. His inquiries are more concerned with the reasons why we experience the illusion of free will. That free will is an illusion is substantiated by the psychopathology of disorders that are characterized by a breakdown of the normal sense of agency, such as schizophrenia. This research has identified a mapping system that predicts the sensory consequences of behavior. By mapping current motor instructions onto cortical regions processing sensations we can anticipate what we are about to experience. The sense of causing an action is created when these predictions are validated by actual sensory feedback. These recent models of motor prediction have revealed important insights into the abnormal experience of ownership of motion that inflicts some schizophrenics. This loss must be a particularly disheartening alteration of the content of consciousness, as it strikes at the heart of our sense of identity.

Suggested reading

Frith, C. D. (1992). *The Cognitive Neuropsychology of Schizophrenia*. Hove: Lawrence Erlbaum.

Libet, B. Freeman, A., & Sutherland, K. (1999). *The Volitional Brain: Towards a Neuroscience of Free Will*. Thorverton: Devon, Imprint Academic.

Wegner, D. M. (2002). *The Illusion of Conscious Will*. Cambridge, MA: MIT Press.

PART IV

Altered states of consciousness

12 Sleep and dreams

Conceptualizing ASC

Problems with definitions

If consciousness is notoriously hard to define, try altered states of consciousness (ASC)! Several attempts have been made to crystallize the concept into a workable definition, but to say that they have not been widely adopted is an understatement. As a result we have a poor understanding of what, exactly, is being studied and a broad disagreement about the type of phenomena that should be classified as ASC. From an empirical standpoint, the matter goes from bad to worse owing to the ephemeral nature of ASC. Altered mind states are difficult to induce reliably and any effect an induction procedure might have on consciousness is even more difficult to observe, let alone quantify. In short, the independent variable cannot be readily manipulated and the outcome measures rely on introspective verbal report, a set of circumstances that has all but halted serious research on the subject.

What's more, ASC is a subject still seen by most neuroscientists as career suicide. There are, of course, exceptions, such as sleep research or experimental hypnosis, but by and large ASC are gravely underfunded by grant agencies and few psychologists or neuroscientists can afford to make them their primary area of expertise. This is partly due to the insidious cliché attached to ASC. Many view them with suspicion – some sort of abstruse psychopathology at the lunatic fringe frequented mostly by potheads and meditating yogis. This bias is further exacerbated by the excessive use of esoteric language used to describe them, which does little to disabuse others of the aura of lawlessness and unscientific hogwash that sadly surrounds ASC. Yet, studying ASC is one of the best ways to study consciousness itself. As with consciousness as a whole, there has been a resurgence of sound research on ASC in recent years. This is fueled also by data showing bona fide medicinal benefits for some altered states, for instance, hypnosis, meditation, or cannabis use. The upshot of this progress, apart from restoring a measure of scientific legitimacy to the topic, is a wealth of exciting new data that informs our understanding of the phenomenology and brain mechanisms of ASC. The prospect of understanding altered states in terms of neural correlates holds the promise that we might clarify at a deeper level questions regarding the nature of ASC, such as, for instance, how ASC are related to each other and how each is related to default consciousness.

The aspiration of mapping **states of consciousness** (SoC) on a continuum and/or hierarchy is not novel but is perhaps more tractable with input from cognitive neuroscience. Two models, one by Charles Tart (1975), and a more recent, neurobiologically informed attempt by Allan Hobson (2001), arrange conscious states by positioning them in a multidimensional space (Figure 12.1). Tart (1972), who also coined the term and popularized the concept of ASC while professor of psychology at the University of California at Davis, envisioned SoC as discrete entities. According to him, the multidimensional space is not uniform. In the same way energy states in a quantum system are discrete, some positions in this space are stable and can be occupied, while others are unstable and cannot be occupied. The twilight between sleep and waking is an example of an unstable position in which we cannot function for long. It quickly gives way to the stable state of either sleep or waking. This led Tart to propose the creation of what he called **state-specific sciences**. The idea is that each state of consciousness has its own logic and set of physical laws, which do not apply to a person in a different state. It follows that scientific evidence and theory are only relevant to the state in which they are produced and can only be understood by someone residing in that same state. This places consciousness, as it happens, in the center of science. If you find it challenging to wrap your mind around the idea of state-specific sciences and its implications, consider that the reason for your doubts may have to do with you not being in the right SoC! Tart's position also argues against the commonsense notion that there is one normal state and all other states are altered states. He sees no qualitiative difference among SoC, echoing the thinking of William James (1890), who wrote 100 years earlier: "our normal waking consciousness is but one special type of consciousness."

The second positive effect arising from the new data is the old hope that ASC could be defined in the future through objective measures, perhaps better neuroimaging tools or other clever eavesdropping devices not yet invented, rather than subjectively through introspection. In the interim, ASC must be defined subjectively. Two such definitions are most commonly cited. The first comes from

Figure 12.1

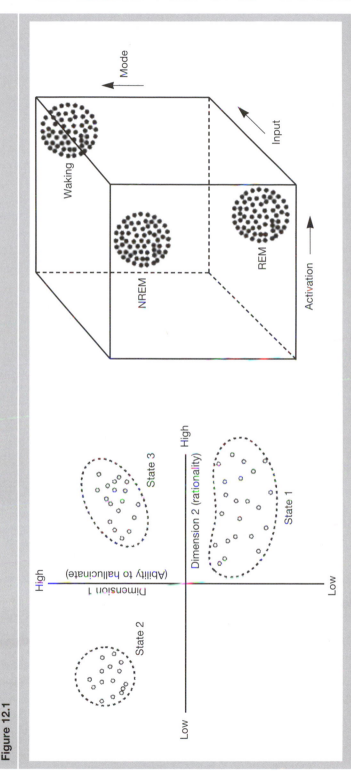

Two attempts to map SoC. Tart's (1975) phenomenal space, shown on the left, consists of two dimensions, irrationality and ability to hallucination. He reasoned that just three position s in this space result in a stable conscious state: ordinary consciousness, dreaming, and lucid dreaming. Hobson's (2001) AIM model, shown on the right, maps SoC in what he calls a brain–mind space along three parameters; **activation**, an energy dimension that depends on the activity of the reticulo-thalamo-cortical system; **input**–output gating, an information source dimension that estimates the extent to which external and internal information is being processed; and **mode**, a chemical modulation dimension that estimates the mix of aminergic (norepinephrine and serotonin) and cholinergic (acetylcholine) influences, which runs from low aminergic to high aminergic.

Tart, who defined them as "a qualitative alteration in the overall pattern of mental functioning, such that the experiencer feels his consciousness is radically different from the way it functions ordinarily" (Tart, 1972, p. 1203). A similar definition is provided by William Farthing (1992, p. 205), who identifies them as: "a temporary change in the overall pattern of subjective experience, such that the individual believes that his or her mental functioning is distinctly different from certain general norms for his or her normal waking state of consciousness."

Although these definitions appear to capture the essence of ASC, several problems preclude their use in science. The exclusive reliance on subjectivity means that only we can determine for ourselves whether or not we have reached an ASC. This renders them unverifiable. Consider two individuals who have the exact same level of alcohol intoxication (matched for tolerance, weight, etc.), but one is claiming an ASC while the other is not? What about antidepressant medication? Do they induce an ASC? It is easy to see how unsatisfactory this state of affairs is. A related problem is that we must decide whether or not our experience is altered by comparing it to normal consciousness. But what is normal? Default consciousness itself is highly variable and the baseline, if one exists, differs not only among people but also with each individual. Two examples that never fail to generate a heated debate among students underscore this predicament. Do you consider the feeling of being madly in love an ASC? Read Tart's and Farthing's definitions again and decide for yourself. Didn't everything seem different when it happened to you? And what would you make of PMS? Apart from bodily changes, many women describe their symptoms in terms of alteration to mental functioning. Does that count as an ASC?

One way to sidestep this troublesome mess is, for the time being, to limit ourselves to putative ASC. We take this route and focus in the following chapters on sleep and dreams, drug-induced states, meditation, hypnosis, daydreaming, and the runner's high. Both definitions also emphasize that ASC are temporary phenomena. More permanent alterations to consciousness, such as those that occur in neurological and psychiatric disorders, are typically not considered ASC, although we can safely assume that they alter consciousness.

We make here a concerted effort to inject a heavy dose of neuroscience into the topic, while at the same time keeping in mind the psychological dimensions of ASC, that is, what it feels like to be in a particular SoC. Explanations of the neural basis of ASC have focused almost exclusively on neurochemical mechanisms, undoubtedly due to the association of ASC to psychoactive drugs. However, we must take a broader neuroscientific approach and thus organize each ASC around a recently proposed framework called the transient hypofrontality hypothesis.

The transient hypofrontality hypothesis

The **transient hypofrontality hypothesis** (THH) is explicity based on recent advances in the neural basis of mental processes. It views consciousness as composed of various attributes, such as self-reflection, attention, memory, perception, and arousal, which are ordered in a functional hierarchy with the frontal lobe necessary for the top attributes. Although this implies a holistic view in which the entire brain contributes to consciousness, it is evident that not all neural structures contribute equally to consciousness. This layering concept localizes the most sophisticated levels of consciousness in the zenithal higher-order structure: the prefrontal cortex. From such consideration, the THH of altered states of consciousness can be formulated (Dietrich, 2003, 2004a). It attempts to unify all altered states into a single theoretical framework and has informed our understanding of the changes in the brain that might occur in ASC. It will thus serve as the guiding model for the following two chapters.

Because the prefrontal cortex is the neural substrate of the topmost layer, any alteration to consciousness should, first and foremost, affect this structure followed by a progressive shutdown of brain regions that compute more basic mental processes. In other words, the top layers of consciousness are most vulnerable when brain activity changes. In light of this "onion-peeling" principle, mental processes such as working memory, sustained and directed attention, and temporal integration are compromised first as consciousness is altered. Anecdotal evidence supports this. All ASC share phenomenological characteristics whose proper functions are regulated by the prefrontal cortex, such as time distortions, disinhibition from social norms, or a change in focused attention. This suggests that the neural mechanism common to all ASC is the transient downregulation of modules in the prefrontal cortex. Importantly, most cases of mental illness and brain damage also produce alterations to mental status but these conditions are different from ASC because they are not characterized by transient shifts in consciousness.

The neutralization of specific contributions to consciousness is known as **phenomenological subtraction** (Hobson, 2001). As an ASC deepens, induced by the progressive disengagement of prefrontal modules, more of those subtractions occur and the phenomenological experience becomes one of ever greater departure from normal consciousness. In altered states that are marked by severe prefrontal hypofunction, such as dreaming or various drug states, this modification results in an extraordinarily bizarre phenomenology. In altered states that are marked by less prefrontal deactivation, such as long-distance running, the change to experience is milder. In any event, the individual simply functions on the highest layer of phenomenological consciousness that remains fully functional.

Take, for instance, **the interpreter** module proposed by Michael Gazzaniga (see Chapter 6) to account for the habit of the left hemisphere to form beliefs about why events occur. For it to operate, the brain must run on all cylinders, as this module requires the availability of all information to infer something as complex as a cause-effect relationship. When a brain is thrown off-keel by, say, the infusion of a few pints from the local brewery, the interpreter appears to be one of the first phenomenological subtractions to take place. Virtually all ASC are interpreter-free mind states; that is, they are characterized by the lack of methodical searches for explanations, reasons, or meaning. Perhaps this is what makes ASC so calm and peaceful.

When seen in this way, a corollary of the THH becomes apparent that argues against a widely held belief about ASC. The concept of hierarchically structured mental functions entails that full-fledged consciousness is the result of a fully operational brain. This means that default consciousness is the highest possible manifestation of consciousness, and all ASC are, by virtue of representing an alteration to a fully functional brain, a reduction in consciousness. This is also true for ASC that are often presumptuously seen as higher forms of consciousness, such as transcendental meditation or the experiences reported after taking "mind-expanding" drugs (whatever that means). This view is in contrast to other theorists, for instance, James (1890) or Tart (1972), who maintained that normal consciousness is not qualitatively different from any other. It is difficult to imagine what higher consciousness might look like in terms of brain activity or phenomenology, but shouldn't it entail an enhancement of mental abilities ascribed to the prefrontal cortex rather than their subtraction?

If all altered states share this common neural mechanism, why, then, does each feel unique? To anyone who frequents them, the experience of, say, hypnosis is unmistakably distinct from that of dreaming or meditation. Similarly, each drug causes unique phenomenological changes that can be readily and reliably distinguished by drug users – or rats, for that matter – from those caused by a different drug (Siegel, 1985). How can we reconcile this with the proposal that prefrontal downregulation is the underlying cause for all altered states? A clue may be found in the induction procedure. There are several ways by which a change in mental status is achieved. We can use a variety of behavioral methods, for instance, we can take advantage of our ability to control executive attention, a method we use to enter the states of daydreaming, hypnosis, or meditation. Alternatively, we can use our ability to engage in prolonged, rhythmic motion, such as running or dancing, to get into a trance state. One altered state, dreaming, we enter entirely involuntarily through a circadian rhythm controlled by the brainstem. And then there is the direct manipulation of neurotransmitter systems by taking psychoactive substances. It is almost certainly the case that these different techniques alter brain function in different ways, but the overall effect should, in principle, be the same. That is, according to the THH, mental functions at the level of the prefrontal cortex that comprise the top layers of consciousness are altered first followed by a progressive downregulation of mental functions lower down the hierarchy. What, then, could account for the distinct phenomenology of each state is that each induction method targets different sets of prefrontal modules, so removing quite specific computation from the conscious experience. To give one example, the sense of self is reported to be lost to a higher degree in meditation than in hypnosis; whereas the opposite is often reported for cognitive flexibility and willed action, which are absent to a higher degree in hypnosis. According to the THH, the kind of prefrontal circuits downregulated first or most is what would account for the subjective uniqueness of each altered state. Much of this theorizing is, admittedly, speculation at this stage but it fits well with what little evidence there is.

Sleep and dreams

The sleep cycle

Sleep is considered the most profound natural alteration of consciousness. For around eight hours every day we radically decrease awareness of our surroundings and conjure up a world that is unlike anything we imagine during wakefulness. In order to get a solid grasp of this – come to think of it – rather curious behavior, we start this section by describing the sleep cycle. The main focus, however, will be on the activation-synthesis model proposed by Allan Hobson and his colleagues, which is rightfully considered the reigning theory of how the brain generates the nightly slideshow of the bizarre. We also examine the equally curious phenomenon known as lucid dreaming and several peculiar disorders of sleep that bear significantly on the problem of consciousness.

Despite the existence of snazzy neuroimaging tools capturing the living mind in 256 million colors, most of what we know about the sleeping brain comes from EEG. Imagine yourself a subject in sleep lab. You arrive in the evening and once you are wired up to an EEG machine and a host of other devices, the experiment can begin or, as William Dement (1978), one of the Magellans of early sleep research, put it in the title of his book: "Some must watch while some must sleep."

At the start, your EEG record picks up a pattern of brain waves called beta activity, which is an irregular pattern that appears during alertness and active thinking. Once you close your eyes, beta activity gives way to alpha activity, which is a fairly regular pattern that occurs when a person is relaxed and minimally aroused. From here you gradually descend into sleep stage 1, which is actually a transition stage between sleeping and waking, lasting approximately 10 minutes. The onset of stage 2 is easily seen in the EEG with irregular and sudden waveforms called sleep spindles and k-complexes. They are believed to further reduce the brain's sensitivity to sensory input and function to keep a person asleep in the early stages (Bowersox et al., 1985). At this point you are sound asleep but if awakened during stage 2, you would likely report not having slept yet.

After 25 minutes of sleep, the EEG starts showing **delta activity**, which is a quite regular, low-amplitude wave. This delta rhythm is the neurosignature of stages 3 and 4, which are called deep or **slow-wave sleep**. It emanates from a very low metabolic rate in the cortex, which indicates that not much cortical processing is taking place in these sleep stages. Given this low cortical activity, it is not surprising that it is very difficult to wake somebody up in stage 4. Most people feel groggy when they get jerked from stage 4 back into default consciousness. The reentry shock can be so harsh that a certain brain fog is present for a while. Stage 4 is also the longest stage, lasting about 45 minutes, which makes it the stage most likely to wake up in. People who awaken in stage 4 also do not report dreams. It would be a bit baffling if they did, given the profound level of cortical inhibition. Yet, some of our most terrifying nightmares occur in stage 4, but they tend to be

Figure 12.2

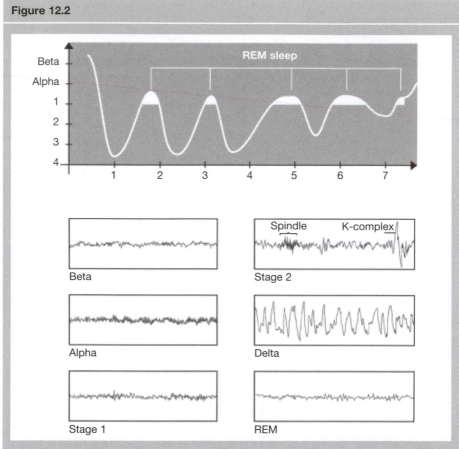

During an idealized eight-hour night of sleep, we cycle through the sleep stages roughly four to five times. Sleep never skips a stage. We descend from stage 1 to 4 into ever deeper sleep and ascend back up to stage 2 again before entering REM. This 90-minute cycle shortens somewhat each time, with later cycles containing longer periods of REM and stage 2 sleep.

of the non-narrative kind and typically involve isolated sensations like falling, suffocating, or being crushed (Fisher et al., 1970).

Approximately 90 minutes into it, the sleep cycle reverses and you ascend, in a matter of minutes, back up through stages 3 then 2. But instead of entering stage 1 again, you enter **REM**, or rapid eye-movement sleep. Here the EEG again starts showing a desynchronized and irregular pattern that resembles beta activity. Eugene Aserinsky discovered this stage in the 1950s rather serendipitously as a graduate student at the University of Chicago (Aserinsky & Kleitman, 1953). While trying to repair his EEG equipment, he tested it on his 8-year-old son, who promptly fell asleep. In contrast to this sudden flurry of brain activity, your muscles become paralyzed during REM. Our nightly habits of twisting, sleepwalking, and snoring do not occur in REM, because such acts require muscular activation. The most interesting aspect of REM, however, is that 90 percent of all people who wake up in it report narrative dreams (Empson, 2001). Although there is some narrative dreaming in non-REM (NREM) and one should be careful equating the mental state of dreaming with the physical state of REM (Empson, 2001; Solms, 2000), imaging data suggest that REM sleep is a state phenomenologically different from NREM sleep (Hobson et al., 2000). Twenty minutes of REM completes the sleep cycle.

This is as good a place as any to dispel a few widely held but wholly mistaken notions about sleep. One such myth is the claim that people never dream or go without dreaming for long periods of time. Like many things in life, it is all a matter of timing. We all dream, four to five times a night, in fact, but we only recall our dreams if we wake up during REM. Allan Hobson (1988) estimated that we lose 95 percent of our dreams, making this now-you-see-it now-you-don't experience a common occurrence.

Several other strange phenomena of sleep become instantly demystified if we stop seeing sleep as a little coma but rather for what it is, an ASC that compromises our ability to interact with our environment. While asleep we still process some information. For instance, we might weave real-life events into our dream, such as the buzzing of an alarm clock; a mother will wake up to the faint crying of her baby while snoozing through the deafening noise of a freight train going by; or just think of the last time an important event was scheduled for the next morning and you woke up *before* your alarm clock. We must also disabuse anyone of the notion that **sleepwalking** is the acting-out of dreams. This is not possible because dreams occur during the paralyzed stage of REM. Indeed, this is likely the purpose of the paralysis. In any case, sleepwalking occurs mostly in stage 4. If you wake up a sleepwalker, you will not be treated to a dream story filled with phantasmagoric images but instead will find a person who is confused with no cue as to where she is or how she got there. This should not be surprising, considering how little the cortex turns over in stage 4. Waking up sleepwalkers is also not dangerous as many people believe – it is just difficult. The sleep researcher Jacob Empson (2001) reported the case of an entire family of sleepwalkers. On one occasion, all members of the family woke up in the morning sitting around the kitchen table, each having sleepwalked there on their own! From this and other tales, one might be tempted to conclude that sleepwalking is a sophisticated behavior, but it is not. Sleepwalkers regularly bump into furniture. They can, however, navigate well in a familiar place such as their own house. Should we consider this as evidence for the presence of consciousness?

Sleeptalking is not any different. When people talk in their sleep they also do not report the content of a dream. This would require muscle activity, which cannot occur in REM. Yet, some sleeptalkers can respond to some limited input (as much as their inhibited cortex permits). This should also lie to rest another myth, namely that we can learn, say, Spanish, using audiotapes. Cortical activity during slow-wave sleep is too diminished for that.

Box 12.1   Oddities of sleep

Sleep and dreams are filled with fascinating oddities. For instance, what do you make of the sleep disorder called pseudoinsomnia? People afflicted with this condition sleep normally but dream that they lie in bed trying to fall asleep. They wake up after as much as seven hours of solid sleep reporting not having slept much. Unfortunately, they also feel as beaten as if they actually did endure a sleepless night. Ouch! The opposite also exists and is called false awakening. Here a person dreams that she woke up and goes through the motion of leaving the house. When the person really awakens she does it all over again but with a strange feeling of déjà-vu.

Narcolepsy is a sleep disorder in which people fall asleep at inappropriate times. They are suddenly overcome by an overwhelming urge to sleep. Many narcoleptics sense the sleep attack coming and have a brief moment to find a slightly better spot to crash, if you'll forgive the phrase. People suffering from cataplexy, a rather spectacular form of narcolepsy, rarely have the luxury of a fair warning. They go from consciousness straight into REM, including the accompanying atonia. Oftentimes they buckle and collapse so rapidly that it poses a real risk of injury to them and others. To the cataleptic, the experience can be terribly frightening because, strictly speaking, they do not enter REM sleep but rather experience the paralysis part of REM. They suffer the atonia while staying fully conscious and awake.

An equally terrifying form of narcolepsy is called sleep paralysis. This phenomenon isn't even rare and many people have endured an episode of it. It occurs either right before sleep or shortly after awakening. It also consists of full paralysis but with a different twist. Here, in the twilight of sleep the paralysis is accompanied with hypnagogic hallucinations, which are a little difficult to describe if you never had them. In principle, the person is awake and aware of it too, but experiences a display of imaginary creatures and voices that are the results of either leftovers or the premature cranking of the brainstem's dream-state generator. This can last for a few minutes and is truly horrifying if the images are ugly monsters entering your room through the open window while you are aware that you are awake and cannot move. Hypnagogic hallucinations can feel so real that most people are jolted back to wakefulness. People can also be snapped out of it by throwing a pillow at them.

There is also a most peculiar sleep dysfunction that is probably best considered as the opposite of cataplexy. It is known by the splendidly descriptive name REM sleep behavior disorder. Here the peribrachial area fails to activate the aspect of REM sleep that controls the muscle paralysis. This enables the sleeper to move during REM and freely act out his dreams. You can check that yourself if you ever see one. Watch him for a while, wake him up and compare his dream story to his immediately preceding behavior. This, however, is a very rare disorder. Chances are you are dealing with a sleepwalker instead, which you can tell by the way he is bumping into furniture. And lastly, though no such case exists, imagine the possibility of a lucid dreamer suffering from REM sleep behavior disorder.

Restoration or adaptation

You must admit that sleep is an odd behavior. If you ask anyone why we do it you will probably get an answer that is simple, neat, and in all likelihood wrong. Any behavior that consumes roughly a third of our lifetime had better be having some kind of useful purpose. To add to the oddness, sleep is also a very insistent drive, perhaps the most insistent drive we have. It is possible to kill yourself by refusing to eat, but no matter how hard you try you cannot sleep-deprive yourself to death. It works the other way, too. In a simple experiment, the sleep researcher Wilse Webb (1975) brought students into his lab and offered them $10 for every minute they went to sleep faster – the easiest $10 you would ever make. No one cashed in.

Theories on why we sleep fall into two types: (1) commonsensical but probably wrong and (2) evolutionarily sound but a bit anticlimatic. First, let's tackle the commonsense theory. In its simplest terms, it assumes that we sleep in order to rest. It is so intuitive an idea that it seems almost pointless to question it. But the evidence to support it is thin. The question one has to ask is this: What, exactly, needs rest? Consider first the brain. We know that sleep is an active process and brain metabolism does not decrease during sleep (Carlson, 2004). Neurons just do not get tired of, say, firing action potentials or releasing their neurotransmitters. This leaves us with the second option, the body; perhaps it needs restoration. To see that it does not, imagine yourself on a foul-weather Sunday during which you do nothing but slouch on the couch alternating between watching TV and talking to friends and family. Yet your sleep that night will be entirely normal. What did you do all day that needs rest? Not convinced? Then consider quadriplegics. Shouldn't they sleep less if the theory holds any validity? But they do not. They snooze as squarely as anybody else (Adey et al., 1968).

Unlike the restoration theory, the second theory for why we sleep has a mountain of evidence behind it. It proposes that sleep is a useful adaptation (Webb, 1975). Nearly all mammals sleep; in fact, all vertebrates sleep, although only mammals exhibit REM. Sleep is simply a useful behavior when it is cold and dark and you can see neither predator nor prey. The best thing to do is to save some energy, stay out of harm's way, find a cozy spot, and alter consciousness to fend off boredom. As might be expected, animals near the top of the food chain are better sleepers than their prey. While bears and the big cats of Africa are big snoozers, zebras and gazelles cannot afford to doze off too much (Siegel, 1995). Dolphins and some birds have found a neat solution to this. They sleep one hemisphere at a time: as one side catches some zees, the other watches the neighborhood (Mukhametov, 1984). Although researchers favor the adaptation theory, note that this explanation does little to clarify why, every 90 minutes during REM, we slip into a kaleidoscope of ghostly images and sounds.

If sleep is an odd behavior, then dreaming is surely an odd mental process. What could possibly be the evolutionary significance of our nocturnal theater of the absurd? The theory that enjoys the most support on this problem centers on the notion that REM sleep serves to consolidate memory (Siegel, 2001). Dreams mostly replay the events of the day and this mental cartwheeling, according to the theory, might help put them into some sort of perspective. Let's look very briefly at the evidentiary basis in favor of the **memory consolidation theory**.

Researchers use an ingenious albeit slightly wicked little trick to sleep-deprive animals of REM. It is known by the cheerfully uplifting name of flowerpot procedure. A rat is placed on a platform surrounded by shallow water. The platform is barely large enough for the animal to stand on and it has no choice but to go to sleep in an upright position. As the rat cycles through the sleep stages it eventually enters REM, becomes paralyzed and drops into the water. As it climbs back onto the platform and falls asleep again the pattern repeats itself for the duration of the night. A rat will get a decent amount of sleep this way but is effectively prevented from entering REM. If REM sleep consolidates memory, the flowerpot method should result in memory deficits. This has indeed been found. Rats trained to navigate a maze and put through the flowerpot procedure show slower learning than rats allowed to enter REM (Rideout, 1979; Smith, 1996).

Whatever the functions of REM sleep, there are people who live happily without it. Consider the case of one man who sustained damage to the brainstem, thalamus, and left frontal lobe. He sleeps an average of 4.5 hours a night but spends only a total of 6 minutes of REM per week! On some nights he might not enter REM at all (Solms, 2000). REM is obviously not necessary for survival. There is surely a joke in the fact that he is a lawyer, but we leave this one to you.

My mother is riding a kangaroo

In 1977, three-quarters of a century after Freud published *The Interpretation of Dreams*, Allan Hobson and Robert McCarley, two Harvard neuroscientists, published a paper in the *American Journal of Psychiatry* that was to revolutionize our conception of the dream state (Hobson & McCarley, 1977). The view at the time – held by, well, nearly everyone – was that dreams are not the sort of stuff that lend themselves easily to scientific inquiry. To many, dreams represented the very embodiment of a mystical world that might lie forever beyond the rational and orderly realm of science. Mindful of the sacred cow they were about to slay, Hobson and McCarley trod lightly but in the process provided the first truly scientific account of our nightly madness. Known as the **activation-synthesis model**, it is perhaps one of the most outstanding examples of a complex mental process that would almost certainly still baffle psychologists if it had not been brilliantly elucidated by neuroscience. The model is, regrettably so, also a good example of how little the fundamental knowledge of neuroscience has reached a wider audience. It is not uncommon to find philosophers, psychologists, or neuroscientists, to say nothing of laymen, wholly unaware that something as ostensibly murky as dreams is grounded in solid science.

Sleep is a profound alteration of consciousness. Not surprisingly, it is instigated by neural activity in the brainstem, an area near the bottom of the hierarchy of consciousness (Hobson et al., 2000). The **reticular formation**, a structure running the length of the brainstem, is the brain's arousal system. Its extensive system of ascending fibers produces the arousal necessary for attention and consciousness. Activity in the reticular formation is also the mechanism that awakens you from sleep and brings you back to full consciousness. Thus, damage here typically sends a person into coma because this is the on/off switch, so to speak, for all higher brain centers.

Part of this activating system is the **peribrachial area**, a structure in the dorsal pons that functions as the executive mechanism of REM sleep. It contains neurons dubbed **REM-ON cells** because they exhibit such high firing rates during REM. Projections from the peribrachial area turn on and coordinate all components of REM. Specifically, the peribrachial area projects to the magnocellular nucleus in the medulla, which inhibits the alpha motor neurons in the spinal cord leading to the paralysis associated with REM. It also projects to the superior colliculus, which mediates the rapid eye movements that occur in REM. Of most importance to a psychological account of dreaming, however, are two other pathways. The first entails brief, phasic bursts that travel from the pons to the LGN and to the visual cortex. This **PGO wave** (pons-geniculate-occipital) precedes the onset of rapid eye movements and explains why dreams almost always contain visual imagery. The second pathway sends projections to the basal forebrain that are responsible for the cortical arousal during REM (see Figure 12.3).

Armed with this knowledge, we can now examine the activation-synthesis model. According to Hobson and McCarley, the brainstem contains a "**dream-state generator**" that spontaneously activates subcortical and cortical structures. During waking, this activation is provided by sensory input but during REM the thalamus blocks such external stimulation and the activation becomes self-generated. The areas in which this brainstem-initiated neural activation is most pronounced are the visual and motor cortices, basal ganglia, and various limbic system structures, particularly the amygdala and the hippocampus (Braun et al., 1997; Maquet et al., 1999; Nofzinger et al., 1997). If you are committed to a materialistic account of the mind, the phenomenal consequences are clear. The bustle of these neurons activates memories that make up the content of the dream. Indeed, the pattern of activation during REM corresponds closely with dream content and matches the neural activity of the same behaviors during waking (Hobson et al., 2000).

For instance, it is possible to predict dream motion by looking at the fMRI scan of the motor cortex of a person in REM. If the dream includes say, walking, the neurons that control real-life leg and torso motion are activated. Likewise, people who talk in their dream show activation in Broca's area, the region controlling speech production. This also sheds light on the common dream theme of the inability to move, as, for instance, the powerlessness to run away from a threat or trying to scream but producing no sound. Recall that we still respond to some sensory information and because we are actually paralyzed in REM this phenomenon is probably the odd bit of reality creeping in. According to Hall and van de Castle (1966), who completed the monumental task of collecting and analyzing over 10,000 dreams, most dreams contain emotions. Not all emotions are equally represented, however. Fear or anxiety occurs in 64 percent of dreams whereas pleasurable feelings occur in only 18 percent. The visual cortex is also highly active due to the direct stimulation of PGO waves. Eye movements during REM also tend to match those in the dreams narrative (Roffwarg et al., 1966). For instance, people watching a tennis match in their dreams show regular and strong saccades to the left and right on the EOG record. This, then, raises the question of why dreaming is so bizarre and nothing like waking mentation.

Figure 12.3

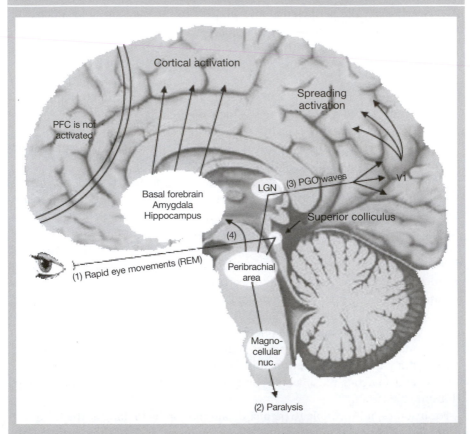

The activation-synthesis model views dreams as the result of a two-step process. Dreaming is initiated when the peribrachial area, the executive area of REM sleep, turns on several brain areas that then provide the raw imagery of dreams. First, a pathway to the superior colliculus is responsible for the defining rapid eye movements of REM (1), and projections to the nucleus magnocellularis in the medulla produce the muscular paralysis (2). The cortical activation that is the source of the content of dreams is induced via two other routes. One initiates the PGO waves which travel to the LGN and the visual cortex (3). The other is a projection to the basal forebrain which activates other cortical regions and several subcortical structures (4). This activation has two characteristic features; it is capricious and, importantly, *excludes* the prefrontal cortex. The psychological consequence is the presence of a set of random, unrelated images coupled with the absence of the ability to engage higher cognitive functions, not an auspicious start for step 2: the synthesis. We must now weave together nonsensical fragments into some kind of narrative while our higher brain centers are mercifully disengaged. That the result is mostly nonsense should not be too surprising. Although Hobson (2001) thinks that the absurd theater of dreams is the phenomenological byproduct of physiological processes in the brainstem, he does not think that dreams are meaningless.

The answer is found in the fact that the dream-state generator fails to activate one critical region: the prefrontal cortex. PET studies show inactivity over vast areas of DLPFC (Braun et al., 1997; Maquet et al., 1999). This pattern is so striking that "REM sleep may constitute a state of generalized brain activity with the specific exclusion of the executive system" (Braun et al., 1997, p. 1190). This is consistent with the phenomenology. Dreams are mostly void of prefrontal-dependent cognition. Self-reflection is absent (Rechtschaffen, 1978), time is distorted with past, present, and future freely exchanged (Hobson, 1988), and volitional control is diminished (Hartman, 1966). The absence of the sense of willing one's own action is likely due to a weak mapping system during REM (see Chapter 11). There is next to no abstract, "bigger picture" thinking, active decision making, or consistent logic. The oneironaut (explorer of dream space) also possesses a distorted self-construct and has no insight that the experience is in virtual reality. Navigating passages of dreamland is ontologically as compelling as the real world. Focused attention and the capacity for semantic and episodic retrieval of specific memories, which heavily rely on DLPFC areas (Cabeza & Nyberg, 2000), are also greatly compromised. Moreover, it has been argued that the extent to which a dream is bizarre is related to the extent of the prefrontal hypofunction (Hobson et al., 2000). It is evident that the principal difference between dream mentation and waking is the pattern of deactivation across the DLPFC.

This brings us to the synthesis component of the model. The spontaneously activated brain regions generate dream images that we now must weave together into some kind of narrative. The trouble is, however, that unlike in waking consciousness when we enjoy the full benefit of our higher cognitive functions, we must do so with a prefrontal cortex that does not operate at full capacity. And, to compound the trouble, the synthesis must proceed with images that are generated at random. Put another way, we must confabulate a tale out of the wholly unrelated googlyguck controlled by an involuntary circadian rhythm, while, in effect, in a state of frontal lobotomy. Yet, more often than not, a coherent story line emerges, presumably due to the associative nature of subsequent, spreading activation. The upshot of buzzing through the nth dimension of absurdity is that we make unregulated and unlimited ideational combinations that are not prefiltered by societal values and conventional wisdom. In Hobson's (1988) own words: "Dreaming may be our most creative conscious state, one in which the chaotic, spontaneous recombination of cognitive elements produces novel configurations of information: new ideas."

To Hobson dreams are epiphenomena, byproducts of random neural firing, which occur as the mind makes frantic attempts to come to grips with incidental neural activity without the help of the integrative capacities of the prefrontal cortex. Although this view renders dreams nothing more than a glitzy slideshow, Hobson stops short of calling dreams meaningless. The way the mirage of visions is fitted into a story, that is, the way we synthesize the random bits and pieces into some sort of thread holds out the possibility of, perhaps, a personal significance for dreams. This prospect notwithstanding, the take-home message of the model is that the neuroscience of REM sleep lends little support to the usefulness of the popular pastime of dream interpretation. One should perhaps be careful of linearizing phantasmagoric images for the purpose of finding some sort of hidden meaning. One might be better off taking dreams at face value.

For some fun and games, try to synthesize this odd group of mental fragments into a dream: (a) you were talking to your mother on the phone a week ago; (b) the subject was money and you asked her for some; (c) you once watched, many years ago, the movie *Crocodile Dundee*, (d) before going to bed you couldn't find the pants you wanted to wear the next day; and (e) assume that the amygdala is activated. Here is one possible dream, which is as good as any:

> I was in my room searching for something – what exactly I cannot remember. I don't know what it was, but all of a sudden, I looked up and there was my mother, riding a kangaroo. I jumped through the window and started chasing her. I was totally naked, but I wanted to catch her under all circumstances. The kangaroo looked back at me and kept laughing. I tried shouting but my mother did not hear or see me. I was afraid I would never see her again. I felt ashamed and lonely.

Now, Freud would reach some strange conclusions here. In his theory of dreams, there is an explicit content, the actual story, which is only the manifestation of the latent content, the deeper and real meaning of the dream. Every image is a symbol of something else – something sexual, specifically – and the task of psychoanalysis is to discover this hidden meaning. To Freud randomness did not exist and it is perhaps fair to say that the activation-synthesis model could not have broken more with the tenets of psychoanalytic theory.

Lucid dreaming

For the study of consciousness, lucid dreaming is an imperative alteration of the dream state. We are usually passive pawns in our own twisted film noir. There is no conscious control over the unfolding of the plot, nor is there any insight that the experience is entirely fictitious. In a lucid dream, however, a person becomes aware that the transpiring events are part of a dream, that is, the dreamer knows that she is, in fact, dreaming (LaBerge, 1985). The degree of lucidity can vary greatly and it is not necessarily accompanied by **dream control**, the intentional directing of the dream. In other words, a dreamer can be lucid during a dream but not have the power to change the course of the dream. Similarly, dream control can occur without lucidity. Here the dreamer may be able to script their own dream but not be aware that they are in the dream (LaBerge, 1985).

Once a dreamer becomes fully lucid she can whiz about in dreamland at will, being secure in the knowledge that she lies in bed at home and all these fantastic images are only in her mind. This does not diminish the reality or intensity of the experience! On the contrary, the dream continues to feel ontologically compelling but now the lucid dreamer can enjoy any experience without the infuriating little hassles of real life – like the laws of physics or the morals of society. There is a limit to this fun and freedom, however. Most lucid dreamers find it impossible to direct their dream story completely at will or change it to a different one in midstream by, say, creating an imaginary door. They still get their supply of dream images from the brainstem – randomly generated, of course.

According to Steven LaBerge, lucidity master and cartographer of oneirospace, lucidity is triggered when the dreamer runs into a **dreamsign**, an event or image, such as a tango-dancing phantasm or a purple cat, that is impossible in the real world. Lucidity can occur without dreamsigns, too. However, you can never be sure in that case whether you are actually awake or in a lucid dream, because both states of consciousness feel entirely real. When unsure of your ontological status, you should perform what is known as a **reality test**. To do this, you must find a watch or a book. This can be tricky in either world but once you have managed it, look at the watch or a page of text, turn briefly away, and then look at it again. If the time or the text changes dramatically, you are dreaming. This reality test probably works because images in the real world are based on real sensory inputs, which do not dramatically change, but in the dream world images are generated from scratch without sensory input, and it is rather unlikely that the brain confabulates the exact same image twice. You can do this test right now: Read this sentence, look away and then come back to it. If the text does not change, you are awake reading this textbook. Congratulations! Why does this matter? Well, surely you want to be certain in which dimension you are before leaping out the window and start flying, don't you?

Lucid dreaming is not some fancy gobbledygook for sleep aficionados but a genuine state of consciousness. Steven LaBerge (1985) and Keith Hearne (1990), working independently, demonstrated this to the skeptical scientific establishment. The problem was that a lucid dreamer is in REM sleep and thus paralyzed, which makes it difficult for her to provide a "live feed" from dreamscape. They found a way around the problem by using eye movements. They instructed their subjects to look, in their dreams, first to the left, then to the right, and then left again as soon as they gained lucidity. The EEG needle would pick up the resulting saccades as large spikes to the left, right, and then left again. Because this signal could be produced at will, lucid dreaming became a bona fide phenomenon of consciousness.

Few people lucid-dream naturally, and even then only manage to reach a low level of lucidity. But lucid dreaming can be learned or enhanced. One reason to invest in it, apart from the fun and games, is for the treatment of otherwise incurable nightmares. Instead of being a slave to the demons you can learn to face them and, if so inclined, make them do the twist.

Let's consider what process in the brain might enable a dreamer to become lucid. There exists no functional imaging data on this phenomenon – a gap in our knowledge that will hopefully soon be filled – but a few inferences can be made from people's subjective reports. Hobson (2001, p. 93) has defined lucid dreaming "as the bolstering of the self-reflective awareness that is normally diminished or absent in dreaming," a definition that appears to go straight to the heart of the matter. Psychological reports from lucid dreamers indicate that higher cognitive and emotional functions that are lacking in normal dream mentation manifest themselves in their dreams. People are able to self-reflect, direct attention, think abstractly, will their own actions, plan strategically, retrieve memories deliberately, and make decisions. These mental functions are, of course, all subserved by the prefrontal cortex. When seen in this way, it can be hypothesized that lucid dreaming is the result of DLPFC activation during REM sleep, or in the words of Allan Hobson (2001), "the residual activation of the dorsolateral prefrontal cortex [that] is amplified by the REM activation" (p. 97). Moreover, the degree and quality of the lucid experience might be a function of the extent as well as the pattern of prefrontal activation. The observation that dream control and lucidity, although highly correlated, are independent might underscore this notion. With the top layers of consciousness activated, lucid dreaming should perhaps be regarded more akin to waking consciousness and indeed, according to LaBerge, awakening is one of the most common results of suddenly gaining lucidity in a dream. In that sense, lucid dreaming might be better thought of as daydreaming during REM sleep.

Summary

Two obstacles impeding empirical progress on altered states of consciousness have been the problem of a clear, operational definition and the ephemeral nature of these phenomena. The problem of defining ASC is inherent in the problem of defining consciousness in general. Because no other definitions are widely accepted, this chapter employed a new approach based on the transient hypofrontality hypothesis. The THH offers a common neural mechanism for ASC that can be subjected to empirical study. It is based on the view that consciousness is a functional hierarchy. Like peeling an onion, an alteration to consciousness disengages, first and foremost, prefrontal-based layers, followed by a progressive deactivation of brain structures that contribute more basic layers of consciousness. This is what seems to happen in ASC, whose hallmark is the subtle modification of functions that are typically ascribed to the prefrontal cortex. It follows from this view that a fully operational brain is associated with default consciousness and an alteration to this default state is an ASC. Since consciousness is a continuum, the question of defining ASC then becomes one of gradation, that is, how far one must be removed from default consciousness to call the experience an altered state.

This chapter considered the most profound alterations to consciousness, sleep and dreaming. During dreams we generate a phenomenal reality unlike anything we experience during waking. Sleep research has provided a wealth of data that has informed our understanding of the stages of sleep, including the distinctive bodily and mental characteristics associated with each. The functions and evolution of sleep and dreams are less well understood.

The paradigm in neuroscience for how the brain creates the nocturnal tales from the crypt is the activation-synthesis model. It explains that dreaming is initiated by a brainstem mechanism, which turns on, at periodic intervals and in a semi-random fashion, several brain areas, which then provide the raw imagery of dreams. This activation is then synthesized into a narrative. Dreams are so bizarre because the activation fails to reach the prefrontal cortex and we are left with making sense out of arbitrarily generated images without the help of higher cognitive functions. A fascinating variation of the dream state is lucid dreaming, in which a person knows that he is dreaming. This phenomenon is likely related to residual prefrontal activation during REM sleep.

Suggested reading

Dietrich, A. (2003). Functional neuroanatomy of altered states of consciousness. The transient hypofrontality hypothesis. *Consciousness and Cognition*, 12, 231–56.

Empson J. (2001). *Sleep and Dreaming* (3rd ed.). New York: Palgrave Macmillan.

Hobson, J. A., Pace-Schott, E. F., & Stickhold, R. (2000). Dreaming and the brain: Toward a cognitive neuroscience of conscious states. *Behavioural and Brain Sciences*, 23, 793–866.

LaBerge, S. (1985). *Lucid Dreaming*. Los Angeles: Jeremy P. Tarcher.

13 Drug states and other alternities

Drug-altered consciousness

The high, the low, and the far-out

Drugs have been used to alter consciousness since recorded history, and probably, for much longer than that. Alcohol, perhaps the oldest such substance, was discovered independently by most cultures and the psychological effects of many naturally occurring preparations were known to the Chinese, Indians, Egyptians, and Greeks. According to Ronald Siegel (1989), a UCLA behavioral pharmacologist and possibly *the* world expert on the mechanics of hallucinations, the pursuit of intoxicated happiness is so pervasive – even among other animals – that he calls it the fourth drive, after hunger, thirst, and sex. The history of drug use and abuse from antiquity to the present day, drug pharmacology – especially drugs' mechanisms of action – and the legal and health implications are all relentlessly fascinating topics, but even a cursory treatment of those topics is wholly beyond the scope of this text. We focus instead on the changes to phenomenology, especially the mind spectaculars induced by hallucinogens and psychedelics. Apart from these chemical nirvanas this chapter also examines the multitude of behavioral ways to reach alternity, such as meditation, hypnosis, daydreaming, and exercise.

Psychoactive drugs are a class of compounds that act on the central nervous system and alter behavior and cognition. They are highly fat-soluble and thus readily cross the blood–brain barrier that border-patrols the gray matter. In addition to their primary effects on mental processes – arousal, perception, mood, cognition, consciousness – these drugs produce a variety of nonbehavioral effects that are often far more dangerous to health (Diaz, 1997).

There exist several different classification schemes for psychoactive drugs (pharmacological, legal, medical), but the most common organization is based on their effect on behavior (Schatzberg & Nemeroff, 1995). This scheme yields four broad classes. The first are the **sedatives and hypnotics**. Drugs in this class depress or inhibit brain activity and produce drowsiness, sedation, or sleep; relieve anxiety; and lower inhibition. Although depressants do not share a common neural mechanism, most of them either decrease the metabolic activity in the brain or increase the transmission of the principal inhibitory neurotransmitter, GABA. Common examples include barbiturates, such as Seconal; benzodiazepines (also known as minor tranquilizers), such as Xanax or Valium; non-barbiturate sedatives, such as methaqualone; non-benzodiazepines, such as buspirone; antihistamines and anesthetics; and alcohol. In low doses, alcohol may act as a stimulant; but with increased dosage its main effects are depressive. Marijuana, which is derived from the hemp plant cannabis sativa, is often misclassified as a psychedelic. Given that its most pronounced behavioral symptom is sedation and the fact that it rarely produces – and only in very high doses – sensory distortions of hallucinatory quality, it is also best classified as a sedative.

The second class, **stimulants**, produce behavioral arousal. This class also includes a variety of different compounds, each with a different neural mechanism. Examples are amphetamines; cocaine; the methylxanthines, such as caffeine (the most widely used psychoactive drug in the world), theophylline (present in tea), and theobromine (present in chocolate); nicotine or tobacco; appetite suppressants; and a variety of exotic plants, such as the betel nut, khat, yohimbe, and ephedra. None of these preparations induces radical changes to mental status, except perhaps cocaine and amphetamines when taken in high doses.

The third class consists of the **opiates**. Drugs in this class act on opiate receptors, mediating relief from pain and producing feelings of euphoria. In pharmacology, the term **narcotics** is also used for these substances but legal systems typically use it to refer to all illicit drugs. Opiates can either be natural, semi-synthetic, or synthetic. Natural opiates, such as morphine and codeine, are derived from crude opium. The most famous semi-synthetic opiate is heroin, which is five to ten times more potent than morphine. Examples of synthetic opiates, also known as **designer drugs**, include methadone, naloxone, and the prescription pain medication Demerol.

The fourth class consists of the **hallucinogens and psychedelics**. Drugs in this class have the common feature of inducing hallucinations or have "mind-manifesting" or "expanding" properties. But this is also where the commonality ends. They can either occur naturally in a plant, such as mescaline, which is derived from the peyote cactus, or be synthesized in the lab, such as LSD. Behaviorally, no overarching framework seems to be emerging that can systematize their wide-ranging phantasmagoric effects on consciousness. Pharmacologically, they are also all over the place. For every classical neurotransmitter system, there exists a drug in this category. Therefore, they are probably best classified according to the neurotransmitter system they primarily modulate. Cholinergic psychedelics include physiostigmine, scopolamine, and atropine. Drugs that alter norepinephrine transmission include mescaline and ecstasy (MDMA). Drugs that alter serotonin transmission include LSD, psilocybin, and morning glory. There are also drugs with psychedelic properties that alter dopamine (cocaine), glutamate (ketamine), GABA (muscimol), opioid (morphine) or cannabinoid (hashish) transmission; however, these preparations are not primarily hallucinogenic and are typically classified elsewhere according to their main effect. A peculiar subclass of this category are the psychedelic anesthetics, such as PCP (angel dust), ketamine, and several gases and solvents, such as ether or nitrous oxide. With the exception of the cholinergic psychedelics, all drugs in this class have a high margin of safety and are generally nonlethal – even when taken in large doses.

In addition to these four broad categories, there are several other drugs that affect the mind including antidepressants, antipsychotic medication, and drugs for epilepsy, Parkinson's disease, or the dementias.

Before we explore the various psychopharmacological heavens and hells, a note of caution is in order. Most theories on the neural basis of ASC rely solely on neurochemical modulation. The reason for this is that drugs are the most common way to induce ASC and their known mechanism of action was for a long time the only hope to find a sound mechanistic explanation for the mercurial nature of ASC. But there is a danger of leaning too hard on neurochemistry. An increase in serotonin does not cause happiness any more than an excess of dopamine causes paranoia. Neurotransmitters do not carry content in their messages. Drugs that work on the same neurotransmitter system, even via the same synaptic mechanism, can have very different effects on consciousness (Diaz, 1997). For instance, Prozac increases serotonergic transmission and is an antidepressant, while with LSD, also a serotonergic agonist, you enter a dimension of another kind. Behavioral pharmacologists have long given up on the naïve idea that complex psychological phenomena can be attributed to changes in the concentration of a simple little molecule. Every transmitter system can be modulated by drugs that do and do not alter consciousness. We must also consider function of the neural structure in which the changes in chemical neurotransmission occur.

Table 13.1 Some psychoactive drugs

Category	Drug & origin	Mechanism of action	Phenomenology
Sedatives & hypnotics	Valium	Binds to benzodiazepine site of the GABAa receptor facilitating the effects of GABA	Produces all degrees of behavioral depression from sedation, to relaxation, to coma; reduces anxiety, disinhibition, sleepiness, tiredness, sense of well-being
	Alcohol	Binds to barbiturate site of the GABAa receptor facilitating the effects of GABA	Relief of anxiety, sedation, disinhibition. Stimulant in low doses. Impairments in vision, speech, motor control, and judgment
	Marijuana (*Cannabis sativa*)	Receptor agonist on the CB1 receptor; also inhibits 5-HT3 receptors	Main effects are sedation and analgesia; others include heightened sensations, uncontrollable laughing, sense of well-being, intensified introspection, mental slowing
Stimulants	Amphetamine	Stimulates the release of DA and blocks its reuptake; also activates adrenergic receptors	Causes alertness, arousal, insomnia, loss of appetite, and combats fatigue; known as "speed" when taken IV or as "speedball" in combo with opioids (to reduce side effects)
	Cocaine (cocca plant)	DA reuptake blocker	Same as for amphetamines; more euphoria and paranoia; freebasing and crack result from purification procedures and intensify the experience, especially the euphoria
Opiates	Morphine, heroin (opium pocpy)	Activates opioid receptors	Analgesia, peacefulness, feelings of warmth and well-being, boundless energy, dream imagery; when taken IV, heroin induces a "rush" of intense pleasure that is without equal

Table 13.1 *continued*

Category	Drug & origin	Mechanism of action	Phenomenology
Hallucinogens & Psychedelics	Scopolamine Atropine (nightshade)	Cholinergic antagonist	Restlessness, delirium, vivid hallucinations, disconnection with reality, no memory of the experience; OBE are common; bad trips can easily be filled with ugly monsters
	Mescaline (peyote cactus)	In a class of its own; structurally related to NE and alters NE transmission	Vivid hallucinations consisting of bright colors, geometric designs, and animals; synesthesia; no OBE, insight is retained; more color and less form distortion than LSD
	MDMA (ecstasy)	Pharmacologically promiscuous but primarily stimulates the release and blocks the reuptake of 5-HT2	Induces feelings of empathy and sympathy; creates desire for intimacy and need for personal contact, heightens self-awareness; no hallucinations or loss of reality
	LSD	Activates 5-HT2a receptors	Vivid, kaleidoscopic sensory changes (e.g., mosaic patterns on all surfaces), powerful feeling of love, mystical oneness, synesthesia; bad trips include anxiety, panic, violence
	Psilocybin Psilocin (mushrooms)	Structure resembles 5-HT and activates 5-HT receptors	Pleasant feelings of relaxation, distortions of space, visual hallucinations with more intense color than LSD; effects resemble more mescaline than LSD; fewer bad trips
	DMT (virola tree)	5-HT agonist	Short-acting and intense psychedelic rush (businessman's LSD); loss of all reality, overwhelming visual hallucinations; communication with gods, spirits, or the deceased
	PCP (angel dust) Ketamine	Primarily an NMDA receptor agonist but also alter opioid and monoamine transmission	Anesthesia with depersonalization, loss of ego boundaries, changes in body image, floating, OBE, NDE, distortion of time and space, full amnesia, euphoria; frequent bad trips

Inside the psychedelic theater

Since hallucinations usually do not occur spontaneously, they are typically not included in the repertoire of normal experiences. In Western societies, hallucinations are mostly associated with madness, as part of some disease process in the brain, such as schizophrenia, or malfunctioning of a bodily system, such as in starvation or sleep deprivation. We also tend to think of them in conjunction with drug use; but here, too, they are seen as neurological junk or signs of temporary insanity. But not all cultures understand hallucinations in this negative light. In other traditions they are valued highly as sources of insight and truth. Often people attach great spiritual significance to them and interpret hallucination as visions that allow them a glimpse into other realms, worlds inhabited by gods and ancestors. Given this sacred meaning, hallucinations are sought out in elaborate rituals and only a selected few **shamans** are chosen to experience them. Such rituals often involve repetitive and rhythmic motion, such as spinning, whirling, dancing, or jumping, combined with cadenced drumming, but hallucinations can also be induced through such behavioral techniques alone – without the aid of a psychedelic substance.

The psychedelic mindscape is not so much an altered state as it is a family of altered states. Depending on the choice of chemical, people can experience a wide variety of hallucinations, delusions, and emotional changes. On the bright side, hallucinations may include intense colors, kaleidoscopic visions, fantastic images of animals and landscapes, mosaic patterns on all surfaces, as well as vibrating, rotating, or exploding designs that retreat into infinity. This is particularly true for the three major psychedelics, LSD, psilocybin, and mescaline. Delusions often include the merging with one's surroundings, such as a mystical oneness with God or the forces of nature, but may also be less sacrosanct experiences, such as becoming one with the candleholder or dissolving into the wallpaper. Emotional changes may include anything from pleasant relaxation to mild amusement to sweeping euphoria. On the dark side, changes may range from anxiety to paranoia to outright terror. People may see ugly beasts chasing after them, roaring dementedly, or an abyss opening up in the floor in front of them. Other wickedly macabre delusions contain distortions of the sense of self, such as grotesque changes in body image (legs getting longer), bizarre depersonalizations with the body floating in a void, and out-of-body or near-death experiences. As with most drug effects, whether you go to heaven or hell depends on set and setting. Given that the psychedelics are by and large not very lethal, the psychological scars that may result from bad trips may represent the biggest drawback of these alternate realities.

Some psychedelics sever all ties with reality and catapult the user into an altogether different mental time zone. PCP and scopolamine delusions are good examples. The danger of losing all sense of what is real and what is imagined is that PCP-powered phantasms are ontologically fully real and when you, in your desperation, run from them and jump out of a real window, you are really dead. Other psychedelics keep the user on this side reality and preserve some type of lucidity. Mescaline, of peyote fame, and ecstasy tend to be of this kind. Insights are often retained upon return and at low doses some people may even be able to "snap out" of it. Marijuana is different still; here the user does not reach the hallucination mode unless high doses are taken. Most register some mild sensory changes, a sense of well-being or peacefulness, and a somewhat vague feeling of goodwill toward others.

Tales from the hallucination zone are nuggets of pure gold to the aficionado but certainly not the sort of scientific sound-bites printed in peer-reviewed pharmacology journals. But these anecdotal and esoteric descriptions give the wrong impression that psychopharmacological karma comes in an infinite plethora of variety. It may be true that different drugs evoke different realities, but all still share characteristics that suggest the disengagement of the prefrontal cortex. The sense that time loses its meaning is as universal for these states as the lack of cognitive flexibility. People simply lack any power to extract themselves from the here and now of the experience. They describe experiences as though the mind is a singularity. Another feature common to most drug states is the loss of ego boundaries. People report that they dissolve into the Universal Ocean, merge with the Almighty, or become one with Void. This experience can be understood in terms of changes in prefrontal activity, as it is there that we form a sense of the self and delineate it from other selves. But taken together, drug states are also quite different from nondrug states such as meditation, hypnosis, or rhythmic movement. While all ASC are marked by phenomenological subtraction, drug states are also accompanied by phenomenological addition, depending on the systems the drug stimulates.

No one knows the insides of the psychedelic theater better than Ronald Siegel, who has built his scientific career around collecting and categorizing the surreal images of the hallucinating mind in an effort to find patterns in what seems to be infinite multiplicity. For years he performed well-controlled studies with psychedelics at a time when no other researcher could get their hands on them. He trained psychonauts, a Siegel term, on a standardized hallucination code that classified their experiences in more precise language. For instance, they would report seeing, say, 560 millimicrons rather than a muddy red. What he discovered in his UCLA "hallucination chamber" is that there is a hidden order in the chaos. Amazingly, the brain hallucinates in only four basic geometric forms. Sure, there are some superimposed, nonlinear fiddly bits providing some creative uniqueness but all visions are variations on four recurrent themes. These **form constants** were first deciphered by the psychologist Heinrich Klüver, who experimented with mescaline in the 1920s (Klüver, 1926). He named them the spiral, the cobweb, the tunnel (or funnel or cone), and the lattice (grating or honeycomb). Siegel has also found them in nondrug ASC, such as those induced by migraines, fever, auras, temporal lobe epilepsy, or sensory deprivation. You can best see them in psychedelic-inspired art all around the globe, from Huichol Indian paintings, to mandalas, and tie-dye T-shirts.

The reason for form constants can be found in the functional architecture of the visual cortex. Computer models using a columnar organization similar to

Figure 13.1

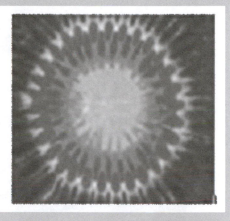

Whether UCLA undergraduates or Indian shamans, visions are made of four basic shapes: the spiral, the cobweb, the tunnel, and the lattice. The spiral is obvious in these examples of drug-inspired art from Huichol paintings (left) and modern flower-power designs (right).

that of the cortex show that the same form constants also crystallize in computer simulations (Bressloff et al., 2002; Cowan, 1982). Furthermore, the content of hallucinations corresponds to neural activity that matches closely the pattern of activation expected when actually seeing the same thing. In other words, normal vision and hallucinating engage the same regions of the cortex (Ffytche, 2000).

As dosage increases, visions become more intricate and contain characters, story lines, and composite scenes. If the basic form constants are phase one, these complex hallucinations are phase two. Siegel has also cartographed and indexed this phase and discovered that it is also governed by some underlying rules. For instance, people or objects grow huge or shrink infinitesimally in size, a hallucination phenomenon known as megalopsy and micropsy. There is also what Siegel called duplication and multiplication. A tunnel always leads to more tunnels and one sunflower becomes an entire field of sunflowers. The manner in which motion and metamorphosis occur is not random either. Birds become bats (never the other way around) and things first pulsate before they revolve. The hallucinating brain is not an unconstrained image generator.

Siegel and Jarvik (1975) showed that specific drugs produce predictable changes in the color spectrum and intensity that can be described in terms of dose-reponse curves. As you can see from Figure 13.2, the three major psychedelics LSD, psilocybin, and mescaline tend to be very colorful and bring out red, orange, and yellow hues; while marijuana is more bluish. When psychonauts closed their eyes and used nothing but their imagination, blacks, whites, and violets dominated.

Figure 13.2

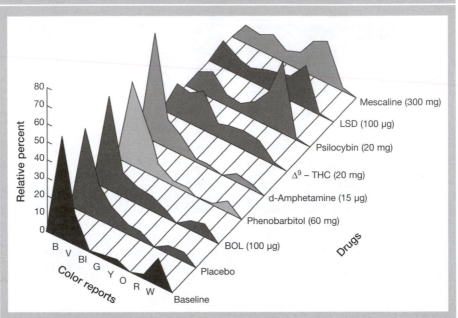

Color in hallucinations is a function of the drug and its dosage. Siegel's psychonauts saw warm reds, oranges, and yellows on LSD, psilocybin, and mescaline; somber blues on marijuana and uninspiring blacks, whites, and shades of gray on amphetamine and sedatives. (Adapted from Siegel & Jarvik, 1975)

Other doors to alternity

Meditation

Meditation is not as shrouded in mystery as it used to be. Although comparable practices exist in the world's three major monotheistic religions (Christianity, Judaism, and Islam), meditation in its disciplined form originated in Eastern religions, particularly Buddhism, Hinduism, and Sufism (West, 1987). As its practice spread in the West during the 1960s and 1970s, introduced mainly in the form of transcendental meditation or TM by Maharishi Mahesh Yogi, it was increasingly stripped of its spiritual overtones and subjected to scientific scrutiny. Images of baldheaded Tibetan monks against a Himalayan backdrop chanting mantras for days on their path to higher consciousnesses have been complemented by countless secular practitioners seeking the experience of meditation for other reasons. Because so much ink has been spilled over the different practices and forms of meditation, their purpose and meaning within Eastern thought, as well as associated physical and mental health benefits, this section focuses primarily on the neuroscience of the meditative state. Although enlightenment may not be visible in functional magnetic neuroimaging, recent experiments with skilled meditators have shed some light on the neural activity accompanying deep meditation (Austin, 1998).

Meditation has long been regarded as an altered state of consciousness. There are many different forms and practices but all variations can be categorized into two broad types (Farthing, 1992; Ornstein, 1986). **Open meditation** entails being aware of everything around you but the experience is not met with a response. The meditator attends to whatever comes to mind without judgment, opinion, or evaluation. The practice of *just sitting* or *shikantaza*, a Buddhist technique of mindfulness meditation, is perhaps the most common form of this. You do not have to pretzel your legs into the lotus position, but any comfortable posture will do. **Concentrative or one-point meditation**, on the other hand, entails focusing awareness on one particular thing. One can quietly observe a candle flickering in the dark; listen to the breathing rhythm; repeat a mantra (usually a smooth-sounding Sanskrit word or phrase, for instance, the famous *Om Mani Padme Hum*, which means "jewel in the center of the lotus" and, presumably, refers to the Buddha himself); ponder a koan (an unanswerable riddle, for instance, what is the sound of one hand clapping?); chant a song; focus on the flow of thoughts and feelings; attend to bodily sensations; or make dancelike movements as in Tai Chi or yoga. Despite this diversity, all practices share a number of common features. First, sensory input is gradually diminished in meditation, creating what the medical researcher Patricia Carrington (1998, p. 68) calls "a mental isolation chamber." The relentless sensory bombardment of daily life is gradually replaced by a nonjudgmental, receptive, quiescent state that deliberately banishes the intrusion of new input. This feature by itself probably explains many well-known health effects of meditation, such as relaxation or reduced anxiety (Jevning et al., 1992). Look at it this way: if your mind is empty, save for a mantra or koan, nothing could possibly bug you and your blood pressure will go down. Second, meditation entails sustained concentration and heightened awareness by focusing attention on a specific event. This increase in attentional effort is the mechanism by which the meditator accomplishes the exclusion of other, intruding information.

Clearly, the key to understanding how meditation alters consciousness is executive attention. This can be seen in several definitions of meditation such as Farthing's (1992, p. 421): "meditation is a ritualistic procedure intended to change one's state of consciousness by means of maintained, voluntary shifts of attention." In meditation, this attention is directed, deliberate, and sustained, suggesting the activation of the frontal attentional network. The few existing studies to date using neuroimaging techniques during meditation all show converging evidence of DLPFC activation (e.g., Newberg et al., 2001). At first glance, these data appear to contradict the hypothesis outlined earlier that ASC are due to transient hypofrontality. Paradoxically, early EEG studies of meditation consistently detected alpha-wave activity across the frontal lobe (e.g.,

Banquent, 1972; Corby et al., 1978). Alpha activity, however, indicates decreased brain activation. This raises the following issue. If focused attention is the most distinguishing feature of the meditative state, as suggested by anecdotal psychological reports and neuroimaging data, why don't we detect beta activity, the neurosignature of attention, across the frontal lobe during meditation? Or, in more esoteric terms, if meditation is, as so often claimed, a vehicle for reaching higher consciousness one would expect the neural structure that enables the highest cognitive functions and thus the top layers of consciousness to be fully functional. Put another way, if we consider the neuroimaging data we must conclude that meditation is associated with activation of prefrontal regions, but if we examine the EEG data we are obliged to come to the opposite conclusion.

It is evident that only more research can resolve the apparent paradox, but a preliminary hypothesis can already be formulated (Dietrich, 2003). Executive attention (see Chapter 10) is a costly and taxing mechanism that cannot be maintained indefinitely. The longer it is engaged the more difficult it is to maintain. At some point, attention inevitably gives way to daydreaming. In meditation, the task is to hold executive attention until some mantra or koan becomes the exclusive content of consciousness. It appears that this ability can be trained like a muscle. Beginners to the practice of meditation can rarely keep their mind calm for more than a few minutes before their attention slips and their thoughts start to wander. Experienced meditators, on the other hand, have mastered the art of attention and can sustain any content in consciousness almost at will (Carter et al., 2005). Now, executive attention appears to be a global prefrontal function, that is, it recruits many, spatially overlapping prefrontal modules. This should produce widespread DLPFC activation, as indeed evidenced by neuroimaging scans. But the singular focus of the mind also results in the deactivation of prefrontal modules subserving other cognitive function; for, they have little to do if you no longer process anything other than some mantra or koan. This, then, is perhaps the reason for the EEG alpha wave over the prefrontal cortex. The coherent pattern of activity is produced because only one network, the attentional network, is active, while all other modules fire at baseline rates. The resulting conscious state is one of full alertness and a heightened sense of awareness, but without content, which is consistent with subjective reports. The longer meditation lasts, the more profound are the psychological changes. Cognitive functions requiring metarepresentations of the highest order are among the first phenomenological subtractions to occur in meditation. There is no sense of time or self, no self-reflection or planning, in fact, no analysis of any type. With these analytical capacities eliminated, it is little wonder that the mind becomes clear and a sense of unity and inner peace emerges. In this view, meditation is a state of transient hypofrontality with the exception of executive attention.

Box 13.1   Flow

The subject of optimal human functioning has a long history in humanistic and health psychology. Maslow (1959), who called such moments of self-actualization "peak experiences," described these memorable experiences as instances of happiness, fulfillment, and achievement that create a feeling of realizing one's human potential. More recently, psychologist Mihaly Csikszentmihalyi (1996, p. 110) has described it as a state of flow because it is characterized by "an almost automatic, effortless, yet highly focused state of consciousness." Flow is a commonly reported phenomena and the concept is intuitively appealing. A flow state ensues when one becomes so deeply focused on a task and pursues it with such passion that all else disappears, including a sense of time or the fear of failure. The person experiences an almost euphoric state of joy and pleasure, in which the task is performed, without strain or effort, to the best of the person's ability. According to Csikszentmihalyi, any activity, mental or physical, can produce flow as long as it is a challenging task that demands intense concentration and commitment, contains clear goals, provides immediate feedback, and is perfectly matched to the person's skill level. But despite the rich descriptions in the psychological literature, very little is known about the brain mechanisms that give rise to such exceptional human functioning.

Some say that flow – if not an ASC – is at the very least a special SoC. Csikszentmihalyi delineated several key characteristics of flow, many of which we also find in other ASC. For instance, people report the typical one-pointedness of mind that occurs when the muscle of attention is flexed and one event or object becomes the exclusive content of consciousness. Any distractions are eleminated from consciousness, especially evaluative metalevel cognitive processes such as self-reflection or worry of failure (or success). Time loses its meaning and one operates solely in the here and how. Because these higher mental functions are encoded in the prefrontal cortex, their absence indicates that flow, too, is a state of prefrontal hypofunction (Dietrich, 2004a).

Hypnosis

(We suggest that) hypnosis is a very odd effect. Whatever we tell you, there is certainly one good thing about it: Hypnosis is what you want it to be! So, listen carefully to whatever you want to hear, and consider yourself invited to a paradox. On the one hand, if you believe us, hypnosis is a somewhat strange altered state of consciousness, and on the other hand, if you believe us again, it might not be as peculiar as you think.

Although still viewed with some skepticism, hypnosis has gained respectability in science and medicine in large part due to its demonstrated effects on analgesia. It is less clear, however, whether hypnosis constitutes an altered state of consciousness. Forty percent of hypnotized subjects describe it as an altered state, while sixty percent compare it to a period of focused attention (Kirsch & Lynn, 1998). This divides psychologists into two camps, **state theorists** and **nonstate theorists**, respectively. Agreement on a sound explanation has been equally difficult to come by. While some researchers postulated a divided stream of consciousness (Hilgard, 1980), others cautioned that the evidence only supports a state of social compliance and suggestibility (Barber, 1970; Spanos, 1994).

When the cloud of hypnosis overtakes the mind, people report or exhibit reductions in pain sensation, vivid images, loss of time perception, hallucinations in all sensory modalities, amnesia, detachment from the self, and an uncanny willingness to accept distortions of logic and reality (Kihlstrom, 1985; Tart, 1979). More commonly, however, hypnotized individuals remain fully alert, interacting normally with other people. By all accounts, hypnosis is not wondrously pleasant, enlightening, or mystical, as is reported for other ASC. Hypnosis is more like a trance state, perhaps the closest you will get to the philosopher's zombie. People become highly receptive to suggestions and respond to them as if possessed by some spirit. Afterwards, they report their actions happened by themselves without doubts, complaints, objections, or critical evaluation. The term "hypnosis" is derived from the Greek *hypnos* for sleep, but the main distinguishing characteristic of the hypnotic state is the lack of initiative and willful motion.

Early studies using EEG failed to uncover an unambiguous physiological marker of hypnosis (Benson et al., 1981). However, recent neuroimaging studies did demonstrate that subtle changes occur in the neural profile, particularly in the left hemisphere (e.g., Maquet et al., 1999). This activation is located predominantly in TOP cortices without corresponding DPLFC activation. During hypnotic suggestion, increases in VMPFC activity were also observed, which, presumably, reflects the demand on attentional resources to process the verbal input (Rainville et al., 1999; Wik et al., 1999).

The process of hypnotic induction – regardless of how it is implemented by the hypnotist – serves to narrow a person's attention to a single source. Thus, similar to meditation, it is the mechanism of executive attention that achieves the alteration to consciousness. So what, then, is the deal in hypnosis? The idea that an underactive frontal cortex causes the psychological effects of hypnosis has been an influential explanation for some time (Gruzelier, 2000; Kallio et al., 2001). The hypothesis suggests that the hypnotist's suggestions, due to the person's exclusive focus on them, become the sole content in working memory. This singular focus causes computations from other neural modules to be eliminated from consciousness. Again, this disengagement must progress, as the attentional effort increases, from the topmost layers of consciousness implemented by the prefrontal cortex to ever more basic layers until the trance state becomes so deep that the person experiences comprehensive phenomenological subtraction. Because, at this stage, there is a complete lack of cognitive flexibility, an inability to critically reflect or independently think, and a suspension of logic, the hypnotist's suggestions arrive in consciousness and affect behavior without being first filtered by these downregulated modules, which otherwise would subject them to some critical analysis. This corresponds well with subjective description of the hypnotic experience that a behavior appears to happen by itself. There are limits to this automatism, however, as hypnotized subjects apparently cannot be induced to act contrary to their moral beliefs and values (Kirsch & Lynn, 1998).

Given this, let us examine two interesting effects of hypnosis. The first is the existence of a so-called **hidden observer** discovered in a classroom demonstration by the psychologist Ernest Hilgard. He hypnotized a student and instructed him to be deaf to the loud noise of a starter pistol. Another student in class asked Hilgard whether or not there was a part of the hypnotized student who could still hear. Hilgard instructed the hypnotized student to raise his right index finger to see if there was. To Hilgard's surprise, the student did raise his right index finger and showed that there was some independent agent that had escaped the mind's general descent into the trance state. This and similar demonstrations led Hilgard to propose two separate streams of consciousnesses, one hypnotized and one that stayed rooted in default consciousness (Hilgard, 1980). The experience of a detached entity that is not in the same altered state than the rest of the mind is not unique to hypnosis. This phenomenon has been reported for other altered states, for instance, in lucid dreaming and several drug-induced states. In these cases, the person has the feeling of retaining some form of lucidity, a bird's-eye view if you will, that continues to process reality. What may occur here is that these experiences are due to some "indomitable" prefrontal circuits that are not affected by the hypnotic induction and thus provide some insight, but without the ability to influence real actions.

The second effect is analgesia. Alterations in pain perception under hypnosis are a somewhat odd form of analgesia. For instance, a patient might experience pain-free surgery yet still complain about the cold temperature in the operating room (Hardcastle, 1999). Likewise, a hypnotized subject might report pain in one hand but not in the other, although both are subjected to the same treatment. Hardcastle (1999) pointed out that to intentionally ignore some specific pain one would have to notice it first in order to know what pain to ignore. That is, the sensation must be recognized, distinguished from other sensations, and then selectively blocked from entering consciousness. This suggests a top-down process of the highest order further intimating the prefrontal cortex. Patients with frontal lobe damage show similar **hypoalgesia**. They report experiences of pain but show little, if any, signs of being distressed by them (Vertosick, 2000).

Psychologists subscribing to the nonstate theory have challenged the recruitment of these data to support a special state of consciousness for hypnosis. Empirical studies have consistently shown that every act performed under hypnosis can be equally well performed by highly motivated volunteers. This is true for analgesia as much as it is for the more spectacular demonstrations, like the stiff-as-a-board stunt. Even the experience of a hidden observer has parallels in default consciousness when we sometimes feel that there is more than one voice inside the head. In this view, hypnosis is simply a state of high suggestibility.

Box 13.2   OBE and NDE

Some 15 percent of people claim to have had an out-of-body experience (**OBE**) or a near-death experience (**NDE**), making them rather common phenomena (Blackmore, 1993). OBEs involve the sensation of leaving one's physical container. Most OBEers report floating just above the body taking in the surroundings from a bird's-eye view. We can understand OBEs as the most profound distortion of the sense of self. This third-person perspective can occur under surprisingly many circumstances, including dreams, various

Box 13.2   *continued*

other ASC, several psychiatric conditions, and, of course, drug use. Importantly, out-of-body-travel can be induced during brain surgery. In the 1930s, the neurosurgeon Wilder Penfield operated on many epileptic patients who had to remain conscious for the surgical procedure. In one case, Penfield lowered the electrode to stimulate a part of the temporal lobe and the man reported leaving his body (Penfield, 1955). At least one more such extraordinary case is known, except this time the OBE was produced several times by stimulation of the anterior angular gyrus, which is also in the temporal lobe (Blanke et al., 2002). This and several other peculiar phenomena (e.g., religious experiences, such as meeting God) reported by people with temporal lobe seizures led the neuroscientist Michael Persinger (1999) to propose that activity in the temporal lobe is an underlying feature of all mystical experiences. Persinger has even induced such experiences at will using TMS.

Like OBEs, NDEs are fascinating experiences if not for anything else but the implications that, if true, bodies and brains are unnecessary for consciousness. The physician Raymond Moody (1975), who also coined the term in his popular book *Life after Life*, undertook the first modern examination of NDE by interviewing dozens of people who felt that they took a walk on the other side and came back. Several other studies, some conducted with more scientific rigor than Moody's, have been reported since. As might be expected, most come from cardiologists who are most at home with snatching people from clinical death. In one study, van Lommel examined 344 consecutive survivors of cardiac arrest. A surprisingly high number of 62 (18 percent) had an NDE (van Lommel et al., 2001). In a similar study, 4 out of 63 (6 percent) reported a NDE after successful resuscitation (Parnia et al., 2001). Michael Sabom (1981) interviewed over a five-year period a random sample of many people who were "resurrected" in the wards of his cardiac unit after a brush with death. The stories of NDE returnees make for gripping tales, containing heavenly landscapes, tunnels, and brilliant lights. Other core features of the NDE experience are body separation (OBE), feelings of bliss, rendezvous with spirits (Jesus if you are Christian, a warm presence if you are an atheist), departed friends or family members, an instantaneous but comprehensive life review, and a conscious decision to return and give it another go.

Given that nothing short of the afterlife is at stake, it is not surprising that the debate regarding the nature of NDEs is emotionally charged. There are, of course, two ways to look at them. For some, NDEs are genuine glimpses of the great Beyond. This is an understandable explanation given the divine lights, biblical figures, and reality of the experience. Two arguments are given most often to support NDEs as proof of the hereafter and life everlasting. First, NDE accounts square unnervingly with actual medical reports. Survivors of flat EEGs tell stories of being ejected from their bodies in full capacity of their mental faculties and floating detached below the ceiling of the operating room, while observing the medical staff working over their lifeless bodies. Sometimes their recall of the event matches the details, right down to the number of shocks to the chest, the number of people in the room, or the description of the paraphernalia of modern resuscitation.

Scientists rightfully reject such anecdotal evidence for many reasons. Most stories cannot be corroborated, claims are frequently exaggerated, no false-alarm rates are reported in the studies (i.e. details that do not match), and controlled experiments with concealed targets have failed regularly (Parnia et al., 2001). Put simply, as honestly as they are told, these tales suffer from the usual suspects of confounds – educated guesses, chance, false memories – and thus cannot be taken as evidence.

Box 13.2   *continued*

The second argument for authenticity is that NDE seem remarkably universal (although no true cross-cultural studies exist). There is the ominous passage through a tunnel, celestial scenes flooded with luminaries in white robes, or the playback of major life events before one's eyes. However, to the neuroscientist this universality is simply indication that brains in a near-death crisis undergo similar alteration to phenomenological content. From all we know about brains, it would be more amazing if everyone "comes back" with a different version of the Other Side. Recall, for instance, the work of Siegel, who showed that many features, such as tunnels ending in lights, are stable properties of hallucinations. This, then, is known as the **dying-brain hypothesis** (Blackmore, 1993), which says that NDEs are simply the effects of a compromised brain. Before we conclude that NDE are bona fide visitations to the borderstation of life, we are well advised to eliminate all alternative explanations. Extraordinary claims require extraordinary evidence and we are right to be skeptical when asked to believe something that would necessitate a wholesale reexamination of the standard scientific model.

Daydreaming

Daydreaming is a mental state quite unlike meditation or hypnosis. In meditation and hypnosis subjective experience is altered intentionally through the ability to control and direct attentional resources. This engenders an altered state in which the individual is highly alert but centers this attention on only one event. Because concentration on this single focal point is so total and our attentional resources so limited, other phenomenological content is prevented from entering consciousness. In contrast, daydreaming is the opposite. Daydreaming is (1) not necessarily intentional, but rather inevitable with time and (2) not a heightening of attentional focus, but simply a loss of attentional power. In other words, the hallmark of daydreaming are mental drifting and ephemeral thoughts. Despite this, all three ASC share two prominent features: (1) the toning-down of external stimulation and (2) the subtraction of phenomenological features typically ascribed to prefrontal areas.

Humans daydream frequently. One way to measure this is to fit people with a beeper and ask them to report their thoughts whenever it goes off (Hurlburt, 2001). The results show that we space out a lot (Ray & Faith, 1995; Gold et al., 1987). This is likely due to the fact that concentration is taxing and will eventually lead to mental exhaustion. Students studying for a difficult exam know this well; sooner or later they get to a point when they feel that their "head is full" and if one more crumb of information is added, the brain will explode. Thus, the periodic shifting of attention away from external events to a daydream scenario (Singer, 1978) could be seen as simply the inevitable result of the overwhelming demands placed on the attentional system to selectively process novel input. No matter how interesting a lecture is, if we listen long enough, we eventually enter the daydream zone, regardless of how great the resolve to stay attentive. Think of how many pages in this book you read only to realize that you did not process the content. Your eyes traced every word but your mind was somewhere else. It appears, then, that the brain needs some time to itself, time off from the merciless bombardment of the senses. Seen in this way, daydreaming is an altered state caused by the recurrent loss of attentional control rather than its deliberate redirection, as is the case in meditation or hypnosis. One interesting fact about daydreaming is that it decreases dramatically with age, suggesting that it might be necessary for normal, healthy brain development (Singer, 1975). Irrespective of this, it is clear that daydreaming is an integral part of conscious life (Singer & Pope, 1981).

While daydreaming, humans are capable of an astonishingly high level of cognitive processing. To return once more to our example of driving, you surely have little trouble relating to Lina the autopilot. Lina has a full day at work. She gets in her car and joins the rush-hour of people heading home. On her way, she reflects on her day, the meetings at work, the dry-cleaning she needs to pick up, and the upcoming dinner at home. Before long, her mind wanders off and eventually arrives at the tropical beach that – why not – also features Brad Pitt as lifeguard. Meanwhile, back in the real world of bumper-to-bumper traffic, she navigates complex traffic situations with ease. She pulls up into the driveway of her home only to realize that she has no conscious recollection of how she got home. But there she is. How can Lina drive while frolicking in her own private fantasy world? Doesn't that contradict the notion that daydreaming involves the loss of attentional power and toning down of sensory input?

Psychologists know well that attention is a serial process and humans cannot successfully perform two tasks if both require attention. The only way to do two things simultaneously is to automatize one of them so that we are not forced to allocate attentional resources to it. This is what happens when we drive and daydream (see also Box 10.1). After hours of practice, the act of driving becomes so routine that its control is transferred from circuits in the prefrontal cortex to the basal ganglia, which then execute the behavior in a set of pathways that cleanly bypasses consciousness. This frees computational space in working memory, which can be used to reload a favorite daydream scenario. Similar sophisticated but unconscious mental operations may occur in other ASC for the same reason, such as sleepwalking or certain memorization feats in hypnosis.

Given the putative view that the content of working memory is the content of consciousness, daydream events transpire in working memory and thus engage prefrontal areas. Yet, daydream phenomenology lacks many key features common to default consciousness that are associated with prefrontal activation, such as the ability to plan and execute concurrent subgoals while keeping in mind the main goal. Consider, for instance, the common blunder of driving straight past the dry-cleaner on the way home, despite the fact that you just reminded yourself to stop there. Anecdotal events such as this highlight the fact that daydreaming is the consequence of inescapable lapses in attentional control. The particular narrative of a daydream may contain a consistent threat but might just as likely disappear in favor of a new storyline. Lala-land is void of many other prefrontal-dependent mental processes, such as the deliberate search for cause-and-effect relationships or a sense for the passage of time.

The runner's high

If you are a LSD (long slow distance) runner this should be familiar to you. It's a beautiful Sunday morning and you are running along your favorite patch of asphalt. The day calls for a one-hour run and right around the 30-minute mark you settle into a comfortable rhythm. You feel remarkably relaxed, the little nagging aches in your knees seem to have evaporated, and you are overcome by a pleasant feeling of happiness. As you keep plugging along, you forget the fact that you are running altogether and experience a pervasive sensation of peace and inner strength. Life's little worries appear to you as just what they are, little, and before you know it, you pass the one-hour mark and feel invincible, perhaps even ecstatic.

The experience of an exercise-induced ASC is popularly known as the "runner's high." The term is a rather unfortunate descriptor for the changes in mental status that occur with extended, moderate exercise because it conjures up images of intense psychological experiences normally associated with drug abuse. It is perhaps this over-expectation that makes many doubt the existence of the runner's high. However, virtually all LSD exercisers can vouch for the fact that exercise has mind-altering properties, a sort of meditation in motion. At a moderate level, the experience has been described as a glow, a feeling of unity with yourself or nature, a sense of calm, timelessness, and boundless energy. Full blown, a rare occurrence requiring hours of continuous motion, the runner's high is not unlike a trance state with distorted perceptions, atypical thought patterns, diminished awareness of one's surroundings, and an intensified introspective understanding of one's sense of identity and emotional status. Ultra-distance runners have even reported full-blown hallucinations. Consider, for instance, the changed mental state of Vito Bialla, who, when running the 135-mile Badwater Ultramarathon, reported the following experience: "As I bend over to stretch, I look at the pavement and there are thousands of bats flapping their wings . . . During the night, plants and bushes turn into dinosaurs, snapping at me as I go by. I see pianos and furniture in the middle of the road."

As is the case with all phenomena related to consciousness and its alterations, the runner's high is a private experience, and the evidence for its existence rests predominantly on verbal reports. Scientific inquiry into the phenomenon has been restricted even further due to its ephemeral nature. Not all runners have the experience and it does not occur consistently in runners who have had it previously. Traditionally, the runner's high has been operationally defined as a "euphoric sensation experienced during running, usually unexpected, in which the runner feels a heightened sense of well being, enhanced appreciation of nature, and transcendence of barriers of time and space" (Pargman & Baker, 1980, p. 342). It is obvious that such a broad definition, in conjunction with the extensive use of esoteric language, does not qualify as an operational definition that can be used to derive testable hypotheses. If we use a more limited operational definition, one that is centered upon quantifiable behaviors such as analgesia, sedation, and anxiolysis, one could subject this ASC to empirical research.

So how can the simple act of running induce such a blissful experience? What happens in the brain as a result of putting one foot in front of another at a certain heart rate? The most popular but probably mistaken explanation involves the peptide neurotransmitter beta-endorphin. But there are a number of serious problems with the endorphin hypothesis and it has fallen out of favor (Dietrich & McDaniel, 2004). In recent years, prominent neuroscientists, including the co-discoverer of the opioid receptor Solomon Snyder and neuroscientist Huda Akil, have publicly criticized the hypothesis as being "overly simplistic," "poorly supported by scientific evidence," and a "myth perpetrated by pop culture" (Kolata, 2002).

Recent studies have brought to light a new, more promising candidate, the endocannabinoids. Activation of the endocannabinoid system causes intense subjective experiences – analgesia, relaxation, reduced anxiety, a state of silent introspection, a general feeling of well-being, the sense that time stands still – all of which are also reported by endurance athletes. Given these remarkable similarities, it was just a matter of time before scientists wondered whether the endocannabinoid system can be activated through exercise. And indeed, new research has shown exactly that (Sparling et al., 2003). This has led to the speculation that the exerciser's high might be a cannabinoid high. One should remain cautious, however, when describing exercise-induced changes in psychological functions as being a direct consequence of alterations in a single bodily system. It is more likely that an activity as elementary as motion involves changes in many different neurotransmitter systems.

In addition to explicating a neurochemical basis for the runner's high, the THH also contributes to a mechanistic explanation for the mental effects of exercise. It is well known that exercise profoundly increases neural activity in the brain's motor, sensory, and autonomic regions (Sokoloff, 1992; Vissing et al., 1996). Yet, contrary to popular conception, blood or oxygen supply to the brain does not increase during exercise (Ide & Secher, 2000). The THH, then, proposes the following. Large-scale bodily motion is computationally taxing, entailing massive and sustained brain activation. Since the brain operates on a finite metabolic budget, this enormous activation places a severe strain on the resources available for other information-processing tasks. It is really a zero-sum game, if fuel is limited, neural activity in one structure must come at the expense of others. Thus, the shift of resources to sensory, motor, and autonomic systems during exercise must cause a concomitant transient decrease in neural activity in structures that are not directly essential to the maintenance of the exercise. Put another way, the brain downregulates neural structures performing functions that an exercising individual can afford to disengage, such as the higher cognitive and emotional centers of the frontal lobe. This notion is simply a consequence of the fundamental principle that processing in the brain is competitive. The longer the exercise lasts, the more profound would be the resulting phenomenological subtraction (Dietrich, 2006). Several lines of evidence support the hypothesis and the effect is so striking that aerobic exercise should be regarded as a state of generalized brain activation with the specific exclusion of the executive system.

The disengagement of higher cognitive processes due to exercise can account for some of the phenomenological features of LSD running. Analgesia, the sense of timelessness, fleeting attention, and a feeling of disinhibition are all consistent with a state of prefrontal hypofunction. In consequence, one would predict that mental processes subserved by the prefrontal cortex, such as working memory and executive attention, should be selectively impaired during exercise. This has indeed been found (Dietrich & Sparling, 2004). The hypothesis of an exercise-induced state of transient frontal hypofunction also explains changes to the emotional content of consciousness. Anxiety, stress, and depression are all associated with hyperactivity in frontal regions (Baxter, 1990; Mayberg, 1997). During exercise this excessive neural activity can simply not be maintained and the brain must to run on safe mode the neural circuits responsible for computing these psychological states. The mental health benefits of exercise might simply be the phenomenological tax the brain has to pay for large-scale bodily motion (Dietrich, 2006).

Summary

We are curious about what it would be like to *feel* different. Perhaps this is the reason why drugs have always been part of human existence. At first sight, drug-induced ASC seem to defy classification. There are several classes of psychoactive drugs, each containing a host of structurally very different compounds working via separate mechanisms of action that involve all known neurotransmitter systems. And then there is this bewilderingly complex phenomenology. Siegel, however, discovered patterns in this diversity. He showed that the brain hallucinates in a very limited number of stable configurations – the four form constants – that give way to more intricate visions according to a number of rules. Colors also vary in an orderly fashion, depending on the type of drug and level of intoxication. All this suggests an underlying blueprint, a kind of universal hallucination code. What's more, all drug realities share common themes, such as the loss of time perception, the lack of cognitive flexibility, and the disintegration of the self-concept, which suggests that the one common neural mechanism underlying these altered states is the downregulation of the prefrontal cortex.

This chapter also covered the whole bonanza of nondrug alternities. These ASC come about through a variety of behavioral techniques that, given the resulting phenomenological changes, also seem to selectively disengage higher mental abilities subserved by the prefrontal cortex. In meditation, hypnosis, and daydreaming, we use our ability to control attentional resources to alter consciousness. By focusing on one item or event, we block all extraneous information from being processed consciously. This, in turn, permits prefrontal circuits to be run in "safe mode," which eliminates their computations from the content of consciousness. While in meditation and hypnosis attention is deliberately redirected, daydreaming accomplishes this feat by reducing attentional ability. In long-distance running, this single-mindedness is simply the result of need-based reallocation in metabolic resources. Prolonged, whole-body motion is costly in terms of the neural resources and the brain must shift resources away from structures that contribute higher content of consciousness. What makes each ASC so phenomenologically unique is that each induction technique or each drug likely targets a different set of prefrontal circuits, resulting in a distinct pattern of phenomenological subtractions.

Suggested reading

Austin, J. H. (1998). *Zen and the Brain: Towards an Understanding of Meditation and Consciousness*. Cambridge: MIT Press.

Goodman, L. S. et al. (eds.) (2000). *Goodman & Gilman's The Pharmacological Basis of Therapeutics* (9th ed.). Elmsford, NY: McGraw Hill.

Hobson, J. A. (2001). *The Dream Drugstore*. Cambridge, MA: MIT Press.

Siegel, R. K. (1992). *Fire in the Brain: Clinical Tales of Hallucination*. New York: Penguin.

Dietrich, A., & McDaniel, W. F. (2004). Cannabinoids and exercise. *British Journal of Sports Medicine*, 38, 50–7.

References

Adey, W. R., Bors, E., & Porter, R. W. (1968). EEG sleep patterns after high cervical lesions. *Archives of Neurology*, 19, 377–83.

Aleksander, I. (2000). *How to Build a Mind*. London: Weidenfeld & Nicolson.

Alkire, M. T., Haier, R. J., Fallon, J. H. (1998). Towards a neurobiology of consciousness: Using brain imaging and anesthesia to investigate the anatomy of consciousness. In S. R. Hameroff, A. W. Kaszniak, & A. C. Scott (eds.), *Towards a Science of Consciousness II: The Tucson Discussions and Debates* (pp. 255–68). Cambridge, MA: MIT Press.

Anderson, J. R. (1996). ACT: A simple theory of complex cognition. *American Psychologist*, 51, 355–65.

Aserinsky, E., & Kleitman, N. (1953). Regular occurrence of eye mobility and concomitant phenomena during sleep. *Science*, 118, 273–4.

Ashby, G. F., & Casale, M. B. (2002). The cognitive neuroscience of implicit category learning. In L. Jiménez (ed.), *Attention and Implicit Learning* (pp. 109–41). Amsterdam & Philadelphia: John Benjamins.

Ashby, F. G., & Shawn, E. W. (2001). The neurobiology of human category learning. *Trends in Cognitive Science*, 5, 204–10.

Atkinson, R. C., & Shiffrin, R. M. (1968). Human memory: A proposed system and its control processes. In K. W. Spence, & J. T. Spence (eds.), *The Psychology of Learning and Motivation*, Vol. 2 (pp. 89–195). New York: Academic Press.

Austin, J. H. (1998). *Zen and the Brain: Toward an Understanding of Meditation and Consciousness*. Cambridge, MA: MIT Press.

Axelrod, B. N., Jiron, C. C., & Henry, R. R. (1993). Performance of adults ages 20 to 90 on the abbreviated Wisconsin Cart Sorting Test. *Clinical Neuropsychology*, 7, 205–9.

Baars, B. J. (1988). *A Cognitive Theory of Consciousness*. Cambridge: Cambridge University Press.

Baars, B. (1997). *In the Theater of Consciousness: The Workspace of the Mind*. New York: Oxford University Press.

Baars, B. J. (2002). The conscious access hypothesis: Origins and recent evidence. *Trends in Cognitive Science*, 6, 47–52.

Baars, B. J. (2005). Subjective experience is probably not limited to humans: The evidence from neurobiology and behavior. *Consciousness and Cognition*, 14, 7–21.

Baddeley, A. (2000). The episodic buffer: a new component of working memory. *Trends in Cognitive Sciences*, 4, 417–23.

Banquent, J. P. (1972). EEG and meditation. *Electroencephalography and Clinical Neurophysiology*, 33, 454.

Barber, T. X. (1970). Who believes in hypnosis? *Psychology Today*, 4, 20–7.

Barbur, J. L., Watson, J. D. G., Frackowiak, R. S. J., & Zeki, S. (1993). Conscious visual perception without V1. *Brain*, 16, 1293–1302.

Baron-Cohen, S. (1995). *Mindblindness*. Cambridge, MA: MIT Press.

Baron-Cohen, S., & Harrison, J., eds. (1997). *Synaesthesia: Classic and Contemporary Readings*. Oxford: Blackwell.

Baxter, L. R. (1990). Brain imaging as a tool in establishing a theory of brain pathology in obsessive-compulsive disorder. *Journal of Clinical Psychiatry*, 51 (Suppl.), 22–5.

Bechara, A., Damasio, A. R., Damasio, H., & Anderson, S. (1994). Insensitivity to future consequences following damage to the human prefrontal cortex. *Cognition*, 50, 7–12.

Benson, H., Arns, P. A., & Hoffman, J. W. (1981). The relaxation response and hypnosis. *International Journal of Clinical and Experimental Hypnosis*, 29, 259–70.

Berns, G. S., & Sejnowski, T. (1996). How the basal ganglia makes decisions. In A. Damasio, & H. Damasio, & Y. Christen (eds.), *The Neurobiology of Decision Making* (pp. 101–13). Cambridge, MA: MIT Press.

Berti, A., & Rizzolatti, G. (1992). Visual processing without awareness: evidence from unilateral neglect. *Journal of Cognitive Neuroscience*, 4, 347–51.

Bierce, A. (1911/2000). *The Devil's Dictionary*. Escondido, CA: The Book Tree.

Bisiach, E. (1992). Understanding consciousness: clues from unilateral neglect and related disorders. In A. D. Milner & M. D. Rugg (eds.), *The Neuropsychology of Consciousness* (pp. 133–7). London: Academic Press.

Bisiach, E., & Luzzatti, C. (1978). Unilateral neglect of representational visual space. *Cortex*, 14, 129–33.

Blackmore, J. S. (1993). *Dying to Live: Science and the Near-Death Experience*. London: Grafton.

Blackmore, J. S. (1999). *The Meme Machine*. Oxford: Oxford University Press.

Blackmore, J. S. (2006). *Conversation on Consciousness*. New York: Oxford University Press.

Blakemore, S.-J., & Decety, J. (2001). From the perception of action to the understanding of intention. *Nature Reviews: Neuroscience*, 2, 561–7.

Blanke, O., Ortigue, S., Landis, T., & Seeck, M. (2002). Simulating illusory own-body perceptions. *Nature*, 18, 269–70.

Block, N. (1995). On a confusion about a function of consciousness. *Behavioural and Brain Sciences*, 18, 227–72.

Bogen, J. E. (1995a). On the neurophysiology of consciousness. I. An overview. *Consciousness and Cognition*, 4, 137–58.

Bogen, J. E. (1995b). Some historical aspects of callosotomy for epilepsy. In A. G. Reeves & D. W. Roberts (eds.), *Epilepsy and the Corpus Callosum* (pp. 107–22). New York: Plenum Press.

Bohm, D. (1980). *Wholeness and the Implicate Order*. London: Ark Paperbacks.

Boone, B. K. (1999). Neuropsychological assessment of executive functions. In B. L. Miller, & J. L. Cummings (eds.), *The Human Frontal Lobes: Functions and Disorders* (pp. 247–60). New York: The Guilford Press.

Bowersox, S. S., Kaitin, K. I., & Dement, W. C. (1985). EEG spindle activity as a function of age: Relationship to sleep continuity. *Brain Research*, 63, 526–39.

Braun, A. R., Balkin, T. J., Wesensten, N. J., Gwadry, F., Carson, R. E., Varga, M., Baldwin, P., Selbie, S., Belenky, G., & Herscovitch, P. (1997). Regional cerebral blood flow throughout the sleep-wake cycle. *Brain*, 120, 1173–97.

Brecht, B. (1939/1966). *Galileo*. New York: Grove Press.

Bressloff, P. C., Cowan, J. D., Golubitsky, M., Thomas, J. P., & Wiener, M. C. (2002). What geometric hallucinations tell us about the visual cortex. *Neural Computation*, 14, 473–91.

Bridgeman, B. (1991). Complementary cognitive and motor image processing. In G. Obrecht, & L. W. Stark (eds.), *Presbyopia Research: From Molecular Biology to Visual Adaptation* (pp. 189–98). New York: Plenum Press.

Bridgeman, B., Peery, S., & Anand, S. (1997). Interaction of cognitive and sensorimotor maps in visual space. *Perception and Psychophysics*, 59, 456–9.

Broadbent, D. A. (1958). *Perception and Communication*. New York: Pergamon.

Brooks, R. A. (2002). *Flesh and Machines*. New York: Pantheon.

Brown, R., & Kulik, J. (1977). Flushbulb memories. *Cognition*, 5, 73–99.

Cabeza, R., & Nyberg, L. (2000). Imaging Cognition II: An empirical review of 275 PET and fMRI studies. *Journal of Cognitive Neuroscience*, 12, 1–47.

Carlson, N. R. (2004). *Physiology and Behavior* (8th ed.). Boston: Allyn & Bacon.

Carrasco, M., Ling, S., & Read, S. (2004). Attention alters appearance. *Nature Neuroscience*, 7, 308–13.

Carrington, P. (1998). *The Book of Meditation: The Complete Guide to Modern Meditation* (revised ed.). New York: Element Books.

Carruthers, P. (2000). *Phenomenal Consciousness*. Cambridge: Cambridge University Press.

Carter, O. L., Presti, D. E., Callistemon, C., Ungerer, Y., Liu, G. B., & Pettigrew, J. D. (2005). Meditation alters perceptual rivalry in Tibetan Buddhist monks. *Current Biology*, 15, R412–13.

Carter, R. (2002). *Exploring Consciousness*. Los Angeles: University of California Press.

Castiello, U., Paulignan, Y., & Jeannerod, M. (1991). Temporal dissociation of motor responses and subjective awareness. *Brain*, 114, 2639–3655.

Chalmers, D. J. (1995a). Facing up to the problem of consciousness. *Journal of Consciousness Studies*, 3, 200–19.

Chalmers, D. J. (1995b). The puzzle of conscious experience. *Scientific American*, 273, 62–8.

Chalmers, D. J. (1996). *The Conscious Mind: In Search of a Fundamental Theory*. New York: Oxford University Press.

Cheesman, J., & Merikle, P. M. (1986). Distinguishing conscious from unconscious perceptual processes. *Canadian Journal of Psychology*, 40, 343–67.

Cherry, E. C. (1953). Some experiments on the recognition of speech, with one and two ears. *Journal of Acoustic Society American*, 25, 975–9.

Churchland, P. M. (1984). *Matter and Consciousness*. Cambridge, MA: MIT Press.

Churchland, P. M. (1996). The rediscovery of light. *Journal of Philosophy*, 93, 211–28.

Churchland, P. M., & Churchland, P. S. (1990). Could a machine think? *Scientific American*, 262, 32–9.

Churchland, P. S. (1981). On the alleged backwards referral of experiences and its relevance to the mind-body problem. *Philosophy of Science*, 48, 165–81.

Churchland, P. S. (1994). Can neurobiology teach us anything about consciousness? In H. Morowitz, & J. L. Singer (eds.), *The Mind, the Brain, and Complex Adaptive Systems* (pp. 99–121). Reading, MA: Addison-Wesley/Longman.

Churchland, P. S. (1996). The hornswoggle problem. *Journal of Consciousness Studies*, 3, 402–8.

Churchland, P. S. (2002). *Brain-Wise: Studies in Neurophilosophy*. Cambridge, MA: MIT Press.

Claparede, E. (1911/1951). Recognition and "me-ness". In D. Rapaport (ed.), *Organization and Pathology of Thought* (pp. 58–75). New York: Columbia University Press.

Cleeremans, A. (1997). Principles for implicit learning. In D. Berry (ed.), *How Implicit is Implicit Learning?* (pp. 195–234). Oxford: Oxford University Press.

Cleeremans, A., & Jiménez, L. (2002). Implic learning and consciousness: A graded, dynamic perspective. In R. M. French & A. Cleeremans (eds.), *Implicit Learning and Consciousness* (pp. 1–40). New York: Psychology Press.

Collins, A. M., & Loftus, E. F. (1975). A spreading activation theory of semantic processing. *Psychological Review*, 82, 407–28.

Connors, B. W., & Gutnick, M. J. (1990). Intrinsic firing patterns of diverse neurocortical neurons. *Trends in Neuroscience*, 13, 99–104.

Corballis, M. C. (1999). Phylogeny from apes to humans. In M. C. Corballis, & S. E. G. Lea (eds.), *Descent of Mind* (pp. 40–70). Oxford: Oxford University Press.

Corby, J. C., Roth, W. T., Zarcone, V. P., & Kopell, B. S. (1978). Psychophysiological correlates of the practice of Tantric Yoga meditation. *Archives of General Psychiatry*, 35, 571–7.

Cotterill, R. (1995). On the unity of conscious experience. *Journal of Consciousness Studies*, 2, 290–312.

Courtney, S. M., Petit, L., Haxby, J. V., & Ungerleider, L. G. (1998). The role of prefrontal cortex in working memory: examining on the contents of consciousness. *Philosophical Transactions of the Royal Society of London Series B-Biological Sciences*, 353, 1819–28.

Cowan, J. D. (1982). Spontaneous symmetry breaking in large scale nervous activity. *International Journal of Quantum Chemistry*, 22, 1059–82.

Cowan, N. (1995). *Attention and Memory: An Integrated Framework*. Oxford Psychology Series, No 26. New York: Oxford University Press.

Cowan, N. (2001). The magical number 4 in short-term memory: A reconsideration of mental storage capacity. *Behavioural and Brain Sciences*, 24, 87–185.

Craig, A. D. (2002). How do you feel? Interoception: the sense of the physiological condition of the body. *Nature Reviews Neuroscience*, 3, 655–66.

Crick, F. (1994). *The Astonishing Hypothesis*. New York: Scribner.

Crick, F., & Koch, C. (1990). Towards a neurobiological theory of consciousness. *Seminar in the Neurosciences*, 2, 263–75.

Crick, F., & Koch, C. (1995). Are we aware of neural activity in primary visual cortex? *Nature*, 375, 121–3.

Crick, F., & Koch, C. (1998). Consciousness and neuroscience. *Cerebral Cortex*, 8, 97–107.

Crick, F., & Koch, C. (2003). A framework for consciousness. *Nature Neuroscience*, 6, 119–26.

Critchley, H. D., Wiens, S., Rotshtein, P., Öhman, A., & Dolan, R. J. (2004). Neural systems supporting interoceptive awareness. *Nature Neuroscience*, 7, 189–95.

Csikszentmihalyi, M. (1996). *Creativity*. New York: Harper Perennial.

Cytowic, R. E. (1993). *The Man who Tasted Shapes*. New York: Putnam.

Damasio, A. R. (1994). *Descartes' Error: Emotion, Reason, and the Human Brain*. New York: G. P. Putnam.

Damasio, A. R. (1999). *The Feeling of What Happens: Body and Emotion in the Making of Consciousness*. New York: Harcourt Brace.

Davidson, R. J., & Irwin, W. (1999). The functional neuroanatomy of affective style. *Trends in Cognitive Science*, 3, 11–21.

Dawkins, R. (1989). *The Selfish Gene*. Oxford: Oxford University Press.

Deacon, T. W. (1990). Problems of ontogeny and phylogeny in brain-size evolution. *International Journal of Primatology*, 11, 237–82.

Dehaene, S., & Naccache, L. (2001). Towards a cognitive science of consciousness: basic evidence and a workspace framework. *Cognition*, 79, 1–37.

Dement, W. C. (1978). *Some Must Watch while Some Must Sleep*. New York: W. W. Norton.

Dennett, D. C. (1984). *Elbow Room: The Varieties of Free Will Worth Wanting*. Cambridge, MA: MIT Press.

Dennett, D. C. (1988). Quining qualia. In A. J. Marcel, & E. Bisiach (eds.), *Consciousness in Contemporary Science* (pp. 42–77). Oxford: Oxford University Press.

Dennett, D. C. (1991). *Consciousness Explained*. Boston: Little, Brown.

Dennett, D. C. (1994). Instead of qualia. In A. Revonsuo & M. Kampinnen (eds.), *Consciousness in Philosophy and Cognitive Neuroscience* (pp. 129–39). Hillsdale, NJ: Lawrence Erlbaum.

Dennett, D. C. (1995). *Darwins' Dangerous Idea*. New York: Simon & Schuster.

Dennett, D. C. (1996a). Facing backwards to the problem of consciousness. *Journal of Consciousness Studies*, 3, 4–6.

Dennett, D. C. (1996b). *Kinds of Minds: Towards an Understanding of Consciousness*. New York: Basic Books.

Dennett, D. C. (1998). *Brainchildren: Essays on Designing Minds*. New York: Bradford Books.

Dennett, D. C. (2001a). Are we explaining consciousness yet? *Cognition*, 79, 221–37.

Dennett, D. C. (2001b). The fantasy of the first-person science. Debate with D. Chalmers, Evanston, Ill: Northwestern University.http://ase.tufts.edu/cogstud/papers/chalmersdeb3dft.htm.

Dennett, D. C. (2003a). *Freedom Evolves*. New York: Penguin.

Dennett, D. C. (2003b). Who's on first? Heterophenomenology explained. *Journal of Consciousness Studies*, 10, 19–30.

Dennett D. C., & Kinsbourne, M. (1992). Time and the observer – the where and when of consciousness in the brain. *Behavioural and Brain Sciences*, 15, 183–201.

Desimone, R., & Duncan, J. (1995). Neural mechanisms of selective attention. *Annual Review of Neuroscience*, 18, 193–222.

Diaz, J. (1997). *How Drugs Influence Behavior: A Neurobehavioral Approach*. Upper Saddle River, NJ: Prentice Hall.

Dienes, Z., & Perner, J. (1999). A theory of implicit and explicit knowledge. *Behavioural and Brain Sciences*, 5, 735–808.

Dienes, Z., & Perner, J. (2002). A theory of the implicit nature of implicit learning. In R. M. French, & A. Cleeremans (eds.), *Implicit Learning and Consciousness* (pp. 68–92). New York: Psychology Press.

Dietrich, A. (2003). Functional neuroanatomy of altered states of consciousness. The transient hypofrontality hypothesis. *Consciousness and Cognition*, 12, 231–56.

Dietrich, A. (2004a). Neurocognitive mechanisms underlying the experience of flow. *Consciousness and Cognition*, 13, 746–61.

Dietrich, A. (2004b). The cognitive neuroscience of creativity. *Psychonomic Bulletin & Review*, 11, 1011–26.

Dietrich, A. (2006). Transient hypofrontality as a mechanism for the psychological effects of exercise. *Psychiatry Research*, 145, 79–83.

Dietrich, A., & McDaniel, W. F. (2004). Cannabinoids and exercise. *British Journal of Sports Medicine*, 38, 50–7.

Dietrich, A., & Sparling, P. B. (2004). Endurance exercise selectively impairs prefrontal-dependent cognition. *Brain and Cognition*, 55, 516–24.

Dietrich, A., Taylor, J. T., & Passmore, C. E. (2001). AVP (4–8) improves concept learning in PFC-damaged but not hippocampal-damaged rats. *Brain Research*, 919, 41–7.

Dulany, D. E. (1996). Consciousness in the explicit (deliberative) and implicit (evocative). In J. D. Cohen, & J. W. Schooler (eds.), *Scientific Approaches to the Study of Consciousness* (pp. 179–212). Hillsdale, NJ: Lawrence Erlbaum.

Dunbar, R. I. M. (1992). Neocortex size as a constraint on group size in primates. *Journal of Human Evolution*, 20, 469–93.

Dunbar, R. I. M. (1996). *Grooming, Gossip, and the Evolution of Language*. Cambridge, MA: Harvard University Press.

Eccles, J. C. (1994). *How the Self Controls its Brain*. Berlin: Springer Verlag.

Edelman, G. M. (1993). Neural Darwinism: selection and reentrant signaling in higher brain function. *Neuron*, 10, 115–25.

Edelman, G. M., & Tononi, G. (2000). *A Universe of Consciousness*. New York: Basic Books.

Elbert, T., Pantev, C., Wienbruch, C., Rockstroh, B., & Taub., E. (1995). Increased cortical representation of the fingers of the left hand in string players. *Science*, 270, 305–307.

Empson, J. (2001). *Sleep and Dreaming* (3rd ed.). New York: Palgrave Macmillan.

Farthing. G. W. (1992). *The Psychology of Consciousness*. Englewood Cliffs, NJ: Prentice Hall.

Feinberg, T. E., Schindler, R. J., Flanagan, N. G., & Haber, L. D. (1992). Two alien hand syndromes. *Neurology*, 42, 19–24.

Feynman, R. P. (1985). *Surely You're Joking, Mr. Feynman!* New York: Bantam Books.

Ffytche, D. H. (2000). Imaging conscious vision. In T. Metzinger (ed.), *Neural Correlates of Consciousness* (pp. 221–30). Cambridge, MA: MIT Press.

Fisher, C., Byrne, J., Edwards, A., & Kahn, E. (1970). A psychophysiological study of nightmares. *Journal of the American Psychoanalytic Association*, 18, 747–82.

Flanagan, O. (1992). *Consciousness Reconsidered*. Cambridge, MA: MIT Press.

Flohr, H. (2000). NMDA receptor-mediated computational processes and phenomenal consciousness. In T. Metzinger (ed.), *Neural Correlates of Consciousness* (pp. 246–58). Cambridge, MA: MIT Press.

Fodor, J. A. (1975). Special sciences, or the disunity of science as a working hypothesis. *Synthese*, 28, 97–115.

Frankland, P. W., Josselyn, S. A., Bradwejn, J., Vaccarino, F. J., & Yeomans, J. S. (1997). Activation of amygdala cholecystokinin$_B$ receptors potentiates the acoustic startle response in the rat. *Journal of Neuroscience*, 17, 1838–47.

Freeman, W. J. (2000). Perception of time and causation through the kinesthesia of intentional action. *Cognitive Processing*, 1, 18–34.

Frensch, P. A., Haider, H., Rünger, D., Neugebauer, U., Voigt, S., & Werg, J. (2002). Verbal report of incidentally experienced environmental regularity: The route from implicit learning to verbal expression of what has been learned. In L. Jiménez (ed.), *Attention and Implicit Learning* (pp. 335–6). Amsterdam & Philadelphia: John Benjamins.

Frith, C. D. (1992). *The Cognitive Neuropsychology of Schizophrenia*. Hove: Lawrence Erlbaum.

Frith, C. D., & Dolan, R. (1996). The role of the prefrontal cortex in higher cognitive functions. *Cognitive Brain Research*, 5, 175–81.

Frith, C. D., & Frith, U. (2001). Cognitive Psychology – Interacting minds – A biological basis. *Science*, 286, 1692–5.

Frith, C. D., Perry, R., & Lumer, E. (1999). The neural correlates of conscious experience. *Trends in Cognitive Science*, 3, 105–14.

Fuster, J. M. (1995). Temporal processing – Structure and function of the human prefrontal cortex. *Annals of the New York Academy of Sciences*, 769, 173–81.

Fuster, J. M. (2000). Executive frontal functions. *Experimental Brain Research*, 133, 66–70.

Gallup, G. G. (1970). Chimpanzees: self-recognition, *Science*, 167, 86–7.

Gazzaniga, M. S. (1992). *Nature's Mind*. New York: Basic Books.

Gazzaniga, S. M., Ivry, R. B., & Mangun, G. R. (1998). *Cognitive Neuroscience: The Biology of the Mind* (2nd ed.). New York: W. W. Norton.

Gazzaniga, M. S., & LeDoux, J. E. (1978). *The Integrated Mind*. New York: Plenum Press.

Geldard, F. A., & Sherrick, C. E. (1972). The cutaneous "rabbit": A perceptual illusion. *Science*, 178, 178–9.

Gennaro, R. J. (1996). Consciousness and self-consciousness: A defense of the higher-order-thought theory of consciousness. In R. J. Gennaro, & C. Hueneman (eds.), *Advances in Consciousness Research* (pp. 333–47). Amsterdam: John Benjamins.

Georgopoulus, A. P. (1995). Motor cortex and cognitive processing. In M. S. Gazzaniga (ed.), *The Cognitive Neurosciences* (pp. 507–17). Cambridge: MA: MIT Press.

Giacino, J. T. (2005). The minimally conscious state: defining the borders of consciousness. *Progress in Brain Research*, 150, 381–95.

Gilbert, P. F. C. (2001). An outline of brain function. *Cognitive Brain Research*, 12, 61–74.

Gold, S. R., Gold, R. G., & Milner, J. S. (1987). Daydreaming and mental health. *Imagination Cognition and Personality*, 6, 67–73.

Goldman-Rakic, P. S. (1992). Working memory and the mind. *Scientific American*, 267, 111–117.

Gould, S. J. (1997). Evolution: The pleasures of pluralism. *New York Times Review of Books*, 44, 47–52.

Gray, C. M., König, P., Engel, A. K., & Singer, W. (1989). Oscillatory responses in cat visual cortex exhibit inter-columnar synchronization which reflects global stimulus properties. *Nature*, 228, 334–7.

Graziano, M. (2002). Complex movements evoked by microstimulation of precentral cortex. *Neuron*, 34, 841–51.

Grimes, J. (1996). On the failure to detect changes in scenes across saccades. In K. Akins (ed.), *Perception: Vancouver Studies in Cognitive Science* (pp. 89–110). Oxford: Oxford University Press.

Gruzelier, J. H. (2000). Redefining hypnosis: theory, methods and integration. *Contemporary Hypnosis*, 17, 51–70.

Gush, R. (1997). The architecture of representation. *Philosophical Psychology*, 10, 5–23.

Gush, R., & Churchland, P. S. (1995). Gaps in Penrose's toilings. *Journal of Consciousness Studies*, 2, 10–29.

Güzeldere, G. (1997). The many faces of consciousness: a field guide. In N. Block, O. Flanagan, & G. Güzeldere (eds.), *The Nature of Consciousness: Philosophical Debates* (pp. 1–67). Cambridge, MA: MIT Press.

Haggard, P., Newman, C., & Magno, E. (1999). On the perceived time of voluntary action. *British Journal of Psychology*, 90, 291–303.

Hall, C., & van de Castle, R. L. (1966). *The Content Analysis of Dreams*. Meredith Publishing.

Hameroff, S. R., & Penrose, R. (1996). Conscious events as orchestrated space-time selections. *Journal of Consciousness Studies*, 3, 36–53.

Hardcastle, V. G. (1996). The why of consciousness: A non-issue for materialists. *Journal of Consciousness Studies*, 3, 7–13.

Hardcastle, V. G. (1999). *The Myth of Pain*. Cambridge, MA: MIT Press.

Harlow, J. M. (1868). Recovery from the passage of an iron bar through the head. *Bulletin of the Massachusetts Medical Society*, 2, 3–20.

Harnad, S. (1990). The symbol grounding problem. *Physica*, *D42*, 335–46.

Hartman, E. (1966). The psychophysiology of free will: an example of vertical research. In R. Lowenstein, L. Newman, M. Schur, & A. Solnit (eds.), *Psychoanalysis: A General Psychology* (pp. 521–36). New York: International University Press.

Haugeland, J. (1985). *Artificial Intelligence: The Very Idea*. Cambridge, MA: MIT Press.

Hearne, K. (1990). *The Dream Machine: Lucid Dreams and How to Control Them*. Wellingborough, Aquarian.

Hebb, D. O. (1939). Intelligence in man after large removal of cerebral tissue: report of four left frontal lobe cases. *Journal of General Psychology*, 21, 73–87.

Hebb, D. O. (1958). *Textbook of Psychology*. New York: Saunders.

Heywood, C. A., & Kentridge, R. W. (2000). Affective blindsight? *Trends in Cognitive Science*, 4, 125–6.

Hilgard, E. R. (1980). Consciousness in contemporary psychology. *Annual Review of Psychology*, 31, 1–26.

Hippocrates (1952). On the sacred disease. In *Hippocrates and Galen: Great Books of the Western World, Vol 10*. Chicago: William Benton.

Hobson, J. A. (1988). *The Dreaming Brain*. New York: Basic Books.

Hobson, J. A. (2001). *The Dream Drugstore*. Cambridge, MA: MIT Press.

Hobson, J. A., & McCarley, R. (1977). The brain as a dream-state generator: An activation-synthesis hypothesis of the dream process. *American Journal of Psychiatry*, 134, 1335–48.

Hobson, J. A., Pace-Schott, E. F., & Stickhold, R. (2000). Dreaming and the brain: Toward a cognitive neuroscience of conscious states. *Behavioural and Brain Sciences*, 23, 793–866.

Hofstadter, D. R. (1979). *Gödel, Escher, Bach*. London: Penguin.

Hofstadter, D. R., & Dennett, D. C. (1981 Eds). *The Mind's I: Fantasies and Reflections on Self and Soul*. London: Penguin.

Hubel, D. H., & Wiesel, T. N. (1977). Functional architecture of macaque monkey visual cortex. *Proceedings of the Royal Society of London*, B, 198, 1–59.

Hubel, D. H., & Wiesel, T. N. (1979). Brain mechanisms of vision. *Scientific American*, 241, 150–62.

Hughlings-Jackson, J. (1889). On a particular variety of epilepsy "intellectual aura", one case with symptoms of organic brain disease. *Brain*, 11, 179–207.

Hume, D. (1739/1888). *A Treatise of Human Nature*. London: Oxford University Press.

Humphrey, N. (1978). Nature Psychologists. *New Scientist*, June 29, 900–3.

Humphrey, N. (2002). *The Mind Made Flesh: Frontiers of Psychology and Evolution*. Oxford, Oxford University Press.

Hunt, M. (1993). *The Story of Psychology*. New York: Anchor Books.

Hunt, R. R., & Ellis, H. C. (1998). *Fundamentals of Cognitve Psychology* (6th ed.). New York: McGraw Hill.

Hurlbert, R. (2001). Telling what we know: Describing inner experience. *Trends in Cognitive Science*, 5, 400–3.

Huxley, T. H. (1910). *Methods and Results*. New York: Appleton.

Iacoboni, M., Woods, R. P., Brass, M., Bekkering, H., Mazziotta, J. C., & Rizzolatti, G. (1999). Cortical mechanisms of human imitation. *Science*, 286, 2526–8.

Ide, K., & Secher, N. H. (2000). Cerebral blood flow and metabolism during exercise. *Progress in Neurobiology*, 61, 397–414.

Jackendoff, R. (1987). *Consciousness and the Computational Mind*. Cambridge, MA: MIT Press.

Jackson, F. (1982). Epiphenomenal qualia. *Philosophical Quarterly*, 32, 127–36.

Jacobson, C. F., Wolf, J. B., & Jackson, T. A. (1935). An experimental analysis of the function of the frontal association areas in primates. *Journal of Nervous and Mental Disease*, 82, 1–14.

James, W. (1884). What is an emotion? *Mind*, 9, 188–205.

James, W. (1890). *Principles of Psychology*. New York: Holt.

James, W. (1892/1961). *Psychology: The Briefer Course*. New York: Harper.

Jenkins, I. H., Brooks, D. J., Nixon, P. D., Frackowiak, R. S. J., & Passingham, R. E. (1994). Motor sequence learning: A study with positron emission tomography. *Journal of Neuroscience*, 14, 3775–90.

Jevning, R., Wallace, R. K., & Beidebach, M. (1992). The physiology of meditation: a review. A wakeful hypometabolic integrated response. *Neuroscience and Biobehavioral Reviews*, 16, 415–24.

Johanson, A., Gustafson, L., Passant, U., Risberg, J., Smith, G., Warkentin, S., & Tucker, D. (1998). Brain function in spider phobia. *Psychiatry Research: Neuroimaging Section*, 84, 101–111.

Kaas, J. (1995). The reorganization of sensory and motor maps in adult mammals. In M. S. Gazzaniga (ed.), *The Cognitive Neurosciences* (pp. 51–71). Cambridge: MA: MIT Press.

Kallio, A., Revonsuo, A., Hämäläinen, H., Markela, J., & Gruzelier, J. (2001). Anterior brain functions and hypnosis: A test of the frontal hypothesis. *International Journal of Clinical and Experimental Hypnosis*, 49, 95–108.

Kanwisher, T. (2000). Domain specificity in face perception. *Nature Neuroscience*, 3, 759–63.

Karmiloff-Smith, A. (1992). *Beyond Modularity: A Developmental Perspective on Cognitive Science*. Cambridge, MA: MIT Press.

Kiehl, K. A., Smith, A. M., & Hare, R. D. (2001). Limbic abnormalities in affective processing by criminal psychopaths by functional magnetic resonance imaging. *Biological Psychiatry*, 50, 677–84.

Kihlstrom, J. F. (1985). Hypnosis. *Annual Review of Psychology*, 36, 385–418.

Kihlstrom, J. F. (1996). Perception without awareness of what is perceived, learning without awareness of what is learned. In M. Velmans (ed.), *The Science of Consciousness: Psychological, Neuropsychological and Clinical Reviews* (pp. 23–46). London: Routledge.

Kihlstrom, J. F. (1999). The psychological unconscious. In L. R. Pervin, & O. John (eds.), *Handbook of Personality* (2nd ed.) (pp. 424–42). New York: Guilford.

Kirsch, I., & Lynn, S. J. (1998). Social-cognitive alternatives to dissociation theories of hypnotic involuntariness. *Review of General Psychology*, 2, 66–80.

Klüver, H. (1926). Mescal visions and eidetic vision. *American Journal of Psychology*, 37, 502–15.

Kolata, G. (2002). Runners high? Endorphins? Fiction say some scientists. *The New York Times*, May 21, p. D1.

Kolers, P. A., & von Grünau, M. (1976). Shape and color of apparent motion. *Vision Research*, 16, 329–35.

Konishi, S., Nakajima, K., Uchida, I., Kameyama, M., Nakahara, K., Sekihara, K., & Miyashita, Y. (1998). Transient activation of the inferior prefrontal cortex during cognitive set shifting. *Nature Neuroscience*, 1, 80–4.

Kornhuber, H., & Deeke, L. (1965). Hirnpotentialänderungen bei Willkürbewegungen und passiven Bewegungen des Menschen: Bereitschaftspotential und reafferente Potentiale. *Plügers Archiv*, 284, 1–17.

LaBerge, S. (1985). *Lucid dreaming*. Los Angeles: Jeremy P. Tarcher.

Lamme, V. A. F. (2003). Why visual attention and awareness are different. *Trends in Cognitive Science*, 7, 12–18.

Lange, C. G. (1887). *Über Gemütsbewegungen*. Leipzig: T. Thomas.

Latto, R. (1985). Comentary on Unconscious cerebral initiative and the role of conscious will in voluntary action. *Behavioural and Brain Sciences*, 8, 544–5.

LeDoux, J. (1996). *The Emotional Brain*. New York: Touchstone

Leiguardia, R., Starkstein, S., Nogues, M., Berthier, M., & Arbelaiz, R. (1993). Paroxymal alien hand syndrome. *Annals of Neurology*, 32, 749–57.

Leopold, D. A., & Logothetis, N. K. (1999). Multistable phenomena: changing views in perception. *Trends in Cognitive Science*, 3, 254–64.

Levine, J. (1983). Materialism and qualia: The explanatory gap. *Pacific Philosophical Quarterly*, 64, 354–61.

Lhermitte, F. (1983). "Utilization behaviour" and its relation to lesions of the frontal lobes. *Brain*, 106, 237–55.

Lhermitte, F., Pillon, B., & Serdaru, M. (1986). Human autonomy and the frontal lobes. Part I: Imitation and utilization behavior: A neuropsychological study of 75 patients. *Annals of Neurology*, 19, 326–34.

Libet, B. (1982). Brain stimulation in the study of neuronal function for conscious sensory experiences. *Human Neurobiology*, 1, 235–42.

Libet, B. (1985). Unconscious cerebral inititative and the role of conscious will in voluntary action. *Behavioural and Brain Sciences*, 8, 529–39.

Libet, B. (1999). Do we have free will? *Journal of Consciousness Studies*, 6, 47–55.

Libet, B., Gleason, C. A., Wright, E. W., & Perl, D. K. (1983). Time of conscious intention to act in relation to onset of cerebral activity (readiness potential): the unconscious initiation of a freely voluntary act. *Brain*, 106, 623–42.

Libet, B., Wright, E. W., Feinstein, B., & Perl, D. K. (1979). Subjective referal of the timing for a conscious sensory experience: a functional role of the somatosensory specific projections in man. *Brain*, 102, 191–222.

Llinás, R. R. (2001). *I of the Vortex*. Cambridge, MA: MIT Press.

Llinás, R. R. & Paré, D. (1991). Of dreaming and wakefulness. *Neuroscience*, 44, 521–35.

Loftus, E. F., & Palmer, J. C. (1974). Reconstruction of automobile destruction: An example of the interaction between language and memory. *Journal of Verbal Learning and Verbal Behavior*, 13, 585–9.

Lumer, E. D., Friston, K. J., & Rees, G. (1998). Neural correlates of perceptual rivalry in the human brain. *Science*, 280, 1930–4.

Luria, A. R. (1968). *The Mind of a Mnemonist: A Little Book about a Vast Memory.* Chicago: Henry Regency.

Mack, A., & Rock, I. (1998). *Inattentional Blindness.* Cambridge, MA: MIT Press.

MacLean, P. D. (1949). Psychosomatic disease and the "visceral brain": Recent developments bearing on the Papez theory of emotions. *Psychosomatic Medicine*, 11, 338–53.

Malenka, R. (1986). Central error-correcting behavior in schizophrenia and depression. *Biological Psychiatry*, 21, 263–73.

Maquet, P., Faymonville, M. E., Degueldre, C., Delfiore, G., Frank, G., Luxen, A., & Lamy, M. (1999). Functional neuroanatomy of hypnotic state. *Biological Psychiatry*, 45, 327–33.

Marshall, J. C., & Halligan, P. W. (1991). Blindsight and insight in visuo-spatial neglect. *Nature*, 336, 766–7.

Marshall, J. C., Halligan, P. W., & Robertson, I. H. (1993). Contemporary theories of unilateral neglect: a critical review. In I. H. Robertson, & J. C. Marshall (eds.), *Unilateral Neglect: Clinical and Experimental Studies* (pp. 311–29). Hove: Lawrence Erlbaum.

Maslow, A. H. (1959). Cognition of being in the peak experiences. *Journal of Genetic Psychology*, 94, 43–66.

Mayberg, H. S. (1997). Limbic-cortical dysregulation: A proposed model of depression. *Journal of Neuropsychiatry and Clinical Neuroscience*, 9, 471–81.

McClelland, J. L. (1995). Constructive memory and memory distortions: A parallel-distributed processing approach. In D. L. Schacter (ed.), *Memory Distortion: How Minds, Brains, and Societies Reconstruct the Past* (pp. 71–89). Cambridge, MA: Havard University Press.

McConkie, G. W., & Zola, D. (1979). Is visual information integrated across successive fixations in reading. *Perception and Psychophysics*, 25, 221–4.

McGaugh, J. J. (2002). In R. M. Restak (ed.), *The Secret Life of the Brain.* New York: Public Broadcasting Service.

McGinn, C. (1999). *The Mysterious Flame. Conscious Minds in a Material World.* New York: Basic Books.

McLeod, P., Reed, N., & Dienes, Z. (2001). Towards a unified fielder theory: What we do not yet know about how people run to catch a ball. *Journal of Experimental Psychology: Human Perception and Performance*, 6, 1347–55.

Means, L. W., & Holstein, R. D. (1992). Individual aged rats are impaired on repeated reversals due to loss of different behavioral-patterns. *Physiology and Behavior*, 52, 959–63.

Melzack, R. (1992). Phantom Limbs. *Scientific American*, 266, 120–6.

Melzack, R., & Wall, P. (1965). Pain mechanisms: A new theory. *Science*, 150, 971–9.

Merikle, P. M. (2000). Subliminal perception. In A. E. Kazdin (ed.), *Encyclopedia of Psychology* (pp. 497–9). New York: Oxford University Press.

Merzenich, M., & Jenkins, W. M. (1995). Cortical plasticity: Learning and learning dysfunction. In B. Julesz, & I. Kovacs (eds.), *Maturational Window and Adult Cortical Plasticity* (pp. 1–24). Reading: Addison-Wesley.

Metzinger, T. (2000 ed.). *Neural Correlates of Consciousness*. Cambridge, MA: MIT Press.

Metzinger, T. (2003). *Being No One: The Self Model-Theory of Subjectivity*. Cambridge, MA: MIT Press.

Miller, E. K., & Cohen, J. D. (2001). An integrative theory of prefrontal cortex function. *Annual Review of Neuroscience*, 24, 167–202.

Miller, G. A. (1956). The magical number seven, plus or minus two: Some limits on our capacity off processing information. *Psychological Review*, 63, 81–97.

Milner, B. (1970). Memory and the medial temporal lobe region. In K. H. Pribram, & D. E. Broadbent (eds.), *Biology of Memory* (p. 29). New York: Academic Press.

Milner, B., Corkin, S., & Teuber, H. (1968). Further analysis of the hippocampal syndrome: 14-year follow up study of HM. *Neuropsychologia*, 6, 215–34.

Milner, J., & Goodale, M. A. (1995). *The Visual Brain in Action*. Oxford: Oxford University Press.

Minsky, M. (1986). *Society of Mind*. New York: Simon & Schuster.

Mishkin, M., Malamut, B., & Bachevalier, J. (1984). Memory and Habit: Two neural systems. In G. Lynch, J. J. McGaugh, & N. M. Weinberger (eds.), *Neurobiology of Learning and Memory* (pp. 66–77). New York: Guilford Press.

Monchi, O., Petrides, M., Petre, V., Worsley, K., & Dagher, A. (2001). Wisconsin card sorting revisited: Distinct neural circuits participating in different stages of the task identified by event-related functional magnetic resonance imaging. *Journal of Neuroscience*, 21, 7733–41.

Moody, R. A. (1975). *Life after Life*. Altanta: Mockingbrid.

Mukhametov, L. M. (1984). Sleep in marine mammals. In A. A. Borbély, & J. L.Valatx (eds.), *Sleep Mechanisms*. München: Springer Verlag.

Nadel, L., & Zola-Morgan, S. (1984). Infantile amnesia: A neurobiological perspective. In M. Moscovitch (ed.), *Infant Memory* (pp. 145–72). New York: Plenum Press.

Nagel, T. (1974). What is it like to be a bat? *Philosophical Review*, 83, 435–51.

Nagel, T. (1986). *The View from Nowhere*. New York: Oxford University Press.

Neisser, U., & Harsch, N. (1992). Phantom flashbulbs: False recollections of hearing the news about Challenger. In E. Winograd, & U. Neisser (eds.), *Affect and Accuracy in Recall: Studies of "Flashbulb" Memories* (pp. 9–31). New York: Cambridge University Press.

Newberg, A. B., Alavi, A., Baime, M., Pourdehnad, M., Santanna, J., & d'Aquili, E. G. (2001). The measurement of regional cerebral blood flow during the cognitive task of meditation: a preliminary SECT study. *Psychiatry Research Neuroimaging Section*, 106, 113–22.

Newell, A., & Simon, H. A. (1972). *Human Problem Solving*. Englewood Cliffs, NJ: Prentice Hall.

Nicolelis, M. A. L. (2003). Brain-machine interfaces to restore motor function and probe neural circuits. *Nature Reviews Neuroscience*, 4, 417–22.

Nofzinger, E. A., Mintun, M. A., Wiseman, M. B., Kupfer, D. J., & Moore, R. Y. (1997). Forebrain activation in REM sleep: A FDG PET study. *Brain Research*, 770, 192–201.

Norman, D. A., & Shallice, T. (1986). Attention to action: Willed and automatic control of behavior. In R. S. Davidson, G. E. Schwartz, & D. Shapiro (eds.), *Consciousness and Self-Regulation* (pp. 1–18). New York: Plenum Press.

Ogden, J. A., & Corkin, S. (1991). Memories of HM. In W. C. Abraham, M. Corbalis, & K. G. White (eds.), *Memory Mechanisms: A Tribute to G. V. Goddard* (p. 195). Hillsdale, NJ: Erlbaum.

O'Reagan, J. K. (1992). Solving the "real" mysteries of visual perception: the world as an outside memory. *Canadian Journal of Psychology*, 46, 461–88.

O'Reagan, J. K., & Noë, A. (2001). A sensorymotor account of vision and visual consciousness. *Behavioural and Brain Sciences*, 24, 883–917.

O'Reagan, J. K., Rensink, R. A., & Clark, J. J. (1999). Change-blindness as a result of "mudsplashes." *Nature*, 298, 34.

Ornstein, R. E. (1986). *The Psychology of Consciousness* (3rd ed.). New York: Penguin.

Ornstein, R. E. (1991). *The Evolution of Consciousness*. New York: Simon & Schuster.

Palmer, S. E. (1999). Color, consciousness, and the isomorphism constraint. *Behavioural and Brain Sciences*, 22, 923–43.

Papez, J. W. (1937). A proposed mechanism of emotion. *Archives of Neurology and Psychiatry*, 38, 725–44.

Parfit, D. (1987). Divided minds and the nature of persons. In C. Blackmore, & S. Greenfield (eds.), *Mindwaves* (pp. 19–26). Oxford: Blackwell.

Pargman, D., & Baker, M. (1980). Running High: Enkephalin indicted. *Journal of Drug Issues*, 10, 341–9.

Parnia, S., Waller, D. G., Yeates, R., & Fenwick, P. (2001). A quantitative study of the incidence, features, and aetiology of near death experiences in cardiac arrest survivors. *Resuscitation*, 48, 149–56.

Pascual-Leone, A., & Walsh, V. (2001). Fast back projections from the motion to the primary visual area necessary for visual awareness. *Science*, 292, 510–12.

Penfield, W. (1955). The role of the temporal cortex in certain psychical phenomena. *Journal of Mental Science*, 101, 451–5.

Penfield, W. (1975). *Mysteries of the Mind: A Critical Study of Consciousness and the Human Brain*. Princeton, NJ: Princeton University Press.

Penfield, W., & Jasper, H. (1954). *Epilepsy and the Functional Anatomy of the Human Brain*. Boston: Little, Brown.

Penrose, R. (1989). *The Emperor's New Mind*. London: Vintage.

Penrose, R. (1994). *Shadows of the Mind*. Oxford: Oxford University Press.

Persinger, M. (1999). *Neuropsychological Basis of God Beliefs*. New York: Praeger.

Pezdek, K. (2003). Event memory and autobiographical memory for the events of September 11, 2001. *Applied Cognitive Psychology*, 17, 1033–45.

Pillemer, D. B. (1984). Flashbulb memories of the assassination attempt on President Reagan. *Cognition*, 16, 63–80.

Pinker, S. (1999). *How the Mind Works*. New York: W. W. Norton.

Poldrack, R. A., & Packard, M. G. (2003). Competition among multiple memory systems: converging evidence from animal and human brain studies. *Neuropsychologia*, 41, 245–51.

Popper, K. R., & Eccles, C. (1977). *The Self and its Brain*. New York: Springer.

Posner, M. (1994). Attention: The mechanism of consciousness. *Proceedings of the National Academy of Sciences*, 91, 7398–403.

Povinelli, D. J., & de Bois, S. (1992). Young children's (Homo sapiens) understanding of knowledge formation in themsleves and others. *Journal of Comparative Psychology*, 106, 214–24.

Povinelli, D. J., & Eddy, T. J. (1996). Chimpanzees: Joint visual attention. *Psychological Science*, 7, 129–35.

Povinelli, D. J., & Preuss, T. M. (1995). Theory of mind: evolutionary history of a cognitive specialization. *Trends in Neuroscience*, 18, 418–24.

Premack, D., & Woodruff, G. (1978). Does the chimpanzee have a theory of mind? *Behavioural and Brain Sciences*, 4, 515–26.

Pribram, K. H. (1985). Holism could close the cognition era. *APA Monitor*, 16, 5–6.

Putnam, H. (1960). Mind and machines. In S. Hook (ed.), *Dimensions of the Mind* (pp. 138–64). New York: Collier.

Quintana, J., & Fuster, J. M. (1993). Spatial and temporal factors in the role of prefrontal and parietal cortex in visuomotor integration. *Cerebral Cortex*, 3, 122–32.

Rainville, P., Hofbauer, R. K., Paus, T., Duncan, G. H., Bushnell, M. C., & Price, D. D. (1999). Cerebral mechanisms of hypnotic induction and suggestion. *Journal of Cognitive Neuroscience*, 11, 110–125.

Ramachandran, V. S. (1992). Blind spots. *Scientific American*, 266, 86–91.

Ramachandran, V. S. (1993). Behavioral and magnetoencephalographic correlates of plasticity in the adult human brain. *Proceedings of the National Academy of Sciences USA*, 90, 10413–20.

Ramachandran, V. S. (2000). Mirror neurons. Retrieved from: http://www.edge.org/3rd_culture/ramachandran/ramachandran_p1.html

Ramachandran, V. S., & Blakeslee, S. (1998). *Phantoms in the Brain: Probing the Mysteries of the Human Mind*. New York: Morrow.

Ramachandran, V. S., & Hubbard, E. M. (2001). Synaesthesia – a window into perception, thought, and language. *Journal of Consciousness Studies*, 8, 3–34.

Ravizza, K. (1977). Peak performances in sports. *Journal of Humanistic Psychology*, 4, 35–40.

Ray, W. J., & Faith, M. (1995). Dissociate experiences in a college age population: Follow-up with 1190 subjects. *Personality and Individual Differences*, 18, 223–30.

Reber, A. S. (1993). *Implicit Learning and Tacit Knowledge*. Oxford: Oxford University Press.

Rechtschaffen, A. (1978). The single-mindedness and isolation of dreams. *Sleep*, 1, 97–109.

Rensink, R. A., O'Reagan, J. K., & Clark, J. J. (1997). To see or not to see: the need for attention to perceive changes in scences. *Psychological Science*, 8, 368–73.

Riddoch, G. (1917). Disssociation of visual perception due to occipital injuries, with special reference to appreciation of movement. *Brain*, 40, 15–57.

Rideout, B. (1979). Non-REM sleep as a source of learning deficits induced by REM sleep deprivation. *Physiology and Behavior*, 22, 1043–7.

Rizzolatti, G., Fadiga, L., Gallese, V., & Fogassi, L. (1996). Premtor cortex and the recognition of motor actions. *Cognitive Brian Research*, 3, 131–41.

Rizzolatti, G., Fogassi, L., & Gallese, V. (2001). Neurophysiological mechansims underlying the understanding and imitation of action. *Nature Reviews: Neuroscience*, 2, 661–70.

Roffwarg, H. P., Muzio, J. N., & Dement, W. C. (1966). Ontogenic development of human sleep-dream cycle. *Science*, 152, 604–19.

Rosenbaum, D. A., Slotta, J. D., Vaughan, J., & Plamondon, R. (1991). Optimal movement selection. *Psychological Science*, 2, 86–91.

Rosenthal, D. (1993). Thinking that one thinks. In M. Davis, & G. Humphreys (eds.), *Consciousness* (pp. 15–36). Oxford: Blackwell.

Rosenthal, D. (2004). *Consciousness and Mind*. New York: Oxford University Press.

Rubenstein, J. S., Meyer, D. E., & Evans, J. E. (2001). Executive control of cognitive processes in task switching. *Journal of Experimental Psychology: Human Perception and Performance*, 27, 234–40.

Russell, B. (1989). *Wisdom of the West*. New York: Crescent Books.

Rylander, G. (1948). Personality analysis before and after frontal lobotomy. *Research Publication – Association for Research in Nervous and Mental Disease*, 27, 691–705.

Ryle, G. (1949). *The Concept of Mind*. New York: Barnes & Nobel.

Sabom, M. B (1981). *Recollections of Death: A Medical Investigation*. New York: Harpercollins.

Sacks, O. (1992). The last hippie. *New York Review of Books*, 39, 51–60.

Sarter, M., Givens, B., & Bruno, J. P. (2001). The cognitive neuroscience of sustained attention: where top-down meets bottom-up. *Brain Research Reviews*, 35, 146–60.

Schacter, D. L. (1987). Implicit memory: History and current status. *Journal of Experimental Psychology: Learning, Memory, and Cognition*, 113, 501–18.

Schacter, D. L., & Bruckner, R. L. (1998). On the relationship among priming, conscious recollection, and intentional retrieval: Evidence from neuroimaging research. *Neurobiology of Learning and Memory*, 70, 284–303.

Schatzberg, A. F., & Nemeroff, C. B. (1995). *Textbook of Pharmacology* (2nd ed). Washington, DC: American Psychiatric Press.

Schmolck, H., Buffalo, E. A., & Squire, L. R. (2000). Memory distortions develop over time: Recollection of the O. J. Simpson trial verdict after 15 and 32 months. *Psychologial Science*, 11, 39–45.

Schwender, D., Madler, C., Klasing, S., Peter, K., & Pöppel, E. (1994). Anesthetic control of 40-Hz brain activity and implicit memory. *Consciousness and Cognition*, 3, 129–47.

Searle, J. R. (1980). Minds, brains, and programs. *Behavioural and Brain Sciences*, 3, 417–57.

Searle, J. R. (1992). *The Rediscovery of the Mind*. Cambridge, MA: MIT Press.

Searle, J. R. (1997). *The Mystery of Consciousness*. New York: New York Review of Books.

Searle, J. R. (2000). *In Discussion, Towards a Science of Consciousness Conference*. Tucson, AZ.

Searle, J. (2002). Why I am not a property dualist. *Journal of Consciousness Studies*, 9, 57–64.

Selfridge, O. (1959). Pandemonium: A paradigm for learning. In *Proceedings of the Symposium on the Mechanization of Thought Processes Held at the National Physics Laboratory, November 1958*. London: HMSO.

Seligman, M. E. P. (1972). Phobias and preparedness. *Behavior Therapy*, 3, 207–20.

Shallice, T., & Burgess, W. (1991). Deficits in strategy application following frontal lobe damage in man. *Brain*, 114, 727–41.

Sheinberg, D. L., & Logothetis, N. K. (1997). The role of temporal cortical areas in perceptual organization. *Proceedings of the National Academy of Sciences, USA*, 94, 3408–13.

Shin, L. M., Kosslyn, S. M., McNally, R. J., Alpert, N. M., Thompson, W. L., Rauch, S. L., Macklin, M. L., & Pitman, R. K. (1997). Visual imagery and perception in posttraumatic stress disorder. *Archives of General Psychiatry*, 54, 233–41.

Shoemaker, S. (1982). The inverted spectrum. *Journal of Philosophy*, 79, 357–381.

Siegel, J. M. (1995). Phylogeny and the functions of REM sleep. *Behavioural Brain Research*, 69, 29–34.

Siegel, J. M. (2001). The REM sleep-memory consolidation hypothesis. *Science*, 294, 1058–63.

Siegel, R. K. (1985). LSD hallucination: From ergot to electric Kool-Aid. *Journal of Psychoactive Drugs*, 17, 247–56.

Siegel, R. K. (1989). *Intoxication: Life in the Pursuit of Artificial Paradise*. Yew York: Penguin.

Siegel, R. K., & Jarvik, M. E. (1975). Drug induced hallucinations in animals and man. In R. K. Siegel, & L. J. West (eds.), *Hallucinations: Behavior, Experience, and Theory* (pp. 81–161). New York: Wiley.

Simons, D. J., & Chabris, C. F. (1999). Gorillas in our midst – sustained inattentional blindness for dynamic events. *Perception*, 28, 1059–74.

Simonton, D. K. (2003). Scientific creativity as constrained stochastic behavior: The integration of process, and person perspectives. *Psychological Bulletin*, 129, 475–94.

Singer, J. L. (1975). Navigating the stream of consciousness: Research in daydreaming and related inner experiences. *American Psychologist*, 30, 727–38.

Singer, J. L. (1978). Experimental studies of daydreaming and the stream of thought. In K. S. Pope, & J. L. Singer (eds.), *The Stream of Consciousness: Scientific Investigations into the Flow of Human Experience* (pp. 209–27). New York: Plenum.

Singer, J. L.., & Pope, K. S. (1981). Daydreaming and imagery skills as predisposing capacities for self-hypnosis. *International Journal of Clinical and Experimental Hypnosis*, 29, 271–81.

Singer, W. (2000). Phenomenal awareness and consciousness from a neurobiological perspective. In T. Metzinger (ed.), *Neural Correlates of Consciousness* (pp. 121–37). Cambridge, MA: MIT Press.

Singer, W., & Gray, C. M. (1995). Visual feature integration and the temporal correlation hypothesis. *Annual Review of Neuroscience*, 18, 555–86.

Smith, C. (1996). Sleep states, memory processes and synaptic plasticity. *Behavioural and Brain Sciences*, 78, 49–56.

Sokoloff, L. (1992). The brain as a chemical machine. *Progress in Brain Research*, 94, 19–33.

Solms, M. (2000). Dreaming and REM sleep are controlled by different brain mechanisms. *Behavioural and Brain Sciences*, 23, 843–50.

Solyom, L., Turnbull, I. M., & Wilensky, M. (1987). A case of self-inflicted leucotomy. *British Journal of Psychiatry*, 151, 855–57.

Spanos, N. P. (1994). Multiple identity enactment and multiple personality disorder: A sociocognitive perspective. *Psychological Bulletin*, 116, 143–65.

Sparling, P. B., Giuffrida, A., Piomelli, D., Rosskopf, L., & Dietrich, A. (2003). Exercise activates the endocannabinoid system. *Neuroreport*, 14, 2209–11.

Spence, S. A., Brooks, D. J., Hirsch, S. A., Liddle, P. F., Mechan, J., & Grasby, P. M. (1997). A PET study of voluntary movement in schizophrenic patients experiencing passivity phenomena (delusions of alien control). *Brain*, 120, 1997–2011.

Spence, S. A., & Frith, C. D. (1999). Towards a functional anatomy of volition. *Journal of Consciousness Studies*, 6, 11–29.

Sperry, R. W. (1966). Brain dissection and consciousness. In J. C. Eccles (ed.), *Brain and Conscious Experience* (pp. 298–313). New York: Springer.

Sperry, R. W. (1969). A modified concept of consciousness. *Psychological Review*, 76, 532–6.

Squire, L. R. (1992). Memory and the hippocampus: A synthesis from findings with rats, monkeys and humans. *Psychological Review*, 99, 195–231.

Squire, L. R., & Kandel, E. R. (1999). *From Mind to Molecules*. New York: Scientific American Library.

Stoerig, P., & Cowey, A. (1997). Blindsight in men and monkey. *Brain*, 120, 552–9.

Stone, V. E., Baron-Cohen, S., & Knight, R. T. (1998). Frontal lobe contributions to the theory of mind. *Journal of Cognitive Neuroscience,* 10, 640–56.

Storr, E. (1971). Why hooding is mental torture? *Sunday Times*, November 21.

Sweller, J. (1993). Some cognitive processes and their consequences for the organization and presentation of information. *Australian Journal of Psychology*, 45, 1–8.

Tart, C. T. (1972). States of consciousness and state-specific sciences. *Science*, 176, 1203–10.

Tart, C. T. (1975). *States of Consciousness*. New York: Dutton.

Tart, C. T. (1979). Measuring the depth of an altered state of consciousness, with particular reference to self-report scales of hypnotic depth. In E. Fromm & R. E. Shor (eds.), *Hypnosis: Developments in Research and New Perspectives* (2nd ed.). New York: Aldine.

Taylor, J. G. (2001). The central role of the parietal lobes in consciousness. *Consciousness and Cognition*, 10, 379–417.

Thompson, E., Pessoa, L., & Noë, A. (1999). Beyond the grand illusion: What change blindness really teaches us about vision. *Visual Cognition*, 7, 93–106.

Treisman, A. (1992). Perceiving and re-perceiving objects. *American Psychologist*, 47, 862–75.

Treisman, A. (2003). Consciousness and perceptual binding. In A. Cleeremans (ed.), *The Unity of Consciousness: Binding, Integration, and Dissociation* (pp. 95–113). Oxford: Oxford University Press.

Tulving, E. (1995). Organization of memory: Quo vadis? In M.S. Gazzaniga (ed.), *The Cognitive Neurosciences* (pp. 839–47). Cambridge: MA: MIT Press.

Tulving, E. (1997). Human memory. In M. S. Gazzaniga (ed.), *Conversation in the Cognitive Neurosciences*. Cambridge: MA: MIT Press.

Turing, A. (1950). Computing machinery and intelligence. *Mind*, 59, 433–60.

Ungerleider, L. G., & Mishkin, M. (1982). Two cortical visual systems. In D. J. Engle, M. A. Goodale, & R. J. Mansfield (eds.), *Analysis of Visual Behavior* (pp. 549–86). Cambridge, MA: MIT Press.

van Lommel, P., van Wees, R., Meyers, V., & Elfferich, I. (2001). Near-death experience in survivors of cardiac arrest: a prospective study in the Netherlands. *The Lancet*, 358, 2039–45.

Varela, F. J. (1996). Neurophenomenology: A methodological remedy for the hard problem. *Journal of Consciousness Studies*, 3, 330–49.

Varela, F., Thompson, E., & Rosch, E. (1991). *The Embodied Mind*. Cambridge, MA: MIT Press.

Velmans, M. (1991). Consciousness from a first-person perspective. *Behavioural and Brain Sciences*, 14, 702–26.

Velmans, M. (2000). *Understanding Consciousness*. London: Routledge.

Vertosick, F. T. (2000). *Why We Hurt: A Natural History of Pain*. San Diego: Hartcourt Brace.

Vissing, J., Anderson, M., & Diemer, N. H. (1996). Exercise-induced changes in local cerebral glucose utilization in the rat. *Journal of Cerebral Blood Flow and Metabolism*, 16, 729–36.

Vogeley, K., Kurthen, M., Falkai, P., & Maier, W. (1999). Essential functions of the human self model are implemented in the prefrontal cortex. *Consciousness and Cognition*, 8, 343–63.

Voltaire, F. (1752/1924). *Voltaire's Philosophical Dictionary*. New York: Knopf.

Von der Malsberg, C. (1986). Am I thinking assemblies? In G. Palm, & A. Aertsen (eds.), *Brain Theory* (pp. 161–76). Berlin: Springer Verlag.

Waldron, E. M., & Ashby, F. G. (2001). The effects of concurrent task interference on categorization learning. *Psychonomic Bulletin & Review*, 8, 168–76.

Warrington, E. K. (1985). Agnosia: The impairment of object recognition. In P. J. Vinken, G. W. Bruyn, & H. L., Klawans (eds.), *Handbook of Clinical Neurology* (pp. 333–49). New York: Elsevier Science.

Warrington, E. K., & Shallice, T. (1984). Category specific semantic impairment. *Brain*, 107, 829–54.

Webb, W. B. (1975). *Sleep: The Gentle Tyrant*. Englewoods Cliff, NJ: Prentice Hall.

Wegner, D. M. (2002). The *Illusion of Conscious Will*. Cambridge, MA: MIT Press.

Wegner, D. M. (2003). The mind's best trick: How we experience conscious will. *Trends in Cognitive Sciences*, 7, 65–9.

Wegner, D. M., & Wheatley, T. (1999). Apparent mental causation: Sources of the experience of free will. *American Psychologist*, 54, 480–92.

Weiskrantz, L. (1997). *Consciousness Lost and Found*. Oxford: Oxford University Press.

West, M. A. (1987). *The Psychology of Meditation*. Oxford: Clarendon Press.

Wik, G., Fischer, H., Bragee, B., Finer, B., & Frederikson, M. (1999). Functional anatomy of hypnotic analgesia: A PET study of patients with fibromyalgia. *European Journal of Pain – London*, 3, 7–12.

Wolford, G., Miller, M. B., & Gazzanigga, M. (2000). The left hemisphere's role in hypothesis formation. *Journal of Neuroscience*, 20, RC64.

Zeki. S. (1993). *A Vision of the Brain*. Oxford: Blackwell Scientific.

Zihl, J., von Cramon, D., & Mai, N. (1983). Selective disturbance of movement vision after bilateral damage. *Brain*, 106, 313–40.

Index